Un_____g _____ction,
Promoting Human Rights

REFERENCE

Understanding Social Action, Promoting Human Rights

EDITED BY RYAN GOODMAN,
DEREK JINKS,
and
ANDREW K. WOODS

OXFORD
UNIVERSITY PRESS

OXFORD
UNIVERSITY PRESS

Oxford University Press is a department of the University of Oxford.
It furthers the University's objective of excellence in research,
scholarship, and education by publishing worldwide.

Oxford   New York

Auckland   Cape Town   Dar es Salaam   Hong Kong   Karachi
Kuala Lumpur   Madrid   Melbourne   Mexico City   Nairobi
New Delhi   Shanghai   Taipei   Toronto

With offices in

Argentina   Austria   Brazil   Chile   Czech Republic   France   Greece
Guatemala   Hungary   Italy   Japan   Poland   Portugal   Singapore
South Korea   Switzerland   Thailand   Turkey   Ukraine   Vietnam

Oxford is a registered trade mark of Oxford University Press in the UK and certain other countries.

Published in the United States of America by Oxford University Press
198 Madison Avenue, New York, NY 10016

Library of Congress Cataloging-in-Publication Data
Understanding social action, promoting human rights /edited by Ryan Goodman, Derek Jinks, and Andrew K. Woods.
p.   cm.
Includes bibliographical references and index.
ISBN 978-0-19-537189-5 (hardback)—ISBN 978-0-19-537190-1 (pbk.) 1. Human rights. 2. Civil rights.
3. Sociological jurisprudence. I. Goodman, Ryan. II. Jinks, Derek. III. Woods, Andrew K.
K3240.U53   2012
341.4'8—dc23   2011047159

1 3 5 7 9 8 6 4 2

Printed in the United States of America
on acid-free paper

CONTENTS

CONTRIBUTORS

Jonathan Baron is Professor of Psychology at the University of Pennsylvania. He is editor of the journal *Judgment and Decision Making*, and this is his broad field of interest. He is especially interested in moral judgments that affect public policy, such as the judgments of citizens.

Byron Bland is associate director of the Stanford Center on Conflict and Negotiation and a research associate at the Center on Democracy, Development, and the Rule of Law.

Herbert Gintis received his PhD in Economics from Harvard University in 1969. He is External Professor, Santa Fe Institute; and Professor of Economics, Central European University.

Ryan Goodman is the Anne and Joel Ehrenkranz Professor of Law and Co-Chair of the Center for Human Rights and Global Justice at New York University School of Law. He is also a Professor of Politics and Professor of Sociology at NYU.

Robert C. Hornik, PhD, is the Wilbur Schramm Professor of Communication and Health Policy at the Annenberg School for Communication, University of Pennsylvania. He directs Penn's NCI-funded Center of Excellence in Cancer Communication Research. He is the author of *Development Communication*, edited *Public Health Communication*, and coedited *Prediction and Change of Health Behavior*.

Derek Jinks is the Marrs McLean Professor in Law at the University of Texas School of Law and a Senior Fellow at the Robert S. Strauss Center for International Security and Law at the University of Texas.

David Lazer is a member of both the College of Computer and Information Science and the Department of Political Science at Northeastern University. Before joining the faculty there in fall 2009, he was an Associate Professor of

Public Policy at Harvard's John F. Kennedy School of Government and director of its Program on Networked Governance. He holds a PhD in political science from the University of Michigan.

Margaret Levi is the Jere L. Bacharach Professor of International Studies, Department of Political Science, University of Washington and jointly the Chair in Politics, U.S. Studies Centre, University of Sydney. She is a former president of the American Political Science Association and currently general editor of *Cambridge Studies in Comparative Politics* and of *Annual Review of Political Science*.

John Mikhail is a Professor and Associate Dean for Transnational Programs at Georgetown University Law Center.

Deborah A. Prentice is the Alexander Stewart 1886 Professor of Psychology and Department Chair at Princeton University.

Brenna Powell is Principal and Chairman at the IPRE Group. She received her PhD in Government and Social Policy from Harvard University. She has held fellowships at Harvard University's Malcolm Wiener Center for Inequality and Social Policy, Stanford University's Center for International Security and Cooperation, as well as the position of Visiting Scholar at Stanford University's Center for Democracy, Development and the Rule of Law. In addition, she worked for five years with the Stanford Center for International Cooperation and Negotiation, leading conflict resolution and peace-building programs in Northern Ireland.

Lee Ross, a Professor of Psychology at Stanford University since 1969, teaches courses in the application of social psychology to bargaining, negotiation, conflict resolution, and broader public policy issues. He is a cofounder of the Stanford Center on Conflict and Negotiation and the coauthor (with Richard Nisbett) of the books "Human Inference" and "The Person and Situation" as well as nearly 100 journal articles and book chapters. In 1994 Ross was elected to the American Academy of Arts and Sciences, in 2003 he was named the American Psychological Society William James Fellow, and most recently he received the 2008 Distinguished Scientist Award from the Society of Experimental Social Psychology.

Audrey Sacks is a consultant at the World Bank Institute. She has written articles on topics including legitimating beliefs, tax administration, government effectiveness and social welfare, and social network analysis. She completed her PhD in Sociology at the University of Washington and her MSc in Comparative Politics at the London School of Economics.

William F. Schulz served as Executive Director of Amnesty International USA from 1994–2006. An ordained Unitarian Universalist minister and former president of the denomination, he is currently a Senior Fellow in human rights policy at the Center for American Progress, Acting President of the Unitarian Universalist

Service Committee and Adjunct Professor at New York University's Wagner School of Public Service and Meadville Lombard Theological School.

Paul Slovic is president of Decision Research and a Professor of Psychology at the University of Oregon. He studies human judgment, decision making, and risk perception. Dr. Slovic received a BA degree from Stanford University, MA and PhD degrees from the University of Michigan, and honorary doctorates from the Stockholm School of Economics and the University of East Anglia. He is past president of the Society for Risk Analysis and in 1991 received its Distinguished Contribution Award. In 1993, Dr. Slovic received the Distinguished Scientific Contribution Award from the American Psychological Association, and in 1995 he received the Outstanding Contribution to Science Award from the Oregon Academy of Science.

Tom R. Tyler is the Macklin Fleming Professor of Law and Professor of Psychology at Yale Law School. His research explores the dynamics of authority in groups, organizations, and societies. In particular, he examines the role of judgments about the justice or injustice of group procedures in shaping legitimacy, compliance and cooperation. He is the author of several books, including *The social psychology of procedural justice* (1988); *Social justice in a diverse society* (1997); *Cooperation in groups* (2000); *Trust in the law* (2002); and *Why people obey the law* (2006).

Andrew K. Woods is a Fellow at Stanford Law School. He holds a JD from Harvard Law School and a PhD in politics from the University of Cambridge where he was a Gates Scholar.

David Zionts is a magna cum laude graduate of the Harvard Law School where he was an editor of the *Harvard Law Review*. He currently serves as Special Advisor to the Legal Advisor, U.S. Department of State.

Understanding Social Action, Promoting Human Rights

Introduction

Social Science and Human Rights

RYAN GOODMAN, DEREK JINKS, AND ANDREW K. WOODS

A considerable gap remains between the international human rights regime's aspirations and its achievements. Narrowing this gap is one of the central challenges for legal and policy actors, and it animates a growing body of scholarship. International lawyers and policy experts have been central to this effort, naturally enough. But our contention is that this gap cannot be closed with the tools of traditional legal and policy analysis alone. So we set out to find leaders in a wide range of disciplines to help us identify innovative research that could have a major and lasting influence on the study and promotion of human rights.

The concept for this book began with a question: could recent social scientific study of individual and organizational behavior—research that has had a transformative impact on many disciplines, including politics, economics, communications, psychology, sociology—similarly transform the field of human rights? We sought specifically to tap into cutting-edge empirical research that has generally not addressed human rights as a descriptive matter nor converted descriptive analyses into policy recommendations.

Of course, it has long been recognized that human rights issues cut across many facets of life. The field of human rights studies is, according to some schools of thought, a quintessential humanist subject. Many human rights issues have seen rich expression in film, art, and literature—currently on the syllabi of many human rights courses. But our aim was not to add to the considerable scholarship about the inherent interdisciplinary nature of human rights as a subject. Instead, we began with the assumption that the challenges faced by the human rights regime demand reflective advocacy and institutional design crafted with the benefit of the academy's most robust empirical insights. We were accordingly interested in research insights on topics such as cognitive errors in decision making, psychological and evolutionary pressures for good and evil, the influence of social structure on collective beliefs, effects of social marketing campaigns in creating individual preferences, and modes of governance in effectuating resistance and compliance. A group of extraordinary, leading scholars from across the academy agreed to participate in this initiative. This book is the result.

All the contributors accepted our challenge to present research related to the book's core objectives, yet many of their chapters do not include the words "human rights." This is by design. The chapters in this volume were selected because they suggest new avenues for human rights research, and could lead to important advocacy tools or policy reforms in the human rights arena. In order to capture the benefit of research that does not directly deal with human rights, we did not ask the authors to extend their work to that topic artificially. The authors employ different empirical methodologies and exhibit different areas of specialized knowledge. Those differences explain, in significant part, how explicitly each author chose to analyze implications for the human rights field. To expand the potential reach of each contribution, we drafted an editors' Coda for each chapter. The Codas take the findings from the relevant chapter as inspiration for potential human rights regime designs.

In short, our aim in this volume is to provide readers with an overview of the exciting range of empirical insights drawn from the social sciences and with a deep sense of the implications for the human rights regime. The volume can therefore be read as a basis for future academic exploration and for developing new tools for promoting human rights. We view this project as another step toward an interdisciplinary revolution in human rights scholarship and practice.

I. Advances in Social Science and Normative Change

Over the last 20 years, the social scientific understanding of human behavior has taken a significant leap forward. Important advances in several fields have increased the complexity and accuracy of prevailing models of individual actors, group dynamics, and communication. Unfortunately, too few of the key insights of that scholarship have been incorporated into the theory or practice of human rights promotion (Woods, 2010). This book aims to start the process of incorporation, by collecting research from a broad set of disciplines and underscoring its implications for human rights scholarship and practice. By focusing on nonlegal scholarship that touches on norm creation, diffusion, and institutionalization, we present a broad range of interdisciplinary insights relevant to human rights scholars and practitioners.

The time is ripe. There are a number of coinciding developments that simultaneously threaten human rights and expand the reach and effectiveness of rights advocacy. The revolutions of communication and transportation have enabled rights abusers to be more "effective," to push their ideas faster and farther. But the same revolutions promise to provide new avenues for positive rights promotion. In sum, there has been a proliferation of actors promoting human rights norms; tools for promoting human rights norms; lawmaking fora for human rights norms; and, more generally, audiences interested in and able to absorb new ideas about the scope, content, and institutionalization of human rights norms. Human rights scholarship has not taken advantage of the latest work in the social sciences—work that facilitates both a deeper understanding of, and an enhanced capacity to manage and direct, these recent developments.

This is not to say that human rights scholarship lacks an interdisciplinary or empirical dimension. Indeed, this scholarship has increasingly emphasized interdisciplinary and empirical work. For example, there has been much important empirical work on the ratification patterns and effects of formal human rights regimes (See, e.g., Hathaway, 2002; Landman, 2005; Simmons, 2009). Other interdisciplinary work examines the origins and functioning of formal human rights regimes. These works provide macro-level, positive accounts of human rights regimes—often with a view toward closing the compliance gap that plagues human rights law. Some of these works focus exclusively on human rights norms (Goodman and Jinks, forthcoming, 2008, 2005, 2004; Keck and Sikkink, 1998; Risse et al., 1999), while others analyze human rights as part of a more general theory of international law (Goldsmith and Posner, 2005; Goldstein et al., 2001; Guzman, 2008; Koh, 1997; Slaughter, 2004). All this work helps illuminate general patterns of state practice—patterns strongly suggesting that current approaches to human rights advocacy are likely to succeed only under particular conditions. These works, however, provide little fine-grained understanding or assessment of prevailing actor- and organization-level tactics. This volume, therefore, aims to supplement this empirical work in two fundamental respects. On the theoretical level, it provides interdisciplinary, empirically grounded insights into the behavioral and organizational foundations of the observed regime patterns. On the practical level, the volume helps translate some of the general lessons of this empirical work into a more concrete program of action for human rights policy makers and advocates.

To be sure, there is no shortage of ideas about how existing institutions and practices might be altered to better promote human rights. The legal reform literature on human rights, for example, is vast (See, e.g., Alston and Mégret, 2006; Bayefsky, 2001; Ulfstein, 2007). That kind of work provides a low-to-the-ground, internalist perspective on formal regime design questions in human rights law. As a consequence, it is both indispensable and limited. The great weakness of this work, in our view, is that it does not systematically examine, or even make explicit, the considerable (and often questionable) behavioral and organizational assumptions of the suggested reforms. Prevailing approaches are predicated on a broad range of fundamental assumptions about how actors think, reason, process information, communicate with, and influence one another. The question is whether human rights advocacy is ultimately predicated on, at best, an insufficiently nuanced—and, at worst, a completely outmoded—conception of the human actor, means of communication, and group dynamics.

Of course, drawing on the social sciences to inform a richer understanding of legal and political phenomena is not a new idea. In recent years, some of the most powerful regime design insights have come from behavioral inquiries across a number of fields. Just as Tversky and Kahneman fundamentally transformed economics with psychological insights, scholars of law and policy increasingly—and more to the point, fruitfully—turn to the social sciences to inform a broad array of regulatory issues, including choice architecture (Thaler and Sunstein, 2008); corporate governance (Stout and Blair, 2001); development and antipoverty policies (Banerjee and Mullainathan, 2008; Duflo et al., 2009); entrepreneurship and innovation (Benkler, 2009); and criminal law (Braman, Kahan, and Hoffman, 2010; Robinson, Kurzban and Jones, 2007). Amidst this significant trend, human rights scholarship has fallen behind. Despite its increasing empirical sophistication, that scholarship—much of which turns on unexamined claims about social norms and personal beliefs—relies largely on assumptions about human behavior that are out of date.

Advances in various social science fields strongly suggest that a reexamination, or even a wholesale rejection, of some of these assumptions is in order. A few examples illustrate the point:

New research in *empirical economics* examines different mechanisms for stimulating socially desirable behavior. Experimental and field studies demonstrate, for example, that introducing material inducements can, under different conditions, either "crowd out" (displace) or "crowd in" (reinforce) individuals' noninstrumental motivations for engaging in pro-social behavior. Central insights from this research program can inform the use of sanctions to threaten state actors for poor human rights performance; the use of material incentives alongside moral sentiments to mobilize public support for a human rights campaign; and efforts to weaken illiberal organizations—such as terrorist groups—by influencing their techniques for attracting sympathizers and collaborators.

Scholarship on *social marketing* employs concepts from commercial marketing for the purpose of social change. Related research programs have been developed primarily by academics at business schools and schools of public health. Their scholarship can provide broader lessons for effectuating behavioral and attitudinal changes with regard to human rights. Lessons from social marketing can help a ministry of education, for example, in conducting human rights education to shape public perceptions of the disabled, terrorism suspects, sexual minorities, and so on. Social marketing concepts can also help a national human rights commission, for example, to establish a "brand" for itself within a complex of multiple state institutions.

New scholarship on *networks* analyzes the structure and effects of social ties among interconnected actors. Existing research suggests that the transmission of information, material, and influence may be a function of properties—such as the density, strength, and distance—of various ties that make up a network. Central ideas in network studies can foster new approaches to promoting the spread of human rights norms. This research program provides cause to reconsider linkages between civil society and governmental actors and connections among different official networks. For example, there is cause to consider perforating or lowering the institutional walls that insulate human rights officials (e.g., members of treaty bodies, staff of national human rights commissions) from executive agencies to facilitate the flow of human rights norms. This research may also provide reason to reconsider the ability to produce sweeping normative changes through "small world" networks and weak ties; and this research may generate ideas for training advocates to function as nodes within a network.

These and related fields provide theoretically and empirically compelling reasons to question assumptions along three important dimensions: assumptions about the human actor, assumptions about means and modes of communication, and assumptions about group dynamics. Several of the academic fields and authors represented in this volume straddle two or more of these dimensions. Advances in social psychology, for example, offer important insights into both the nature of individual actors and the importance of the social setting for any influence strategy. Likewise, work on moral judgments offers insights that are relevant not only to understanding the individual decision maker but also the design of global institutions that exploit the moral intuitions of various audiences. The trifurcation is theoretically useful in our view because it facilitates integration of insights from multiple fields into ever richer models of effective human rights promotion. Grouping new behavioral fields into these categories provides the following framework:

1. **The Human Actor:** Social Psychology; Cognitive Studies; Empirical Economics; Behavioral Economics; Political Psychology
2. **Means of Communication:** Linguistics; Communication Theory; Social Entrepreneurship; Social Marketing; New Media Studies, Persuasion Studies

3. **Group Dynamics:** Organizational Theory; Complexity Theory; Political Economy; Social Dilemmas/Game Theory; Social Network Theory; Social Movements

Scholarship along each of these dimensions clarifies and qualifies the social scientific theories that tacitly guide conventional wisdom about human rights. Insights cast at such a high level of generality, though, are unlikely to translate easily into human rights practice—or even into legal and policy scholarship on human rights. The cutting-edge social science included herein offers granular insights, which in our view provide meaningful guidance on a range of more concrete questions about how best to promote social change. Consider four axes of application that might guide the incorporation of social science research into more conventional human rights advocacy frames.

1. **Change Agents:** What are the most effective actors or institutions for communicating new ideas, new attitudes, and new behaviors?

   Who are *effective* change agents? What are the best institutions or actors for promoting social change? Is the involvement of particular actors helpful or counterproductive, necessary or unnecessary to achieve results? Students, professionals, experts/epistemic communities, quasi-governmental bodies such as national human rights commissions; international actors (like Amnesty International), local social movements, elites, the general public?

   What distributional issues might arise in the selection (or self-selection) of change agents? Will members of particular classes or groups more likely engage in such initiatives, and with what effect?

   What skills training would assist in the development of effective change agents? For example, if a professional school or a university-based human rights center set out to educate and train prospective practitioners, what skills should it help students develop?

2. **Target Audiences:** What factors determine an actor's receptivity to new ideas, new attitudes, and new behaviors?

   Do successful tactics vary across different audiences? How might different strategies or mechanisms of influence be exploited in rallying sympathetic individuals, securing allies, convincing recalcitrant actors? Are these strategies or mechanisms compatible with one another?

   Do strategies for change differ if the responsible actor is governmental or nongovernmental (for example, if the targets for change are multinational corporations or armed opposition groups)?

3. **Promoting Change through Organizations/Institutions:** What factors determine the capacity of an organization or institution to promote change?

Does effective social change require formal/state enforcement? Might familial and social relations, or other informal institutions, be harnessed for social change?

What institutional devices might be utilized for mobilizing groups of actors—perhaps against their self-interest?

What are the causal pathways for meaningful social change? Are direct connections between particular individuals important? (How) do elites matter? Civil society? Governmental bureaucracies?

How might new technologies (such as the Internet) shape prospects for social change?

4. **Norm Characteristics/Message Content:** Does the nature of the cause or the substance of the influence strategy matter?

Do the elements of social change differ if the cause or social movement is illiberal (e.g., spreading fascism)? Are there empirical insights from the study of illiberal settings (e.g., social networks of terrorists, group psychology, and abusive prison guards) that might be reverse engineered in the human rights domain (e.g., social networks of political dissidents/human rights advocates, group psychology, and rights respecting officials)? What gaps in data/knowledge or differences in context preclude reverse engineering? What might those gaps or differences tell us about the information needed or conditions required to promote human rights?

Do these factors apply universally (regardless of the use, regardless of the context)—or are they substantively/situationally/culturally dependent? If they are culturally dependent, are there examples of successful "translation" projects—which might offer tools for ensuring that culturally dependent ideas are more culturally relevant or culturally resonant?

This volume collects for the first time some of the most important insights located in contemporary academic research and renders them available to human rights scholarship and practice. The book is designed to assist human rights academics, policy makers, and advocates. It aims to inform their consideration of topics such as the design of advocacy strategies, reforms of global and regional human rights institutions, influences on state actors' behavior and preferences, and risks of political cooptation and decay of human rights campaigns. Toward this end, we provide a sample of scholarship that, in our view, has the potential to yield new and important insights for the project of human rights promotion.

Our book thus selects leading scholars who can generally represent and reflect upon central ideas in these fields of study. In particular, we assemble authors who study social influence, social change, collective action, and norm diffusion. These leading thinkers provide broad and fresh perspectives on their respective field and its potential applications to the human rights realm. Given the nature of this project, we did not want to impose a specific conception of "human rights." Instead, we allowed the contributors and our accompanying discussion of their work to embrace a broad conception with the potential to include the promotion of individual-and group-based rights and economic, social, civil, and political rights—whether codified in existing international law or not.

In the balance of this Introduction, we identify, in Section II, some specific implications for human rights research and practice that emerge from the chapters that will follow. Our objective here is not to provide an exhaustive catalogue of potential implications—detailed "Codas" following each chapter suggest many more possibilities. Instead we aim in Section II only to highlight some important themes that recur across the chapters. We then consider, in Section III, a few important challenges for, and possible objections to, the project—challenges for the book project specifically as well as challenges for the more general project of fostering an increasingly rigorous, increasingly useful conversation between human rights scholars and practitioners. In Section IV, we briefly describe the organization and content of the chapters in this volume. In Section V, we offer some provisional reflections on the direction of future research.

II. Implications for Human Rights

The work assembled in this volume is, in our view, pregnant with possible applications to important questions in human rights scholarship and practice. Following each chapter, we have provided Codas that offer some provisional thoughts on possible lines of application. In this section, we underscore some themes that arise in several of the chapters. These themes might, in turn, prompt a more fundamental reconsideration of some common social scientific assumptions in the human rights field.

A. The Power of Norms

In many ways, the contributions in this volume demonstrate the power of ideas—whether for good or ill—in producing and stymieing social change. Such insights are important to the study and practice of human rights in three respects.

First, research in this volume shows the potential of ideas to override material self-interest. Indeed, contrary to some theories (and assumptions) of human motivation in international relations scholarship and practice, the research demonstrates the propensity of individuals to act upon individual beliefs and social norms that do not serve their material self-interest. Some of the research is modest along one dimension—it accepts that individuals will prioritize material self-interest. However, in making costly decisions, people, for example, frequently believe in a fallacy that their choice will accrue to their material benefit (Baron, chapter 8). Other research more fundamentally challenges the notion that individuals act primarily to maximize their material self-interest. Instead, notions of reciprocity (Gintis, chapter 6), equality (Gintis, chapter 6; Mikhail, chapter 7; Bland, Powell, and Ross, chapter 10), and legitimacy (Levi, Tyler, and Sachs, chapter 4) motivate individuals and groups across a wide range of human activities. For instance, individuals may act spitefully—at material cost to themselves—to sanction normatively undesirable behavior of others (Gintis, chapter 6). Individuals may comply with the law even if the legal outcome does not materially benefit them, but the legal process respects them (Levi, Tyler, and Sacks, chapter 4).

Second, research in this volume shows the potential of ideas and cognitive processes to override other individual preferences. This research domain escapes the tired, old dualism of material versus nonmaterial self-interest that dominates some areas of international relations scholarship and more popular thinking about human rights. Instead, the research considers how particular group norms, institutions, or cognitive frames steer individual decision making away from various preferences. For example, individuals may wish to help victims of human rights abuse, but succumb to cognitive limitations and decision-making errors that impede action (Slovic and Zionts, chapter 5). And members of groups may not properly calculate the full impact of their omissions on members of outside groups (Baron, chapter 8).

Third, research in this volume shows the potential of ideas to thrive, backfire, or demise based not on their content—but on existing social structures, means of communication, or unintended social meaning. Social structure, for example, can be shown to determine outcomes when members of a social network change their minds or practices when influential actors in the network begin to do so (Lazer, chapter 9). Unintended social meanings can be important, for example, when a social campaign to end an undesirable behavior perversely sends the message that the behavior is prevalent and socially attractive (Hornik, chapter 3; Prentice, chapter 2). Indeed, a related set of insights evidenced in this volume demonstrates the very unimportance of ideas under certain conditions. That is, as Deborah Prentice's chapter shows, sometimes behavior depends much more on mimicry, or sensitivity to peer preference, than on the ideational content of a particular social message.

B. Overcoming and Exploiting Bias

Several of the chapters identify common biases that shape patterns of behavior. In some cases, the central application of the relevant social science insights is to identify and overcome a bias. For example, the parochialism discussed in Jonathan

Baron's chapter 8 is presented as a cognitive feature that must be overcome to prevent certain harms such as those resulting from strong nationalism. Similarly, chapter 5 by Paul Slovic and David Zionts on psychic numbing invites the conclusion that in order to combat genocide, one must overcome the bias that causes people to value lives less as the scale of an atrocity increases. Indeed, contributions to this volume not only describe biases, but also provide concrete ways to combat them.

But as the findings in this book show, biases can also be harnessed to benefit the human rights regime. Taking again the parochialism example, we identify applications where the powerful forces that drive the parochialism bias can be harnessed to guide behavior for the benefit of human rights. In the Coda to Baron's chapter 8, we briefly discuss the potential to harness this bias by speaking to group interests when those interests might correspond with a more general interest in promoting human rights. Self-sacrifice for the in-group does not necessarily entail, as parochialism traditionally suggests, an outcome at odds with human rights. Even though many prominent examples of parochialism (nationalism, ethnic conflict) have been tied to gross human rights abuses, one could imagine a pro-social campaign harnessing the parochialism and in-group preference to care for human rights victims. Or consider the numbing described by Slovic and Zionts (chapter 5). As mentioned, Slovic and Zionts explore how large numbers of deaths in the context of atrocities resonate less than individual horror stories. From the standpoint of the human rights regime, numbing is a problem when it masks underlying preferences by domestic audiences who would otherwise, but for the numbing, respond to mass atrocity abroad. But one could also imagine how numbing could serve a useful social function in those rare situations when an emotional process threatens to crowd out more deliberative processes. In the context of investigations after atrocity, for example, or in the determination of admissibility of witness statements in an emotionally charged trial, one might imagine harnessing (or accepting) numbing effects in order to contain emotional thinking where that thinking undermines other important cognitive processes. In domestic law, scholars have suggested designs for trials to prevent moral emotions (moral outrage, indignation) from crowding out more consequentialist thinking (Sunstein, 2009). Harnessing the numbing effects highlighted in the work of Slovic and Zionts suggest a similar design insight for the international human rights realm.

In the end, granular insights about bias, like fine-grained insights about norms, allow not only for specific policy proposals but in some cases they encourage expansive thinking about the means of rights enforcement and promotion. This is not to say that social science insights can easily be translated into policy—a topic we discuss next—and the design insights offered here are not proposed as fully developed policies ready for implementation, today or ever. The point is, instead, that these social science insights offer a new, creative foundation for approaching, and sometimes overcoming, what have become in some cases rather entrenched debates.

III. Impediments to the Translation of Social Science Research into Human Rights

In many ways, the topic of human rights inherently calls for interdisciplinary inquiry: human rights issues affect business, education, medicine, criminology, and much more. And yet, despite widespread interest in the topic, the subject of human rights is generally relegated to law schools and perhaps also public policy schools, but rarely beyond that. Universities tend not to draw from all of their faculties in a coordinated way to address the massive and multifaceted challenges faced by the human rights regime.

What explains this failure? The most obvious explanation is the sheer difficulty of interdisciplinary work. Part of this is due to the fact that disciplines develop in silos, and interdisciplinary research centers have only recently come into existence in significant numbers. Secondly, few people are adequately versed in other disciplines to be able to digest work from another field and synthesize it with their own. Finally, interdisciplinary work is typically hazardous and often not rewarded by colleagues in one's own department, making the incentives for academics to undertake interdisciplinary work dubious.

Now that some significant academic centers recognize the importance of interdisciplinary research—and some scholars have begun the important work of attempting to harmonize the various social sciences (Gintis, 2009)—the challenge still remains to identify ways to make this research relevant to practice in a meaningful way. That is at least a two-step process. First, it requires an attempt on the part of academics to take the real-world implications of their work seriously, to offer policy conclusions or suggestions, however tentative, and to frame their research such that the conclusions are more likely to be useful to policy makers and advocates. Second, it requires a space where practitioners can think deeply about how their work could be influenced in meaningful ways by academic insights. This space would offer a permeable membrane between the academy and the world of practice, and it would also develop its own common language so that productive conversations could take place across disciplines and between scholars and practitioners. Creating such a space is not particularly easy, and this volume offers insight into both the promise and limitations of interdisciplinary work designed with policy in mind.

A. Challenges

Proof of the difficulty of interdisciplinary work among scholars can be found along a number of different dimensions of the volume. First, take the variation of the papers. The chapters do not have a common point of departure. They are pitched at different levels of abstraction. They do not share a common methodology. Beyond the challenge of harmony among nomenclature and level of abstraction, the contributors—in keeping with social science tradition, and with only a few exceptions—tend to hesitate to apply their findings to concrete human rights problems. This likely comes as no surprise to anyone who has been involved in interdisciplinary efforts to bring academic insights to bear on pressing policy problems.

The standard critique of the scholarship/practice divide places the blame on the scholarly community. The academy is frequently cited as "out of touch" with practice; rarely is practice said to be out of touch with the academy. This makes sense in one respect because the academy is much smaller than the world of practice, so adaptation by the academy is more realistic. Moreover, the very point of the academy is to provide thinkers with the time and space to reflect deeply on certain issues—the kind of time and space that practitioners very often do not have. It is typically assumed that scholars can and should adapt to the world of practice because they have the time to do so; practitioners are just too busy.

Practitioners, perhaps as a consequence, are often reluctant to take seriously the idea that social science insights might significantly inform their practice. Such skepticism, in our view, simply shows the need for more bridge builders and more structural opportunities for bridge building. That the findings in this volume pose important challenges to conventional human rights thinking and practices is clear. That these findings might stimulate real innovation in human rights advocacy and regime design is, in our view, also clear. Clear too, however, is the need for institutions, scholars, and practitioners dedicated to bridging the considerable impediments to the translation of theory and empirical research into practice. In the blogosphere, for example, one of the most important nodes in any network are the translators. That is because the blogosphere is in fact many blogospheres, walled off by language, with very little overlap. The "bridgebloggers" are those crucial multilingual nodes that act as gateways and bridges between different online worlds (Zuckerman, 2008). The human rights regime needs the scholar/practitioner analog.

B. From Descriptive Research to Normative Analysis

Several lessons of the volume concern the difficulty of managing the relationship between descriptive research and normative analysis. Part of that difficulty involves unintended consequences that potentially flow from the descriptive research. These merit detailed consideration.

First, one unintended consequence involves the wrong lesson being drawn from the descriptive research. The implications here could be severe, including normalizing the perpetration of human rights violations and silence on the part of third parties. For example, Paul Slovic and David Zionts's work on psychic numbing is intended to improve the global response to genocides. And yet, the same insights about psychic numbing might have perverse effects on key actors. That is, there are benefits to social regulation through shaming such that leaders feel guilt for not acting to stop genocide. The human rights regime is strengthened by the fact that Bill Clinton and Kofi Annan expressed remorse for not acting to stop the genocide in Rwanda, and that the Dutch government resigned for its inaction in Srebrenica. Slovic and Zionts's research, however, might be taken to suggest that these omissions were not a result of personal moral failure or aberrant neglect, but a result of universal features of human psychology— how any individual would behave under the circumstances. Those "lessons" from the research can undercut the benefits of shame. Actors may not feel the need to salve their conscience by calling for stronger action in the future (e.g., NATO's intervention in Bosnia) and by making commitments to the survivors (e.g., establishing the ICTR and rebuilding Rwanda).

A second unintended consequence involves the right lesson but in the wrong hands. Research insights, properly understood, could be employed by actors to reverse or abandon rights protections. As an example, consider Bland, Powell, and Ross's exposition (chapter 10) of psychological barriers that impede the successful conclusion of peace negotiations. In the hands of spoilers, does that exposition amount to a strategic manual for obstruction? As another example, do empirical insights into the structure of human rights advocacy networks (Lazer, chapter 9) provide valuable information for tyrannical regimes to attack advocacy groups? And in our Coda to Levi, Tyler, and Sacks's chapter, we discuss how their analysis of the public's willingness to comply with (unpopular and undesirable) laws might be reverse engineered to assist despotic regimes.

A third consequence involves the right lesson, in the right hands but with unintended second-order consequences. Slovic and Zionts's chapter, for example, calls for visual narratives and storytelling to compel people to respond more strongly to massacres. As we discuss in the accompanying Coda to that chapter, such strategies might siphon attention from less visible concerns (such as structural poverty) that are not as easily captured by such media, and the losers may also be individuals whose images do not appeal to mainstream social groups. Jonathan Baron's chapter suggests, in part through our Coda, ways of overcoming negative forms of parochialism through measures that could diminish such biases among a general population. However, under certain conditions, these biases also promote pro-human rights outcomes. The latter benefit would be lost as a result of interventions to stop the biases from operating.

IV. Organization of the Volume

A. The Chapters

In chapter 2, social psychologist Deborah Prentice describes her empirical work on social-norms marketing campaigns. Prentice highlights two key empirical findings: (1) actors often overestimate the prevalence of many undesirable behaviors, and (2) actors use their perceptions of peer norms as a standard against which to compare their own behaviors. Social-norms campaigns reduce problem behaviors (or increase desirable ones) by conveying information that counters this "pluralistic ignorance."

In chapter 3, communications scholar Robert C. Hornik gives a brief history of the health communications field and outlines insights and pitfalls relevant to human rights communications efforts. In addition to ensuring that messages are well-tailored to and will receive sufficient attention in the target audience, he also outlines several counterintuitive findings including the need to be mindful of "boomerang effects"—the risk that any given communication will, in fact, worsen the behaviors the message was intended to fix.

In chapter 4, political scientist Margaret Levi, social psychologist Tom Tyler, and sociologist Audrey Sacks, relying on two datasets (one from the United States and one from sub-Saharan Africa), contend that two factors affect individuals' compliance with law. First, voluntary compliance with the law is influenced by individuals' views of the government's legitimacy. Second, individuals' conception of legitimacy depends significantly on the government's trustworthiness (including its perceived competence) and its commitment to procedural justice.

In chapter 5, psychologist Paul Slovic and legal scholar David Zionts discuss psychological constraints that impede individuals' ability to respond to the plight of large numbers of people. As a result, individuals price lives differently depending on the numbers involved—specifically, they succumb to a numbing effect whereby they register a greater emotional and financial response to the loss of a few than to the loss of many.

In chapter 6, behavioral economist Herbert Gintis calls into question the standard economic model of human motivation. Gintis argues that human social behavior exhibits certain fundamental, transcultural features including: (1) a natural predisposition to support certain fundamental human rights; and (2) an evolved predisposition to cooperate with others similarly disposed, even when cooperation is costly, as well as a commitment to punish those who violate cooperative norms, even when punishing is costly to the punisher (what he calls "strong reciprocity").

In chapter 7, cognitive science and legal scholar John Mikhail reviews the mind sciences for evidence of what he calls "universal moral grammar"—a moral organ that is now an innate feature like linguistic ability. If such an inherent moral fabric exists, Mikhail argues, it may suggest that current skepticism in human rights scholarship about moral foundationalism is unwarranted.

In chapter 8, psychologist and expert on judgment and decision making Jonathan Baron identifies cognitive biases whereby individuals sacrifice self-interest for the benefit of in-group members—especially in the presence of an affected out-group and especially when the effect on out-group members results from omission rather than action. According to Baron's research, people are also misled by a "self-interest illusion," fallaciously believing that their sacrifices for the group redound to their personal benefit even when their actions incur a net personal cost.

In chapter 9, political scientist and scholar of social networks David Lazer gives an overview of the standard tools of social network analysis. He explains how network dynamics can be useful for understanding human rights issues as they relate to global flows of people, information and goods, as well as for understanding the relationships between states and sub state actors within the human rights regime.

In chapter 10, social psychologist Lee Ross, ethicist Byron Bland, and political scientist Brenna Powell offer an interdisciplinary analysis of persistent psychological barriers to conflict resolution. Effective resolution of deep political disputes, they maintain, requires awareness of the psychological processes and biases—including "naïve realism," judgmental overconfidence, loss aversion, and reactive devaluation—that shape the ways in which relevant actors interpret and understand disputes and disputants.

Finally, reflecting on each of the chapters and the larger project, William Schulz, former executive director of Amnesty International USA, offers a human rights practitioner's perspective in the concluding chapter.

B. The Codas

Following each chapter is a Coda written by the editors, which presents a catalogue of suggestions for human rights practice based on the empirical evidence presented in the chapter. We should say a bit about what the Codas are not. The applications highlighted in the Codas are not intended to be fully developed policy prescriptions. Nor are the editors necessarily endorsing any of the applications discussed. These applications are offered instead as illustrative examples of potential human rights policy applications that can be drawn from the research outlined in each chapter. The Codas do not critique, question, or qualify the methods, data, or analysis offered in the chapters. They highlight instead some concrete applications that might follow from the insights of each chapter.

We have organized these suggestions according to the actors who would be targets for change. That is, some research findings shed light on the preferences, beliefs, and practices of (i) indirect supporters of human rights campaigns, (ii) indirect supporters of human rights violations, (iii) human rights advocates, and (iv) perpetrators of abuse. We divide the policy recommendations with these subjects—as targets of change—in mind. For instance, a chapter may provide insights into causal mechanisms that motivate citizens to support altruistic outlays to foreign populations—the Coda discusses those insights under headings such as "potential supporters of human rights." And, other research may provide evidence showing the conditions under which political leaders make cognitive errors that result in human suffering—the Coda accordingly discusses those insights under such headings as "potential perpetrators of human rights abuses." Of course, we do not assume that perpetrators (or lay human rights supporters) would represent the direct consumers or audience for such suggestions. Instead, these suggestions are directed at regime architects and operators who could draw upon these suggestions in their efforts to change the behavior, preferences, beliefs, and structural opportunities of potential violators and supporters.

Notably, each Coda is not simply an expansion of the individual chapter to which it is attached. The Codas also begin the necessary work of synthesis across methodological approaches and levels of analysis. Indeed, the volume contains a diverse set of contributions. And, in the Codas, we accordingly draw connections between the different research insights presented in this book. This allows us to identify striking instances of triangulation in which scholars using different methodologies arrive at similar empirical findings. And it also allows us to identify important areas of discord.

Finally, we should note that the authors were aware that we would write a Coda for their chapter, but they had no role in drafting or developing it. We thus assume sole responsibility for the content of the Codas, including any errors and omissions that they contain.

V. New Research Horizons

This volume forms part of a significantly larger project that is now needed—an organized engagement in interdisciplinary and practically oriented research on human rights. The collection of scholarly works in this book already provides important and actionable insights. The contributions help to close existing gaps in theoretical and empirical knowledge. And the products of this research lend themselves to some clear recommendations for human rights practitioners. That is, the contributions also help to expose gaps that need to be filled by future research and future researchers. Building on the works in this volume, we suggest some priorities for charting new research horizons.

We consider the following priorities:

1. Testing empirical findings—about human behavior in general—in the specific context of human rights norms;
2. Studying whether (and under what conditions) empirical findings about human behavior apply to state actors;
3. Sharing and building upon common subjects of analysis and research concerns across disciplines;
4. Developing explanations of human variation within different research programs;
5. Testing the ("real world") application of social science insights.

First, it would be helpful to test general research insights about human behavior in the specific context of human rights norms. The chapters in this book analyze various factors that influence individuals, means of communication, and group dynamics in a wide range of human endeavors. The empirical research, however, does not always focus on human rights norms or practices.

Generalized research can, of course, contribute indirectly to the field of human rights. Existing practices (and theories) of human rights protection are often predicated on unexamined or unproven assumptions about human behavior in general. And, research in this volume challenges several such presuppositions. Indeed, this research often dislodges those assumptions with stronger evidence, more sophisticated theoretical models, and systematic analyses. Additionally, some of the research does not challenge an existing assumption but lays the foundation for new understandings of human behavior. Such research applies broadly, and the burden is on those who would contend that it should exclude certain sub-domains of human cognition and social practice.

The study of human rights, however, would benefit from further research that proves whether, and under what conditions, these general descriptive accounts apply to human rights. For example, Hornik's and Prentice's chapters (3 and 2) each provide important insights about the effectiveness of communication campaigns. The available data, however, are drawn primarily from research in areas other than human rights (e.g., public health and commercial marketing) and often involve distinct subpopulations (e.g., college students or young adults). Similarly, Lazer's chapter 9 delivers useful insights about the power of informational networks and the structural organization of social networks. The empirics of network analysis, however, remain relatively untested in the context of human rights. Slovic and Zionts are among the closest with respect to studying human rights directly. However, they depend largely on studies of a more general personal willingness to contribute to the basic needs of individuals. The available research does not directly measure individual responses to rights violations or genocidal extermination. The next generation of scholarship should study how general empirical insights apply in human rights contexts. That scholarship should also explore whether differences occur across sub-domains of rights—economic and social versus civil and political, substantive versus procedural rights, individual versus group rights, and so on.

Second, it would be beneficial to test whether (and under what conditions) empirical findings about human behavior apply specifically to state actors and the practices of states. Significant parts of the present volume concern individual psychological phenomenon, including notions of personal identity and individual-level internalization of norms. Some studies prompt the reader to theorize how these individual-level dynamics might translate into actions on the part of the state. For example, do citizens internalize the identity of the nation-state and personally feel humiliation when their state suffers a blow (cf. Bland, Powell, and Ross, chapter 10)? Is such an indirect and collective form of shame the same as personal shame for one's own wrongdoing with respect to its content, durability, and interaction with other psychological motivations? Perhaps individuals do not personally internalize the identity of the state. In that case, do policy makers act "as if" the state is motivated by its status in international society? For example, do they respond to social influences in making decisions "for the state" based on social norms ostensibly practiced by other states (Prentice, chapter 2)?

These are some of the unanswered questions about the links between motivations for human behavior that have been studied at the individual level and macro-level state practices. The uncertainty whether such research applies to state-level behavior should challenge scholars to develop a better account of causal connections to micro-level motivations. Slovic and Zionts's chapter most directly touches on this issue. They conclude that cognitive failures that people generally suffer would not apply in the context of policy makers in specific organizational settings. That said, the negative case—i.e., the contention that a feature of human cognition or communication does not extend to the state—also needs a theoretical explanation and empirical foundation. One bright frontier for new research, then, involves examining these links systematically and determining the conditions under which micro-level motivations and changes in state practice are associated or disassociated with one another. Third, there is a need for sharing and building upon common subjects of analysis and research concerns across disciplines. Consider contemporary examples from the academy: interdisciplinary discussions concerning the concept of trust and the concept of hypocrisy have helped to produce creative projects and important empirical insights. With that inspiration, our volume suggests some common topics for future research in human rights. First, a focus of Baron's chapter on omission bias suggests the enormous power of this characteristic of a decision to harm or help others (chapter 8). And Baron examines whether omission bias is associated with other decision characteristics, such as effects of the decision on resource allocations between in-groups and out-groups. It would benefit other research programs to consider omission bias (along with these other decision characteristics) in the study of human rights. For example, building upon Slovic and Zionts's study (chapter 5), researchers should investigate how cognitive impediments to apprehending mass suffering might be associated with these decision characteristics—for example, whether a decision not to help X numbers of individuals operates differently than a decision to hurt X numbers of individuals. Building upon Levi, Tyler, and Sachs's study of state legitimacy and legal compliance (chapter 4), researchers could explore whether public perceptions of governmental competence are affected by omission versus commission of official acts. If important findings vary significantly according to an omission bias, it would dovetail nicely with Baron's research. If not, it would be an interesting contrast with Baron's research and advance our knowledge of the conditions under which such factors matter.

Another topic that is ripe for integrated analysis involves the aversion of humans to social and material inequality. This aversion motivates individuals to shift resources to others even when they would personally benefit from an inequitable distribution—which has the potential to produce altruistic social practices. And the aversion shapes individuals' preferences for relative gains over objective gains for themselves—which has the potential, in some circumstances, to diminish aggregate public welfare. Notions of inequality aversion, and concepts similar in structure to it, appear in independent research programs presented in this book (Bland, Powell, and Ross, chapter 10; Gintis, chapter 6; cf. Mikhail, chapter 7). However, an organized conversation between those programs has not (yet) emerged.

This volume illuminates other cross-cutting topics similar to omission bias and inequality aversion. For example, social scientists across various research programs could incorporate social networks into their research designs—as evidenced in part by Lazer's presentation of networks analysis (chapter 9). And a deeper conversation about the significance of evolutionary biology—to which several chapters allude—could also make advances for the study of human rights. We are certain that researchers will identify other cross-cutting topics from the collection of works in this volume.

Fourth, there is a need for better explanations of variance as part of the next phase of research. An understated feature of the studies presented in this volume—as well as many related social science accounts of the human actor—is variation, or deviance. The studies emphasize predominant—if not near universal—behavioral, psychological, and communicative regularities. Some studies suggest that particular features of human cognition are "universal" (Mikhail, chapter 7). Other studies suggest particular tendencies are the product of evolutionary pressures on humankind (Gintis, chapter 6). And other studies analogize particular cognitive biases (so-called psychophysical functions) to visual illusions where the naked eye inexorably commits an error of perception (Slovic and Zionts, chapter 5). The question is why a meaningful fraction of the subjects do not exhibit these common traits. Why do some individuals fail to follow an evolutionary path toward strong reciprocity, to exhibit an innate moral grammar, to fall trap to psychic numbing, to succumb to pluralistic ignorance, or to experience shame? Is the variation explained by underlying systematic conditions, for example, the particular status or prior experiences of subjects? Are the factors that cause deviance malleable or fixed? Some methodologies—such as comparison of means—might obscure this concern. But it should be made explicit.

Indeed, a new phase of research could examine variations that currently lack explanation. These inquiries can help the larger project of engaging interdisciplinary scholarship to promote human rights. In particular, these issues of variance constitute important factors for designing institutions to produce different preferences, to affect decision making, to screen in or screen out particular individuals, and to overcome or to exploit biases. In short, this agenda item for future researchers will directly help to create better institutions and to build cultures of human rights.

Finally, before research insights are used to change human rights advocacy strategies and policy, it would be helpful to consider how such insights can and/ or cannot be used to guide behavior through the manipulation of social institutions. For example, when will the very identification of a bias—for the purposes of studying it and devising human rights policy—cause the bias to change? Also, many studies observe social behaviors that have been affected, oftentimes incidentally, by prior institutional changes. The studies, however, often cannot predict the effects of future institutional reforms that are deliberately adopted to generate those behaviors. Indeed, especially in the case of democratic or transparent decision making, the explicit discussion of the reform's strategies and objectives might undermine its desired social and psychological effects. Additionally, we offer policy applications here based on the information we currently have of the world—but once the application goes into effect, the world changes as a result, and the central insight that informed the application may no longer hold. For this reason, significant contributions are waiting to be made by studying the implementation of applied social science insight. This would, in fact, be an ideal topic of future research and collaboration between scholars and practitioners.

The Psychology of Social Norms and the Promotion of Human Rights

DEBORAH A. PRENTICE

I. Introduction

Promoting human rights means changing behavior: changing the behavior of governments that mistreat suspected criminals, opponents of their policies, supporters of their political rivals, and members of particular gender, ethnic, or religious groups; changing the behavior of corporations that mistreat their workers, damage the environment, and produce unsafe products; and changing the behavior of citizens who mistreat their spouses, children, and neighbors. In this chapter, I consider what an understanding of how social norms function psychologically has to contribute to this very worthy project. Social norms have proven to be an effective mechanism for changing health-related and environmental behaviors, so there is good reason to think that they might be helpful in the human rights domain as well.

In the social sciences, social norms are defined as socially shared and enforced attitudes specifying what to do and what not to do in a given situation (see Elster, 1990; Sunstein, 1997). They are one source of constraint on behavior, in a family with laws, markets, and structural features of the environment (Lessig, 1998). Social norms are similar to laws, only less formal: The standards they promote are not codified, and their enforcement occurs informally, through social sanctions within groups and communities. They are similar to markets, only the incentives involved are social, not material: the approval of one's friends and neighbors is what is at stake. Social norms are akin to structural features of the environment, in that they are social constraints that channel behavior in some directions and prevent it from going in other ones. One might assume that because social norms are less explicit and observable than laws, markets, and physical structures, they are also less powerful; in fact, the opposite is the case. Social norms do not require legislation, and the resources used to enforce them are unlimited; thus, they are much more pervasive than laws and markets. Moreover, because humans are highly social creatures, they are keenly sensitive to the behavior of those around them and are often prepared to put their material and even physical well-being aside in pursuit of social approval (Miller and Prentice, 1994). The fact that social sanctions are freely available does not diminish their power.

Traditionally, advocates of human rights have conceived of their project strictly within a legal framework, narrowly defined. However, as the scope of that project has broadened to include the civil, economic, and social rights of particular groups of people within societies, the importance of social norms has drawn their attention. For scholars, norms provide a way of conceptualizing both sides of the human rights equation: the practices that violate people's rights and the international standards that seek to uphold those rights (see, e.g., Checkel, 1999; Clark, 2001; Cortell and Davis, 1996; Risse, Ropp, and Sikkink, 1999; Simmons, 2000). For practitioners, norms are a highly attractive target for intervention, especially for rights violations that are embedded in the everyday practices of ordinary people. Of course, in all of these cases, the promise of social norms stems, in large part, from the fact that more formal and resource-dependent mechanisms are not available or suitable. Norms seem to offer a simple, economical way to explain, create, and sometimes unravel behavioral regularities.[1] Exactly how they work remains a bit of a mystery. Let me begin the task of demystifying norms by outlining how they function to regulate behavior. Here, I will adopt a psychological level of analysis to examine how norms affect the behavior of individuals.

II. The Mechanics of Social Norms

As I noted, social scientists typically define norms as socially shared and enforced attitudes specifying what to do and what not to do in a given situation. Psychologists, by contrast, favor a definition that is broader, more abstract, and more intrapsychic: Social norms are representations of where one's group is located or ought to be located on an attitudinal or behavioral dimension (Miller and Prentice, 1996). These representations tend to be socially shared, and the attitudes and behaviors they specify tend to be socially enforced, but neither of these properties is definitional; neither is required of a norm. Instead, these are outcomes of the way norms function. Moreover, norms do not just specify what people ought and ought not to do; they also specify what people actually do, what they think, and how they feel. This definition of norms highlights a number of features that prove useful for understanding how they work.

First, social norms are representations of *a group*, one's own group; they are characterizations of what "we" think, feel, and do. Thus, for there to be a norm, there must be a group—a "we"—to characterize. This point is important and often overlooked. The power of social norms to constrain behavior resides in social psychological dynamics that occur within groups—in the tendency of group members to look to each other for guidance, affirmation, and approval; and in the psychological pressures toward uniformity within the group that result (Turner, 1991). The group can be a club, an organization, a community, a neighborhood, a network; it can be loosely or tightly formed, formal or informal, face-to-face or virtual. What is important is that the members of the group consider themselves to be peers—equals, fellows, similar in important ways—and therefore consider the opinions and behaviors of the other group members to be relevant to their own.

This feature of social norms—their embeddedness in the dynamics of peer groups—begins to delimit the rights-relevant behaviors that norms can illuminate. For example, social norms might shape the interrogation practices used by a police force: police officers use the behavior of their peers as a guide to what constitutes an appropriate level of force. Similarly, social norms might influence the level of education girls receive in a community: parents use the behavior of other parents as a guide. Social norms can explain uniformities of behavior among employees within corporations and among corporations within industries. They can also explain why groups differ—why some police forces use more aggressive interrogation tactics than others, some communities treat girls better than others, and some corporations and industries treat workers better than others.

For other behaviors, social norms probably play a less significant role. Consider, for example, the rights-related policies of governments. Are these policies shaped by international human rights norms? This question has generated considerable controversy within the field of international relations and has produced a growing literature on how, when, and where norms matter (see Cardenas, 2004, for a review). What the present analysis can contribute to that project is not answers, but more questions. One key question, for example, is whether the government has a peer group—that is, a group of similar others, whose behavior is relevant for comparison and whose good opinion is valued. If so, then the comparison and reinforcement processes within the international peer group might have a significant influence on adherence to human rights standards independent of other incentives. Another key question is whether the nation has internalized the international norms—that is, whether the nation itself now holds these standards as important for its own functioning. In this case, human rights norms might be enforced not by the international community alone, but also by domestic constituencies, and therefore may loom much larger in the government's political calculus. The point I want to underscore is that the influence of norms begins and ends with membership in groups, and identifying the relevant groups is a critical step in understanding the nature of that influence.

Finally, on this issue, it is important to emphasize that social norms are particular to one's own group (the in-group). They are distinct from representations of other groups; those are stereotypes. They are also distinct from the thoughts, feelings, and behaviors of the individual members of the group. An individual may represent her group as holding attitudes and engaging in practices that she herself does not condone. For example, we may be in favor of the death penalty, and yet I may be vehemently opposed.

A second point to make about social norms is that they come in two types: norms can be injunctive, characterizing where a group *should be* located on a dimension; or descriptive, characterizing where the group *is* located on the dimension (Cialdini, Kallgren, and Reno, 1991; Miller and Prentice, 1996). This is the difference between behavior in principle and behavior in practice, a difference that looms very large in the human rights domain. In principle, a police force may prohibit aggressive interrogation tactics; in practice, officers may use these tactics when all else fails. In principle, a firm may have a norm of zero tolerance for sexual harassment; in practice, suggestive remarks and sexist humor may be commonplace. Descriptive norms can be consistent with, inconsistent with, or independent of injunctive norms. Both descriptive and injunctive norms produce behavioral regularities: the former because violations of them are seen as odd, and the latter because violations of them are seen as bad.

A third point to make about norms is that they are *representations*—ideas about the group, pictures people have in their heads about what their group does and values. These pictures have two distinguishing features. One, the group is represented as having a central tendency—an average or modal location on the dimension in question. For example, in the United States, most people graduate from high school (82% of those who complete the 8th grade); most of those who do will enroll in a 4-year college (58%); and most of those who enroll go on to graduate (59% by age 26; see Goldin and Katz, 2008). Thus, it is the norm in the United States to take an educational path that results in a bachelor's degree; it is typical, expected. Of course, not all members of the group conform to this norm—indeed, the majority do not. But enough do that the central tendency is a meaningful feature of how the group is represented by its members. The central tendency is the content of the norm and determines the direction of its influence.

A second feature of the representation of the group is its dispersal—that is, how uniform the group is seen as being on the dimension in question. For example, suppose in one community, children receive, on average, 8 years of education, with a range from 7 to 9 years. In another community, children also receive an average of 8 years of education, but here the range is 4 to 12 years. The central tendency of the group, and therefore the direction of the norm's influence, is the same in these two communities. However, the strength of that influence is likely to be very different. In the first community, children's education is highly uniform; most children are treated the same way. In the second community, the range is so great that almost anything goes. As a consequence, the norm for how much to educate children is likely to have a much stronger influence in the first community than in the second.

Finally, it is important to emphasize that representations do not always map perfectly onto reality. People sometimes have ideas about their group that are outdated, exaggerated, or just plain wrong. In particular, under certain circumstances, people misjudge the location of the social norm, overestimate the uniformity of the group, and overestimate the extent of private support for group norms. These errors are of potential interest to human rights advocates for at least two reasons: One, they often play a role in perpetuating extreme, anomalous, and dysfunctional group behaviors that interfere with people's rights. In some cases, they foster these behaviors; in others, they inhibit people from openly expressing disapproval of them. Two, erroneous assumptions about the group give rise to discrepancies between injunctive and descriptive norms, on the one hand, and private attitudes, on the other—discrepancies that, when brought to light, can catalyze behavior change. I will have more to say about these misrepresentations and their consequences in the sections that follow.

Social norms enter into discussions of human rights in two main ways: one, as a source of problematic behavior, and two, as a way to counter that behavior. Let me analyze how norms function in each of these capacities.

III. Social Norms as a Source of Problematic Behavior

Many of the behaviors that human rights advocates find problematic are enshrined in cultural practices and supported by (locally) injunctive norms. Female genital cutting is one widely discussed example, but there are many others: male circumcision, corporal punishment of children, infanticide, animal sacrifices, slavery, polygamy, and so on. Debates about these kinds of behaviors typically revolve around the tension between promoting human rights (conceived as universal, inalienable, and natural), on the one hand; and respecting local cultural practices, on the other. However, as Shweder (2006) has pointed out, local cultural practices are protected by rights as well—among them, the right of groups and nations to autonomy, self-determination, freedom of religion, and the right of parents to raise their children within their own cultural traditions. Therefore, so long as the behavior in question remains a cultural norm—that is, so long as it remains prevalent, valued, and linked to important social outcomes within the group—it is very difficult for human rights advocates, coming from outside the group, to find legitimate grounds to overturn it.

There is, however, reason to question the actual degree of support any particular cultural norm enjoys. As I noted in the foregoing section, norms are representations that do not always map perfectly onto reality. They are subject to systematic biases, and one of these biases is a tendency for people, both within and outside of the group, to overestimate the uniformity of support for normative practices. This bias in representation is rooted in three well-documented biases in the information people reveal to their fellow group members the inferences they draw from that information.

First, people are more likely to reveal their normative behaviors—those that reflect what is considered typical and desirable for group members—and to conceal their counternormative, and therefore stigmatizing, behaviors. College students talk about their drinking escapades and remain silent about Saturday nights spent at the student center; juvenile delinquents brag about acts of vandalism and conceal acts of obedience; residents in vegetarian co-ops eat tofu with their housemates and meat only with their close friends (Kitts, 2003; Miller and Prentice, 1996).

Second, people are more likely to express opinions they believe to be consistent with descriptive and injunctive group norms than those they believe to be inconsistent with these norms. Public opinion researchers have long recognized that believing oneself to be deviant is silencing, even when that belief is inaccurate (Noelle-Neumann, 1984). Empirical studies have confirmed that the willingness of group members to voice their opinions is a direct function of how prevalent they believe those opinions to be among their peers (Glynn, Hayes, and Shanahan, 1997). When the relationship between voice and perceived support for one's position does not hold, it is either because people mistakenly believe that everybody agrees with them (Miller and Morrison, 2009) or because they see their opinions as violating the descriptive but not the injunctive norm of the group—that is, they see themselves as different but good (Morrison and Miller, 2008). For example, in a group that is mildly in favor of capital punishment, a rabid capital punishment supporter may recognize that his opinion is deviant, but because he is on the right side of the issue, he will feel different in a good way, superior to those who take a more moderate view. Thus, he will not hesitate to give voice to his opinion.

Third, people assume that their observations of their fellow group members—the behaviors they witness, the opinions they hear expressed—reflect what those individuals privately think, feel, and do. That is, they fail to recognize how, and how much, people's public behaviors and expressions are influenced by social constraints (Gilbert, 1998; Ross, 1977). The uncertainties and misgivings that people often feel about the norms of their groups, and their reluctance to challenge those norms under any and all circumstances, go unrecognized in all but the self. This tendency to take other people's behavior at face value leads individuals to think that they feel differently than others do, even when they act identically. Researchers have termed this phenomenon *pluralistic ignorance* (see Prentice and Miller, 1996).

In short, systematic biases in the information people reveal to each other and the inferences they draw from that information can conspire to produce widespread overestimation of private support for social norms. Under these conditions, norm-challenging interventions run much less risk of infringing on people's rights, not to mention desires. A key question, then, is when does overestimation of support for social norms occur? That is, when does public behavior diverge systematically from private views?

One condition that contributes to this divergence is constraint on public behavior. Of course, norms always constrain public actions, but sometimes the constraints are more explicit than others. When constraints are very strong and explicit, public actions and private views typically diverge quite substantially. For example, in countries living under totalitarian rule, such divergences are commonplace. However, this is not the situation that leads to an overestimation of private support for public practices. More insidious are those cases in which constraints on public behavior are subtle and accompanied by the illusion of choice; these are the cases in which norms are often thought to have more support than they do. In his excellent book on divergences between public actions and private views, Kuran (1995) noted that he developed his theory of preference falsification not through experience with despotic regimes, but instead in societies with free press and open debate about official policies. Open societies can be deceptive in this regard: the constraints on behavior imposed by social roles, social norms, and public opinion go unrecognized, and people's actions are seen by any and all observers as a straightforward reflection of their private preferences.[2]

An example of this phenomenon, one with considerable relevance to human rights concerns, comes from studies of prison guards and inmates (Kauffman, 1981; Klofas and Toch, 1982; Toch and Klofas, 1982; Wheeler, 1961). Behavior by members of both of these groups is highly constrained by social roles. The traditional role of the guard demands harsh and punitive behavior toward inmates, and the traditional role of the prisoner demands resistant and recalcitrant behavior toward guards. It is very common for the behavior of both groups to polarize along this adversarial axis. Guards assume that other guards hold anti-inmate attitudes that correspond to their antagonistic stance, and prisoners assume that other prisoners hold anti-guard attitudes that correspond to their antagonistic stance. In fact, opinions surveys have shown that attitudes on both sides are much more congenial and sympathetic to the other group and, in fact, that both sides feel beleaguered by their peers' hostility. Because they do not recognize the constraints introduced by their polarized roles in this situation, they also do not recognize that the feelings of their peers, like their own, are more moderate.

Constraints on public behavior are one source of a divergence between public actions and private views; a second is a lack of determinacy in people's feelings and preferences. Such indeterminacy arises, for example, when preferences are not well formed, when people do not know how to act on what they want, when they have mixed feelings, and when the situation itself is unclear or changing rapidly. Under all of these circumstances, people find themselves without a clear, internal guide to action; their inclination is to hesitate, to wait for clarity to emerge, and to look to other people for guidance. When everybody does this simultaneously, one of two things happens: either inaction itself emerges as the norm, or inaction is interpreted as support for the status quo.

A famous example of the emergence of inaction as a social norm comes from research on bystander intervention. Bystanders in emergency situations are notorious for failing to act, failing to intervene. In the 1960s and 1970s, two researchers, Bibb Latané and John Darley, did a series of laboratory and field experiments that demonstrated that the likelihood that a witness to an emergency will do something to help is inversely proportional to the number of witnesses present (see Latané and Darley, 1970). In their analysis of the phenomenon, Latané and Darley highlighted the uncertainty inherent in emergency situations and the role that trying to cope with that uncertainty publicly plays in the dynamic. As they put it: "Occasionally the reactions of others provide false information as to the true state of their feelings . . . If each member of a group is trying to appear calm and not overreact to the possibility of danger, each other member, in looking to him for guidance, may be misled into thinking that he is not concerned. Looking at the *apparent* impassivity and lack of reaction of the others, each individual is led to believe that nothing is really wrong" (Latané and Darley, 1970, p. 44). In short, inaction, which is originally driven by uncertainty, becomes a norm as everybody observes it in each other. Note that people in these situations need never decide anything; often, they are still uncertain, still waiting for clarity to emerge, when the situation ends. Moreover, time is not on their side: The longer they wait, the less likely they are to act (Latané and Darley, 1970).

An interesting version of this dynamic occurs during times of social change, when existing norms are being questioned and contested. It is common, under these circumstances, for attitudes to change more quickly than norms do, as people are persuaded by arguments for change but are not sure how or whether to act on their evolving convictions. As they look to others for clarity and guidance, they see only continued support for the status quo: support that they, in their inaction, are signaling as well. In other words, each individual's inability or reluctance to act differently maintains the illusion of widespread support for norms to which people no longer feel allegiance. This phenomenon is known as a *conservative lag* (Fields and Schuman, 1976).

The civil rights movement in the United States engendered a well-documented case of a conservative lag. National surveys conducted in the late 1960s revealed a sizable gap between the views people expressed about racial segregation and the beliefs they held about other people's views. For example, the Survey Research Center's 1968 National Election Study revealed that explicit support for racial segregation among whites was quite low across the country, ranging from just under 10% in the New England and Pacific states to just over 30% in the Southern states.[3] By contrast, nearly 50% of white respondents expressed the belief that all or most whites in their area favored segregation (O'Gorman, 1975). Estimates of others' support co-varied with the observed degree of segregation within and across regions, suggesting that respondents based these estimates on what they saw around them. Fields and Schuman (1976) reported a similar result from a 1969 survey of Detroit residents. Asked whether they thought a white mother should allow her young daughter to bring a black classmate home from school, 76% said yes. Asked how "most people in Detroit" would answer, just 33% said yes. Again, predictions of others mirrored the high degree of racial segregation that characterized life in Detroit in the late 1960s. Why did people respond differently for themselves? Fields and Schuman (1976) argued strongly for the veracity of these self-reported attitudes. They maintained that the majority of whites in Detroit truly believed that a white mother should allow her young daughter to bring a black classmate home from school. These whites did not act on this belief because they, and everyone else—black and white alike—thought it was a minority view.

Surveys of racial attitudes no longer reveal a conservative lag; however, that is not to say that norms of racial segregation are a thing of the past. In many settings, some of them engineered to be racially diverse, norms of segregation continue to characterize behavior. One example of such a setting is the modern-day college campus, where racial and ethnic groups coexist side by side, and students interact much more with in-group members than with out-group members. When asked why they do not interact more across racial boundaries, students typically say that they would like to have more contact, that they are not content with the status quo. However, they believe that members of other groups are not interested in having more contact with them. Black and white students alike attribute their own failure to cross group boundaries to a fear of being rejected, but they attribute the other group's failure to cross group boundaries as reflecting a genuine lack of interest (Shelton and Richeson, 2005). It is easy to see how this dynamic would be self-perpetuating.

One final example illustrates how this misinterpretation of inaction can lead to an overestimation of citizen support for government policies. In the period between September 11, 2001, and the invasion of Iraq, there was considerable uncertainty over how the United States should conduct its War on Terror. U.S. citizens knew how they felt—they were sure they were terrified—but they did not know how to translate that fear into action. The U.S. government, as it turns out, did not know what to do either, and what emerged was a policy whereby the United States would decide what it wanted to do; would seek approval from the international community; and, if approval was not forthcoming, would take unilateral action. One of the results of that policy was the invasion of Iraq in 2003.

In the weeks leading up to the invasion, Todorov and Mandisodza (2004) conducted a survey using a representative national sample in which they asked, "What do you think is the more important lesson of September 11: that the U.S. needs to work more closely with other countries to fight terrorism or that the U.S. needs to act on its own more to fight terrorism?" Respondents reported their own opinions and then estimated the proportion of Americans who endorsed each of the stated positions in the question. The results showed that private attitudes were overwhelmingly multilateral, with over three-quarters of respondents endorsing multilateralism as the more important lesson of September 11. However, these same respondents indicated that they thought unilateralism was the view of a majority of other Americans. The survey also asked specifically about attitudes toward a unilateral invasion of Iraq, without the support of the UN Security Council. Among respondents who expressed multilateral views, responses to this question depended on what they thought others thought. Specifically, when they thought others held unilateral views, they were more likely to agree with a unilateral invasion and more likely to support one even if they disagreed than when they thought others held multilateral views (Todorov and Mandisodza, 2004). In short, the majority's mistaken assumption that others supported government policies led them to support these policies themselves.

There is a different, but related, question one might ask about the gap between social norms and private views that emerged in the wake of September 11: Why did the government's policies and the norms they spawned fail to represent the private views of citizens? Why were they so extreme? Most answers to these questions foreground particular features of the Bush administration: its power structure, ideology, history, decision-making processes, and so on. Alternatively, it seems worth exploring the possibility that there were also general forces at work, forces that tend to promote the emergence of extreme norms in highly uncertain or unstable situations. What might those forces be? Consider the qualities of individuals who are likely to act in an uncertain or unstable situation: the ones who will rush into a burning building, be the first in their neighborhood to invite a black classmate over to play, and think they know what to do in the face of a terrorist attack. These are, at the very least, highly unusual, unrepresentative people. They are certain when others are not, express their views when others remain silent, and take action while others are still wondering what to do. Sometimes their actions are heroic, and sometimes they simply make a bad situation worse. Importantly, they are a source of new, often extreme, and at least initially unsupported social norms. Norms promoting excessive alcohol use, extreme political views, and delinquent gang behavior have all been traced to the actions of a vocal and unrepresentative minority (see Korte, 1972; Matza, 1964; Miller and Morrison, 2009).

In summary, social norms do not always reflect what the individuals who abide by and enforce them consider desirable and appropriate behavior; indeed, they often diverge markedly from individual feelings and preferences. Conceptualizing social norms as representations of the group clarifies how and when these divergences occur. Their implications for understanding and promoting human rights are considerable: they help to explain why ordinary people stand by while atrocities occur, why groups in adversarial relationships tend to polarize, why customary practices remain entrenched even after individuals have been persuaded of their disutility, and why groups and governments often take extreme actions in times of uncertainty or crisis. Moreover, these situations also offer to human rights advocates opportunities to intervene without the usual concerns about infringing on the rights and sensibilities of those they seek to help. To the extent that there is, within the group, unacknowledged disaffection for existing norms and a majority sentiment for change, promoting that change becomes a much more manageable project.

IV. Social Norms as a Mechanism for Behavior Change

I now turn to a consideration of what this analysis of social norms and how they function psychologically has to contribute to efforts at behavior change, and specifically, change in the behaviors that violate human rights. For human rights advocates, the target of behavior change is typically the descriptive norm; that is, the goal is to change what the group is doing. One might want to move the location of the descriptive norm: to increase the average number of years that girls go to school in a community, for example, or to reduce the incidence of circumcision or corporal punishment or spousal abuse. One also might want to change the dispersion of the group: to reduce the dispersion by tightening conformity to environmental or public health standards, for example; or to increase the dispersion by liberating people to express unpopular political views or to interact with whomever they choose. In the former case, one seeks to bring the descriptive norm into line with the injunctive norm, to get people to practice what they preach. In the latter case, one seeks to weaken or eliminate the descriptive norm so that people will be guided by personal attitudes and predilections or perhaps by other norms or incentives.

There are two complementary schools of thought on the social psychology of changing behavior. One focuses on changing people's attitudes and beliefs in order to change their actions (cf. Hovland, Janis, and Kelley, 1953). For adherents to this school of thought, changing behavior is fundamentally about changing minds; it is about controlling the information to which people are exposed and how they process that information. This tradition survives and is most prominently represented in the fields of communications, marketing, and consumer behavior (see, e.g., Hornik, this volume). A second school of thought focuses not on attitudes and beliefs but on motives—on the pressures pushing people in the direction of some goals and away from others (cf. Lewin, 1951). For adherents to this school of thought, changing behavior is fundamentally about changing the force of the different pressures, so as to change the equilibrium of the tension system (see Ross and Nisbett, 1991). This tradition survives and is most prominently represented in the fields of group dynamics, organizational behavior, and behavioral economics.

Social norms fit comfortably within this latter tradition.[4] Social norms are motivational pressures acting on all members of a group simultaneously to produce collective movement toward some behaviors and away from others. Behavior change, then, involves strengthening or weakening the force of particular social norms so as to change the equilibrium of the system. Given that the force of norms comes from the perception that everyone agrees with and adheres to them—that is, from the perceived dispersion of the group around the norm—the most straightforward way to strengthen or weaken them is to alter perceptions of that dispersion: to highlight the fact that everyone wants the same thing or that they all want different things. Note that this type of intervention often has the effect of changing the location of the norm as well. Specifically, strengthening a norm usually changes its location because behavior is not symmetrically distributed around the central tendency to start with (e.g., people are more likely to pollute more than the norm prescribes, not less, so strengthening the norm moves the location of the descriptive norm in the direction of less pollution); similarly, weakening a norm does not send behavior in all directions equally, but rather predominantly in the direction counter to the force of the norm (see Katz and Schanck, 1938, for a discussion of the dynamics of the J-curve).

The other point to make about this formulation is that it highlights the fact that social norms are part of a larger motivational system. They do not exist in isolation but rather form systems of complementary and competing pressures on behavior. Moreover, that system includes not just social norms but other types of motives as well, including needs, goals, values, and material incentives; all of these forces act in concert to determine behavior. Thus, the consequences of strengthening or weakening a particular norm depend on what other forces are operating within the system.

V. Strengthening Social Norms

Strengthening social norms involves leveraging human sociality to mobilize conformity to a particular standard. Often, this is exactly what human rights advocates want to do: they want individuals, groups, corporations, and nations to adhere to the human rights standards they have agreed are desirable; they want people to practice what they preach; they want to close the gap between descriptive norms and injunctive norms. Conformity turns out to be reasonably straightforward to produce: all one needs to do is to highlight the direction and uniformity of the group's behavior, and group members will follow suit. Of course, that only serves to strengthen existing behavioral patterns and only works in the short run. Human rights advocates typically aspire to a more ambitious project: they seek to produce long-lasting change in the behavioral patterns of the group. This project runs into two challenges.

One challenge is to make the injunctive, rather than the descriptive, norm the salient guide for behavior. In many cases of human rights violations, people agree on the desirable and appropriate course of action; they simply fall short. They respond to short-term incentives, give other goals and norms priority, and react badly in times of crisis. The group's behavior ends up deviating systematically and predictably from the injunctive norm. How to close the gap? One solution is to enhance the salience and therefore the force of injunctive norms by highlighting the group's collective approval or disapproval of a certain behavior. This potential effectiveness of this strategy was demonstrated by Schultz and colleagues (2007). The injunctive norm these researchers sought to promote was energy conservation. They partnered with a local utilities company in San Diego, which gave them access to the company's routine meter readings of household energy consumption. The researchers gave householders feedback on their energy consumption at two time points, by way of a handwritten note delivered on a door hanger. For one set of households, they provided information about that household's energy consumption and the average consumption of households of their size, with tips for how to conserve; this was the descriptive-norm intervention. For a second set of households, they provided the same information, plus a hand-drawn happy face if that household's consumption was below average and a sad face if that household's consumption was above average; this was the descriptive+injunctive-norm intervention. Both of these interventions induced conformity: When presented with only descriptive information, above-average households decreased their subsequent consumption, and below-average households increased their consumption. However, when presented with descriptive and injunctive information, above-average households decreased their subsequent consumptions, and below-average households showed no change. Behavior tightened around the injunctive norm. This is exactly the outcome that human rights advocates so often seek. Utilities companies were impressed with this outcome also: several companies have now begun to include social comparison information, complete with smiling and frowning faces, in the design of their utility bills (Kaufman, 2009).

A second challenge is to maintain the salience of one particular norm amidst competing motivational pressures. Although people readily conform to social norms, both descriptive and injunctive, the motivational potency of those norms depends critically on their salience (Cialdini et al., 1991). And given the very crowded condition of most people's motivational landscape, the salience of any particular norm waxes and wanes. These two facts have led some theorists to argue that what the field needs is a theory of norm salience, and in particular, its situational determinants (Bicchieri, 2000). Absent such a theory, and with a more pragmatic goal in mind, I would simply note that sustained behavior change, at a collective level, rarely rests on mobilizing conformity to one particular injunctive norm. That is, shaming rarely works in isolation. Rather, strengthening injunctive norms is an important part of a multifaceted strategy to produce behavior change, a strategy that typically combines the recruitment of directional social pressure with material and legal incentives. The success of the campaign to reduce smoking behavior over the last 50 years provides an excellent illustration of the importance of social norms in such a strategy (Brandt, 2007).

VI. Weakening Social Norms

Of course, social norms are very often the problem, not the solution, to promoting human rights. That is, often human rights advocates seek to weaken the influence of norms that support rights-violating behaviors. The strategy here is the flip side of the strategies for strengthening norms. Specifically, if highlighting the direction and uniformity of the group's behavior serves to strengthen norms, then decreasing the salience of the group's behavior and/or highlighting its heterogeneity will serve to weaken them.

One way to implement this latter strategy is to give individuals voice: that is, to provide them with an opportunity to express their private views and to learn the private views of others. To the extent that prevailing norms do not have strong consensual support, this process will make salient to people the diversity of opinions within the group and thereby dispel the illusion of universality. Public opinion surveys can serve this function, sometimes inadvertently and occasionally despite the best efforts of those trying to conserve the norms. The history of prohibition laws in the United States provides a good illustration. As Katz and Schanck (1938) described: "During the prohibition era the forces in favor of prohibition never wanted any objective check on public sentiment. They tried to kill off straw polls on the subject of prohibition. As a consequence of their tactics even the politicians were fooled by an illusion of universality of opinion in favor of the Eighteenth Amendment. When an objective check was made, however, prohibition collapsed like a punctured balloon" (p. 175).

A liberating voice can also serve as an effective intervention strategy, particularly when social norms have less private support than people believe them to have. Schroeder and Prentice (1998) used just such a strategy to liberate college students from the norm of excessive alcohol consumption. Their intervention capitalized on an earlier finding that college students systematically and substantially overestimate their peers' comfort with heavy drinking (Prentice and Miller, 1993). In the norm-focused intervention, students saw evidence that they themselves overestimated their peers' comfort with heavy drinking and then discussed, as a group, the phenomenon of pluralistic ignorance and what might give rise to it in drinking situations. This intervention produced a 40% drop in drinking behavior, relative to a control intervention, at a follow-up assessment four to six months after the discussions. Additional findings suggested that this reduction in drinking was a result of weakening the power of the drinking norm. First, there was no evidence for a change in the location of the norm; that is, perceptions of the average student's comfort with drinking did not vary as a function of the intervention, nor was there any evidence that a change in the perceived location of the norm mediated drinking behavior. Thus, students were not simply conforming to a lower drinking norm. Second, the intervention was most effective at reducing heavy drinking among students high in social anxiety, suggesting a reduction in perceived peer pressure. Third, the intervention left nondrinking students feeling more comfortable on campus, again suggesting a reduction in perceived peer pressure (see Prentice and Miller, 1996). All of these findings point to a weakening of the norm's influence as a consequence of the intervention.

Liberating people from oppressive group norms may sound appealing, but it has at least two potential downsides. First, weakening norms deprives people of something they very much want and need: a way to fit in with their peers and fellow community members. Group norms are double-edged swords: they thwart individuality, but at the same time, provide identity and belongingness (Prentice, 2006). If people are deprived of one way to connect themselves to the group and establish themselves as good group members, they will find another way to do it. Or, they may seek out like-minded peers, who share their perceptions and habits, with whom they can establish more well-grounded norms. Or, they may revert to the discredited norm once the glow of liberation has worn off. The point is that intervention efforts may be able to liberate people from a particular norm, but they will not be able to eliminate normative influence altogether. Indeed, this would be neither a desirable nor a feasible goal. Second and relatedly, the ultimate success of this type of intervention, from a human rights perspective, rests entirely on the question of what will guide people's behavior once the influence of the norm is eliminated. As problematic as the norm may seem in prospect, there is always the possibility that what comes afterward will be considerably worse.

Economic incentives are another effective way to weaken social norms, though they, too, have a downside for human rights advocates. Specifically, economic taxes and subsidies work by replacing moral considerations with material ones (Bowles, 2008); they have the effect of removing behavior from the domain of right and wrong. Consider, for example, the case of blood donation. In the early 1970s, when Britain was considering trying to increase its blood supply by moving from a strictly charitable system to a compensated one, Richard Titmuss (1971), a social policy authority, argued that this move would have adverse effects on the both the quantity and quality of the blood supply. Specifically, in a very controversial book, he argued that compensating blood donation would make it less attractive to people because the compensation would deprive them of the gratification they received from what heretofore had been an act of civic virtue. In other words, he argued that the offer of an economic subsidy would shift the behavior from a moral economy to a market economy. Moreover, he maintained that the magnitude of the economic subsidy would not be high enough even to maintain current levels of blood donation, much less to increase them. Titmuss (1971) offered little data in support of his claims; however, recent theory and evidence have borne them out, at least to some extent (Mellstrom and Johanneson, 2008). For blood donation, as well as for any other behaviors linked to injunctive norms, the psychological benefit people receive from the action is undermined if they begin to receive economic benefit from the action as well.

Economic taxes and fines work the same way. Consider the findings of an intervention study conducted in 10 private day care centers in Israel (Gneezy and Rustichini, 2000). The targeted group was the parents of children enrolled at each center, many of whom were routinely tardy to pick up their children. The intervention strategy was one of traditional deterrence: The investigators sought to reduce the frequency of tardiness by imposing a fine on latecoming behavior. At 6 of the day care centers, a modest fine was imposed in the 5th week of the 20-week observation period and was removed in the 17th week; the other 4 centers served as a control group. The results showed that the number of late pickups *increased* significantly with the imposition of a fine and remained at the increased level even after the fine was removed. The investigators interpreted these results as evidence for the demoralizing effects of economic incentives. Before the fine, behavior was regulated by injunctive norms against latecoming, to which parents imperfectly conformed. They tried to arrive on time and felt guilty when they did not make it. Once a fine was introduced, however, latecomers no longer felt guilty; they simply paid a material price for their lateness. The fine changed the meaning of the behavior—it made latecoming a commodity rather than a transgression—and this new meaning persisted even once the fine was removed.

Note that the (ostensible) goal of this intervention was to mobilize conformity to the injunctive social norm: to bring parents' behavior into line with the no-tardiness standard. The foregoing discussion suggests that a more effective way to accomplish this goal might be to strengthen the timeliness norm, perhaps by giving parents feedback about their own frequency of late arrivals compared with the late arrivals of other parents, with frowning faces meted out to anyone who exceeds the average and happy faces to those who fall short of it. Posting the names of the most frequent latecomers might be another way to mobilize conformity to the injunctive norm; however, it would be important not to allow to list to grow too long, lest it communicate the commonness of the practice.

In short, economic incentives, both subsidies and fines, weaken social norms, but they do so by taking behavior off the moral grid. In the two examples I described, the introduction of economic incentives, designed to increase a desirable behavior, were insufficient even to maintain it. Of course, this is not always the case: when fines and subsidies are set high enough, they are usually sufficient to produce the desired behavior. Moreover, when the relevant actors are institutions, corporations, or governments—entities that are often more responsive to their material interests than to the good example and opinion of their peers—the use of economic incentives to promote human rights is essential. Nevertheless, it seems unlikely that the project of promoting human rights among ordinary people will be advanced by taking behavior out of the realm of right and wrong.

The question, then, for human rights advocates is: How can we free people up from the pressure of a particularly problematic social norm without weakening or even challenging the broader normative framework? That is, rather than liberating behavior from social control or relegating control to market forces, can interventions reduce or eliminate particular practices by changing in more subtle ways the balance of motivational forces within the normative system? The answer is yes: legal remedies, wisely deployed, can be effective in this regard. Consider, for example, the case of dueling in the Southern United States (Lessig, 1995). Eradicating dueling in the South proved an elusive goal for many decades. Dueling was a normative means of resolving disputes or matters of honor for

Southern gentlemen. Because of the strong injunctive norms promoting dueling, participation in duels was often rational for the duelists; it enhanced their social status. However, dueling was costly to society at large, or at least it was perceived as costly by the states that struggled to ban the practice. Steep legal penalties for dueling, sometimes including death, had little deterrent value. One problem was the difficulty of maintaining enforcement of the law. Another was the strength of the norm—the high social cost incurred by refusing the challenge to a duel. No material tax on conviction for dueling could compete with the social (not to mention psychological) cost of being branded a coward and no gentleman. Moreover, Southern males of high social standing could not use the illegality of the behavior as a reason not to duel because the code of honor was meant to be above laws made by commoners.

A more effective solution, as it happened, was to make disqualification from holding public office one of the penalties for a dueling conviction (Lessig, 1995). This strategy served to liberate gentlemen from one powerful social norm by pitting an even more powerful norm against it: the obligation of the Southern gentlemen to be willing to hold public office. Conflicted duelers were unable to fulfill that obligation. Thus, refusing to duel could now be viewed as consistent with, or at least not entirely inconsistent with, the code of honor, the normative framework within which this class lived. In short, the law functioned not so much to constrain Southern males from dueling as to liberate them from having to duel in order to prove their allegiance to the norms of their group. Note that this strategy could only have worked if there were a desire among the majority of group members to extract themselves from social pressure to engage in this practice. Southern gentlemen must have wanted a way out, or this particular penalty would not have been effective. One can only assume that dueling either never had widespread support, or that support had waned over time, and a conservative lag still held the norm in place (Fields and Schuman, 1976).

The history of the Southern United States provides many other examples of how the introduction of laws was effective because those laws liberated people from particular social norms to which they no longer felt allegiance without alienating them from society (Lessig, 1995). In some of the most striking cases, the members of the group themselves actually advocated for the laws that would force them to change their behavior. One such case is the role that Southern businesspeople played in the 1960s civil rights legislation. According to Lessig (1995), in the hearings surrounding this legislation, many white business, restaurant, and hotel owners in the South testified in support of legislation that would make it illegal to do what they currently did—namely, refuse to serve African Americans. In other words, these individuals were advocating to be forced to do what they would not do voluntarily. Why didn't they simply start serving African Americans on their own? Voluntarily serving African Americans would have been a deviant action; it would have opened them up to accusations that they were too greedy or perhaps too sympathetic to blacks; and, in any case, that they put their own interests and desires ahead of the good of the community. It would have alienated them from their society. This social cost deterred them from doing something that was in their economic interest: to serve as many customers as they could. Antidiscrimination laws allowed them—indeed, forced them—to pursue their self-interest. In effect, they were lobbying for one kind of constraint to free them from a more costly one.

In short, laws can be an effective mechanism for liberating people from specific social norms without challenging the normative framework and without alienating people from their social group. Note that this strategy works only if people want to be liberated from the norms, and even then, the sanctions imposed must be carefully titrated in light of prevailing (and also perceived) public opinion. New laws must fit into the broader normative framework; otherwise, they will not be enforced. Thus, laws prohibiting dueling in the South were ineffective because they challenged directly a broader normative framework that people were not prepared to relinquish: the code of honor. A more modest legal effort to target dueling in particular, while leaving this normative framework intact (indeed, capitalizing on it), was much more enforceable and therefore more effective (Lessig, 1995). More recent laws prohibiting date rape, drunk driving, and domestic violence have run up against the same problem. Although people agree that these undesirable behaviors should be reduced or eliminated, they are not prepared to accept legal remedies that challenge the prevailing normative framework. However, more modest efforts to stigmatize these behaviors from within the framework—often by construing them as violations of even more widely held and strongly supported injunctive norms—have proven quite effective. These successes may pave the way for more ambitious legal remedies in the future (see Kahan, 2000).

VII. Concluding Remarks

Understanding the role that social norms play in regulating behavior can be a maddening enterprise: norms are, at once, ubiquitous and elusive; they are both cause and effect, a source of their own perpetuation. Although the claim that norms play an important part in promoting and subverting human rights seems uncontroversial, it is a challenge to say anything more precise and useful than that. I have argued that a psychological level of analysis—a consideration of how people represent the norms of their groups and how those representations influence behavior at an individual level—can bring some measure of clarity to this enterprise. Moreover, the analysis I have sketched suggests several conclusions about the most effective ways to design and deploy norms-based interventions in the service of promoting human rights.

One conclusion pertains to the conditions under which norms-based interventions are most likely to be effective for changing behavior: these interventions work only when there is some consensus around the desirability of change. That consensus can come from the injunctive norm (we are not doing what we should be doing) or from personal preferences (we are not doing what I want to be doing); it can be acknowledged or unacknowledged, explicit or latent. There simply needs to be some collective resonance to the notion that we would be better off if we did things differently. When there is, norms-based interventions can highlight the gap between the descriptive norm and either the injunctive norm or personal preferences to mobilize behavior change. When there is no gap—when people see the group as doing what it should do and what they personally want to do, at least on average—there is little scope for such an approach. In this case, intervention efforts need to start by changing people's views of what is desirable, through education, information campaigns, or other kinds of consciousness-raising exercises.

A second conclusion concerns implementation. Social scientists have recently shown considerable interest in the question of how to produce behavior change and specifically how forceful an intervention to use. Current thinking suggests that less is more, that a nudge is often more effective than a shove (Kahan, 2000; see Thaler and Sunstein, 2008). This proposal resonates with an older psychological literature that contrasted the ineffectiveness of many highly ambitious and heavy-handed intervention efforts with the power of minor and often subtle manipulations of channel factors (see Ross and Nisbett, 1991, for a review). The analysis I have offered suggests a more complex and nuanced conclusion. On the one hand, it underscores the fact that one should never underestimate the effectiveness of a well-placed nudge. For example, when it comes to liberating people from norms that no longer have private support, a modest intervention is often all that is required. In addition, a nudge is often all that is possible, particularly when the collective desire for change is weak or ambivalent (Kahan, 2000). On the other hand, sometimes behavior change requires a hard shove. Sometimes it requires a direct and forceful assault on behavior itself, to which injunctive norms and private attitudes then adjust. Laws mandating desegregation of public schools and those prohibiting smoking in public places are two examples of the hard-shove approach, where a forced change in descriptive norms was on the leading edge of changes in attitudes and injunctive norms. Of course, hard shoves, like gentle nudges, cannot be enacted without support, if not from the majority of the group then at least from its most powerful and influential members.

A final conclusion focuses on the broader picture. Social norms are just one part of an individual's motivational system, a system that includes personal goals and values, social rules and norms, material incentives, legal constraints, and many other forces as well. This system can be perturbed intentionally by the types of psychological, material, and legal interventions I have outlined, but it also changes and evolves in response to shifting internal and external conditions over time. This gives the system an unpredictable quality: a strategy that works to change one behavior will not work to change another, a strategy that works in Group X will not work in Group Y, and a strategy that fails at Time A may very well succeed at Time B. Variations in outcome are almost always comprehensible in retrospect, but they are much more difficult to predict in prospect. This unpredictability should not discourage efforts at intervention—indeed, there is much that can be done—but it does highlight the fact that behavior change is an art, as well as a science. An understanding of the psychology of social norms, and of motivational systems more generally, is vital to this project, but so too is particularistic knowledge of the behavior one seeks to change; the forces acting on that behavior in the status quo; the group that enacts the behavior; and the social, political, and legal climate surrounding the behavior. Only when they are armed with this local knowledge *and* scientific insight will behavior-change agents, including those who seek to promote human rights, be in a position to assess whether, when, and how to intervene.

Notes

This chapter was written while I was visiting faculty in the School of Social Sciences at the Institute for Advanced Study, Princeton, NJ. I would like to thank Jeremy Adelman, JoAnne Gowa, Bob Keohane, Eric Maskin, Dale Miller, Catherine Ross, Teemu Ruskola, Rick Shweder, and Eric Weitz for helpful discussions and comments on earlier drafts of the chapter.

1. The apparent simplicity of norms rests, at least in part, on their circularity. Sociologists, in particular, define social norms in terms of behavioral regularities and then posit norms as the cause of those regularities (Turner and Edgley, 2005). This is simple, to be sure, but not very productive. Defining norms as psychological entities—as mental representations—is one way to get around this problem.

2. For many reasons, norms-based approaches are likely to have little utility for combating rights violations committed by entrenched totalitarian regimes. However, they can be used to undermine the legitimacy of such regimes, as Kuran's (1995) analysis suggests.

3. Note that there is ample reason to take a skeptical stance toward self-reported racial attitudes, as they are subject to various forms of bias, some that people are aware of and some that they are not. However, in the case of the 1968 NES survey, additional evidence supported the validity of the self-reported attitudes, at least in regions outside the South (see O'Gorman 1975).

4. Note that, as representations of the group, social norms do tap into attitudes and beliefs: in particular, beliefs about what the group thinks is the right and reasonable thing to do. As such, communication programs and information campaigns often have a key role to play in changing these representations and therefore in changing the direction and strength of their influence. Indeed, such campaigns can be central to the effort to create the consensus around which norms can form.

CODA

The Psychology of Social Norms and the Promotion of Human Rights

RYAN GOODMAN, DEREK JINKS, AND ANDREW K. WOODS

Deborah A. Prentice's chapter offers a social psychological approach to social norms. The crucial theoretical insight is to conceptualize social norms as representations of the group. This insight makes possible her rich empirical work on the circumstances in which social norms deviate from the actual preferences of the relevant group. Prentice's chapter documents two consistent findings: (1) actors often overestimate the prevalence of many undesirable behaviors, such as alcohol use among peers; and (2) actors use their perceptions of peer norms as a standard against which to compare their own behaviors. Social-norms marketing campaigns seek to reduce the occurrence of undesirable behaviors by correcting the misperceptions of target actors about either the relevant descriptive norm (the prevalence of undesirable behaviors) or the relevant injunctive norm (the approval or disapproval of the undesirable behavior within the peer group). Social-norms campaigns, in these ways, seek to correct one form or another of "pluralistic ignorance." That is, social-norms campaigns reduce problem behaviors (or increase desirable behaviors) by conveying information that undesirable behaviors are occurring less often than is commonly thought, or that the peer group strongly disapproves of the undesirable behaviors irrespective of the prevalence of those behaviors. Prentice identifies several direct applications of her work to human rights. We provide some additional thoughts on possible applications here.

I. Target: Human Rights Advocates

A. Information Conveyance about the Extent of Human Rights Abuses—Correcting Misperceptions about the Descriptive Norm

Prentice explains how social norms respond to information (or the lack thereof) about peer beliefs and behavior. The findings described in Prentice's research challenge one of the core features of the prevailing human rights regime. International human rights institutions as well as human rights advocacy groups are designed to document and report—even widely publicize—human rights abuses. This information gathering and information conveyance strategy increases public awareness of human rights abuses and facilitates various political strategies aimed at "shaming" relevant actors into improved practices. Prentice highlights a potentially important downside to this approach. This approach arguably reinforces the sense that human rights abuses (even of the most extreme variety) are commonplace, and that other priorities of good governance—such as economic growth, public order, and national security—routinely trump the protection of individual rights. In other words, the prevailing approach creates a "boomerang effect."[1] This chapter therefore recommends perhaps modifying this approach. Two kinds of reforms might be explored: (1) reforms that encourage greater selectivity in the documentation and reporting of human rights abuses; and (2) reforms that encourage greater specificity in documentation and reporting about the extent, comparative frequency, or comparative severity of human rights abuses. Scaling or ranking of the human rights records of states on a range of issues is one possibility here. This type of reform might give actors a more accurate sense of the descriptive norm. These reforms could be implemented by the UN Human Rights Council, international human rights treaty bodies, national governments, and human rights NGOs.

B. Information Conveyance about the Disapproval of Human Rights Abuses—Correcting Misperceptions about the Injunctive Norm

Given the obvious complications associated with the reform strategies described in section I.A, strategies emphasizing injunctive norms provide an important supplement or replacement for those strategies. Along these lines, the findings described in the paper recommend conveying greater information about the disapproval of human rights abuses—irrespective of the extent of them. International human rights institutions and human rights advocacy groups might convey such information by (a) emphasizing the formal commitments of the relevant actors; in international and domestic law, to protect human rights (and to refrain from specific rights restricting actions); (b) emphasizing when states deny the accuracy of human rights reports rather than dispute the validity of the underlying human rights norm; (c) emphasizing the steps taken by offending states (and other relevant actors) to redress past abuses and to prevent future abuses. These reforms could also be implemented by the UN Human Rights Council, international human rights treaty bodies, national governments, and human rights NGOs.

C. Information Conveyance about the Extent of Positive Developments in Human Rights

An analogue to the reform strategies outlined in sections I.A and I.B is the conveyance of more information about positive or favorable developments in human rights practices. Although uncommon in the documentation and reporting of human rights abuses, the paper underscores some important benefits of this approach. These reforms could also be implemented by the UN Human Rights Council, international human rights treaty bodies, national governments, and human rights NGOs. For example, treaty bodies might emphasize to a much greater extent the positive aspects of state human rights records when considering periodic state reports. Treaty bodies might also consider issuing so-called General Comments to praise favorable patterns in state practice (rather than doing so only to underscore common problems).

II. Target: Human Rights Regime Architects

Prentice emphasizes that effective norm intervention is more likely where some underlying consensus can be leveraged. The difficulty, of course, is how to do this where the relevant axis of disagreement is the scope and content of human rights norms. Prentice's research suggests, for example, that consensus building around even a modest normative commitment might, in turn, facilitate more effective social pressure to conform over time to evolving group expectations. This line of thinking is consistent with a broad range of specific institutional reforms and advocacy strategies designed to leverage shallow commitments to promote incrementally deeper commitments. Examples would include relatively imprecise initial treaty obligations, relatively permissive escape clauses allowing for context specific articulation of general norms in light of local exigencies, and institutionalized deference to national or local actors (such as the margin of appreciation doctrine in European human rights law).

Notes

This Coda, like the others in the book, offers some specific applications drawn from the insights in the contributor's chapter. It is not intended to be a list of fully developed policy prescriptions, but instead an example of the rich sorts of human rights policy applications that can be drawn from cutting-edge social science research. It does not question the insights offered in the chapter but instead asks what implications those insights might have for human rights law and policy. The Codas are the sole authorship of the editors of the volume.

   1. See Levy, Paluck, and Ball (2010) (providing a thoughtful, sustained application of this line of research to social awareness campaigns against gender violence).

‖ 3 ‖

Why Can't We Sell Human Rights Like We Sell Soap?

ROBERT C. HORNIK

I. Introduction

In 1951, G. D. Wiebe asked whether we can sell brotherhood like we sell soap; he thought we could if we just worked like commercial marketers do. Before that, but very much after, various institutions have been trying to use the strategies of public communication and of marketing to accomplish noncommercial goals. More than a half century after Wiebe's question—what seemed like a straightforward proposition—has turned out not to be. In some cases, public communication has been a successful strategy in influencing "good" behavior; in many more it has turned out be ineffective (Hornik, ed., 2002). What have we learned from that experience that might be applied to issues of human rights?

My purpose in this chapter is to describe some current thinking and some evidence in the field of communication for social and behavioral change and consider how these findings may relate to interventions to affect human rights. I begin with a brief review of the intellectual strands that have dominated the field and then move to discussions of three major topics: how do communication and social change scholars think about behavior, when do we think that communication programs are likely to work (digressing briefly to note the possibility of boomerang effects of campaigns), and then consider directly the human rights implications of the history of communication for social change.

II. Three Traditions of Communication and Social Change Scholarship

A. Investments in Information Technology and in Communication Institutions

The oldest tradition of scholarship (and of applied investments in communication) focused on the role of communication infrastructure rather than on the content of communication; it was not interested in deliberate persuasive campaigns but only in building up the capacity to do communication. Scholars in this tradition argued that if access to information technology was high and governments assured the free flow of information and a free press—this would create "modern societies" featuring "democratic institutions" (Inkeles and Smith, 1974; Pye, 1963).

In the post-World War II period, this strong argument led, for example, to Western foreign aid agencies assisting in the diffusion of newspaper presses, then radio towers and television studios, and even later to investments in telephone systems and in satellite transmission capacity. More recently, it has led to increasing Internet access and to the distribution of cute, cheap computers to developing countries. In each case, there was a justification that said that if communication capacity expanded, the opportunities for improved exchange of information among citizens, and between the government and its citizens, would expand and accelerate the pace of development.

A similar argument focused less on the technology and more on the institutional rules for the use of technology. For example, Amartya Sen argued that "No substantial famine has ever occurred in any independent and democratic country with a relatively free press (1999)." The assumption here was that if the free press could maintain surveillance over the government and attack its failings, then the government would have no choice but to be responsive (and in this case, assure that policies favoring adequate food for all would be in place). A parallel argument is made with regard to Internet access—it provides ordinary citizens with the opportunity for surveillance, for shared communication with others, and a channel for criticism of actions by authorities. If the population has the ability to criticize and to organize, then, the logic goes, it has greater ability to influence policy.

In each of these cases, the optimistic argument for investment in technology is that broader access to communication capacity is supportive of the development of human rights. However, this argument, while attractive, may need some further elaboration. While this optimism seems to reoccur with the development of each new form of communication technology, there is almost invariably a swing away from such technological determinism after some time for observation of its effects. There are two major countercurrents: that enhancement of communication technological capacity does not define how it will be used; and that even when technology advances provide access to communication by a wider range of constituencies, there is no assurance that they will use it to enhance human rights.

What does access to communication capacity imply? One may have broad access to communication technology, but if that access is limited to the ability to receive messages only—the ability to receive television broadcasts from government-owned channels, read newspapers controlled by elite or commercial interests, or have access to Internet content censored for offending political content, then communication capacity may mean less for human rights. A. J. Liebling wryly noted: "Freedom of the press is guaranteed only to those who own one" (1960).

If communication capacity is to fulfill its "best" human rights role, then it would seem as though it ought to involve something beyond the ability to receive messages; it ought to assure broadened access to the production of messages as well. In the case of messages distributed by mass mediated channels, are there a range of interests represented in the messages typically consumed by the population? There is nothing in the technology itself that assures representation of a breadth of constituencies. There are frequent claims that the opening of the Internet assures such breadth of production capacity. In an obvious way, it clearly expands the ability of individuals or institutions to produce messages at lower cost, but this implies only the capacity to produce messages; it does nothing to assure wide circulation of such messages. The assessment of communication production capacity has to weigh literal production capacity against actual consumption—does the creation of an Internet web page (one of billions of such pages) assure reception by more than a tiny fraction of the population?

Perhaps it is more useful to consider the role of the Internet in shaping policy debate as broader than its simple enhancement of mass access to specific site pages. The content of a blog or site page may reach a small percentage of the population directly but may have substantial influence if other sources—political elites, mass circulation media—are attending to those sources and are shaped by them. This may mean that elites and mass media make use of information from the Internet, or accept the frames for debate set by bloggers, or present content differently to preempt what might be expected from bloggers (e.g., present information that might have been suppressed except that it will surely be uncovered by bloggers). Direct exposure to Internet-produced messages can be minimal, but indirect exposure may be more substantial.

Undermining optimistic interpretations of increasing diffusion of communication technology are questions about who actually has the ability to receive and produce messages. No less of a concern is the question about how the technology would be used even if both reception and production capacities were widely diffused. Optimists may focus on the Internet as an important political organizing tool or on the free press and blogs as a method for assuring a responsive political elite. However, these are not the only possibilities. Political movements that make use of newly available communication capacity to organize their path to power may turn out to support human rights or to limit them if they come to power: the Islamic revolution in Iran made use of taped messages from the Ayatollah Khomeini to organize its opposition to the Shah (Sreberny-Mohammadi, 1990); its human rights record is widely criticized, and the groups opposed to Khomeini's successors have turned to the web and its video sharing technology to organize their opposition. Majorities may find that enhanced communication capacity increases their ability to organize the suppression of minorities (for an extreme example, the Hutu use of radio broadcasts to spread their messages encouraging murder of Tutsis in Rwanda). The 24-hour news cycle and the "gotcha" approach of partisan bloggers and talk show hosts may constrain the willingness of political leaders to support politically unpopular human rights policies; for a recent example, there is the wariness of U.S. politicians to support immigrant rights in recent years. It is clear that enhanced communication capacity can be used to support human rights, or it can be used to undermine them.

This first tradition of communication and social change research focuses on the potential gains associated with the spread of technology and of the institutions that support the use of that technology. The optimism about this potential remains, but it is tempered by a recognition that much depends on how the technology is used: who owns it, what content is made available through it, and who has access to it are all constraints on whether it will enhance or suppress human rights. The second and third traditions of communication and social change are reflections of this understanding.

B. "Natural" Media Effects

The second tradition of research extends the focus on technology diffusion and institutional rules around technology to consider the effects of the content spread by the technology. It is not concerned, especially, with deliberate efforts to "sell brotherhood like soap" but rather with the effects of content typically diffused by media sources. After all, most exposure to communication content is not exposure to content shaped to inform or educate or persuade. Yet, that non-purposive content may well have effects on noncommercial outcomes, including perceptions of and actions relating to specific human rights issues. The media effects literature is very substantial, and there can be no reasonable attempt here to present it or even outline its dimensions. However, it may be helpful to point to some pieces of this literature and suggest how they might relate to communication and human rights.

One of the most important influences of media may not be to persuade audiences as to which position on an issue to adopt, but rather to convince them that they ought to be paying attention to an issue altogether (called agenda setting); or to convince them that when they think about an issue, they ought to be understanding it in a particular way (called framing). Both of these are quite relevant to thinking about communication influences on human rights.

A widely quoted aphorism summarizes the point well: "the press may not be successful . . . in telling people what to think, but it is stunningly successful in telling readers what to think about" (Cohen, 1963). Should U.S. voters elect their next president because of his or her position on a human rights issue (e.g., immigrants' rights), or should they weigh his or her position on another issue (e.g., war in the Middle East) more heavily? The media tell us which issue we should be paying attention to by the fact that they repeatedly address one topic but ignore another. It may be that two users of media have quite different opinions about immigration, but neither of them will use their opinion as a basis for their vote unless they have become convinced that it is an important criterion. Media tell us what is important by their allocation of column inches and blog space and news broadcast time. Even outside of the election context, politicians may be unwilling to focus their attention on an issue unless it matters to the public, and the public interest may be a reflection of media interest.

Even if a topic gains public interest, the way that people consider it may also reflect media coverage of the issue—the way that media "frame" the issue. As Dearing and Rogers (1996) note, quoting Schattschneider: "The definition of alternatives is the supreme instrument of power." Is immigration to be understood in terms of legal status of immigrants, is it to be understood as a demand for labor issue, or is it to be understood in terms of the human costs of children long established in the United States being forced to return to "home" countries they do not know? Depending on which frame for the issue gains popular currency, the outcome of the policy debate will likely change. Clearly, media coverage of the issue will affect what frames are available for debate.

A particularly intriguing version of the framing hypothesis has been called the "Spiral of Silence" (Noelle-Neumann, 1974). The hypothesis suggests that many people have a tendency to be unwilling to express their opinion if they believe it to be a minority opinion, and thus that it is likely to be badly received if voiced publicly. However, if minority opinions are not voiced, then others who may hold similar opinions are even less likely to express such opinions, reducing even further their presence in the public debate. Analogously, if media fail to give attention to minority views, then those views appear to be less legitimate views to hold and to express. Eventually, according to this hypothesis, such views are likely to be silenced. There is mixed evidence for this particular hypothesis, but the broader argument concerning the role of media in framing debates is strong.

Another frequent concern of media effects research that bears on the issue of human rights is the idea that much of the influence of media is interpreted in the context of social network affiliations. A great deal of mass communication research has focused on the issue of how social contexts affect reception, interpretation, and action with regard to media messages. This research tradition has argued that audience members are not isolates responding as individuals to hypodermic media messages, but rather that we are embedded in social relationships that affect how we are affected by media (cf. Katz and Lazarsfeld, 1955, 2006). There are two major elements of this argument: the first says that how we interpret what we see or hear reflects the frameworks of understanding that come from our social networks. For example, perhaps prior discussions in one individual's social network have focused on the human costs of returning undocumented families to their home countries; new messages from media sources focusing on the illegality of immigrants' status do not resonate with that individual's framework for thinking about this issue. Separately, our social networks are responsible for passing on messages that we may not have been exposed to directly. A friend quotes a media source on immigration approvingly or disapprovingly or does not pass the message on at all. In this way, also, social relationships reinforce, silence, or reinterpret media messages.

A distinct thread of mass media research is worth attention in the context of human rights concerns. Gerbner (1976) argued that the stories that are the core of media content may influence us; and, in particular, he had argued that such stories may reinforce social status inequalities and reinforce the existing distribution of power in a society. If such inequalities and power statuses limit public interest in addressing human rights issues, then this research tradition deserves further attention in this context. For example, Gerbner argued that the balance in authority between male and female characters on fictional television places men in more central roles; he hypothesized that this may lead viewers to expect and accept such distinctions in reality. He showed, as others have, how prevalent violence is on television; while others argued that such violence would lead viewers to aggressive behavior, he argued that the effects might be quite different. The exposure to violence on television would create in its audience an increase in fear of the world around them, and this fear would increase their willingness to support law and order policies. It is not hard to see how this argument might be extended to expect a reluctance to support human rights concerns if such concerns need to compete with media-reinforced fears about how dangerous a place the world is. Fear of the world may serve as a counterbalance to support for human rights.

C. Purposive, Content-Specific Uses of Communication Technology

The third major research tradition, and the one that bears most directly on building interventions to ameliorate human rights concerns, is about purposive uses of communication technology to educate, persuade, and produce social change. This is a tradition of research that goes beyond the diffusion of technology, beyond the effects of the typical media content, and toward deliberate attempts to influence behavior. There are substantial literatures that deal with schooling (or school-equivalent education) through media; agricultural innovation diffusion; public health communication; and more recently, communication in support of governance. The rest of this chapter focuses on this literature. It provides an overview of some of the major concerns of this field and relates those concerns to thinking about construction of efforts to influence human rights. Much of the content is based on work in the field of health communication where a great deal of work is ongoing and where the analogy to human rights efforts may be easiest to see. The section is organized around a series of major questions: How do purposive communication and social change scholars and practitioners think about behavior? What does the evidence say about when communication programs will work (and what are the risks of doing communication interventions)? What issues will efforts to affect human rights through communication need to address?

III. How Do Scholars of Purposive Communication and Social Change Think about Behavior?: Specific Behavior, Not Categories of Behavior

It would be desirable if it were possible to develop communication campaigns that might influence a broad mindset among individuals and that such a mindset would then turn into a variety of specific behaviors. For example, it would be efficient if it were possible to gain a commitment to a healthy lifestyle, and then expect that people will turn that commitment into good lifestyle decisions across the board—no smoking, regular exercise, maintenance of a healthy weight, consumption of a diet heavy in fruit and vegetables, etc. It would be lovely if one could generate a commitment to a pro-environmental ethos and that assured good decisions in all the very many individual behaviors that affect the environment. However, behavior change theory and health behavior theory has been more focused on thinking about determinants of specific behaviors (smoking cessation, condom use with the next casual partner, recycling of paper goods, choice of low trans-fat foods) than it has been in thinking about categories of behavior (healthy lifestyles, safe sex, pro-environmental behavior, obesity control.) We know a fair amount about how to change specific behaviors—there is good evidence, for example, for communication campaigns to reduce smoking initiation (NCI, 2008) and encourage condom use (cf. Wellings, 2002). However we don't have evidence supporting the effects of campaigns to increase healthy lifestyles or engage in safer sex, when those abstract categories are not defined by specific behaviors. We know much less about how to change categories of behaviors. This experience is likely to generalize from areas where there is substantial experience to behaviors related to human rights.

There are two likely explanations for why this mismatch may occur between what we would like to do (see many behaviors adopted in response to categorical advocacy) and what we have been successful in doing (stimulating targeted behavior change).

The behaviors that interventionists and policy advocates may see as fitting into a category and as appropriately adopted as a coherent set of behaviors are not always seen as similar behaviors by ordinary people. Human rights advocates may see immigration issues, prisoner's rights, and political participation and free speech and access to smoke-free homes as all human rights issues. However, ordinary people may see those issues as quite distinct—their support for one of those issues may not generalize to support for others. One may see oneself as a supporter of human rights but not accept that support for a particular immigrant right fits into that category.

Also it may be that the behaviors that fall into a single category for outsiders are distinct in the factors that influence them for the individuals who might consider performing them. Fishbein and Ajzen's Integrative Model (IM) brings together constructs from their own prior theories (Theory of Reasoned Action, Theory of Planned Behavior) and those of other health behavior scholars (Social Cognitive Theory, Health Belief Model) in defining a common set of likely categories of influence on behavior (Fishbein and Ajzen, 2009).

The IM argues that there are three central determinants of behavior: beliefs about the good and bad outcomes of a behavior, beliefs about what important others do and expect the individual to do with regard to the behavior, and beliefs about whether or not one has the skills and the opportunity to engage in a behavior successfully. Each of these is assumed to influence behavior, either directly or through the intention to engage in the behavior. This model can be applied to thinking about human rights advocacy.

Human right supporters seek not merely abstract support for an ideal but want to see specific behaviors to enact that support. For example, one can consider the issue of support for the restoration of voting rights for felons after serving their prison terms. Perhaps a human rights group would like to develop a public communication campaign to advocate for this goal, encouraging people to write supporting letters to the editor in local newspapers or send letters to legislators when the issue is up for debate. The influences on individuals' willingness to write a letter to the editor may reflect their belief that voting rights for felons is a good thing (which may reflect a broader commitment to human rights), but it also may reflect their belief that a letter to the editor is likely to influence the achievement of those rights, their belief that they have the time and the ability to compose a persuasive letter that will be published, and their belief that important social network members will respond positively to them if they see a letter under their signature supporting felons' voting rights. The influences on writing to a legislator may be quite distinct—for example, given that letters to legislators do not involve public advocacy, the role of the expectations from a social network may be quite different. More broadly, the set of influences that come into play when a quite different human rights-related behavior is the target may be substantially different.

Consider the issue of the right to smoke-free living space for children, encouraging parents to avoid smoking at home. A human rights advocate may describe this as a human right, but a parent's behavior change may not be much influenced by a belief in human rights. The decision to stop smoking at home may reflect the parent's belief that smoking at home will affect a child's health or that it will model smoking behavior for the child. The parent's behavior will be influenced as well by the ability to tolerate nicotine withdrawal and the expectations of a spouse. Variation in individual beliefs in human rights generally may simply not come into play for the decision to smoke or not in the home.

The implications for human rights advocacy of this set of arguments encouraging a focus on specific behaviors are twofold. There may be little expectation that a broad campaign for human rights will have any important behavioral effects, absent a focus on specific issues. This may not be much of challenge to current human rights work; it would seem that most human rights campaigns are about a specific issue already and not about some generic human rights goal. However, the second implication may have more traction. It is rarely the case that human rights advocates' goals are merely attitudinal. Goals are typically behavioral—that individuals should take a specific action or a set of actions—that are expected to lead to a change in institutional policy or practice. Successful advocacy campaigns need first to define the specific behaviors they want to encourage and then understand what is likely to influence each behavior. Crucially, they need to understand that different behaviors (even if they are meant to address the same issue) will have different influences, and that the influences on each behavior may be weighted differently across the people who are addressed. In particular, general support for human rights may be relevant to some issues and irrelevant to others; and even where it may be relevant, it may be an essential determinant or a minor determinant of the likelihood that people will engage in desired behaviors.

IV. What Does the Evidence Say about When Communication Programs Will Work?

This section of the chapter turns from general considerations of behavior change theory and its relevance to human rights advocacy, to a focus on communication interventions themselves and what we have learned about the conditions under which they are likely to be successful. The chapter considers evidence about two types of communication efforts: deliberate or controlled communication campaigns and Public Relations/Media Advocacy programs.

Controlled communication campaigns are campaigns where producers develop specific messages and transmit them through well-defined channels with an expectation that they will produce measureable behavior change. Public relations campaigns make use of press releases and other materials to encourage attention to an issue by media and other institutions. They also may hope for behavior change, but they do not expect to control how many messages are received by audiences or through what channels. They may have a goal of changing broad social norms concerning an issue, and, in some cases, may focus on mobilizing public support to achieve policy change.

The literature on deliberate public communication campaigns is quite substantial. This chapter provides only a very high-level summary of some major conclusions based in that literature. There are three types of campaigns for which there is decent positive evidence of influence on behavior: when the focus behavior is high reward and low cost to implement; when the communication campaign can complement substantial changes in the material environment affecting adoption of the behavior, and when the communication campaign can be long lived and operate through multiple channels with an expectation of incremental change.

A. Campaigns Focused on Low-Cost, High-Reward Behaviors

There are (rare) cases where behavior change is simple and highly rewarding but unknown to an audience. Adoption of these behaviors can be sharply affected by conventional communication campaigns. One useful example is the effort to encourage parents to put their infants on their backs to sleep. As evidence accumulated that Sudden Infant Death Syndrome (SIDS) might be reduced if children slept on their backs rather than their stomachs, a number of agencies mounted campaigns to encourage this shift in behavior. Back sleeping was not the common practice, and the dangers with prone sleeping were generally unknown. However, because the promised reward associated with the behavior was highly valued (reducing the risk of SIDS), the behavior was simple and easy to adopt (putting the baby on his or her back rather than prone), and the costs were probably low (some possible increased fussiness), it was quickly adopted by many parents. And deaths from SIDS declined rapidly by 50% or more in a number of countries (Willinger et al., 1994).

B. Campaigns Linked to Substantial Changes in the Material Environment

Communication campaigns have been effective when they were mounted to facilitate behavior change when that communication effort complemented a change in the behavior environment. Communication is used to publicize some "real" change in the environment that has clear implications for behavior change. Here are two good illustrations of a somewhat distinct nature. In urban areas of the Philippines, on-time immunization rates were lower than desired. The Ministry of Health improved its policies around delivering health services (creating a focus vaccination day, allowing clinic staff to open vials of serum even for a single child, and others). However, it complemented such changes in the material environment around provision of vaccination with intense advertising programs letting parents know about where and when vaccines were available. If clinics had not been ready to serve increased demand, then it is unlikely that the communication efforts would have been worthwhile; at the same time, the policy changes alone were not able to increase the rates. Complementing material changes with communication meant a jump in one year in timely complete vaccination from 32% to 56% (Zimicki et al., 1994).

A related example comes from U.S. efforts to encourage the wearing of seat belts. Simple advocacy campaigns have not produced large quick increases in seat belt wearing. Similarly simple enforcement efforts in isolation have not had much greater success. However, campaigns that link enforcement to communication have been sharply more successful. So-called Click It or Ticket campaigns that both establish checkpoints to ticket motorists who are not wearing seat belts and mount advertising efforts to publicize those efforts have been associated with sharp changes in seat belt wearing and even some evidence of a reduction in deaths of motorists (Williams et al., 1996).

C. Long-Lived, Long-Term Programs

The third type of communication program with some consistent evidence for success is a group of long-lived, high-exposure, multiple-channel programs that work to affect individual preferences, as well as social support and institutional policies that support such preferences. These programs are rarely limited to communication efforts alone, but typically complement communication efforts with other changes and also expect to achieve effects over the long term. Again, two examples illustrate this class of programming. The National High Blood Pressure Education Program (NHBPEP, which began in 1972 and still continues, albeit in reduced form) was a kitchen sink sort of program: it involved institutional consensus building around the appropriate way to define and treat high blood pressure; education of health professionals; and some public education through community organizations and major efforts in mass media education, including both distribution of public service announcements and work to encourage media outlets to address the issue of hypertension. The period of the most intensive NHBPEP outreach was closely associated with sharp increases in the proportion of the hypertensive population visiting doctors, taking medication, and having their high blood pressure controlled (Rocella, 2002).

A distinct version of this long-term, large-scale intervention program is the antismoking movement in the United States. There are specific shorter-lived communication interventions with some evidence of immediate success (Farrelly et al., 2005; Warner, 1981), but the most striking results come from taking a 50-year perspective. The proportion of U.S. adults who smoked in 2008 was less than half the proportion that smoked in 1958. It can be argued that this reflects not a single effort by a single authority but the often uncoordinated efforts of a movement that produced slow but over-the-long-term large change. Sometimes this movement involved identifiable mass media campaigns, sometimes it involved deliberate public relations efforts by antismoking groups to affect policy decisions at all levels of institutions, sometimes it involved legal actions, and sometimes it involved community groups pressing their case on policy makers. All of these reflected a massive shift in social norms around smoking, even as tobacco companies fought those changes. This was not a specific communication campaign, but at its core was the diffusion of the idea that smoking was dangerous and merited public action. This diffusion was not the result of a single actor's sponsored communication campaign, but it was a reflection of a massive communication effort, nonetheless.

This antismoking effort exemplifies also a last type of communication program that seems relevant to human rights campaigns: public relations and media advocacy programs. Agencies may seek to use what is called "earned media" to influence the public. They meet with journalists and editorial boards, put out press releases, organize press conferences, or encourage demonstrations or create other attention-getting events all in the hope that news media will both cover the issues of concern to the agency and that they will cover the issues within a framework that favors the agency's position. In contrast to the controlled intervention programs described above, they do not buy advertising time or seek free media time for public service announcements. They can control the message that gets to the public at large only if their public relations campaign is successful in shaping what the media outlets say. There are two versions of these programs. Some intend to shape public sentiment in the belief that policy makers will be responsive to shifts in public opinion. Media Advocacy (Wallack and Dorfman, 1993) is a particular type of public relations that seeks to use to use media coverage to galvanize grass roots organizations and to use media coverage of grassroots demonstrations to put pressure on policy makers. Others try to short circuit that policy influence process, by using the fact of press coverage of an issue to convince policy makers that public sentiment is on their side, whether or not there has actually been a shift in sentiment (sometimes called Astroturf organization to differentiate it from actual grassroots organizing).

As noted above, the antismoking movement has been particularly adept at gaining favorable press coverage and, in turn, affecting policy decisions. There has been a massive and continuing shift in institutional policies meant to discourage smoking: smoke-free buildings and bars and airplanes, tax increases on tobacco products, and enhanced enforcement of underage smoking laws. All of these reflect the continuing actions of a social movement able to make use of the strategies of public relations to affect policy decisions (Warner, 1989).

D. A Digression: At Least Communication Can Do No Harm—Well, Not Quite

Historically, when groups have proposed to undertake communication programs, they have assumed that they will either be unsuccessful or successful, where being unsuccessful meant not producing any behavior change. However a recent experience raises an additional caution flag. The U.S. government invested something over $1 billion in its National Youth Anti-Drug Media Campaign. The evaluation of that campaign reported that either there were no effects on youth beliefs and behavior around drugs (particularly marijuana) or possibly showed boomerang effects (Hornik et al., 2008). The likely mechanism for the observed boomerang effects is of particular interest to those considering human rights campaigns. It appeared that the effects were probably associated with repeated exposure to messages. Even though each message encouraged rejecting the behavior, the repeated exposure may have led to the acceptance of a contrary meta-message: a perception that marijuana use was highly prevalent, because why else would so many messages be used to attack it. The messages led youth to believe that there was high prevalence of a non-desired behavior. There is also evidence that high perceived prevalence of marijuana use predicts subsequent youth initiation of the drug. These findings are consistent with a theoretical argument put forward by Cialdini, who has shown that such prevalence information can legitimate noncompliance (2003).

What are the implications of this highlight summary of evidence relating to other communication campaigns for the development of human rights-related campaigns? First, if there are low hanging fruit of the sort exemplified by the

"Back to Sleep" campaigns in a particular human rights context, then they are an obvious target. In a sense, the quick media response to the Abu Ghraib photographs reflected the photo's portrayal of behavior, which was a deep violation of public norms around prisoner treatment. Exposing violations of public norms makes it impossible to continue what is accepted in private. However, such clearly unacceptable violations may not be uncovered regularly.

Programs that can use communication to support material changes in the environment may be an approach that is more applicable. A communication campaign that lets abused women know about newly available resources available to them will surely be more successful than a communication campaign that merely encourages women to leave their abusing spouses but has no resources to provide.

However, it is likely that many human right issues will not bend to quick communication interventions. Then, the most important implication of this history may be the example of the smoking and high blood pressure campaigns: many human rights issues will require long-term, large-scale continuing interventions; it may be that, for example, cementing policy makers' votes to support legalization of undocumented immigrants already in the United States will require a relatively long horizon, a thoroughgoing understanding of the influences on various relevant constituencies, and a multicomponent effort to affect public norms about the issue.

The next section of this chapter follows the discussion of the theory and the description of prior experience to a focus on some primary (and fairly practical) lessons to be drawn from theory and experience. On the assumption that a human rights organization has chosen a behavioral focus for a campaign, what sorts of problems might it run into? There is unfortunately extensive experience with missteps in this field.

V. What Issues Will "Human Rights Communication" Need to Address?

Following the model of the previous section, this discussion focuses on presenting a small number of typical problems that many communication programs face, and it may well be that human rights-focused communication advocacy and behavior change programs should expect to face as well.

Poor messages. Many communication programs confuse the goal of their program with the messages they need to distribute. Perhaps a program wants to encourage letter writing to legislators. However, a message that merely asks for letters on the basis of what its advocates think are good reasons for writing may be not be successful. The crucial question is: What are the forces that influence potential letter writers? Is it their belief about whether a letter will affect a desired outcome, their belief that there won't be a bad consequence for their own careers, their beliefs about whether other people they care about think they should write, or their confidence that they can write a persuasive letter? A message emphasizing that letter writers can feel good about their commitment to human rights may not matter—if reluctant writers need to be convinced that writing can actually convince policy makers. Message producers need to choose messages that are persuasive to their target audience, but the arguments that are likely to influence them are not always what program producers might guess. Nonetheless, programs often put a lot of resources into producing pretty messages (nice formats, good fonts, balanced designs, and attention-getting images) but spend too little on understanding how target audience members think about the behavior of concern. Programs may invest too little in shaping their messages so that they correspond with the factors that actually influence behavior, rather than merely cajoling people to adopt a desired behavior.

Too little exposure. Good programs may eventually sort out the need for careful message design. However, the next problem looms large. Many serious communication efforts fail because their good messages are not seen or heard at all, or are not seen or heard with sufficient frequency to be persuasive. Even when substantial effort goes into message creation, there may not be sufficient funding to purchase exposure or no adequate strategy to earn free exposure. If, for example, a program is aimed at audiences in the United States, it faces the daunting task of competing with massive media noise for audience attention: public service advertising, if it is aired at all, is often relegated to times of the day when few are in the audience. Purchasing advertising time at a level that can be recalled by the target viewer is likely to be beyond the budget of many human rights advocacy programs. This often means than public relations strategies—efforts to earn free media time by making news—are the only viable approach. At the same time, public relations is an approach where control over the actual content of messages is reduced, and there is rapid wear out of the willingness of news media to pay attention to an issue. Getting sufficient continuing message exposure is a crucial problem to be solved for any human rights agency that intends to make use of public communication.

Individual persuasion when the behavior belongs to social networks or institutions. Much of the history of communication for social change has been focused on persuading individuals to change their behavior. Even for issues when individual behavior is the focus of a campaign, this may not always be the most efficient strategy. If a behavior is open to influence from an individual's social network, then it may prove productive to focus a campaign on changing social norms, and only through social norm change try to influence individual behavior. For example, it has often been argued that adolescent binge drinking reflects social norms, and the best strategy for reducing such drinking is through changing the norm (and the perception of the norm) within social networks. In a parallel way, if a behavior is substantially influenced by institutional policies and structures, convincing institutions to change policies may be a more efficient way of changing individual behavior than efforts at individual persuasion. The efforts to complement individual antismoking messages with advocacy to change institutional policies around smoking are a clear example of this strategy. It is more difficult for individuals to maintain a smoking habit when they have to leave their workplace every time they want to light up.

This logic applies to human rights issues in two ways. There are some individual behaviors that can support a human rights agenda that will happen quickest if they are influenced by shared norm change in a social network or supportive institutional policy changes. Communication interventions designed to affect those social network norm changes and to encourage institutional policy change will look different than interventions designed only to persuade individuals directly.

Perhaps of greater relevance, many human rights issues are about institutional change, per se. In contrast to a health communication campaign that may be using institutional or social routes to get to individual behavior change (smoke-free workplaces to get individuals to stop smoking), human rights campaign are often directly about institutional policy changes (changing the legal status of undocumented immigrants). Nonetheless the communication strategies that proved productive in facilitating policy change for the anti-smoking movement may transfer usefully to the development of human rights interventions.

It is not a communication problem. Thus far, this chapter has made the assumption that there is a communication solution to a particular problem, and the challenge is creating an effective communication strategy. Communication interventions often assume that *if only the right people or policy makers knew or believed the right things, then the needed changes would come about.* However, agencies considering communication interventions need to ask a hard question first: if the problem is one of lack of material resources to permit changes, or if current circumstances are consistent with interests reflecting the distribution of power in a society, is communication really a solution? Sometimes it is the interests of policy actors not to change policy; they fully understand the issues, and the human rights arguments behind change, but they think that change is not in their own interests or the interest of the constituencies who support them. This idea is closely linked to the next one.

Confusing communicating with doing something about a problem. Communication efforts can make actors feel like they are doing something, which is not the same as doing something. When agencies (and in this case, particularly political actors) turn to public communication to address an issue, there are two outcomes they may be seeking. Ideally they are trying to make things better. However, they also may be trying to *look like* they are doing something to make things better. Public communication—speaking to the public through television and radio ads, for example—can be a useful strategy, and it can be a replacement for an effective but less public strategy. A government ministry can invest in a public communication campaign to encourage families to send their daughters to school, and that may be an important intervention. But if the problems with sending girls to school reflect institutional constraints–unwillingness of religious authorities in local areas to countenance mixed schooling or the need for school-age girls to care for younger siblings because of the lack of affordable child care alternatives—the public communication campaign may bring credit for its sponsors but have little impact on the participation of girls in schooling. Because communication is a public intervention, it carries with it a particular risk of allowing the appearance of action to replace effective action.

VI. Conclusions

This chapter presents a range of current ideas drawn from the communication and social change literature. Where possible, examples from better documented areas of scholarship and, in particular, from health communication are extended speculatively to the human rights context. Here I summarize again the points most relevant to thinking about exploiting communication approaches for human rights interventions.

We know how to address and try to influence a specific behavior, but we do not know how to address behavioral categories. We do not know how to address human rights attitudes broadly, and it is not obvious that a broad commitment to human rights will translate into specific behaviors in support of a specific human right. Rather, human rights campaigns, if they follow the history of other intervention areas, will focus on specific outcomes, will consider what behaviors need to be influenced for the outcomes to be achieved, and specify what are likely influences on those specific behaviors are. Communication efforts will then focus on addressing the relevant influences.

Rarely, there will be a behavioral target that is easy to influence. More often, purposive communication is likely to be effective because it influences behavior over the long run, through lots of exposure, through the use of multiple channels, and because it produces incremental rather than dramatic change. Large-scale change may come because of action by multiple agencies rather than the short-term focused campaign by a single actor.

Communication is one tool for human rights advocates, but if it is to be effective it will require skilled and focused use, reasonable expectations, and patience. Use of communication interventions requires hard thinking about relevance, and then specifically about models of behavior change that are assumed: messages that promise to be persuasive for audiences and strategies to gain sufficient exposure to those messages.

Note

This chapter is adapted from one published in the volume *Public Communication Campaigns* (4th edition), edited by Ronald Rice and Charles Atkins. The development of this chapter's human rights aspects in particular grew out of conversations with the editors, Ryan Goodman, Derek Jinks, and Andrew K. Woods, and the contributors to the present volume.

CODA

Why Can't We Sell Human Rights Like We Sell Soap?

RYAN GOODMAN, DEREK JINKS, AND ANDREW K. WOODS

I. Introduction

Robert C. Hornik's chapter offers insights from the literature on health communications. Campaigns to change behavior, he argues, can fail for a number of reasons. These include insufficient exposure, poor or vague messaging, and attempting to change whole categories of behavior ("be environmental") rather than specific, targeted acts ("don't litter"). Hornik also outlines several counterintuitive findings including the need to be mindful of "boomerang effects"—the risk that any given communication will in fact worsen the behaviors the message was intended to fix. The literature suggests that health communications are most likely to succeed when they are focused on low-cost, high-reward behaviors (for example, convincing parents to put their infants to sleep on their back) and with sufficient exposure for a sufficient length of time. These insights have significant implications for the human rights regime. We consider strategies for incorporating these insights into the current human rights regime's practice, focusing on two potential targets for policy.

II. Target: Promoters of Human Rights

A. Overcoming Insufficient Exposure

Hornik discusses the danger of insufficient message exposure, which has plagued many health communications campaigns. Some human rights campaigns face a similar challenge of exposure, especially where money has been spent instead on monitoring and enforcement. Future research is required into the ways in which the human rights regime might secure such exposure. For example, human rights practitioners might seek to gain small commitments of airtime or advertising space from state parties to a particular treaty or trade negotiation, whether the international agreement is human rights related or not. Such a commitment might be cheap for the state relative to other measures and therefore may be a very low-cost way to increase their public commitment to human rights. In order to fulfill this commitment, they would not have to expend state funds, and they could pass the cost of lost revenues onto the paying advertisers or broadcasters.

Second, human rights practitioners might seek to work with private advertising enterprises to seek out mutual benefit; global businesses are often looking for ways to improve their human rights "brand." Perhaps those businesses can be convinced that a cheap way to integrate human rights norms into their practices is to dedicate their networks, expertise, and money in the world of advertising to public communications campaigns for a few targeted human rights-driven campaigns. Similarly, perhaps the relevant association of advertisers might be convinced to design and issue a certain number of public service announcements, the way that the Ad Council in the United States leverages its institutional relationships and expertise to launch widespread pro-social campaigns. Similarly, athletic associations often require their teams, mascots, and stars to donate a certain amount of time to public service—including making public service announcements. Perhaps cities or states could make sports license deals (for stadiums or team licenses) contingent on a certain amount of targeted campaigns designed to limit a specific rights abuse or promote a particular behavior. As an example from the United States, the city of Boston recently required that the Boston Red Sox commit a certain portion of its advertisements in the stadium, as well as a portion of its public endorsements, to charities.

But overcoming exposure limitations is a necessary but not sufficient component for a successful human rights campaign. Message saturation does not guarantee a campaign's success, and indeed, as Hornik points out, it can produce boomerang effects (discussed below) or fall on deaf ears if the problem being addressed is not a communications problem. Human rights communicators might think that all human rights messages, however ineffective, are harmless—but this research suggests that ineffective messages waste valuable resources and political will and risk complacency or even boomerang effects.

One important insight from this chapter relates to boomerang effects—in which a message's prescriptive norm ("stop smoking marijuana") is overshadowed by the descriptive norm implied by the message's tone and prevalence ("everyone is smoking marijuana"). Human rights campaigns designed to change behavior should be aware of this risk. Guarding against boomerang effects can only occur if practitioners monitor and evaluate the impact of their own campaigns.

B. Human Rights Groups Should Develop Criteria for Evaluating the Efficacy of Messages

This chapter suggests that human rights practitioners—whether state or non-state actors—should develop strict evaluation criteria to measure the efficacy of their messages and to guard against boomerang effects or negative unintended consequences. They should be able to draw heavily from the field of health communications in this regard. Future research might investigate how advocates could measure boomerang effects and how they can build timed trials and specific assessments of their message efficacy into their campaign designs. Because some practitioners lack the resources for intense data collection, the Internet or mobile phones might prove particularly useful for collecting survey data about the efficacy of a particular campaign. This is a particularly useful finding for human rights practitioners working with highly organized bureaucratic structures such as the military, which may offer an ideal setting for randomized controlled trials. But such interventions need not involve sophisticated methodologies, either. Surveys at health clinics could seek to measure whether a particular health intervention involves boomerang effects.

III. Target: Potential and Actual Perpetrators of Human Rights Violations

A. Human Rights Campaigns Should Seek to Change Specific Behaviors (Not Categories of Behavior) under Certain Conditions

This chapter suggests that a central communications problem for the international human rights regime is that it emphasizes categories of behavior rather than specific behaviors. Many human rights instruments consist of general and/or vague aspirational statements ("All peoples have the right of self-determination. By virtue of that right they freely determine their political status and freely pursue their economic, social and cultural development"[1]), which are designed to avoid identifying any particular behaviors that might deter a reluctant signatory state. Future research—if not practice—should inquire into how the regime might turn these general statements into specific communication strategies, directed at specific behaviors. Some examples of where these recommendations might appear could include the concluding observations by treaty bodies in state periodic reports, "best practices" guides produced by international and local NGOs, and reports of the UN's various regional and thematic Special Rapporteurs who are tasked with investigating and drafting recommendations about particular human rights issues.

National Human Rights Institutions (NHRIs) may have an important role to play here as translators of international human rights instruments into locally relevant (and specific) campaigns. "Human Rights Education" is the broad category for human rights messaging, and the field is awash in strategies for creating human rights "cultures." This chapter suggests instead that these education programs should consist of targeted campaigns designed to convince a particular subcommunity to change a particular behavior. These campaigns might aim to convince men to curb spousal abuse, or to convince police and interrogators never to use "third degree" interrogation methods, or to encourage newspaper editors to use human rights language in their editorials. (This work may also warrant a meta-campaign to convince NHRIs and other human rights organizations to abandon broad proclamations such as "human rights are everybody's rights," in favor of more targeted messages.)

B. Human Rights Communications Should Be Linked to Changes in the Relevant Material Environment—and Vice Versa—for Maximum Effectiveness

This chapter demonstrates the power of changes in the material environment to augment communications campaigns—such as the rollout of clinics at the same time as urging immunizations. The same coordination could be used in the human rights context. Imagine, for example, instructions for the safe and lawful interrogation of a detainee in a cell that is specifically designed for such an interrogation. Such a cell might be built with cameras, windows, and other transparency designs. Or consider the now-booming cell phone industry in the developing world. Nearly all cell phones rely on state-licensed communication networks in order to make and receive calls. One strategy for NHRIs and human rights practitioners might be to convince telecommunications departments to require private cell providers to bundle new mobile phones with "tips" for using those devices in pro-social ways, such as health reminders, whistle-blowing numbers, or a means of reporting sexual violence discreetly via text.

A second application would be to use this finding to urge policy makers (who might otherwise be reluctant to offer certain services like needle exchange, or new interrogation rooms, or new mobile phone services) to offer simple services or material changes in order to amplify the effect of some generally agreed-upon message. For example, if policy makers have agreed to the dissemination of certain messages, and it can be shown that those messages would have a significantly higher impact on behavior if they were timed with certain services, perhaps those policy makers can be convinced to provide such services. Similarly, state human rights workers could synchronize the timing of the rollout of new services to bundle and amplify their communicative impact. For example, the unveiling of a new NHRI could be coordinated with the launch of a new communication campaign to maximize the exposure of both and to link messages with state service.

Note

This Coda, like the others in the book, offers some specific applications drawn from the insights in the contributor's chapter. It is not intended to be a list of fully developed policy prescriptions, but instead an example of the rich sorts of human rights policy applications that can be drawn from cutting-edge social science research. It does not question the insights offered in the chapter but instead asks what implications those insights might have for human rights law and policy. The Codas are the sole authorship of the editors of the volume.

    1. Article I, Part I, International Covenant on Civil and Political Rights, G.A. res. 2200A (XXI), 21 U.N. GAOR Supp. (No. 16) at 52, U.N. Doc. A/6316 (1966), 999 U.N.T.S. 171, *entered into force* Mar. 23, 1976.

4

The Reasons for Compliance with Law

MARGARET LEVI, TOM R. TYLER, AND AUDREY SACKS

I. Introduction

People's willingness to comply with the law is a litmus test of the effectiveness and viability of the state. Without compliance, there is no rule of law, no matter how well the institutions and regulations are designed. Governments unable to motivate their citizenry to pay taxes, fight on behalf of the state, and generally refrain from lawbreaking are unlikely to survive in the long run (Levi, 1988; Levi, 1997; Tyler, 1990). Even in established societies such as the United States, compliance cannot be taken for granted; the government must continually work to secure and sustain deference to its policies. Most governments, especially those in emerging and transitional societies, are struggling to establish a regime of widespread compliance based on legitimacy and not simply coercion.

We are concerned with one aspect of this broad question: the role of value-based legitimacy in generating and sustaining behavioral legitimacy as reflected by compliance with the law. We investigate how positive judgments of government translate into a sense of obligation and the conditions under which obligations translate into compliance with governmental laws and regulations. Our argument has two core propositions. The first is that value-based legitimacy, that is, the obligation to defer to government rests, at least in part, on evaluations that government is objectively meeting the normative criteria a citizen possesses about what government should be doing. One of the most important antecedent conditions of value-based legitimacy is the trustworthiness of government, based on positive assessments of leadership motivations, administrative competence, and government performance. The other important antecedent is the extent to which government upholds procedural justice.

Our second proposition is that decisions of whether to comply with the law are influenced by value-based legitimacy. Once citizens come to believe they should obey, do they obey? We argue that behavior is responsive to judgments about the degree to which the state is an appropriate political authority, entitled to be obeyed. This judgment, we suggest, is linked to how the state exercises its authority (i.e., to judgments about the justice of state procedures). While the capacity of the state to monitor and punish noncompliance also influences behavior, our concern is with the extent voluntary decisions to comply are at work.

Our conceptual model is summarized in Figure 4.1. We build here on arguments made in an earlier paper (Levi et al., 2009). We first present evidence for our propositions and then consider the implications of our findings for the development of a rule of law that encompasses human rights.

We test our propositions using two data sets. These include cross-sectional data from the United States and cross-national survey data from Africa. In the United States, we expect to observe high levels of value-based legitimacy and a robust positive relationship between value-based legitimacy and behavioral legitimacy. However, we also expect that there will be variation based on region, race, and class, given different experiences with government. In Africa, there is wide variation in terms of objective measurements of government trustworthiness and procedural justice both across and within countries. We expect to observe a positive relationship between favorable assessments of government and value-based legitimacy and between value-based legitimacy and behavioral legitimacy, but we do not expect these relationships to be as robust.

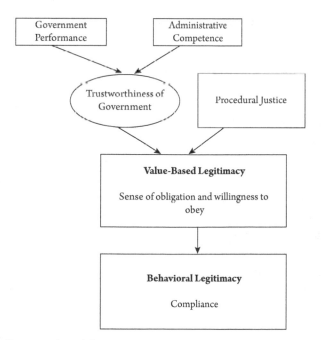

Figure 4.1   Conceptual model.

II. Theoretical Framework

Responsibility and obligation are the core features of theoretical discussions of legitimacy (Tyler, 2006). When members of a polity view the political authorities and institutions of that polity as legitimate, they defer to the policies they enact out of a normative sense of obligation to do so. Individuals defer to political authorities because they believe it is right and proper for those authorities and institutions to design and implement rules, and they will continue to defer even if they discover instances in which they or their groups benefit or are harmed by the rules.

It is this sense of doing what is normatively appropriate that is the essence of legitimacy. From our perspective, the key issue is whether the members of a polity judge government leaders, personnel, and institutions to be legitimate. While we draw upon the large and robust literature on the objective criterion that should be used to decide whether authorities ought to be obeyed, our analysis is psychological in nature and concerns the judgments made by mass publics within the various societies we consider. It is simultaneously a political analysis. The behavior of political authorities influences the judgments citizens make about their legitimacy, and the subsequent decision by citizens to obey governmental rules is a political choice albeit with psychological determinants.

A. Proposition 1: Assessments of Government Behavior as the Basis of Legitimacy

Figure 4.1 illustrates our conceptual model. Judgments concerning the motivations of leaders and the administrative competence and performance of government influence the extent to which citizens perceive government as trustworthy, which then has a direct effect on value-based legitimacy. Judgments about procedural justice have an independent but also direct effect on value-based legitimacy. Having trust and confidence in government is distinct from crediting it with procedural justice and fairness—although there may be a reciprocal relationship. We suspect that perceptions of violations of procedural justice may distort or even swamp positive assessments of government trustworthiness. The nature of that interaction is one we shall be exploring empirically.

The belief that government is trustworthy reflects the judgment that authorities are motivated to deliver on their promises and do what is right for the people they serve, seeking policies that truly benefit their societies. In countries with institutions that are perceived as effectively selecting and constraining government personnel, citizen evaluations of personal motivations are less important than their judgment that the institutions work (Hardin, 2002; Levi, 1998). Of course, the popularity of leaders can sometimes affect trust beliefs, particularly if citizens conflate liking someone with the assessment of trustworthiness. In the United States, survey evidence about trust in national government often reflects shifts in presidential popularity (Levi and Stoker, 2000). Charisma has often proved a basis for trustworthiness, helping to enhance the value-based legitimacy of those who are in fact trustworthy but also those who are not.

Given that we are most interested in exploring the development of legitimating beliefs based on reasoned assessments of motivations, and given the difficulties of truly knowing what inspires a leader's decisions or when or how her personal motivations have changed, the best objective measure of the trustworthiness of the motivations of personnel is the extent to which the relevant institutional arrangements are elaborated and operative. To the extent possible with the data sets we have, we try to determine the extent to which citizen trust of government derives from citizen assessment of the quality of the institutions in which political authorities are embedded.

A positive evaluation of government trustworthiness further depends on assessments of how well government is performing and how administratively competent it is (Cook et al., 2005; Levi, 1988; Rothstein, 2005). To the extent citizens perceive government agencies as producing the goods and services expected of government, the likelihood of feeling obliged to obey rules should increase. Citizens who believe that government is delivering the services they expect in exchange for paying their taxes and obeying other laws are likely to continue to comply with the law. When governments fail to reciprocate, citizens are likely to respond by noncompliance or possibly rebellion.

When other citizens fail to comply in situations in which government has fulfilled its side of the implicit bargain, those citizens who feel obliged to comply may pay the costs of punishing the free riders through personal action or via government coercion subsidized by their tax payments. What we are describing is a variant of strong reciprocity as elaborated by Gintis (this volume) in which individuals are willing to cooperate but also punish the noncompliant even when it is against their narrow self-interest.

Value-based legitimacy should also be responsive to citizen judgments that government is administratively competent to produce promised policies, solve problems, and control corruption. Also critical is confidence that government will enforce laws by punishing those—be it citizens or government officials—who break them. In terms of legitimacy, coercion is important for reassuring citizens that others will be punished. It signals government competence and protects citizens from being a sucker while others free ride. Then, value-based legitimacy can operate and produce voluntary compliance. Governments that provide services and protections that bolster citizen welfare or are quickly developing the capacity to do so should be more likely to elicit the willing deference of citizens than ineffective and poorly performing governments, *ceteris paribus*.

Procedural justice—that is, the commitment of government to uphold the laws fairly and to apply them equally to all—should also enhance deference and the obligation to obey. A large body of psychological research links legitimacy to the procedural justice of government (Tyler, 2000; Tyler, 2006). A number of studies suggest that people are more likely to judge authorities and institutions to be legitimate if they exercise their authority through fair procedures. This includes neutral, rule-based decision making and respect for people and for their rights. If individuals believe that they or people like them are being treated unfairly because of discrimination or favoritism, they are less likely to develop value-based legitimacy. If they feel government officials routinely violate due process, they will have fewer reasons to respect or desire to uphold the law.

B. Proposition 2: The Obligation to Obey as the Basis of Compliance

Once individuals have formed judgments about the trustworthiness of government and the extent to which it is procedurally just, they then have to make a decision about whether to comply with its laws. We argue that compliance rates will reflect the strength of the obligation to comply: that behavioral legitimacy follows from value-based legitimacy. Deference, a psychological attribute, is the precursor to the political act of obedience.

III. Quantitative Analyses

A. Proposition 1

1. United States

We test our two propositions using survey data collected from the United States and Africa. Our first analysis explores the antecedents of deference within the United States. This analysis is based upon a study of 1,653 New Yorkers, interviewed in 2002 concerning their views about the New York City Police Department (NYPD), as well as their law-related behavior (for methodological details, see Tyler and Fagan, 2008).

We first attempt to determine the factors shaping value-based legitimacy (i.e., the obligation to obey the law). To assess their sense of obligation, respondents were asked seven obligation items: "The NYPD is a legitimate authority and people should obey the decisions that NYPD officers make"; "You should accept the decisions made by police officers, even if you think they are wrong"; "It would be difficult for you to break the law and keep your self-respect"; "You should do what the police tell you to do even when you do not understand the reasons for their decisions"; "You should do what the police tell you to do even when you do not like the way they treat you"; "There are times when it is ok for you to ignore what the police tell you to do"; and "Sometimes you have to bend the law for things to come out right (reverse scored)."[1]

In addition to legitimacy, several other psychological factors are measured. First, the study assessed the perceived risk of punishment for wrongdoing. One important way that law enforcement can demonstrate competence is by creating the perception that it captures and punishes those who break the law. Another important aspect of police performance involves the ability to manage crime. To assess police performance, the perceived crime rate was measured. Finally, standard demographic factors were measured and included in the equation. These included ethnicity, gender, age, education, and income.

Procedural justice was assessed using a nine-item scale. The items assessed whether the police "Usually accurately understand and apply the law"; "Make their decisions based upon facts, not their personal biases and opinions"; "Try to get the facts in a situation before deciding what to do"; "Give honest explanations for their actions"; "Apply the rules consistently"; "Treat people with dignity and respect"; "Respect people's rights"; "Consider the views of the people involved when making decisions"; and "Take account of the needs and concerns of the people they deal with."

For trustworthiness of government, we use self-reported trust. Although our conceptual model emphasizes objective indicators, these were not available for this particular study. Instead, we relied on the measures commonly used to assess trust and confidence in government. We included seven items: "I have confidence that the NYPD can do its job well"; "I trust the leaders of the NYPD to make decisions that are good for everyone in the city"; "The police care about the well-being of everyone they deal with"; "People's basic rights are well protected by the police"; "The police are often dishonest (reverse scored)"; "Some of the things the police do embarrass the city (reverse scored)"; and "There are things about the NYPD that need to be changed (reverse scored)."

a. Results

Our first concern is whether value-based legitimacy derives from positive assessments of government officials acting within the rule of law. In other words, does the sense of obligation to obey the law develop from judgments about how government authorities exercise their authority (procedural justice), and/or is it linked to the perceived ability of those authorities to effectively manage problems (competence and performance)? Our focus is on two elements that are central to the rule of law—perceived procedural justice and the trustworthiness of government. In the case of the police, trustworthiness is assessed by self-report.

We find that both procedural justice and citizen's trust in government influence value-based legitimacy. In fact, at least in this analysis, procedural justice and trust in government are very strong influences, while both government performance and administrative competence have no direct influence (see Table 4.1). Among Americans, procedural justice and trust are central to judging the legitimacy of the police.

Our finding that performance and competence do not directly shape legitimacy is not inconsistent with our model, which argues that performance and competence should shape trustworthiness and, through it, should indirectly influence legitimacy. The results of an analysis of the influence of government performance and administrative competence on trustworthiness support this argument (see Table 4.2). Our results suggest that both performance and competence influence citizens' evaluation of government trustworthiness.

The analysis presented supports the general model outlined. However, it is important to note the manner in which trustworthiness is measured and included in the analysis. Here we use self-reported trust of the type that is assessed in studies of trust and confidence in government. In our analysis of African data, we infer the trustworthiness of government from objective evaluations of its performance and competence.

Table 4.1 **The antecedents of value-based legitimacy**

	Legitimacy
Procedural justice	.17***
Self-reported trust	.23***
Solving problems	−0.03
Enforcing laws	−0.01
Police professionalism	−0.02
Favor the wealthy?	−0.05
Hispanic v. White	0.04
African-American v. White	−0.01
Age	0.02
Gender	−.09**
Education	−.07*
Income	−.16***
Adj. R-sq	19%***

Table 4.2 **Influences on self-reported trust**

	Self-reported trust
Solving problems	0.25***
Enforcing laws	0.09***
Professional	0.16***
Favor the wealthy?	−.19***
Hispanic v. White	−.01
African American v. White	0.08***
Age	−.04
Gender	−.02
Education	0.04
Income	0.05
Adjusted R.-sq.	21%***

2. Africa

Our second analysis explores the antecedents of legitimating beliefs within a wide variety of sub-Saharan African states. Africa is an especially good place to examine these issues because of the large amount of variation, both within and across African countries, in the extent to which governments are perceived as legitimate. Afrobarometer data surveys Africans' views toward democracy, economics, and civil society with random, stratified, nationally representative samples.[2]

We measure the extent to which government trustworthiness and procedural justice are related to legitimating beliefs using the third round of the Afrobarometer. Round 3 surveys were conducted in 2005 in 18 sub-Saharan African countries.[3]

We model three separate dependent variables that tap the obligation or willingness to obey and, thus, value-based legitimacy. Specifically, respondents were asked if they agree with the statements "The tax department always has the right to make people pay taxes"; "The courts always have the right to make decisions people abide by"; and "The police always have the right to make people obey the law." Respondents' answers were originally coded as strongly disagree, disagree, neither disagree nor agree, agree, strongly agree, don't know, and refused to answer. We dichotomized this variable from a five-point scale because we do not believe there is a substantive difference between the various categories.

We include three indicators of procedural justice that measure different dimensions of the concept. Two indicators capture government discrimination: whether respondents perceive that their government treats all citizens fairly and whether they believe their government treats members of their ethnic group fairly. We also include an index that taps citizen perceptions of the fairness of governments' exercise of authority. This index is constructed from questions that ask respondents whether they believe the following are worse or better now than they were a few years ago or about the same: freedom to say what you think, freedom to join any political organization you want, freedom to choose who to vote for without feeling pressured, and, the ability of ordinary people to influence what government does.[4]

The combination of government performance and administrative competence equals a trustworthy government. Our measure of government performance is a dummy variable indicating whether a respondent or a household member ever went without sufficient food in the year preceding the survey. This should capture the extent to which citizens believe their government is meeting its end of the fiscal contract. In an earlier paper, Sacks and Levi (2006) find that government effectiveness in terms of the provision of infrastructure, bureaucratic services, and law and order corresponds to a higher level of food security at the individual level.

Our measures of administrative competence capture citizens' assessment of the probity of officials and the likelihood government will enforce the law. Specifically, we include separate indicators of whether respondents believe that a large portion of tax administrators, police, and judges are corrupt. Although an imperfect measure of states' enforcement capacity, Afrobarometer probes respondents on whether they believe that the state will enforce the law if a citizen does not pay taxes or commits a serious crime. Another set of questions asks respondents about the likelihood that government authorities would enforce the law if a top government official committed a serious crime or did not pay taxes.

We control for standard sociodemographic variables that can affect whether citizens defer to government authority. We have reasonably good proxies for income, including whether respondents own a television, radio, car, and bike; and respondents' health, age, employment, and urban or rural residence. We also control for standard country-level indicators for 2004: logged GDP per capita, logged aid per capita, logged population size, and Freedom House's measures of civil liberties and political rights.

We estimate the effects of procedural justice and a trustworthy government on value-based legitimacy using multilevel logistic regression with random intercepts for the Primary Sampling Unit (PSU) and country levels. Because of the difficulty of interpreting multilevel logistic parameters, we focus our discussion on the point estimates of the first differences and the confidence intervals surrounding them (see Table 4.3).[5]

First, as we expected, assessments of government trustworthiness correlate with deference to government authority. Our indicator of government performance, whether a respondent and household members went without sufficient food in the year preceding the survey, is significant at the p<.001 for our regressions on acceptance of the tax department's and court's authority. Enjoying food security translates into an average 1.75 percentage point increase in the probability that a respondent will accept the authority of the courts, tax department, and police.[6]

There are two dimensions of administrative competence: its honesty and the extent to which it can monitor and enforce laws and regulations among citizens and elites. A perception that the government is competent and honest, as opposed to believing that the government is corrupt and unlikely to enforce its regulations and laws, translates into an average 16.33 percentage point increase

Table 4.3 **Changes in predicted probability of willingness to accept government authority (Afrobarometer data, N = 23,909)**

		95% Confidence Interval	
	Min. to Max. (Percent)	Lower Bound	Lower Bound
Tax Department			
Government Performance	2.60%	1.20%	3.90%
Administrative Competence	15.00%	11.00%	18.00
Procedural Justice	19.00%	16.00%	22.00%
Police			
Government Performance	0.46%	−0.62%	1.50%
Administrative Competence	15.00%	11.00%	19.00%
Procedural Justice	12.00%	10.00%	15.00%
Courts			
Government Performance	2.20%	0.96%	3.40%
Administrative Competence	19.00%	16.00%	23.00%
Procedural Justice	12.00%	9.60%	14.00%
Average for Tax Department, Courts & Police			
Government Performance	1.75%		
Administrative Competence	16.33%		
Procedural Justice	14.33%		

in the probability that a respondent will accept the court's, tax department's, and police's authority, respectively.[7]

Second, in support of our hypothesis, we find considerable evidence of a link between procedural justice and deference to government authority.[8] Each of our indicators of procedural justice are significant at the p<.01 level. A belief that the government is procedurally fair corresponds to an average 14.33 percentage point increase in the probability that a citizen will defer to the authority of the tax department, police, and courts.[9]

None of our country-level indicators including civil liberties, political rights, and GDP per capita are significant at the p<.05 level. The most likely explanation for why we are not finding any robust country-level effects is that there is more variation in legitimating beliefs within countries than between them. The intraclass correlation coefficient for the PSU level is significantly higher than for the country level. For example, only 3.2% of the unexplained variance in deference to the courts can be attributed to country-level factors. By contrast, 18% of the unexplained variance in deference to the courts can be attributed to PSU-level factors. It is likely that we would find more country-level variation if we had a more heterogeneous sample with war-torn countries like Somalia and Sudan.

To summarize, we find considerable evidence of a link between the extent of procedural justice and government trustworthiness and citizens' perceptions of legitimacy in a wide range of developing societies in Africa. Of our three latent factors, the most important is administrative competence (16.33%), followed by procedural justice (14.33%), and government performance (1.75%). We do not find any evidence that country-level indicators including GDP (per capita), civil liberties, and political rights explain variation in deference to government authority.

3. Discussion

In spite of the differences in our analyses of data from New York and Africa, the results from both analyses appear to support our basic model of legitimacy. We find that across both analyses, procedural justice strongly influences citizens' judgments about government. This finding is important because it suggests that how governments exercise their authority influences their legitimacy and shapes their ability to secure widespread compliance from their citizens. Our findings also suggest that government trustworthiness and self-reported trust affect deference to authority in both the New York and Africa study, respectively.

The most surprising result is the insignificant effect of civil liberties. This may, as already noted, reflect our inability to capture internal country variations with the data available. A very different data set offers a more intuitive finding. Our analysis of the 2005 Latin American survey data (the Latinobarometer)

Table 4.4 **Multilevel logistic regression on confidence in the judiciary**
(Latinobarometer data, N = 19,633)

Intercept	−2.038 ***	0.224
Car	0.076	0.046
Health	0.066 **	0.022
TV	−0.003	0.063
Mobile phone	0.040	0.041
Education	0.033 **	0.011
Sewage system	−0.011	0.049
Drinking water	−0.087	0.065
Town size	−0.044 ***	0.009
Gov't progress in reducing corruption—a lot/some	0.339 ***	0.040
No. of corrupt civil servants—25 or less (out of 100)	0.044	0.177
No. of corrupt civil servants—26 to 50 (out of 100)	−0.042	0.172
No. of corrupt civil servants—51 to 75 (out of 100)	0.178	0.177
No. of corrupt civil servants—76 to 75 (out of 100)	−0.510 **	0.172
Everyone is treated equally in country	0.069	0.074
Everyone receives equal treatment under law—agree	0.367 ***	0.045
Courts are fair—somewhat disagree	0.263 ***	0.062
Courts are fair—somewhat agree	0.601 ***	0.065
Courts are fair—strongly agree	0.682 ***	0.083
Citizen lawfulness—very/quite	0.251 ***	0.049
Citizen demanding of rights—very/quite	0.160 ***	0.040
Citizens conscious of obligations and duties—very/quite	0.051	0.043
Elections are clean & not rigged	0.314 ***	0.044
Most people say what they think about politics	0.137 ***	0.040
Courts deliver justice—somewhat disagree	0.196 **	0.074
Courts deliver justice—somewhat agree	0.834 ***	0.073
Courts deliver justice—strongly agree	1.062 ***	0.089
Random Intercepts		
T^2 (Districts) (N = 526)	0.070	0.265
T^2 (Countries) (N = 187)	0.152	0.390

*p<.05, **p<.01, ***p<.001

*We modeled don't know, refused to answer, and NA responses. However, we excluded these results from this table to conserve space.

suggests that a positive assessment of civil liberties helps to shape citizen confidence in government (see Table 4.4). Respondents were probed on their confidence in the police, judiciary, local government or municipalities, and government. They were also asked whether they agree with the following: elections are clean and not rigged, citizens are demanding of their rights, people say what they think about politics, the courts deliver justice, and everyone receives equal treatment under the law. In general, we find a positive and significant relationship between each of these indicators and confidence in government.[10] Our results are similar for the regressions on confidence in the local government, police, and the president.[11]

B. Proposition 2

1. United States

Previous analyses demonstrate that value-based legitimacy shapes self-reported compliance with the law (Sunshine and Tyler, 2003; Tyler, 2006; Tyler and Fagan, 2008), an indicator of behavioral legitimacy. We replicate these analyses in this paper. Behavioral legitimacy as reflected in adherence to the law was evaluated in several ways. First is through self-reports of everyday compliance with the law. Respondents are asked to indicate how frequently they follow a set of laws ranging from lifestyle violations to more serious crimes such as stealing and the use of drugs. Second is through self-reports from respondents about their willingness to voluntarily help the police by reporting crime and criminals and to help the police in their communities. Finally, using precinct level police data, the objective rate of felonies within different areas of the city is used as an estimate of people's rate of compliance.

Consistent with the argument we are making, people who express value-based legitimacy (i.e., who indicate feeling obligated to obey the law) indicate that they are more likely to comply with the law. Of particular interest is the finding that voluntary cooperation with laws increases when the government has value-based legitimacy. This finding accords with other studies that rely upon people's self-reported behavior (Tyler, 2006), as well as studies that assess behavior via official arrest records (Tyler et al., 2007b). Value-based legitimacy is consistently found to enhance behavioral legitimacy (i.e., obligation enhances cooperation).

Our goal is to move beyond the prior analysis of individual-level compliance. We seek to examine whether a climate of legitimacy leads to a climate of law abidingness. We evaluate our second proposition using respondents' answers to the already outlined measures of obligation. To carry out this analysis, we use the objective crime rates reported for each of the 75 police precincts of the city of

New York. We predict that those respondents who have higher levels of value-based legitimacy, as randomly sampled respondents from their precinct, should reflect the general level of value-based legitimacy among members of that neighborhood. And those neighborhoods in which the law was viewed as more legitimate should have lower rates of crime. In other words, as before, we argue that value-based legitimacy should shape behavioral legitimacy.

Our results support this hypothesis (see Table 4.5). This finding suggests that value-based legitimacy is linked to the crime rate within the respondent's neighborhood, which reflects objective behavioral legitimacy. This provides evidence that the climate of legitimacy has objective consequences for a polity because it influences the general rate of rule following within it.

In our analysis, we use multilevel modeling (Raudenbush and Bryk, 2002) to control for the population size within each precinct, as well as the socioeconomic character of each neighborhood. We include the following three objective measures of neighborhood wealth using census data: the percentage of

Table 4.5 **Legitimacy and compliance**

	Behavioral legitimacy			
	Compliance with Regulations	Compliance with Laws	Voluntary Cooperation with the Police	Precinct Level Felony Arrests*
Beta weights				
Value-based legitimacy	0.10***	0.10***	0.18***	0.05*
Crime rate	0.01	0.01	0.04	0.04
Risk of punishment	0.07**	0.07*	0.16***	0.01
Hispanic	−0.01	−0.01	−0.02	0.23***
African American	0	0	0.09***	0.26***
Age	0.19***	0.21***	−.15***	0.02
Gender	0.10***	0.12***	0.01	0
Income	0	0.02	−.11***	−.08**
Education	−.11***	−.10***	−.08*	−.12***
Precinct size	−0.03	−0.03	−.05*	−0.02
Adjusted R.-sq.	7%***	7%***	13%***	15%***

Note: Multiple regression analysis. Compliance measured via self-report. Precinct-level felony arrests via police statistics.

*Higher numbers of our dependent variable equals fewer arrests.

families living in poverty, the percentage of families without a wage earner, and the median value of homes. These three variables are found to be positively related to precinct crime rate (see Table 4.6). However, introducing these controls does not change our basic finding that legitimacy is negatively associated with a neighborhood's crime rate.

Taken together, these findings support the argument that value-based legitimacy promotes compliance. People comply, in other words, because they feel they have an obligation to comply. Our evidence suggests that a climate of obligation encourages a climate of compliance.

And, of course, people also comply for other reasons. For example, we have already noted that people's assessments of the state are linked to the ability of the state to create credible risks for those who break rules. As expected, we find that people view the law as more legitimate when there is a clear risk that those who break rules are punished. For example, in the analysis of self-reported compliance, the risk of punishment shapes both compliance and voluntary cooperation. Consistent with our argument risk of punishment has an especially strong influence on voluntary cooperation. This effect is also found in the multilevel model shown in Table 4.6. If people believe that the police enforce the laws and thereby create a credible risk of being punished for wrongdoing, they are more likely to comply, as reflected in a lower objective crime rate.

Table 4.6 **Neighborhood characteristics and legitimacy**

	Precinct-level felony	
	Arrest Area Stats.	Std. Error
Individual-level data		
Legitimacy	126.25 ***	31.91
Perceived crime rate	81.88 **	29.59
Neighbor-hood conditions	240.44 ***	31.43
Police enforcement of laws	40.52 *	20.32
Size of precinct	4.33 *	1.90
Individual-level intercept	1262.76 ***	58.49
FISC-level data		
Percentage of households below poverty level	7202.95 ***	2218.63
Percentage of households with someone working	9542.57	3242.10
Standardized median price of homes	0.06 *	0.03

Note: HML multilevel modeling. Weighted data. *p<.05; **p < .01; ***p< .001.

2. Africa

a. Crime rates

We ask whether communities with higher average levels of legitimating beliefs have lower average crime rates in our African sample. Our dependent variable is the average of the number of times respondents within the same PSU report experiencing burglaries within the past year. Our main explanatory variable, value-based legitimacy, represents the average level of willingness of accepting the following among respondents within the same PSU: the tax department's right to make people pay taxes, the court's right to impose binding decisions, and the police's right to make people obey the law.[12]

We model the relationship between the existence of legitimating beliefs and low crime rates at the PSU level using the second and third rounds of Afrobarometer. Respondents were sampled from a total of 1,978 PSUs in round 2 and 2,368 PSUs in round 3. We include controls for the sociodemographic characteristics of communities including the averages of the following: the number of female respondents, the number of children under age 18 living in respondents' households, the frequency respondents' reported having had access to a sufficient amount of food within the past year, the level of respondents' education, and, the number of rural respondents.[13] We include a variable indicating whether survey enumerators observed a police station and police within each PSU. We also include a variable indicating the average ease respondents within the same community face in obtaining help from the police. Since we are concerned with crime levels at the community level, we aggregate the individual-level data up to the PSU level and estimate a two-level hierarchical model with random intercepts for countries.

We find that those geographical units with higher average legitimacy have statistically discernable ($p<.05$) lower average crime for both rounds of data (see Table 4.7).[14] Although the findings suggest that there is an impact of the climate of value-based legitimacy upon the crime rate, this relationship is weak.

Only one of our indicators of police presence is significant at the $p<.05$ level in the round 2 analysis. We find that the relationship between the average ease of obtaining help from the police and the average safety of a community is positive. Our analysis of the round 3 data does not point to any discernable relationship between the presence of police and a police station within a PSU and the average level of crime. In fact, our analysis of round 3 data suggests that the relationship between a police station in a PSU and the average level of crime in a PSU is positive; in other words, the presence of a police station corresponds to a higher level of crime. This may suggest that

Table 4.7   **Hierarchical linear regression on crime (No. districts = 2,638) Afrobarometer data (2005)**

	Estimate	Std. Error	95% Confidence Interval	
			Lower Bound	Upper Bound
Intercept	12.29 *	0.33	11.64	12.95
Female	0.11	0.37	−0.63	0.86
Rural	0.13	0.07	−0.01	0.27
TV	0.02	0.14	−0.26	0.30
Car	−0.24	0.17	−0.57	0.10
Book	−0.28 *	0.13	−0.54	−0.02
Radio	0.12	0.16	−0.21	0.45
Bike	0.06	0.15	−0.23	0.36
Police present in the PSU	0.06	0.07	−0.08	0.20
Police station present in the PSU	−0.22 *	0.07	−0.37	−0.08
Easy to obtain help from police	0.34 *	0.06	0.23	0.46
Legitimacy (Tax Dept., Police & Judges)	0.06 *	0.02	0.01	0.10
Random Intercepts				
T^2 (Countries) (N = 16)	0.11	0.34		

*p<.05

police across our sample are ineffective or corrupt. An alternative explanation is that in countries where the government cannot afford to provide police stations in each neighborhood, governments may reserve police stations for neighborhoods with higher preexisting levels of crime.

To summarize, we find a positive but weak relationship between the presence of legitimacy within a community and the average level of crime in that community while accounting for police presence and the sociodemographic character of a community. These data are cross-sectional, reflecting influences measured at one point in time.

It would further advance our case if we could show that changes in legitimacy lead to changes in the rate of crime. We would need longitudinal data over a long period to be able to assess whether the strengthening or weakening of legitimacy in a community corresponds to a reduction or increase in crime. We hope to find such data and to use it to extend our analysis.

b. Bribes

Next, using the third round of Afrobarometer, we ask whether respondents who hold legitimating beliefs towards their government reflecting an obligation to obey the law are less likely to violate the law by offering a bribe, gift, or favor to government officials in order to access certain services. Our dependent variable is the frequency respondents offered a bribe, gift, or favor within the year preceding the survey to obtain a document or permit, a place in school for one's child a household service, medicine or medical attention from a health worker, or to avoid a problem with the police.[15]

We include the same sociodemographic control variables and indicators of police presence and effectiveness as described in our model on crime rate. We anticipate that when citizens face difficulty obtaining bureaucratic services, they are more likely to offer a larger number of bribes than citizens who do not face similar obstacles. Thus, we include two additional variables indicating the ease respondents face in obtaining identity documents and a place in primary school for a child. We estimate a three-level model on the use of bribes with random intercepts for the PSU and country levels.

In support of our hypothesis, we find that those respondents who defer to the tax department and to the courts are more likely to have offered fewer bribes ($p<.05$) (see Table 4.8). This finding suggests that there is a relationship between holding legitimating beliefs and following the law by rejecting bribery as a means to obtain certain bureaucratic services. The estimate for deference to the police is not significant at the $p<.05$ level. In fact, we find a positive relationship between the presence of a police station in a PSU and the use of bribes. Our results suggest that respondents who are able to obtain help from the police are less likely to offer bribes.

Given that the ability to offer bribes or gifts to government officials is related to an individual's wealth, not surprisingly, we find that the ownership of a television, bike, and radio is positively related to bribes. Respondents living in urban areas are more likely to offer bribes than rural residents.

To summarize, we find a positive relationship between citizens' deference to the tax department and courts and their compliance with the law in terms of not turning to bribes, gifts, or favors to obtain services from government officials. We also find a positive relationship between police presence and the use of bribes, which may point to widespread corruption within the police across the 17 countries that are included in our sample.

3. Discussion

The approach we use to test our second proposition is a daunting one for any model rooted in the judgments of particular individuals. We use the combined

Table 4.8 **Hierarchical linear regression on frequency of offering bribes (higher numbers equal fewer bribes) (N = 21,108)**

	Estimate	Std. Error	95% Confidence Interval	
			Lower Bound	Upper Bound
Sociodemographic Variables				
(Intercept)	20.294 *	0.328	19.637	20.950
Age	0.005 *	0.002	0.001	0.008
Female	0.399 *	0.052	0.294	0.504
Rural	0.166 *	0.067	0.032	0.301
TV	−0.209 *	0.070	−0.349	-0.069
Car	−0.181	0.100	−0.381	0.019
Book	−0.060	0.059	−0.178	0.059
Radio	−0.176 *	0.067	−0.310	−0.043
Bike	−0.196 *	0.063	−0.323	−0.070
Administrative Competence				
Ease of obtaining help from police—yes	0.557 *	0.063	0.432	0.682
Ease of obtaining help from police—don't know	0.621 *	0.205	0.211	1.032
Ease of obtaining help from police—never tried	0.397 *	0.088	0.221	0.573
Police station present in the PSU	-0.223 *	0.073	−0.370	−0.077
Ease of obtaining an ID document—easy	0.563 *	0.062	0.440	0.686
Ease of obtaining an ID document—don't know	-0.059	0.215	−0.489	0.372
Ease of obtaining an ID document—never tried	0.293 *	0.109	0.074	0.511
Ease of obtaining a place in primary school—easy	0.878 *	0.074	0.730	1.026
Ease of obtaining a place in primary school—don't know	0.482 *	0.183	0.116	0.849
Ease of obtaining a place in primary school—never tried	0.311 *	0.105	0.101	0.520

Table 4.8 (*continued*)

	Estimate	Std. Error	95% Confidence Interval	
			Lower Bound	Upper Bound
Legitimacy				
Defer to Authority of Tax Department	0.127 *	0.062	0.004	0.250
Defer to Authority of Courts	0.176 *	0.066	0.044	0.308
Defer to Authority of Police	0.123	0.069	−0.016	0.261
Random Effects				
T^2 (Districts) (N = 2,478)	0.895	0.946		
T^2 (Countries) (N = 17)	1.409	1.187		

individual responses within particular communities as indicators of the general level of value-based legitimacy within that community. We then link that generalized judgment to the level of crime within that community. Because communities differ in many ways, we adjust for factors such as the economic status of the community and the presence of effective policing (or even any policing). Of course, we recognize that these adjustments can never be complete. As a result, we think it is striking that the evidence from our samples suggests that value-based legitimacy is linked to the rate of crime.

This is perhaps most notable in the case of the New York City sample, where crime rates are drawn from police statistics. Those statistics are not linked in any way to the judgments of the respondents about legitimacy. Still, in those communities in which respondents generally report higher value-based legitimacy, the police report lower crime. In the African samples, we use the respondents to tell us about the level of crime.

The number of respondents who report having experienced crime or having fear of crime within a given geographical area is used to estimate the rate of crime. Again, we find that higher value-based legitimacy is associated with lower crime rates. In other words, a similar finding consistently emerges across variations in our methodology, suggesting that the underlying relationship we predict is robust.

4. Conclusions

We have presented and tested a framework for thinking about compliance with the law. We have found support for the proposition that value-based legitimacy is related to individuals' assessments of their governments as procedurally just and trustworthy. In both the United States and in Africa, we find that positive evaluations of government on these dimensions shape judgments that government ought to be obeyed. However, we also find evidence suggesting that while citizen evaluations of government's competence and performance play a significant role in shaping legitimating beliefs, equally and sometimes more important is the perception that government is procedurally just.

We have also found support for our second proposition: people's compliance with the law is related to their normative judgments about the legitimacy of government. Operationalizing value-based legitimacy as an obligation to defer to authorities, we show that it is linked to the level of compliance; that is, behavioral legitimacy, as reflected in indices of crime. Communities with higher levels of value-based legitimacy have lower rates of crime. This is true both in an American sample and in two multi-country samples within Africa.

The major implication of these findings for the development of human rights is that procedural justice has significant consequences for how citizens evaluate their government and, consequently, for the costs of government. Governments that are reasonably fair in how they devise and implement policies, introduce meritocracy into bureaucracy and education, offer relatively equitable access to services and protection, and provide relatively equal treatment before the law are more likely to ensure a high level of value-based legitimacy in their polities and, consequently, a high level of behavioral legitimacy, *ceteris paribus.*

There are several benefits to basing political authority on legitimacy grounded in procedural justice and some respect for human rights. The principle advantage is that the government is freed from the continual need to provide citizens with rewards or credibly threaten them with punishments to obtain desired behavior. The costs of doing so are high and may be too high where there is no motivation to obey and, possibly, reason to resist (Levi, 1988; Levi, 1997). Trying to coerce compliance can even be self-defeating. Loyalty that is purchased is fleeting. As Machiavelli said long ago: "friendships that are obtained by payments and not by greatness or nobility of mind, may indeed be earned, but they are not secured and in time cannot be relied upon" (Machiavelli, 1950, chapter 17).

A second advantage is that those citizens whose own values lead them to support the state are more likely to do so proactively, finding ways to do what is needed to solve problems and manage difficulties (Tyler, 2007). For example, the battlefield advantage of democratic armies is linked to the superior ability of soldiers to be innovative in adapting to battlefield conditions, as well as their greater motivation to sacrifice on behalf of their country (Tyler et al., 2007a).

A third advantage has to do with the establishment of a positive reciprocal relationship between government and its citizens. Whether it be for blood donations (Titmuss, 1971) or for other forms of contribution or compliance

(Akerlof, 1982; Barzel, 2001), "gifts" are often of higher quality than coerced extractions. This is particularly the case when they derive from norms of reciprocity in which those being asked to give believe they have been treated well and therefore ought to return the favor (Fehr et al., 1998; Gintis, 2002; Homans, 1958). The evidence presented here and in other papers (Levi and Sacks, 2007; Levi and Sacks, forthcoming) suggests that when government is relatively effective and fair, its citizens are likely to come to believe that government deserves compliance. Where such a relationship exists, there is the potential for the development of a virtuous circle. The more effective and fair the government, the greater the willingness to accept governmental authority and, therefore, the more compliance, which then improves government's capacity to become more effective and to evoke deference, which in turn increases compliance.

A procedurally fair government may also help to encourage universalistic norms, a third advantage of legitimacy. By adhering to procedural justice in its decision-making processes and its treatment of citizens, governments set a standard of how citizens should treat one another. Over time, once common attitudes and actions (e.g., slavery or racism) may become unthinkable (Fiske and Tetlock, 1997; Levi, 1997). They may even come to develop a common identity that produces expectations of fair treatment regardless of ethnic, racial, or religious traits. Parochialism (see Baron, this volume) is, therefore, less likely to emerge.

A final advantage of legitimacy is that it gives government some space when wars, natural disasters, economic downturns, or shifts in policy lead to deterioration in the quality and quantity of services or security. The more legitimate a government is perceived to be, the more likely citizens will tolerate its efforts to correct problems that society is experiencing. Without legitimacy, government is both less effective and more costly.

We have further argued that governmental fairness and procedural justice, as indicated by its use of fair decision-making procedures, as well as its respect of citizen rights and entitlements, is a major factor in producing governmental legitimacy. Governments have the ability to rise above their objective circumstances and create public support through the manner in which they exercise their authority. There is a lesson here for extra-state actors—be they domestic NGOs, international agencies, or foreign governments. The provision of donations or, more directly, goods and services will have very little influence on the long-run stability of the government or the welfare of citizens unless there is also the insistence that governments treat their citizens with dignity and respect. Procedural justice in the form of human rights and government accountability are the sine qua non of governments that are most likely to be long-lasting, responsive, and effective.

Notes

We wish to thank Robert Nelson for useful comments on an earlier draft. We thank the Royalty Research Fund at the University of Washington for helping to support this research.

1. The legitimacy index used was drawn from Tyler and Fagan (2008). That index assessed legitimacy using a scale that measures obligation and legal cynicism. First, it included the seven obligation items noted. In addition, respondents were asked three questions reflecting their general cynicism regarding the motivations underlying the law (i.e., low trust and confidence), questions drawn from the Ewick and Silbey (1998) legitimacy framework. These items ask people to agree or disagree with these items: "The law represents the interests of the rich, rather than the concerns of people like myself"; "People in power use the law to try to control people like you"; and "The law does not protect your interests." The analysis reported uses this overall index because this overall scale corrects for agreement bias and is less skewed (see Tyler and Fagan, 2008). However, for the purposes of our argument here, it is important to note that a similar analysis focused only on obligation similarly indicates that legitimacy leads to compliance.

2. The Afrobarometer is a joint enterprise of Michigan State University (MSU), the Institute for Democracy in South Africa (IDASA), and the Centre for Democracy and Development (CDD, Ghana). For more on the Afrobarometer, see www.afrobarometer.org.

3. We excluded Zimbabwe from all of our analyses because of concerns with data quality. We also excluded Uganda from our analysis of neighborhood thefts (2005 data) since the data set did not come with PSU codes. Fieldwork was conducted by national research institutions affiliated with the Afrobarometer project. Samples were designed using a common multistage, stratified, area-cluster approach. Random selection methods were used at each stage, with probability proportional to population size where appropriate. Sampling frames were constructed in the first stages from the most up-to-date census figures or projections available and thereafter from census maps, systematic walk patterns, and project-generated lists of household members.

4. A single unrotated procedural justice factor explains 51% of the common variance, and Cronbach's Alpha is .83.

5. In each case, we repeated the first differences algorithm 10,000 times to approximate a 95% confidence interval around the probability of accepting the tax department's, courts', and the police's authority.

6. Enjoying food security corresponds to a percentage point increase of 2.6, 0.46, and 2.2 in the acceptance of tax department's, police's, and courts' authority, respectively.

7. A positive assessment of administrative competence corresponds to a percentage point increase of 15, 15, and 19 in the probability of accepting the authority of the tax department, police, and courts, respectively.

8. The results we present in this paper are slightly different from our analysis in Levi, Sacks, and Tyler (Levi et al., 2009). In this latter paper, we do not include the extent to which citizens believe the government is respecting citizens' rights as an indicator of procedural justice.

9. A positive evaluation of procedural justice corresponds to a percentage point increase of 19, 12, and 12 in the probability of accepting the authority of the tax department, police, and courts, respectively.

10. Unfortunately, Latinobarometer does not ask respondents whether they feel obligated to defer to government authority.

11. To conserve space, we left these results out of the paper. These results are available by request.

12. For the 2002–2003 data, a single unrotated legitimacy factor explains 40% of the common variance in legitimacy and Cronbach's Alpha is .65. For the 2005 data, a single unrotated legitimacy actor explains 42% of the common variance in legitimacy and Cronbach's Alpha is .68.

13. We use the same variables in the regression on 2003 and 2005 with a few exceptions for the sociodemographic variables. The 2005 survey asked respondents whether they own a number of household items including a car, television, book, radio, and bike.
14. The results for the round 2 analysis are available by request.
15. A single unrotated bribe factor explains 44% of the common variance and Cronbach's Alpha is .79.

CODA

The Reasons for Compliance with Law

RYAN GOODMAN, DEREK JINKS, AND ANDREW K. WOODS

Relying on two sets of cross-sectional data—one from the United States and one from sub-Saharan Africa—Margaret Levi, Tom Tyler and Audrey Sacks provide evidence of two relationships that implicate compliance with law. First, individuals' voluntary compliance with law is influenced by their views of the government's legitimacy. Second, their conceptions of legitimacy depend significantly on two elements: the government's trustworthiness and commitment to procedural justice. Trustworthiness, in turn, is a product of the government's record of performance and administrative competence. We examine how these relationships can produce a "virtuous circle" that helps promote human rights. We also examine, among other applications, how a citizenry might come to accept laws that violate human rights.

I. Target: Promoters of Human Rights

A. Exploiting Beneficial Effects of Links between Legitimacy (Trust and Procedural Justice) and Compliance

Levi, Tyler, and Sacks's line of research could lead to empirically informed analysis that builds better global institutions. That is, if their model applies at the international level, it might help unlock the door to more effective, more humane forms of global governance. A key theoretical insight of the chapter is that trust and procedural justice are keys to legal compliance. As a consequence, governments can harness significant power to effectuate compliance—without the resort to coercion. Applied to the international domain, these insights are remarkably consistent with Thomas Franck's work, which argues that (a) procedural justice is central to the legitimacy of international law; and (b) legitimacy, in turn, exerts "compliance pull" on states (Franck, 1990). Levi, Tyler, and Sacks's research program is an important supplement. It can provide empirical groundwork for testing and explaining psychological and political mechanisms that undergird these relationships in international human rights law. Their chapter also points to normative implications for other research that examines procedural justice mechanisms within international organizations (such as the Global Administrative Law research program at NYU).

Issues of global governance may be especially fertile ground for Levi, Tyler, and Sacks's model. Legitimacy, according to their model, is potentially most important for governments that lack resources to exercise the full panoply of coercive powers and for governments in emergent or transitional societies. These conditions approximate the current state of international affairs. That is, international legal institutions cannot depend heavily on coercive authority. And the international legal order constitutes an emergent regime consciously struggling to secure its legitimacy among various stakeholders. Furthermore, one lesson from the chapter is that even established international institutions with considerable coercive power—for example, the UN Security Council— may strengthen compliance with their dictates by demonstrating a high level of competence through procedures that are respectful of human rights.

B. Overcoming Negative Effects of Links between Legitimacy (Trust and Procedural Justice) and Compliance

The chapter encourages us to consider relationships between international institutions and public confidence in government performance and administrative competence. The authors' data suggest that governments could erode their legitimacy by relying on external institutions to improve domestic conditions. And such a result would undercut the ability of the government to maintain public order. Consider a few examples: (1) Under certain circumstances, the International Criminal Court's investigation in a state (which might have called for the Court's assistance) could have a perverse effect of undermining compliance with criminal laws across the country. (2) International election monitors, even if they ultimately sanction a national election, may cast doubt on the government's competence to conduct such monitoring itself. (3) The emergent "responsibility to protect" doctrine obliges international actors to redress a country's internal human rights conditions, but its activation requires a determination that a national government is unwilling or unable to protect its own people. The empirical data suggest that such a determination (of incompetence), and the drawn-out process of reaching it, might have unintended destabilizing effects within the relevant country. Notably, such dynamics can help explain why and when states reject external election monitoring, or reject humanitarian assistance after a natural disaster. Outside assistance casts doubt on the government's competence and administrative performance—and, hence, undercuts its legitimacy and ability to effectuate compliance. A vicious circle, rather than a virtuous one, might occur.

Various institutional designs could mitigate such negative effects. An obvious design option is to raise the threshold for external intervention to balance against the potential negative effects—in other words, to intervene only when the situation is dire, or governmental inaction is extreme. On the contrary, the opposite design—lowering the threshold for external involvement—could be more prudent. First, lowering the threshold for external involvement can help combat the notion that such relationships with international institutions are a sign of poor performance and incompetence on the part of the state. Indeed, transnational actors would be well advised to frame the reliance on international institutions as evidence of wise policy judgment on the part of domestic actors and a relatively ordinary feature of modern statehood. One can take a page from Abram and Antonia Chayes, who argue that modern conceptions of state sovereignty are increasingly defined by participation in and reliance upon international organizations (Chayes and Chayes, 1996). Second, the collateral effects on legal compliance are potentially more likely to occur and to be significant when a national government is already at its weakest point. Thus, early intervention may lessen the destabilizing effects along this dimension. And, delaying action—exhausting all other remedies (in international legal parlance)—before dire or extreme circumstances are reached may be the worst design choice.

II. Target: Direct Perpetrators of Human Rights Violations

A. Exploiting Beneficial Effects of Links between Legitimacy (Trust and Procedural Justice) and Compliance

Governmental leaders should become attuned to the virtuous circle identified in the chapter. If great leadership comes to include the provision of basic rights, perhaps some leaders will see support for human rights as a cheap way to achieve a measure of legitimacy. They could also be encouraged by the long-term ability to effectuate compliance across a spectrum of governmental domains. Failure to guarantee procedural justice and competence in the provision of public goods could undermine the longevity of a regime. Such lessons could be imparted through leadership training in mid-career teaching programs and graduate schools and via international advisors and consultancy firms. Also, individual leaders and governments with the demonstrated ability to understand such long-term positive returns should receive more favorable treatment from financial institutions, the donor community, and risk assessment models.

A specific lesson for leaders includes the cost effectiveness of procedural justice. Achieving procedural justice can be expensive. But this chapter offers a powerful argument for why the cost is justified: if procedural justice is a significant contributor to a government's legitimacy, it may enable the government to enact all manner of policies with more ease than if the government were seen as illegitimate. This argument might be used to justify investing in procedural mechanisms up front to see returns on the investment in the form of less costly compliance. In that sense, human rights compliance might be pitched to reluctant governmental leaders as a cost-effective policy.

This cost-effectiveness analysis translates into the promotion of economic and social rights, an area of human rights that is generally troubled by resource constraints. The important point here is that governmental competence in domains of economic and social rights (food, security, education) can reduce the cost of compliance and also expand the ability of government to extract resources from the public through taxation. Levi, Tyler, and Sacks show that the trustworthiness of government garnered in the domain of social and economic rights can promote its legitimacy—which the government can, in turn, use to obtain financial and moral support from the public. This is not to say that some economic and social rights protections are completely self-financing. Their cost, however, may be considerably lower than expected.

Finally, this chapter suggests that governmental leaders should take seriously the criticisms that are expressed in human rights advocacy campaigns. A core insight of the research is that public perception of the legitimacy of the state is key to compliance rates across a range of legal and regulatory domains. In other words, winning hearts and minds is a crucial component of effective governance. Human rights campaigns can change societal beliefs about the trustworthiness and fairness of a government. Officials would be wise to understand this dimension of global and transnational politics. In the national security realm, John Vasquez examines self-defeating strategies resulting from individuals who enter government service wedded to a realist paradigm of international politics. In that context, realist frames lead officials to devalue compromise and to risk security spirals. In our context, realist assumptions could lead officials to underestimate the power of human rights advocates and to devalue the state interest in making concessions to associated stakeholders in society. Great leadership requires understanding these challenges.

B. Overcoming Negative Effects of Links between Legitimacy (Trust and Procedural Justice) and Compliance

Could the authors' research help produce a playbook for duplicitous regimes to shore up their legitimacy without serving the public interest? Consider the degree to which the data involve *perceptions* of governmental conduct rather than the conduct itself. There are normatively undesirable lessons that could be derived from such findings. First, officials might calculate that it serves their interest to spend $1 on marketing a better image of themselves rather than $10 on actually solving problems or improving procedural justice. At the least, officials might consider it prudent to siphon off funds for a project that delivers public goods and instead direct those funds to public relations. Even "altruistic" officials could make such tradeoffs in the interest of generating political stability and compliance with legal institutions. Second, governments may falsely take credit for the provision of public goods (such as food security). Third, malevolent officials might be more willing to restrict actual procedural protections if such strategies do not erode the broader public perception that people are being treated fairly. Such officials could, for example, conclude that the erosion of procedural protections for marginalized groups may increase the perception of dominant groups that their own interests are protected.

The data on procedural justice support some of these concerns more directly. On one hand, the authors find "considerable evidence of a link between procedural justice and deference to government authority," which is measured by beliefs that the government is acting fairly. On the other hand, the authors "do not find any evidence that country-level indicators including . . . civil liberties and political rights explain variation in deference to government authority." The difference here lies in perception: the former includes subjective measures while the latter involves more objective measures of human rights conditions. In short, government may benefit from individuals' perceptions of procedural rights protections and not from the actual protection of civil liberties and political rights.

That said, the evidence of these relationships is indirect and still tentative. And some of these relationships, even if true, could produce second-order benefits. In particular, it may prove beneficial overall and overtime if governments are encouraged to promote themselves as procedurally just and highly competent in the delivery of public goods. Furthermore, for many governments, already skilled in the art of propaganda and public relations, these lessons may be nothing new. These lessons do, however, translate into agendas for human rights advocates. The authors' research suggests that advocates should expose misperceptions that people have about their government, as a means of sparking greater demands by citizens for civil liberties and political rights (or at least a tighter connection between actual rights conditions and the legitimacy bestowed on government).

III. Target: Supporters of Human Rights Violations

A. Overcoming Negative Effects of the Legitimacy (Trust and Procedural Justice)-Compliance Link

Levi, Tyler, and Sacks's research suggests that individuals may voluntarily consent to governmental restrictions on their personal freedoms if citizens believe the government is trustworthy or committed to procedural fairness. Trustworthiness may, in part, be a product of charismatic leadership or the delivery of public goods such as crime prevention. And a sense of procedural fairness may be obtained if citizens are convinced that their views are adequately considered in generating the law. The legitimation of governmental authority through trust and procedural regularities could foster a culture of compliance (the authors refer to "deference") even when citizens think that the substantive policy outcomes (e.g., rights restrictions) are wrong. Moreover, the authors posit that citizens may pay (at a net cost to themselves) to sanction others who do not reciprocate by complying with the law (e.g., "righteous retaliation" in other scholars' work). Levi, Tyler, and Sacks write: "When other citizens fail to comply in situations in which government has fulfilled its side of the implicit bargain, those citizens who feel obliged to comply may pay the costs of punishing the free riders through personal action or via government coercion subsidized by their tax payments." (See also chapter 6 in this volume by Herbert Gintis.) In that regard, the normative desirability of compliance with the law depends on the substantive content of the legal regime.

These insights, similar to those we discussed in Baron's chapter 8, are especially provocative because they identify citizens as willing agents in the (excessive) erosion of their own rights. Such insights can be important to human rights advocates in choosing which actors to target for persuasion in an illiberal regime, in considering potential perverse effects of democratic institutions, and in determining what persuasive messages might gain traction with particular audiences. These insights also suggest that advocates should focus not only on delegitimizing the rights violations committed by particular regimes. Advocacy campaigns may also need to target the source of public confidence in the government, if that support is based on a false sense of the government's competence (e.g., combating a perceived crime rate) or a false sense of procedural fairness.

Note

This Coda, like the others in the book, offers some specific applications drawn from the insights in the contributor's chapter. It is not intended to be a list of fully developed policy prescriptions, but instead an example of the rich sorts of human rights policy applications that can be drawn from cutting-edge social science research. It does not question the insights offered in the chapter but instead asks what implications those insights might have for human rights law and policy. The Codas are the sole authorship of the editors of the volume.

5

Can International Law Stop Genocide When Our Moral Intuitions Fail Us?

PAUL SLOVIC AND DAVID ZIONTS

> To avoid further disasters, we need political restraint on a world scale. But politics is not the whole story. We have experienced the result of technology in the service of the destructive side of human psychology. Something needs to be done about this fatal combination. The means for expressing cruelty and carrying out mass killing have been fully developed. It is too late to stop the technology. It is to the psychology that we should now turn.
>
> —Jonathan Glover, *Humanity*, 2001, p. 144

I. Introduction

"If I look at the mass I will never act. If I look at one, I will." This statement, uttered by Mother Teresa, captures a powerful and deeply unsettling insight into human nature: most people are caring and will exert great effort to rescue "the one" whose needy plight comes to their attention. But these same people often become numbly indifferent to the plight of "the one" who is part of a much greater problem. Why does this occur? The answer to this question will help us answer a related question: why do good people and their governments ignore mass murder and genocide?

There is no simple answer to this question. It is not because we are insensitive to the suffering of our fellow human beings—witness the extraordinary efforts we expend to rescue a person in distress. It is not because we only care about identifiable victims, of similar skin color, who live near us: witness the outpouring of aid to victims of the December 2004 tsunami in South Asia. We cannot simply blame our political leaders. Although President George W. Bush was quite unresponsive to the murder of hundreds of thousands of people in Darfur, it was President Bill Clinton who ignored Rwanda, and President Franklin Roosevelt who did little to stop the Holocaust. Behind every president who ignored mass murder were millions of citizens whose indifference allowed them to get away with it. And it is not only fear of losing American lives in battle that necessarily deters us from acting. We have not even taken quite safe steps that could save many lives, such as bombing the radio stations in Rwanda that were coordinating the slaughter of 800,000 people in 100 days, or supporting the forces of the African Union in Darfur, or just raising our powerful American voices in a threatening shout—*Stop that killing!*—as opposed to turning away in silence.

Every episode of mass murder is distinct and raises unique social, economic, military, and political obstacles to intervention. We therefore recognize that geopolitics, domestic politics, or failures of individual leadership have been important factors in particular episodes. But the repetitiveness of such atrocities, ignored by powerful people and nations, and by the general public, calls for explanations that may reflect some fundamental deficiency in our humanity—a deficiency not in our intentions but in our very hardware. And a deficiency that, once identified, might possibly be overcome.

One fundamental mechanism that may play a role in many, if not all, episodes of mass-murder neglect involves the capacity to experience *affect*, the positive and negative feelings that combine with reasoned analysis to guide our judgments, decisions, and actions. Research shows that the statistics of mass murder or genocide, no matter how large the numbers, fail to convey the true meaning of such atrocities. The numbers fail to spark emotion or feeling and thus fail to motivate action. Genocide in Darfur is real, but we do not "feel" that reality. We examine below ways that we might make genocide "feel real" and motivate appropriate interventions.

Ultimately, however, we conclude that we cannot only depend on our intuitive feelings about these atrocities but, in addition, we must create and commit ourselves to institutional, legal, and political responses based upon reasoned analysis of our moral obligations to stop the mass annihilation of innocent people.

II. The Lessons of Genocide

Dubinsky (2005, p. 112) reports a news story from *The Gazette* (Montreal, April 29, 1992, p. A8):

> On April 28, 1994: the Associated Press (AP) bureau in Nairobi received a frantic call from a man in Kigali who described horrific scenes of concerted slaughter that had been unfolding in the Rwandan capital "every day, everywhere" for three weeks. "I saw people hacked to death, even babies, month-old babies. . . . Anybody who tried to flee was killed in the streets, and people who were hiding were found and massacred."

Dubinsky (2005, p. 113) further notes:

> The caller's story was dispatched on the AP newswire for the planet to read, and complemented an OXFAM statement from the same day declaring that the slaughter—the toll of which had already reached 200,000—"amounts to genocide." The following day, U.N. Secretary General Boutros Boutros-Ghali acknowledged the massacres and requested that the Security Council deploy a significant force, a week after the council had reduced the number of U.N. peacekeepers in Rwanda from 2,500 to 270.

Yet the killings continued for another two and a half months. By mid-July, when the government was finally routed by exiled Tutsi rebels and the slaughter had been quelled, 800,000 were dead, and reinforcements from the United Nations were only just arriving.

In his review of the book *Conspiracy to Murder: The Rwandan Genocide* (Melvern, 2004), Dubinsky (2005, p. 113) draws an ominous lesson from what happened in Rwanda:

> Despite its morally unambiguous heinousness, despite overwhelming evidence of its occurrence (for example, two days into the Rwandan carnage, the US Defense Intelligence Agency possessed satellite photos showing sprawling massacre sites), and despite the relative ease with which it could have been abated (the U.N. commander in Rwanda felt a modest 5,500 reinforcements, had they arrived promptly, could have saved tens of thousands of lives)—despite all this, the world ignored genocide.

Unfortunately, Rwanda is not an isolated incident of indifference to mass murder and genocide. In a deeply disturbing book titled *A Problem from Hell: America and the Age of Genocide*, journalist Samantha Power documents in meticulous detail many of the numerous genocides that occurred during the past century, beginning with the slaughter of two million Armenians by the Turks in 1915 (Power, 2003; see Table 5.1). In every instance, American response was inadequate. She concludes, "No U.S. president has ever made genocide prevention a priority, and no U.S. president has ever suffered politically for his indifference to its occurrence. It is thus no coincidence that genocide rages on" (Power, 2003, p. xxi).

A second lesson to emerge from the study of genocide is that media news coverage is similarly inadequate. The past century has witnessed a remarkable transformation in the ability of the news media to learn about, and report on, world

Table 5.1 **A century of genocide**

Armenia (1915)
Ukraine (1932–1933)
Nazi Germany/Holocaust (World War II)
Bangladesh (1971)
Cambodia (1975–1979)
Countries in the former Yugoslavia (1990s)
Rwanda (1994)
Zimbabwe (2000)
Congo (Today)
Darfur (Today)
? (Tomorrow)

events. The vivid, dramatic coverage of the December 2004 tsunami in South Asia and the similarly intimate and exhaustive reporting of the destruction of lives and property by Hurricane Katrina in September 2005 demonstrate how thorough and powerful news coverage of humanitarian disasters can be. But the intense coverage of recent natural disasters stands in sharp contrast to the lack of reporting on the ongoing genocides in Darfur and other regions in Africa, in which hundreds of thousands of people have been murdered and millions forced to flee their burning villages and relocate to refugee camps. But according to the *Tyndall Report*, which monitors American television coverage, ABC news allotted only 18 minutes on the Darfur genocide in its nightly newscasts in 2004, NBC only 5 minutes, and CBS only 3 minutes. Martha Stewart and Michael Jackson received vastly greater coverage, as did Natalee Holloway, the American girl missing in Aruba. With the exception of the relentless reporting by *New York Times* columnist Nicholas Kristof, the print media have done little better in covering Darfur.

A third and even more disturbing lesson is that even when we have all the information that we should need, we still do not act. Power (2003) contends that U.S. government officials have known of the mass murders and genocides that took place during the past century. She attempts to explain the failure to act on that knowledge as follows:

> ... the atrocities that were known remained abstract and remote ... Because the savagery of genocide so defies our everyday experience, many of us failed to wrap our minds around it ... Bystanders were thus able to retreat to the "twilight between knowing and not knowing." (p. 505)

However, despite the failure of mainstream print and television media to give Darfur its due, the duration of the crisis, now in its seventh year; and the availability of new forms of communication have actually provided us with considerable information about what is happening there. Satellites beam images of burning villages to Google Earth (United States Holocaust Memorial Museum, 2008). Celebrities such as Mia Farrow and George Clooney visit Darfur and Chad and provide regular reports on their websites miafarrow.org and notonourwatchproject.org. Eric Reeves publishes meticulously detailed and up-to-date reports about Darfur on his website www.sudanreeves.org. Former Marine captain Brian Steidle returned from Darfur with hundreds of brutally explicit photographs of the atrocities. Convinced that when such images were released to the public, troops would be sent in to stop the killing, he publicized his photographs through the news media, a book (Steidle and Wallace, 2007), a movie, congressional testimony, and hundreds of speaking engagements. There was little meaningful response, no serious movement for international intervention.

As Richard Just (2008) has observed,

> ... we are awash in information about Darfur. Disturbing photos—now ubiquitous—of torture, death, and starvation are just the beginning of it. There are the regular dispatches of wire service reporters, the drumbeat of opinion columns, and the images beamed home by television cameras. There are more websites maintained by activists and human rights groups than anyone can count. And now there is something else, too: a substantial body of literature, academic and popular, about western Sudan. (p. 36)

> All this gives Darfur a morbid sort of distinction. No genocide has ever been so thoroughly documented while it was taking place. . . . The sheer volume of historical, anthropological, and narrative detail available to the public about the genocide is staggering. . . . But the genocide continues. We document what we do not stop. The truth does not set anybody free. (p. 36)

> How could we have known so much and done so little? (p. 38)

One answer to this question, based on human psychology, will be presented below. Another answer, representing a fourth lesson, is that the laws and institutions designed to prevent and halt genocide and other forms of mass murder have failed to do so. The U.N. general assembly adopted the Convention on the Prevention and Punishment of the Crime of Genocide in 1948 in the hope that "never again" would there be such odious crimes against humanity as occurred during the Holocaust of World War II. Eventually some 140 states would ratify the Genocide Convention, yet it has never been invoked to prevent a potential attack or halt an ongoing massacre. That genocide continues to "rage on" is documented in a striking compilation by Barbara Harff (2003), who lists 36 serious civil conflicts that involved genocidal violence between 1955 and 2003, with a death toll in the tens of millions.

Darfur has shone a particularly harsh light on the Genocide Convention and what Eric Reeves has called "60 years of abject failure" (Reeves, 2008). A careful survey of atrocities there initiated by the U.S. State Department (Totten, 2006) led Secretary of State Colin Powell to conclude in September 2004 that "genocide has been committed in Darfur and that the Government of Sudan and the Janjaweed bear responsibility—and that genocide may still be occurring" (Powell, 2004, p. 4). But rather than invoke the Genocide Convention to justify action, Powell concluded that "no new action is dictated by this determination" (p. 5).

Shocked by Powell's easy sidestepping of obligations to act "in light of the most conspicuous evidence of ongoing genocide," Reeves (2004) observed that this "may actually signal the end of the Genocide Convention as a tool of deterrence and prevention" (pp. 2–3).

Recognizing the need to remedy some of the ambiguities and loopholes in the Genocide Convention, a series of initiatives in Canada led to the development of an important report titled *The Responsibility to Protect* (International Commission on Intervention and State Sovereignty, 2001), which was endorsed by the U.N. World Summit in 2005. However, efforts by the United Nations to address the crisis in Darfur have repeatedly been thwarted by some permanent members of the Security Council who have vetoed or rendered impotent resolutions to halt the bloodshed and implement peacekeeping efforts.

III. Lessons from Psychology

In 1994, Roméo Dallaire, the commander of the tiny U.N. peacekeeping mission in Rwanda, was forced to watch helplessly as the slaughter he had foreseen and warned about began to unfold. Writing of this massive humanitarian disaster a decade later, he encouraged scholars "to study this human tragedy and to contribute to our growing understanding of the genocide. If we do not understand what happened, how will we ever ensure it does not happen again?" (Dallaire, 2005, p. 548).

Researchers in psychology, economics, and a multidisciplinary field called behavioral decision theory have developed theories and findings that, in part, begin to explain the pervasive underresponse to genocide.

A. Affect, Attention, Information, and Meaning

The search to identify a fundamental mechanism in human psychology that causes us to ignore mass murder and genocide draws upon a theoretical framework that describes the importance of emotions and feelings in guiding decision making and behavior. Perhaps the most basic form of feeling is affect, the sense (not necessarily conscious) that something is good or bad. Positive and negative feelings occur rapidly and automatically—note how quickly you sense the feelings associated with the word "joy" or the word "hate." A large research literature in psychology documents the importance of affect in conveying meaning upon information and motivating behavior (Barrett and Salovey, 2002; Clark and Fiske, 1982; Forgas, 2000; Le Doux, 1996; Mowrer, 1960; Tomkins, 1962, 1963; Zajonc, 1980). Without affect, information lacks meaning and won't be used in judgment and decision making (Loewenstein, Weber, Hsee, and Welch, 2001; Slovic, Finucane, Peters, and MacGregor, 2002).

Affect plays a central role in what are known as "dual-process theories" of thinking. As Epstein (1994) has observed: "There is no dearth of evidence in everyday life that people apprehend reality in two fundamentally different ways, one variously labeled intuitive, automatic, natural, non-verbal, narrative, and experiential, and the other analytical, deliberative, verbal, and rational" (p. 710).

Stanovich and West (2000) labeled these two modes of thinking *System 1* and *System 2*. One of the characteristics of System 1, the experiential or intuitive system, is its affective basis. Although analysis (System 2) is certainly important in many decision-making circumstances, reliance on affect and emotion is generally a quicker, easier, and more efficient way to navigate in a complex, uncertain, and sometimes dangerous world. Many theorists have given affect a direct and primary role in motivating behavior.

Underlying the role of affect in the experiential system is the importance of images, to which positive or negative feelings become attached. Images in this system include not only visual images, important as these may be, but words, sounds, smells, memories, and products of our imagination.

Kahneman (2003) notes that one of the functions of System 2 is to monitor the quality of the intuitive impressions formed by System 1. Kahneman and Frederick (2002) suggest that this monitoring is typically rather lax and allows many intuitive judgments to be expressed in behavior, including some that are erroneous. This point has important implications that will be discussed later.

In addition to positive and negative affect, more nuanced feelings such as empathy, sympathy, compassion, and sadness have been found to be critical for motivating people to help others (Coke, Batson, and McDavis, 1978; Dickert and Slovic, 2009; Eisenberg and Miller, 1987). As Batson (1990) put it, "considerable research suggests that we are more likely to help someone in need when we 'feel for' that person . . ." (p. 339).

A particularly important psychological insight comes from Haidt (2001, 2007; see also Van Berkum, Holleman, Nieuwland, Otten, and Jaap, 2009), who argues that moral intuitions (akin to System 1) precede moral judgments. Specifically, he asserts that

> . . . moral intuition can be defined as the sudden appearance in consciousness of a moral judgment, including an affective valence (good-bad, like-dislike) without any conscious awareness of having gone through steps of searching, weighing evidence, or inferring a conclusion. Moral intuition is therefore . . . akin to aesthetic judgment. One sees or hears about a social event and one instantly feels approval or disapproval. (p. 818)

In other words, feelings associated with moral intuition usually dominate moral judgment, unless we make an effort to use judgment to critique and, if necessary, override intuition. Not that our moral intuitions aren't, in many cases, sophisticated and accurate. They are much like human visual perceptions in this regard, equipped with shortcuts that most of the time serve us well but occasionally lead us seriously astray (Kahneman, 2003). Indeed, like perception, which is subject under certain conditions to visual illusions, our moral intuitions can be very misguided. We shall demonstrate this in the following sections and argue that in particular, our intuitions fail us in the face of genocide and mass atrocities. This points to the need to create laws and institutions, designed to stimulate reasoned analysis, that can help us overcome the deficiencies in our ability to *feel* the need to act.

B. Affect, Analysis, and the Value of Human Lives

How *should* we value the saving of human lives? A System 2 answer would look to basic principles or fundamental values for guidance. For example, Article 1 of the United Nations Universal Declaration of Human Rights asserts that "All human beings are born free and equal in dignity and rights." We might infer from this the conclusion that every human life is of equal value. If so, the value of saving N lives is N times the value of saving one life, as represented by the linear function in Figure 5.1.

An argument can also be made for judging large losses of life to be disproportionately more serious because they threaten the social fabric and viability of a group or community, as in genocide (see Figure 5.2). Debate can be had at the margins over whether governments have a duty to give more weight to the lives of their own people, but something approximating the equality of human lives is rather uncontroversial.

How do we actually value human lives? Research provides evidence in support of two descriptive models linked to affect and intuitive System 1 thinking, which reflect values for lifesaving profoundly different from the normative models shown in Figures 5.1 and 5.2. Both of these descriptive models demonstrate responses that are insensitive to large losses of human life, consistent with apathy toward genocide.

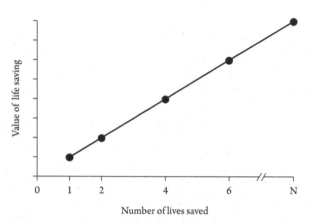

Figure 5.1 A normative model for valuing the saving of human lives: Every human life is of equal value.

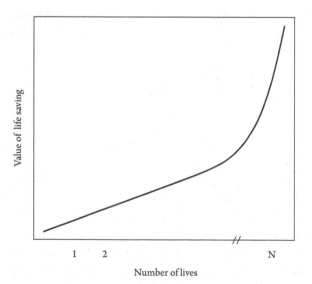

Figure 5.2 Another normative model: Large losses threaten the viability of the group or society.

B.1 The Psychophysical Model

Affect is a remarkable mechanism that enabled humans to survive the long course of evolution. Before there were sophisticated analytic tools such as probability theory, scientific risk assessment, and cost/benefit calculus, humans used their senses, honed by experience, to determine whether the animal lurking in the bushes was safe to approach or the murky water in the pond was safe to drink. Simply put, System 1 thinking evolved to protect individuals and their small family and community groups from present, visible, immediate dangers. This affective system did not evolve to help us respond to distant mass murder. As a result, System 1 thinking responds to large-scale atrocities in ways that System 2 deliberation, if activated, finds reprehensible.

Fundamental qualities of human behavior are, of course, recognized by others besides scientists. American writer Annie Dillard cleverly demonstrates the limitation of our affective system as she seeks to help us understand the humanity of the Chinese nation: "There are 1,198,500,000 people alive now in China. To get a *feel* for what this *means*, simply take yourself—in all your singularity, importance, complexity, and love—and multiply by 1,198,500,000. See? Nothing to it" (Dillard, 1999, p. 47, italics added).

We quickly recognize that Dillard is joking when she asserts "nothing to it." We know, as she does, that we are incapable of feeling the humanity behind the number 1,198,500,000. The circuitry in our brain is not up to this task. This same incapacity is echoed by Nobel prize winning biochemist Albert Szent Gyorgi as he struggles to comprehend the possible consequences of nuclear war: "I am deeply moved if I see one man suffering and would risk my life for him. Then I talk impersonally about the possible pulverization of our big cities, with a hundred million dead. I am unable to multiply one man's suffering by a hundred million."

There is considerable evidence that our affective responses and the resulting value we place on saving human lives may follow the same sort of "psychophysical function" that characterizes our diminished sensitivity to a wide range of perceptual and cognitive entities—brightness, loudness, heaviness, and money—as their underlying magnitudes increase.

What psychological principle lies behind this insensitivity? In the nineteenth century, E. H. Weber and Gustav Fechner discovered a fundamental psychophysical principle that describes how we perceive changes in our environment. They found that people's ability to detect changes in a physical stimulus rapidly decreases as the magnitude of the stimulus increases (Weber, 1834; Fechner, 1860). What is known today as "Weber's law" states that in order for a change in a stimulus to become just noticeable, a fixed percentage must be added. Thus, perceived difference is a relative matter. To a small stimulus, only a small amount must be added to be noticeable. To a large stimulus, a large amount must be added. Fechner proposed a logarithmic law to model this nonlinear growth of sensation. Numerous empirical studies by S. S. Stevens (1975) have demonstrated that the growth of sensory magnitude (ψ) is best fit by a power function of the stimulus magnitude

$$\phi, \psi = \kappa\phi\beta,$$

where the exponent β is typically less than one for measurements of phenomena such as loudness, brightness, and even the value of money (Galanter, 1962). For example, if the exponent is 0.5 as it is in some studies of perceived brightness, a light that is four times the intensity of another light will be judged only twice as bright.

Remarkably, the way that numbers are represented mentally may also follow the psychophysical function. Dehaene (1997) describes a simple experiment in which people are asked to indicate which of two numbers is larger: 9 or 8? 2 or 1? Everyone gets the answers right, but it takes more time to identify 9 as larger than 8 than to indicate 2 is larger than 1. From experiments such as this, Dehaene concludes that "Our brain represents quantities in a fashion not unlike the logarithmic scale on a slide rule, where equal space is allocated to the interval between 1 and 2, 2 and 4, or between 4 and 8" (p. 76). Numbers 8 and 9 thus seem closer together or more similar than 1 and 2.

Our cognitive and perceptual systems seem designed to sensitize us to small changes in our environment, possibly at the expense of making us less able to detect and respond to large changes. As the psychophysical research indicates, constant increases in the magnitude of a stimulus typically evoke smaller and smaller changes in response. Applying this principle to the valuing of human life suggests that a form of psychophysical numbing may result from our inability to appreciate losses of life as they become larger (see Figure 5.3). The function in Figure 5.3 represents a value structure in which the importance of saving one life is great when it is the first, or only, life saved but diminishes marginally as the total number of lives saved increases. Thus, psychologically, the importance of saving one life is diminished against the background of a larger threat—we will likely not "feel" much difference, nor value the difference, between saving 87 lives or saving 88.

Kahneman and Tversky (1979) have incorporated this psychophysical principle of decreasing sensitivity into prospect theory, a descriptive account of decision making under uncertainty. A major element of prospect theory is the value function, which relates subjective value to actual gains or losses. When applied to human lives, the value function implies that the subjective value of saving a specific number of lives is greater for a smaller tragedy than for a larger one.

Fetherstonhaugh, Slovic, Johnson, and Friedrich (1997) demonstrated this potential for diminished sensitivity to the value of life—that is, "psychophysical

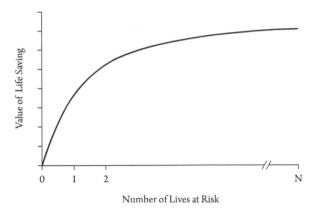

Figure 5.3 A psychophysical model describing how the saving of human lives may actually be valued.

numbing"—in the context of evaluating people's willingness to fund various life-saving interventions. In a study involving a hypothetical grant funding agency, respondents were asked to indicate the number of lives a medical research institute would have to save to merit receipt of a $10 million grant. Nearly two-thirds of the respondents raised their minimum benefit requirements to warrant funding when there was a larger at-risk population, with a median value of 9,000 lives needing to be saved when 15,000 were at risk, compared to a median of 100,000 lives needing to be saved out of 290,000 at risk. By implication, respondents saw saving 9,000 lives in the smaller population as more valuable than saving ten times as many lives in the larger population.

Other studies in the domain of lifesaving interventions have documented similar psychophysical numbing or proportional reasoning effects (Baron, 1997; Bartels and Burnett, 2006; Fetherstonhaugh et al., 1997; Friedrich et al., 1999; Jenni and Loewenstein, 1997; Ubel, Baron, and Asch, 2001). For example, Fetherstonhaugh et al. (1997) also found that people were less willing to send aid that would save 4,500 lives in Rwandan refugee camps as the size of the camps' at-risk population increased. Friedrich et al. (1999) found that people required more lives to be saved to justify mandatory antilock brakes on new cars when the alleged size of the at-risk pool (annual braking-related deaths) increased.

These diverse studies of lifesaving demonstrate that the proportion of lives saved often carries more weight than the number of lives saved when people evaluate interventions. Thus, extrapolating from Fetherstonhaugh et al., one would expect that in separate evaluations, there would be more support for saving 80% of 100 lives at risk than for saving 20% of 1,000 lives at risk. This is consistent with an affective (System 1) account, in which the number of lives saved conveys little affect but the proportion saved carries much feeling: 80% is clearly "good," and 20% is "poor."

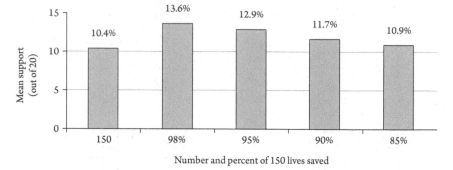

Figure 5.4 Airport safety study: Saving a percentage of 150 lives receives higher support ratings than does saving 150 lives. Note. Bars describe mean responses to the question, "How much would you support the proposed measure to purchase the new equipment?" The response scale ranged from 0 (would not support at all) to 20 (very strong support) (Slovic et al., 2002).

Slovic, Finucane, Peters, and MacGregor (2004), drawing upon the finding that proportions appear to convey more feeling than do numbers of lives, predicted (and found) that college students, in a between-groups design, would more strongly support an airport safety measure expected to save 98% of 150 lives at risk than a measure expected to save 150 lives. Saving 150 lives is diffusely good, and therefore somewhat hard to evaluate, whereas saving 98% of something is clearly very good because it is so close to the upper bound on the percentage scale, and hence is highly weighted in the support judgment. Subsequent reduction of the percentage of 150 lives that would be saved to 95%, 90%, and 85% led to reduced support for the safety measure, but each of these percentage conditions still garnered a higher mean level of support than did the Save 150 Lives Condition (Figure 5.4).

This research on psychophysical numbing is important because it demonstrates that feelings necessary for motivating lifesaving actions are not congruent with the normative models in Figures 5.1 and 5.2. The nonlinearity displayed in Figure 5.3 is consistent with the disregard of incremental loss of life against a background of a large tragedy. However, it does not fully explain apathy toward genocide because it implies that the response to initial loss of life will be strong and maintained, albeit with diminished sensitivity, as the losses increase. Evidence for a second descriptive model, better suited to explain apathy toward genocide, follows.

C. Numbers and Numbness: Images and Feeling

Psychological theories and data confirm what keen observers of human behavior have long known. Numerical representations of human lives do not necessarily convey the importance of those lives. All too often the numbers represent dry statistics, "human beings with the tears dried off," which lack feeling and fail to motivate action (Slovic and Slovic, 2004).

How can we impart the feelings that are needed for rational action? Attempts to do this typically involve highlighting the images that lie beneath the numbers. For example, organizers of a rally designed to get Congress to do something about 38,000 deaths a year from handguns piled 38,000 pairs of shoes in a mound in front of the Capitol (Associated Press, 1994). Students at a middle school in Tennessee, struggling to comprehend the magnitude of the Holocaust, collected six million paper clips as a centerpiece for a memorial (Schroeder and Schroeder-Hildebrand, 2004). Flags were "planted" on the lawn of the University of Oregon campus to represent the thousands of American and Iraqi war dead (see Figure 5.5).

When it comes to eliciting compassion, the identified individual victim, with a face and a name, has no peer. Psychological experiments demonstrate this clearly, but we all know it as well from personal experience and media coverage of heroic efforts to save individual lives. The world watched tensely, in 1987, as rescuers worked for several days to rescue 18-month-old Jessica McClure, who had fallen 22 feet into a narrow abandoned well shaft. Charities such as Save the Children have long recognized that it is better to endow a donor with a single, named child to support than to ask for contributions to the bigger cause.

Even Adolf Eichmann, complicit in the murder of millions of Jews during the Holocaust, exhibited an emotional connection to one of his victims after being interrogated by the victim's son for hundreds of hours during his 1961 trial in Israel. When the interrogator, Captain Avner Less, reveals to Eichmann

Figure 5.5 Flags depicting American and Iraqi war dead.

that his father had been deported to Auschwitz by Eichmann's headquarters, Eichmann cried out "But that's horrible, Herr Captain! That's horrible!" (von Lang, 1983, p. ix).

But the face need not even be human to motivate powerful intervention. A dog stranded aboard a tanker adrift in the Pacific was the subject of one of the most costly animal rescue efforts ever(Vedantam, 2010). Hearing this, columnist Nicholas Kristof (2007) recalled cynically that a single hawk, Pale Male, evicted from his nest in Manhattan, aroused more indignation than two million homeless Sudanese. He observed that what was needed to galvanize the American public and their leaders to respond to the genocide in Darfur was a suffering puppy with big eyes and floppy ears: "If President Bush and the global public alike are unmoved by the slaughter of hundreds of thousands of fellow humans, maybe our last, best hope is that we can be galvanized by a puppy in distress."

D. The Collapse of Compassion

In recent years, vivid images of natural disasters in South Asia, the American Gulf Coast, and Haiti—and stories of individual victims there—brought to us through relentless, courageous, and intimate news coverage unleashed an outpouring of compassion and humanitarian aid from all over the world. Perhaps there is hope here that vivid, personalized media coverage featuring victims of genocide could motivate intervention to prevent mass murder and genocide.

Perhaps. Research demonstrates that people are much more willing to aid identified individuals than unidentified or statistical victims (Kogut and Ritov, 2005a; Schelling, 1968; Small and Loewenstein, 2003, 2005; Jenni and Loewenstein, 1997). But a cautionary note comes from a study by Small, Loewenstein, and Slovic (2007), who gave people leaving a psychological experiment the opportunity to contribute up to $5 of their earnings to Save the Children. In one condition, respondents were asked to donate money to feed an identified victim, a seven-year-old African girl named Rokia. They contributed more than twice the amount given by a second group asked to donate to the same organization working to save millions of Africans from hunger (see Figure 5.6). Respondents in a third group were asked to donate to Rokia but were also shown the larger statistical problem (millions in need) shown to the second group. Unfortunately, coupling the statistical realities with Rokia's story significantly reduced the contributions to Rokia. It may be that the presence of statistics reduced the attention to Rokia, which was essential for establishing the emotional connection necessary to motivate donations. Alternatively, recognition of the millions not being helped by one's donation may have produced negative affect that inhibited any response.

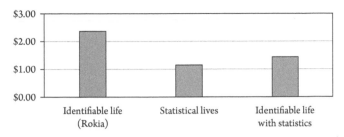

Figure 5.6   Mean donations. (Reprinted from Small et al. (2006), Copyright (2006), with permission from Elsevier.)

A follow-up experiment by Small et al. (2007) provided additional evidence for the importance of feelings. Before being given the opportunity to donate, participants were either primed to feel ("Describe your feelings when you hear the word 'baby'" and similar items) or to do simple arithmetic calculations. Priming analytic thinking (calculation) reduced donations to the identifiable victim (Rokia) relative to the feeling prime. Yet the two primes had no distinct effect on statistical victims, which is symptomatic of the difficulty in generating feelings for such victims.

Writer Annie Dillard reads in her newspaper the headline "Head Spinning Numbers Cause Mind to Go Slack." She struggles to think straight about the great losses that the world ignores: "More than two million children die a year from diarrhea and eight hundred thousand from measles. Do we blink? Stalin starved seven million Ukrainians in one year, Pol Pot killed two million Cambodians. . . ." She writes of "compassion fatigue" and asks, "At what number do other individuals blur for me?" (Dillard, 1999, pp. 130–131).

An answer to Dillard's question is beginning to emerge from behavioral research. Studies by Hamilton and Sherman (1996) and Susskind, Maurer, Thakkar, Hamilton, and Sherman (1999) find that a single individual, unlike a group, is viewed as a psychologically coherent unit. This leads to more extensive processing of information and stronger impressions about individuals than about groups. Consistent with this, Kogut and Ritov (2005a, b) found that people tend to feel more distress and compassion when considering an identified single victim than when considering a group of victims, even if identified.

Specifically, Kogut and Ritov asked participants to contribute to a costly lifesaving treatment needed by a sick child or a group of eight sick children. The target amount needed to save the child (children) was the same in both conditions. All contributions were actually donated to children in need of cancer treatment. In addition, participants rated their feelings of distress (feeling worried, upset, and sad) toward the sick child (children).

Figure 5.7 Mean contributions to individuals and their group. (Reprinted from Kogut and Ritov (2005b), Copyright (2005), with permission from Elsevier.)

The mean contributions are shown in Figure 5.7. Contributions to the individuals in the group, as individuals, were far greater than were contributions to the entire group. Ratings of distress were also higher in the individual condition. Kogut and Ritov concluded that the greater donations to the single victim most likely stem from the stronger emotions evoked by such victims.

Västfjäll, Peters, and Slovic (in press) decided to test whether the effect found by Kogut and Ritov would occur as well for donations to two starving children. Following the protocol designed by Small et al. (2007), they gave one group of Swedish students the opportunity to contribute their earnings from another experiment to Save the Children to aid Rokia, whose plight was described as in the study by Small et al. A second group was offered the opportunity to contribute their earnings to Save the Children to aid Moussa, a seven-year-old boy from Africa who was similarly described as in need of food aid. A third group was shown the vignettes and photos of Rokia and Moussa and was told that any donation would go to both of them—Rokia and Moussa. The donations were real and were sent to Save the Children. Participants also rated their feelings about donating on a 1 (negative) to 5 (positive) scale. Affect was found to be least positive in the combined condition, and donations were smaller in that condition (see Figure 5.8). In the individual-child conditions, the size of the donation made was strongly correlated with rated feelings ($r = .52$ for Rokia; $r = .52$ for Moussa). However, this correlation was much reduced ($r = .19$) in the combined condition.

As unsettling as is the valuation of lifesaving portrayed by the psychophysical model, the studies just described suggest an even more disturbing psychological tendency. Our capacity to feel is limited. To the extent that valuation of lifesaving depends on feelings driven by attention or imagery, it might follow the function shown in Figure 5.9, where the emotion or affective feeling is greatest at $N = 1$

Feelings and donations decline at *N* = 2!

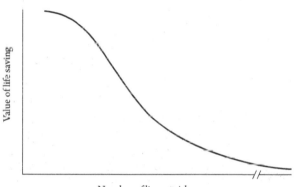

Figure 5.8   Mean affect ratings (left) and mean donations (right) for individuals and their combination (from Västfjäll et al., in press).

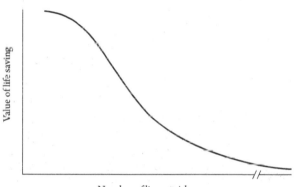

Figure 5.9   A model depicting psychic numbing—the collapse of compassion—when valuing the saving of lives.

but begins to decline at N = 2 and collapses at some higher value of N that becomes simply "a statistic." In other words, returning to Annie Dillard's worry about compassion fatigue, perhaps the "blurring" of individuals begins at two! Whereas Robert J. Lifton (1967) coined the term "psychic numbing" to describe the "turning off" of feeling that enabled rescue workers to function during the horrific aftermath of the Hiroshima bombing, Figure 5.9 depicts a form of numbing that is not beneficial. Rather, it leads to apathy and inaction, consistent with what is seen repeatedly in response to mass murder and genocide.

E. The Failure of Moral Intuition

Thoughtful deliberation takes effort. Fortunately, evolution has equipped us with sophisticated cognitive and perceptual mechanisms that can guide us through our daily lives efficiently, with minimal need for "deep thinking." We have referred to these mechanisms as System 1.

Consider, for example, how we deal with risk. Long before we had invented probability theory, risk assessment, and decision analysis, there was intuition, instinct, and gut feeling, all honed by experience, to tell us whether an animal was safe to approach or the water was safe to drink. As life became more complex and humans gained more control over their environment, analytic ways of thinking, known as System 2, evolved to boost the rationality of our experiential reactions. Beyond the question of how water looks and tastes, we now look to toxicology and analytic chemistry to tell us whether the water is safe to drink (Slovic et al., 2004). But we can still use our feelings as well, an easier path.

As with risk, the natural and easy way to deal with moral issues is to rely on our intuitions: "How bad is it?" "Well, how bad does it feel?" We can also apply reason and logical analysis to determine right and wrong, as our legal system attempts to do. But moral intuition comes first and usually dominates moral judgment unless we make an effort to use judgment to critique and, if necessary, override our intuitive feelings (Haidt, 2001, 2007).

Unfortunately, moral intuition fails us in the face of genocide and other disasters that threaten human lives and the environment on a large scale. As powerful as System 1 is, when infused with vivid experiential stimulation (witness the moral outrage triggered by the photos of abuse at the Abu Ghraib prison in Iraq), it has a darker side. We cannot trust it. It depends upon attention and feelings that may be hard to arouse and sustain over time for large numbers of victims, not to speak of numbers as small as two. Left to its own devices, moral intuition will likely favor individual victims and sensational stories that are closer to home and easier to imagine. It will be distracted by images that produce strong, though erroneous, feelings, like percentages as opposed to actual numbers. Our sizable capacity to care for others may also be overridden by more pressing personal interests. Compassion for others has been characterized by Batson, O'Quin, Fulz, Vanderplas, and Isen (1983) as "a fragile flower, easily crushed by self concern" (p. 718). Faced with genocide and other mass tragedies, we cannot rely on our moral intuitions alone to guide us to act properly.

Philosophers such as Peter Singer and Peter Unger, employing very different methods than psychologists, have come to much the same conclusions about the unreliability of moral intuitions (Singer, 2007; Unger, 1996). Unger, after leading his readers through 50 ingenious thought experiments, urges them and us to think harder to overcome the morally questionable appearances promoted by our intuitive responses. These intuitions, he argues, lead us to act in ways that are inconsistent with our true "Values"; that is, the Values we would hold after more careful deliberation: "Folks' intuitive moral responses to specific cases derive from sources far removed from our Values and, so, they fail to reflect these Values, often even pointing in the opposite direction" (p. 11).

Greene (2007), drawing on data from psychology and neuroscience as well as philosophy, attempts to explain the problems with intuitions in terms of the morally irrelevant evolutionary factors that shaped these intuitions. Thus, we say it is wrong to abandon a drowning child in a shallow pond but okay to ignore the needs of millions of starving children abroad because the former pushes our emotional buttons while the latter do not. And this may be because we evolved in an environment in which we lived in small groups and developed immediate, emotionally based intuitive responses to the needs and transgressions of others. There was little or no interaction with faraway strangers.

III. Combating Genocide

Clearly there are serious political obstacles posing challenges to those who would consider intervention in genocide, and material risks as well. What we have tried to describe here are the additional psychological obstacles centered around the difficulties in wrapping our minds around genocide and forming the emotional connections to its victims that are necessary to motivate us to overcome these other obstacles.

A. Strengthen System 1: Focus on Individuals

Richard Just's question haunts us: "How can we have known so much and done so little?" Are we destined to stand numbly and do nothing as genocides and crimes against humanity rage on for another century? Can we overcome the psychological obstacles to action? There are no simple solutions. Despite the limitations of System 1 noted above, we should nevertheless attempt to bolster it, at the least so it can motivate support for efforts based on System 2. Such attempts should capitalize on the findings described earlier, demonstrating that we care most about aiding individual people in need, even more so when we can attach a name and a face to them. Thus, one possibility is to infuse System 1 with powerful affective imagery such as that associated with Hurricane Katrina, the South Asian tsunami, and the earthquake in Haiti. This would require pressure on the media to report the slaughter of innocent people aggressively and vividly. Another way to engage our experiential system would be to bring people from Darfur into our communities and our homes to tell their stories.

Other strategies to bolster System 1 and overcome psychic numbing by highlighting harm to individuals include:

In-Country or in-Region Meetings

Special sessions of the U.N. Security Council regarding cases of genocide could be required to be held in the region where the events were
taking place.

Avoid Numbing Language

Terms such as "collateral damage" mask the barbarity of harm to civilian
populations and should be used much more cautiously, if at all. Even
the substantive law of genocide might be considered problematic as it
conceptualizes genocide as a collective or group injury, rather than as
harm to individuals. In this light, it is instructive to reflect on the characterization by Holocaust survivor Abel Hertzberg: "There were not six
million Jews murdered: there was one murder, six million times."

Victim Empowerment

Victims should be empowered to trigger a range of institutional responses such as initiating international court proceedings or placing an
issue on the agenda of an international political body.

Alter Reporting Formats

Efforts by international organizations and NGOs to document genocide
and other mass human rights violations typically focus on the scale of
atrocities rather than on narratives or other information about the individuals who have been harmed. Statistics prevail over stories. A good example
of this is the Darfur Atrocities Documentation Project (Totten, 2006),
which compiled a database of over 10,000 eyewitnessed incidents but
reported mostly the percentages of different types of abuses. While it is
obviously necessary to document the scope of such atrocities, neglecting
the stories of individuals certainly contributes to numbing. When civilian
populations are harmed, reporting should describe harms to specific vulnerable groups, such as children, women, and the elderly. Arresting visual
displays (such as that shown in Figure 5.5) and photographs of victims
and atrocities should be included in the reporting and publicly distributed.

On this last point, Paul Farmer (2005) has written eloquently about the
power of images, narratives, and first-person testimony to overcome our "failure
of imagination" in contemplating the fate of distant, suffering people. Such documentation can, he asserts, render abstract struggles personal and help make
human rights violations "real" to those unlikely to suffer them. But he is aware, as

well, of the limitations of this information. He quotes Susan Sontag (2003), who cautions that "As one can become habituated to harm in real life, one can become habituated to the harm of certain images" (p. 82). Sparking emotion with testimony and photographs, Farmer argues, is one thing; "linking them effectively, enduringly, to the broader project of promoting basic rights . . . is quite another" (p. 185). In short, he says, "serious social ills require in-depth analyses" (p. 185).

Further caveats about the use of atrocity images have been expressed by Zelizer (1998), who argues that the recycling of images, such as photos of starving children in refugee camps, bears eerie resemblance to photos from the Holocaust, which undermine their novelty and immediacy and can dull our responses.

Similarly, Richard Just (2008), reviewing the plethora of excellent books and movies on Darfur, observes that the horror they vividly depict should disgust us, but

> . . . one effect of the extraordinary amount of knowledge we have about Darfur is that these stories eventually run together and lose their power to shock. . . . repetition eventually numbs the moral imagination. It is a terrible thing to admit, but sometimes the more information we consume about Darfur, the less shocking each piece of new information seems. . . . Ignorance is not the only ally of indifference; sometimes knowledge, too, blunts the heart and the will." (p. xx)

B. Engage System 2

In sum, research in psychology, neuroscience, and philosophy, supported by common observation and the record of repeated failures to arouse citizens and leaders to halt the scourge of genocide, sends a strong and important message. Our moral intuitions fail us. They seduce us into calmly turning away from massive abuses of human beings, when we should be driven by outrage to act. This is no small weakness in our moral compass. Fortunately, we have evolved a second mechanism to address such problems, based on reason and moral argument, and we must focus now on engaging this mechanism—System 2—to strengthen international laws and political institutions in order to precommit states to respond to genocide. It is obvious that we need more muscle behind international obligations to intervene in and prevent genocides, whether one views our failures thus far as caused by psychology, power politics, or some combination of these and other factors.

We need to strengthen both laws and international institutions dealing with genocide. The United Nations is the institution that was created in part to deal with such issues, but structural problems built into its very charter have made it ineffective. Permanent members of the Security Council have veto power that they have used repeatedly to block or render impotent attempts to halt ongoing genocides. This will be hard to remedy as reform or redesign of the United Nations requires the approval of these permanent members.

A thorough analysis of the strengths and weaknesses of the United Nations in preventing mass violence is provided by David Hamburg (2008), who is not optimistic about prospects for the near term. Recognizing the powerful constraints imposed on the United Nations' own efficacy in matters of peace and security, Hamburg examines the prospect that NATO, the European Union, the African Union, the Organization of American States, the Organization for Cooperation and Security in Europe, and the Association of Southeast Asian Nations might cooperate in military, diplomatic, and economic measures designed to counter genocide. He also notes the important role NGOs can play in pressuring national and international bodies to attend to conflict prevention and resolution. He proposes the establishment of two international centers for the prevention of genocide, with complementary functions; one in the United Nations and one in the European Union.

We shall not discuss the many thoughtful suggestions made by Hamburg, except to say that appreciation of the failure of moral intuition makes development of new institutional arrangements even more urgent and critical. For it may only be laws and institutions that can keep us on course, forcing us to pursue the hard measures needed to combat genocide when our attention strays and our feelings lull us into complacency.

C. Require Open Deliberation

That institutional reforms would be welcome is also not news. But it is unclear how optimistic we can hope to be about such efforts. After all, the failed Genocide Convention is itself a precommitment-based approach, and while this traditional approach should not be written off and attempts to strengthen it encouraged, at least some energy should be expended toward conceiving alternative solutions. In fact, the role of psychology in mediating our reactions to genocide may suggest the promise of one such supplemental remedy: one that, paradoxically, is actually quite modest on its face—a "less-is-more" approach to the international legal regime combating genocide.

As psychological research indicates, even when System 1's moral intuitions are distorted, human cognition can rely on the rational, deliberative mode of thinking characteristic of System 2. Where emotion and affect let us down, we still can be spurred into action if we can trigger a deliberative process capable of weighing the costs and benefits of possible intervention options. One goal we should have, therefore, should be to promote deliberative, cost-benefit thinking about genocide. Of course, people will always disagree about when the costs of a particular intervention outweigh the benefits, but to the extent that psychic numbing plays a role in dissuading interventions to stop or ameliorate the effects of genocides, deliberation-forcing mechanisms in the law may play a role in countering that effect.

What this proposal suggests is that rather than solely focusing on obligations to act, international and domestic law should also require actors to deliberate and reason about actions to take in response to genocide, thereby engaging the System 2 mode of human cognition that can overcome the numbing problem. This goal of promoting deliberation should be aimed at two distinct audiences, and it is analytically important to separate them. The first is the group of political leaders and policy makers at the front lines of government responsiveness, and unresponsiveness, to genocide. Policy makers are human beings working with the same cognitive raw material as the rest of us, and part of their response to genocide may well be the sort of psychic numbing a deliberation-forcing policy can ameliorate. But policy makers might also be meaningfully different—by self-selection or the imperatives of their jobs, they may be more inclined to think about reelection and geopolitics, and psychology might be a smaller part of their story. Even if this is the case, however, most rational-choice-based approaches to politics recognize that policy makers respond to constituent pressures. There is therefore a second group among whom we should strive to promote deliberation on responses to genocide: the general public.

Can legal institutions in fact promote deliberation, either among policy makers or among the general public? Although the law is typically conceived as being concerned with action and not deliberation, institutional designers have taken just such an approach in a number of areas of law and policy—seeking to promote better outcomes not just by regulating the end result of the decision-making process but by regulating the process itself as well. One important example is the U.S. legal requirement that agencies produce "environmental impact statements" before taking actions that might have deleterious environmental effects. The National Environmental Policy Act (NEPA), which requires these statements, is a self-consciously deliberation-forcing mechanism: the statute does not itself bar agency action that would harm the environment; it simply requires that these effects be considered. And while NEPA's success in actually altering outcomes has been debated, advocates for the environment have at least taken it seriously enough to vigorously enforce its requirements in court, even absent a guarantee that the ultimate policy decision will be affected.

A more broadly applicable example from U.S. administrative law is the requirement that cost-benefit analysis (CBA) be performed in the course of deciding to regulate or not regulate. While CBA was initially considered a means for achieving deregulatory results, recent developments in the administrative state have illustrated CBA's potential for promoting the consideration of beneficial regulations (Hahn and Sunstein 2002, pp. 1521–1522). Applied without a deregulatory bias, this policy might be viewed as a deliberation-forcing rule to ensure the government does not fail to consider potential welfare-promoting actions. The U.S. Congress has also chosen to enforce the important American legal principle of federalism through a deliberation-forcing mechanism, requiring that legislation imposing so-called unfunded mandates on state and local governments be accompanied by reports detailing the costs of these mandates (Unfunded Mandate Reform Act of 1995: Pub. L. No. 104–4). And the U.S. Supreme Court has occasionally applied the principle of "structural due process" to require that certain controversial governmental decisions be taken only after full consideration by the President and Congress (*Hampton v. Mow Sun Wong*, 426 U.S. 88, 1976). Finally, to mention an example from outside the U.S. legal system, the South African Constitutional Court, in the landmark *Doctors for Life International* case, enforced a constitutional provision requiring participatory democracy by ordering the legislature to hold public hearings and debates (2006 (12) BCLR 1399). All of these examples demonstrate a concern with the quality of deliberation given to controversial government decisions and manifest an expectation that improved deliberation can result in improved decisions, even without mandating what the final decision itself must be.

These examples indicate that pursuing a deliberation-forcing approach to antigenocide efforts would not be unprecedented as a supplemental legal tool designed to overcome the cognitive obstacles in the way of interventions. At the international level, an additional protocol to the genocide convention could compel states to respond to genocide by producing a detailed action plan, factoring in the likely costs and benefits of different types of intervention. At regular intervals, states could be required to justify failure to act based on an updated assessment of costs and benefits. And the treaty could require public presentation of these findings before both international and domestic audiences, potentially mandating high-visibility strategies such as televised addresses to the nation.

A clear strength of this approach is its palatable nature: for states concerned about preserving their sovereignty and keeping options open, there is comparatively little to fear from an obligation to deliberate and explain. The benefits of the "less-is-more" approach are particularly strong in this regard. In the area of international law, where the means of ensuring compliance are always more or less an issue, a regime that features apparently low-cost obligations could be more easily swallowed by states concerned with sovereignty, and compliance should be correspondingly better.

But while compliance should be more attainable, beneficial results are still quite possible. Forcing deliberation in security establishments and in the top levels of government will force decision makers to confront the costs and benefits of certain types of interventions. Moreover, by forcing the government to present its case and to justify its failure to respond, deliberation will also be forced at the popular level, making it more likely that people will in turn pressure their leaders to take action. In fact, as Kip Viscusi (2000) demonstrates, an interesting effect of cost-benefit analysis is that people are often outraged when actors use cost-benefit analysis to make decisions that cost human lives. Imagine the outrage if the hidden cost-benefit assessments justifying inaction in Rwanda had been made public. Roméo Dallaire (2005) recounts the following deliberation regarding the value of a Rwandan life:

> As to the value of the 800,000 lives in the balance book of Washington, during those last weeks we received a shocking call from an American staffer, whose name I have long forgotten. He was engaged in some sort of planning exercise and wanted to know how many Rwandans had died, how many were refugees, and how many were internally-displaced. He told me that his estimates indicated that it would take the deaths of 85,000 Rwandans to justify the risking of the life of one American soldier. It was macabre, to say the least. (pp. 322–323)

Thus, some degree of System 1 outrage, together with System 2 deliberation, can be achieved at the popular level through the public reporting requirements of a deliberation-forcing regime, and this in turn may help pressure governments to take action.

While there would obviously need to be latitude in terms of how such obligations to deliberate would be implemented across jurisdictions, in the United States a conceivable paradigm would be the enactment of a statute analogous to the NEPA. If the institutions of administration and judicial review can accommodate a requirement to prepare reports detailing the environmental costs of government action, it should also be able to accommodate a requirement to prepare reports detailing the human costs of government inaction in the face of genocide and other grave human rights abuses. Following the NEPA model furthers two important goals. It would provide for judicial review, thus providing a mechanism for forcing deliberation by government actors. It would also cast public light on the issue of genocide and the government's response to it. Consider as an example the recent Supreme Court decision in *Massachusetts v. EPA*, not a NEPA case but one in which the government was told not that it had to act to stop climate change, but simply that it had the authority to do so. Though the case did not result in any concrete action, it did help draw national attention to the government's failure to address global warming, demonstrating that even a proceduralist court opinion can have important deliberative affects in the polity at large.

On the other hand, the NEPA model would avoid the problem of compelling direct action, which in the security sphere would be unfeasible. A statute forcing deliberation on responses to genocide in this manner, while revolutionary in some respects, could be within the realm of political possibility and would also provide some hope for activating beneficial deliberative processes on the part of both government actors and society at large. Indeed, even absent action at the international level, domestic pressure groups concerned with responses to genocide could persuade lawmakers eager to be seen as taking some action to install this sort of deliberative mechanism.

There are, of course, weaknesses to this deliberation-forcing approach, whether implemented internationally or domestically. The most serious concern is that this will place the focus of the international community on producing "yet another" committee report, at best being of no consequence and at worst providing a means for foot-dragging and delay while ongoing atrocities continue. These concerns are real, and it bears repeating that the deliberation-forcing proposal is a supplemental one, designed to add to the current requirements to take action on genocide and not to replace them with a weaker commitment.

In designing the deliberation-forcing regime, it will be necessary to ensure that the mechanisms are closely calibrated to the goal of genuinely activating System 2 processes so as to overcome the psychic numbing of mass tragedies. Adding another report by an emissary of the Secretary-General would not serve this purpose; rather, the reporting requirements would have to involve states themselves, and would have to specify levels of engagement at both the elite decision-making level (e.g., requiring the participation of the security establishment) and the popular level (e.g., requiring, like the participatory democracy provision of the South African Constitution, public hearing and debate designed to reach the entire polity). Moreover, the U.N. Security Council should consider creating a "Genocide Committee" to monitor and receive state reports and to ensure that state reports are timely and do not constitute foot-dragging. Such a committee would be analogous to the "1540 Committee" established to monitor and coordinate national nonproliferation efforts.

At the domestic level, the availability of some sort of judicial review, as in NEPA, could arguably speed matters, and given the comparative need for speed in addressing genocide, provision for some sort of expedited review in domestic law would be appropriate. Ultimately, a deliberation-forcing approach to the genocide regime should take seriously the worry that another round of reporting will be unhelpful or even pernicious. But given the stakes and our current failure to adequately respond to genocide, designing a regime that takes these concerns seriously while also seeking ways to promote reasoned deliberation about responses to genocide could be beneficial.

D. The Responsibility to Protect Individuals

Somewhat more ambitious than requiring deliberation would be a revision of the genocide convention sensitive to the realities of mass murder in the twenty-first century.

Specifically, the genocide convention needs to be refocused around the principle of protecting individuals, regardless of race, ethnicity, or any other collective categorizations. This is consistent with the psychological account of psychic numbing that demonstrates the preeminence of the individual over the collective. It is also consistent with the changing nature of conflict. The genocide convention was designed to prevent the Holocaust from happening again. That conflict was between a nation state and a stable, defined religious/ethnic group, the Jews. In today's world, perpetrators of mass violence are often subnational militias, and their victims are not racially or ethnically pure. Coupled with the fact that the genocide convention requires proof of intent to destroy a defined collective (very hard to demonstrate), the genocide convention becomes impossible to implement. Nations can thus wiggle out of their obligation to act, and they invariably do so (Hong, 2008).

An important attempt to repair the deficiencies of the genocide convention was initiated in 2005, when the UN General Assembly endorsed the concept of "Responsibility to Protect" (R2P). According to this doctrine, states are entrusted with the responsibility to protect the security of their citizens. But if they should fail to exercise this responsibility, the principle of nonintervention yields to the "responsibility to protect."

Although many governments responded positively to this new norm, none of the key provisions in the report of the International Commission of Intervention and State Sovereignty (ICISS) have yet been adopted and implemented (Wheeler, 2005).

IV. Conclusion

Drawing upon behavioral research and common observation, we argue here that we cannot depend only upon our moral intuitions to motivate us to take proper action against genocide and mass abuse of human rights. This places the burden of response squarely upon moral argument and international law. The genocide convention was supposed to meet this need, but it has not been effective. It is time to reexamine this failure in light of the psychological deficiencies described here and design legal and institutional mechanisms that will compel us to respond to genocide with a degree of intensity that is commensurate with the high value we place on individual human lives.

More fundamentally, understanding and appreciating how psychic numbing disables our moral intuitions highlights the importance of long-term efforts that emphasize prevention strategies over reactive strategies (Hamburg, 2008). Prevention strategies engage a potential crisis before the number of casualties is so large that numbing sets in. Moreover, prevention is in many ways easier and less costly and less dangerous than intervention. This strategy recommends a range of policy options including more vigorous international intervention (including humanitarian aid) in situations likely to generate wide-scale atrocities (e.g., civil wars, military coups, etc.).

Central to this strategy are efforts to develop what Hamburg (2008) calls "pillars of prevention":

> These are structures of human relations, good governance, constraints on aggressive behavior, the movement toward worldwide protection of human rights and individual dignity through democratic institutions, construction of equitable socioeconomic development, widespread application of conflict resolution concepts and techniques, . . . efforts to restrain the availability and use of highly lethal weapons—and, . . . development of a global movement to use such knowledge to educate children, youth, political leaders, and indeed, all humanity to learn to live together in peace through mutual benefit from informed cooperation. (p. 265)

The stakes are high. Failure to overcome psychic numbing may condemn us to witness another century of genocide and mass abuses of innocent people as in the previous century.

Note

Portions of this chapter appeared earlier in the paper "If I Look at the Mass I Shall Never Act: Psychic Numbing and Genocide," that was published in *Judgment and Decision Making*, 2007(2): 79–95. We wish to thank the William and Flora Hewlett Foundation and its president, Paul Brest, for support and encouragement in the research that has gone into this chapter. Additional support has been provided by the National Science Foundation through Grant SES-0649509. David Zionts currently serves as Special Advisor to the Legal Adviser, U.S. Department of State. The views expressed here are his own and do not necessarily reflect those of the U.S. Department of State or the U.S. Government.

Many individuals have provided constructive criticisms and helpful suggestions on this work as well as other intellectual and logistical support. Among the many, Ellen Peters and Daniel Västfjäll deserve special thanks. Finally, this chapter has benefited greatly from the advice and comments of Dan Ariely, Cass Sunstein, Ryan Goodman, Derek Jinks, and Andrew K. Woods.

CODA

Can International Law Stop Genocide When
Our Moral Intuitions Fail Us?

RYAN GOODMAN, DEREK JINKS, AND ANDREW K. WOODS

Paul Slovic and David Zionts's chapter discusses psychological constraints that impede individuals' ability to respond to the plight of large numbers of people. Similar to the inability of the human eye to comprehend particular gradations of light, the mind's ability to appreciate the value of multiple lives is constrained by "psychophysical functions." As a result, individuals price lives differently depending on the numbers involved—specifically, they succumb to a numbing effect whereby they register a greater emotional and financial response to the loss of a few than to the loss of many. Slovic and Zionts argue that these psychological impediments help explain the inadequate public response to genocide. Their chapter—a collaboration in psychology and law—also discusses institutional design applications at some length. This Coda develops upon those ideas (including suggesting some cautionary notes) and proposes additional applications. As the outset, we should note that much of the empirical research presumably applies equally to human rights violations involving large numbers of victims in general. The data are not limited to genocide. The lessons for policy makers and practitioners are thus broader than the chapter might otherwise suggest.

I. Target: Perpetrators of Human Rights Violations

A. Overcoming Psychic Numbing

Although Slovic and Zionts's chapter focuses on individuals who might act to stop the perpetration of human rights violations, it is a small step to consider potential research applications for influencing the perpetrators themselves. First, the research can potentially unlock the psychological mechanisms for the mental slide into indifference. Consider the evocative statement: "the death of one man is a tragedy, the death of millions is a statistic" (often misattributed to Stalin). Research that identifies the relevant psychological mechanisms could contribute to more effective human rights training programs and human rights campaigns.

Such research could also inform international criminal tribunals and truth com-missions that seek to uncover the past and shape the calculus of future actors.

This area of research can also help resolve difficult legal issues such as the defense of duress to manslaughter. Consider, for example, the case of the Serbian soldier Dražen Erdemovic who turned himself into the International Criminal Tribunal for the former Yugoslavia and pled that he had participated in the Sre-brenica genocide in fear of his and his family's life if he refused to do so. Psycho-logical research, along the lines of Slovic and his collaborators, might uncover ways in which one set of interests (the victims of Srebrenica) were devalued, and the other set of interests (Erdemovic and his family) were overvalued due to the effects of System 1 processes. Well-trained international judges and prosecutors may more easily engage System 2 decision making to correct this imbalance, but the international criminal regime nevertheless needs to plunge deeply into decision research to attribute blame appropriately and to alter the mindset of future actors. Slovic and his collaborators' research is highly relevant to that agenda.

B. Overcoming Emotional Overreactions

The empirical research also suggests that powerful narratives of humiliation and abuse against individual members of a perpetrator's own group can motivate excessive counteractions—in the form of human rights violations and large-scale commitments to rectify perceived injustices. That is, genocidaires (as well as xenophobes, misogynists, and the like) may be primarily motivated by expe-riences and memories involving affronts to a particular individual person from their group. Research on these mental processes can help to contend with the animating narratives and to supply competing ones. That research can also identify the limits of efforts to convince perpetrators through information in-volving aggregate numbers, cost-benefit analysis, or notions of disproportionate reactions.

C. Cautionary Notes

The research in this chapter also provides a cautionary note with respect to the limits of progressive change and to building human rights cultures. We have already discussed some limitations on the techniques of change—namely, trying to influence perpetrators who are motivated by System 1 through communica-tions that invoke aggregate numbers and System 2 calculations.

The research also suggests the limits of particular results. That is, the research helps explain how individuals can dehumanize large numbers of out-siders while empathizing with the lives of individual members of that same group. Accordingly, progress on the latter front may be fully consistent with stasis or regression on the former. It may be grossly insufficient to change mindsets with respect to personal relations and empathy for particular individuals. This cautionary lesson contrasts with more optimistic research suggesting a causal link between familiarity and density of interactions among diverse ethnic groups and lower prevalence of intergroup violence (e.g., studies involving subareas of the former Yugoslavia) (Stover and Weinstein, 2005).

II. Target: Promoters of Human Rights

Crises in Darfur, the DRC, and elsewhere have prompted reexamination of the way that international law responds to atrocities, but Slovic and Zionts's chapter suggests that much of this thinking takes the wrong approach. In general, there are two types of legal reforms: (1) measures designed to improve the response of international institutions to genocide and crimes against humanity (e.g., the U.N. Secretary-General's establishment of a U.N. Genocide Prevention Advisory Committee and the creation of a U.N. Special Adviser on Genocide Prevention); and (2) measures designed to combat impunity for perpetrators of genocide and crimes against humanity (e.g., the Genocide Convention's requirement of prosecution or extradition, universal jurisdiction and other efforts to relax jurisdictional requirements, and international criminal tribunals). The chapter has much to say about both. Most reform efforts of the first variety aim to increase the monitoring, reporting, and early warning capacity of international legal institutions. The thought is that documentation will prompt action. But, of course, Slovic's research suggests that this kind of reform is unlikely to work and might backfire.

A. Overcoming System 1 Processes

As Slovic and Zionts discuss, the international regime could construct precommitment enforcement strategies designed to prompt System 2 thinking. Consider a few options: the Security Council could preauthorize, subject perhaps to an ex post Council override, the use of force in any situation in which atrocities reach a certain scale. Alternatively, states could conclude a treaty in which state parties would preinvite foreign intervention and/or U.N. peacekeepers in the event that the commission of atrocities ever reached a certain level on their own territory. In addition to the use of armed force, the relevant bodies might preauthorize or order economic sanctions in these circumstances.

Three points deserve emphasis. First, political actors may be more willing to adopt such strategies if preauthorization is not intended to overcome political interests, but to overcome cognitive failures. The need for reform should be grounded in an understanding that cognitive deficiencies can prevent actors' ability to realize their preferences and to feel the need to stop mass human rights violations *even when doing so would fulfill their values and interests.* Indeed, in some circumstances, the more widespread and systematic the atrocity, the weaker the potential response. Default rules favoring action by powerful institutions can help overcome these limitations. Second, Slovic and Zionts's chapter provides a powerful reason for supporting the Responsibility to Protect, an emerging doctrine that shifts from a right to a duty of outside states to intervene to stop a mass atrocity. That is, Slovic and Zionts provide an independent and unique reason to place pressure on states (in the form of a legal responsibility) to intervene once the Security Council has authorized such action. Third, this chapter provides a reason to support a form of "subsidiarity" within humanitarian law and the use of force regime. Regional actors are more likely to overcome System 1 limitations in comprehending the gravity of an atrocity. Accordingly, international law might permit regional organizations (e.g., the Economic Community of West African States (ECOWAS), the African Union) greater leeway to use force to stop genocides even before or without Security Council action.

The chapter also provides good reason to emphasize prevention strategies over reaction strategies—because reaction strategies must necessarily overcome the psychic numbing generated by the instant crisis. This insight perhaps recommends a range of policy options including more vigorous international intervention in situations likely to generate wide-scale atrocities (e.g., civil wars, military coups, etc.) or "anticipatory" humanitarian intervention. Again, such reforms are also more politically plausible if they are understood to overcome cognitive deficiencies.

Finally, the research presented in the chapter suggests harmful effects of large-scale initiatives to employ statistical measures of human rights conditions. A new research program led by Kevin Davis, Benedict Kingsbury, and Sally Engle Merry studies the use and effects of quantitative indicators in global governance (e.g., measures of good governance by the World Bank). Davis, Kingsbury, and Merry's project is open ended thus far in terms of the position they take on how indicators should be optimally generated and used, and under what conditions (if any) they should be abandoned. Slovic and Zionts's research raises similar questions. Specifically, the chapter by Slovic and Zionts suggests dramatic perverse effects (downsides) that may result from the production, collection, and circulation of human rights indicators. Actors involved in these various processes may be desensitized with respect to human rights violations, and such processes often involve some of the most important actors within government and civil society.

B. Exploiting System 1 Processes

By challenging the assumption that information makes positive change more likely, the chapter calls into question one of the strategic pillars of human rights advocacy. Human rights advocates should reorient documentation and reporting of abuses to prompt System 1 thinking. In some cases, in-depth narratives and visual personal stories describing the predicament of individual victims should be emphasized instead of more abstract descriptions of the scale of abuses—that is, stories over statistics. At the same time, scale and systematicity presumably remain important for calibrating the appropriate response to any human rights problem. As a consequence, human rights reporting seemingly should not abandon the documentation and reporting of scale and system-level effects. The central challenge of applying the chapter to human rights advocacy is identifying when or how much "statistics" and when or how much "storytelling" should be employed in the documentation and reporting of abuses.

C. Cautionary Notes in Exploiting System 1 Processes

The research discussed in this chapter also suggests two cautionary notes that should accompany efforts to exploit System 1 processes. First, exploiting System 1 processes may encourage overvaluing particular lives. Some of the analysis by Slovic and Zionts suggests that subjects correctly value helping 1 life, but incorrectly value helping 2 lives. This normative assessment is based on the fact that the latter is assigned less weight than the former (or less than 2 times the former). But, couldn't the latter reflect the true moral value of multiple lives? The problem sometimes might be that humans overvalue the individual life because of System 1 thinking. The extraordinary use of resources to save Jessica McClure from a well shaft may provide such an example. It would have been better, one might reason, to spread those resources across multiple lives. Indeed, human rights advocates might worry about second-order effects involving tradeoffs with other human rights crises. Advocates should also worry about the political and social repercussions when actors exhibit excessive exuberance in dedicating resources to a human rights cause based on System 1 processes.

Second, the use of tactics to promote System 1 processes—such as visual narratives and storytelling—might siphon attention from less-visible concerns (such as structural poverty), which are not as easily captured by such media and from individuals whose images do not appeal to mainstream social groups (members of marginalized ethnic groups, distant foreigners, undocumented immigrants, members of lower classes and castes). As human rights reporting and representation turn to these forms of influence, the consequences for social outcasts and less-visual human rights tragedies may become more severe.

Note

This Coda, like the others in the book, offers some specific applications drawn from the insights in the contributor's chapter. It is not intended to be a list of fully developed policy prescriptions, but instead an example of the rich sorts of human rights policy applications that can be drawn from cutting-edge social science research. It does not question the insights offered in the chapter but instead asks what implications those insights might have for human rights law and policy. The Codas are the sole authorship of the editors of the volume.

‖ 6 ‖

Human Rights

An Evolutionary and Behavioral Perspective

HERBERT GINTIS

I. What is Human Nature?

The human rights movement is among the most powerful and respected global social movements of recent decades. This paper uses evolutionary biology and behavioral economics to suggest that this movement is a logical reaction of basic human motivations to contemporary political realities. These political realities concern the struggle between citizens and despotic states in the context of economically powerful liberal democratic societies. The struggle for basic human rights will remain potent and visible, this analysis suggests, as long as this constellation of political forces remain salient.

Human rights are based on human nature, not abstract philosophical theorizing. For much of the twentieth century, sociologists, social psychologists, and anthropologists steadfastly denied the existence of human nature, beyond the obvious physiological characteristics and cognitive capacities of Homo sapiens (Tooby and Cosmides, 1992). For these social scientists, human nature is a blank slate, a tabula rasa on which society's cultural institutions can impose virtually any set of moral values (Pinker, 2002). In this view, human rights have no universal validity, being totally dependent upon the norms and values of the society in question.

Biologists and economists, by contrast, in this same period strongly affirmed a concept of human nature in which human rights simply do not exist at all. These disciplines identified human nature with the archetypal rational, self-interested individual, Homo economicus. In economics, Adam Smith's "invisible hand" in *The Wealth of Nations* (2000 [1759]) expressed this notion, as did the architects of modern neoclassical economics, such as Francis Ysidro Edgeworth, who considered self-interest "the first principle of pure economics" (Edgeworth, 1925, p.173).

In biology, the selfishness principle has been touted as a central implication of rigorous evolutionary modeling. In *The Selfish Gene* (1976), for instance, Richard Dawkins asserts: "We are survival machines—robot vehicles blindly programmed to preserve the selfish molecules known as genes.... Let us try to teach generosity and altruism, because we are born selfish." Similarly, in *The Biology of Moral Systems* (1987, p. 3), R. D. Alexander asserts that "ethics, morality, human conduct, and the human psyche are to be understood only if societies are seen as collections of individuals seeking their own self-interest." More poetically, Michael Ghiselin (1974) writes: "No hint of genuine charity ameliorates our vision of society, once sentimentalism has been laid aside. What passes for cooperation turns out to be a mixture of opportunism and exploitation.... Scratch an altruist, and watch a hypocrite bleed."

Clearly, the tabula rasa and the Homo economicus views, no matter how firmly held by perceptive and intelligent social theorists, cannot both be correct. In fact, we now have very solid evidence that both misrepresent human nature. On the one hand, there are certain human behaviors that are so widespread as to be virtual human universals (Brown, 1991), and these point to the existence of severe constraints upon what a society can induce its members to accept as factually and morally correct (Pinker, 2002). On the other hand, there is extensive laboratory evidence that humans are not simply selfish, but rather exhibit strong pro-social behavioral propensities even when it is costly to do so, and even when the individual cannot expect to be materially compensated for the cost of pro-social behavior (Gintis, Bowles, Boyd, and Fehr, 2003).

A conception of universal human rights can be based on the model of human nature that flows from the above empirical findings. The reader will note that the task of specifying the nature of these human rights is, according to the above reasoning, a purely scientific exercise, irrespective of the political ideology and personal morality of the social theorist. Human rights, in this conception, are powers that individuals inherently demand and that intrinsically serve their personal needs for dignity, autonomy, and personal authority. Moral and political issues do, of course, enter into the analysis when there is a clash of social values. For instance, whether patriarchal authority should constrain individual rights, or whether religious authority should suppress the right of free expression, are issues fraught with moral significance that cannot be answered by recourse to a scientific approach to human behavior.

Actually constructing such a model of universal human rights is an ambitious task that remains to be accomplished and will likely involve the interaction of many social theorists and policy makers. The reader should consider what follows as a set of notes and materials that can be applied to this task.

II. Gene-Culture Coevolution

There is a classic debate in social theory as to whether genes or culture (nature or nurture) is more important in determining human behavior. For many years we have known that the question has little meaning, since all behavior is an interaction between genes and culture, neither being capable of acting alone. We now know that the reality is in fact even deeper: human nature, by which I mean the genetic predispositions of humans, is itself the product of human culture. In effect, our species has dynamically crafted its own nature through its crafting of cultural evolution. We call this gene-culture coevolution.

Gene-culture coevolution is the application of evolutionary biology to Homo sapiens. All species evolve genetically; that is, information is passed from parents to offspring via genes, with occasional mutations. Those mutations that are fitness enhancing (i.e., those that lead the individual to have more offspring that reach reproductive age) are called adaptations, and are likely to be conserved in the genome of future generations. Humans also acquire information from experience ("learning"), share this information with others ("teaching"), and conserve this information across generations in the form of culture.

Culture evolves dynamically in much the same way as genes: copies of culture units (ideas, pieces of information, rules, norms, icons) are transmitted from one individual to another with mutation, and successful cultural mutations tend to flourish in the population. Until the growth of civilization and settled agriculture during the Holocene epoch some 10,000 years ago, "successful" cultural forms and fitness-enhancing cultural forms were doubtless virtually coincident, because population growth was close to zero for Homo sapiens from its historical inception until the Holocene.

Gene-culture coevolution describes a dynamic interrelationship between genes and culture that is mirrored vaguely, if at all, in the evolution of other species. The centrality of culture and complex social organization to the evolutionary success of Homo sapiens implies that individual fitness in humans depends on the structure of social life. Since culture is limited by and facilitated by human genetic propensities, it follows that human cognitive, affective, and moral capacities are the product of an evolutionary dynamic involving the interaction of genes and culture. This dynamic is known as gene-culture coevolution (Boyd and Richerson, 1985; Cavalli-Sforza and Feldman, 1982; Dunbar, 1993; Richerson and Boyd, 2004). This coevolutionary process has endowed us with preferences that go beyond the self-regarding concerns emphasized in traditional economic and biological theory, and embrace a social epistemology facilitating the sharing of intentionality across minds, as well as such non-self-regarding values as a taste for cooperation, fairness, and retribution, the capacity to empathize, and the ability to value honesty, hard work, piety, toleration of diversity, and loyalty to one's reference group.

Gene-culture coevolution is the application of sociobiology, the general theory of the social organization of biological species, to species that transmit culture without informational loss across generations. An intermediate category is niche construction, which applies to species that transform their natural environment to facilitate social interaction and collective behavior (Odling-Smee, Laland, and Feldman, 2003).

The parallel between cultural and biological evolution goes back to Huxley (1955) and Popper (1979). The idea of treating culture as a form of evolutionary, nongenetic, information transmission was pioneered by Richard Dawkins, who coined the term "meme" in *The Selfish Gene* (1976) to represent an integral unit of information that could be transmitted phenotypically. There quickly followed several major contributions to a biological approach to culture, all based on the notion that culture, like genes, could evolve through replication (intergenerational transmission), mutation, and selection.

Cultural elements reproduce themselves from brain to brain and across time, mutate, and are subject to selection according to their effects on the fitness of their carriers (Cavalli-Sforza and Feldman, 1982; Parsons, 1964). Moreover, there are strong interactions between genes and culture in human evolution, ranging from basic physiology (e.g., the transformation of the organs of speech with the evolution of language) to sophisticated social emotions, including empathy, shame, guilt, and revenge seeking (Zajonc, 1980, 1984).

Because of their common informational and evolutionary character, there are strong parallels between genes and culture (Mesoudi, Whiten, and Laland, 2006). Like genes, culture is transmitted from parents to offspring; and like culture, which is transmitted horizontally to unrelated individuals; so in microbes and many plant species, genes are regularly transferred across lineage boundaries (Abbott, James, Milne, and Gillies, 2003; Jablonka and Lamb, 1995; Rivera and Lake, 2004). Moreover, anthropologists reconstruct the history of social groups by analyzing homologous and analogous cultural traits, much as biologists reconstruct the evolution of species by the analysis of shared characters and homologous DNA (Mace and Pagel, 1994). Indeed, the same computer programs developed by biological systematists are used by cultural anthropologists (Holden, 2002; Holden and Mace, 2003). In addition, archaeologists who study cultural evolution have a similar modus operandi as paleobiologists who study genetic evolution (Mesoudi et al., 2006). Both attempt to reconstruct lineages of artifacts and their carriers. Like paleobiology, archaeology assumes that when analogy can be ruled out, similarity implies causal connection by inheritance (O'Brian and Lyman, 2000). Like biogeography's study of the spatial distribution of organisms (Brown and Lomolino, 1998), behavioral ecology studies the interaction of ecological, historical, and geographical factors that determine distribution of cultural forms across space and time (Smith and Winterhalder, 1992).

In the next section, I will give an example of gene-culture coevolution in an area that we are all familiar with: the evolution of communicative capacities in humans. This example has little to do with the evolution of morality or human emotions and behavior, but similar mechanisms apply to these less physically obvious aspects of human nature. Indeed, in general our genetic constitution, including our moral predispositions and emotions, are the product of the cultural evolution of our primate and human ancestors.

III. The Evolution of Human Communicative Physiology

Communication through language and complex facial expressions exists in more than rudimentary form only in humans. On an evolutionary timescale, when a form of human communication became prevalent among hunter-gatherers, this new cultural form became the new environment within which new genetic mutations were evaluated for their fitness effects. Humans thus underwent massive physiological changes to facilitate speaking, understanding speech, and communicating with facial expressions.

To this end, regions in the human motor cortex expanded to carry out speech production in the evolution of hominins and even Homo sapiens. Nerves and muscles to the mouth, larynx, and tongue became more numerous to handle the complexities of speech (Jurmain, Nelson, Kilgore, and Travathan, 1997). Parts of the cerebral cortex, Broca's and Wernicke's areas, which do not exist or are small in other primates, evolved to permit grammatical speech and comprehension (Campbell, Loy, and Cruz-Uribe, 2005).

The most dramatic changes in human physiology involve speech production. Adult modern humans have a larynx low in the throat, which permits the throat to act as a highly flexible resonating chamber (Relethford, 2007). The first hominids that have skeletal structures supporting this laryngeal placement are the Homo heidelbergensis, who lived from 800,000 to 100,000 years ago. In addition, the production of consonants requires a short oral cavity, whereas our nearest primate relatives have much too long an oral cavity to produce most consonants. The position of the hyoid bone, which is a point of attachment for a tongue muscle, developed in Homo sapiens in a manner permitting highly precise and flexible tongue movements. Another indication that the tongue has evolved in hominids to facilitate speech is the size of the hypoglossal canal, an aperture that permits the hypoglossal nerve to reach the tongue muscles. This aperture is much larger in Neanderthals and humans than in early hominids and nonhuman primates (Campbell et al., 2005).

Human facial nerves and musculature have also evolved to facilitate communication. This musculature is present in all vertebrates, but except in mammals, it serves feeding and respiratory functions (Burrows, 2008). In mammals, this mimetic musculature attaches to skin in the face, thus permitting the subtle and accurate facial communication of such emotions as fear, surprise, disgust, and anger. In most mammals, however, a few wide sheet-like muscles are involved, rendering fine informational differentiation impossible. In primates, by contrast, this musculature divides into many independent muscles with distinct points of attachment to the epidermis and distinct ennervation, thus permitting higher bandwidth facial communication. Humans have the most highly developed facial musculature among vertebrates by far, with a degree of involvement of lips and eyes that is not present in any other species.

IV. The Evolution of the Moral Mind

Gene-culture coevolution applies to the emergence of unique human emotional capacities, including shame, guilt, pride, empathy, jealousy, and a taste for retribution. Neuroscientific studies exhibit clearly the genetic basis for moral behavior. Brain regions involved in moral judgments and behavior include the prefrontal cortex, the orbitofrontal cortex, and the superior temporal sulcus (Moll, Zahn, di Oliveira-Souza, Krueger, and Grafman 2005). These brain structures are virtually unique to, or most highly developed in humans and are doubtless evolutionary adaptations (Schulkin, 2000). The evolution of the human prefrontal cortex is closely tied to the emergence of human morality (Allman, Hakeem, and Watson, 2002). Patients with focal damage to one or more of these areas exhibit a variety of antisocial behaviors, including the absence of embarrassment, pride, and regret (Beer, Heerey, Keltner, Skabini, and Knight, 2003; Camille, 2004), and sociopathic behavior (Miller, Darby, Benson, Cummings, and Miller, 1997). There is a likely genetic predisposition underlying sociopathy, and sociopaths comprise 3–4% of the male population, but they account for between 33% and 80% of the population of chronic criminal offenders in the United States (Mednick, Kirkegaard-Sorenson, Hutchings, Knop, Rosenberg, and Schulsinger, 1977).

It is clear from this body of empirical information that culture is directly encoded into the human brain, which of course is the central claim of gene-culture coevolutionary theory.

V. The Evolutionary Origin of Human Rights

Social species generally exhibit a characteristic form of social organization that varies little across communities. Humans are exceptional in exhibiting several distinctive social forms, including hunter-gatherer, small-scale agriculture, tribal, despotic state, and liberal democratic organization. Because humans are also the only species for which culture is a central element in social organization, it is tempting to attribute the variety of human social forms to the plasticity of culture. While this is surely an element, it is also the case that humans have genetically endowed predispositions toward two highly distinctive and contrasting behavioral schemas. The first predisposition is toward striving for hierarchical dominance, and when this fails, submitting to the hierarchical authority of a dominant individual. We share this predisposition to hierarchical authority with most nonhuman primates, including chimpanzees and, to a lesser extent, bonobos. The second predisposition is toward a sense of personal autonomy and individual responsibility that conflicts directly with submission to hierarchical authority. This predisposition appears to be unique to our species.

Christopher Boehm (2000) has documented that hunter-gatherer societies have generally been based on a self-conscious, socially enforced egalitarianism, which he terms a reverse dominance hierarchy that relentlessly suppressed the dominance ambitions of hierarchically inclined males. A variety of social strategies could be used to such dominance ambitions, including ridicule, ostracism, and even assassination.

The distinctively human characteristic that empowered this egalitarianism was the development of lethal projectile weapons for use in hunting large game. This development allowed even a relatively weak individual to punish and kill dominant males in their sleep—a feat that could not be accomplished in any other primate society. This relative powerlessness of dominant males led to the emergence of a new set of qualities of leadership, among which were willingness to listen to the ideas of others, consensus seeking, ability to form majoritarian coalitions, and generosity.

Homo sapiens, then, evolved under conditions of an enforced egalitarianism prevailing over the despotic pretensions of natural leaders on the basis of the lethality of stone-age weaponry. With the emergence of private property in the era of settle agriculture, however, despots became capable of protecting themselves and oppressing the population by means of mercenary armies and police, using iron-age weapons: the horse, and the chariot. The period from 3000 BC to the present can be seen as a series of experiments in the organization of despotism, from the ancient kingdoms, to the early modern European state and the totalitarian pretensions of Communism and National Socialism.

Especially important in thwarting the despotic ambitions of nation-states was the invention of the handgun, which shifted the balance of power from mounted cavalry and elite bowmen to mass armies of rifle-toting infantry. Recruiting such armies led state elites to offer voting rights and democratic participation as the price of garnering the loyalty of the masses in World Wars I, II, and beyond. As a result, there was a flourishing of democratic liberal culture in the course of the twentieth century, and the economic power and political unity of the liberal democratic countries led to the decisive defeat of totalitarianism, both economically and militarily (Bowles and Gintis, 1986).

VI. Human Rights as Reverse Dominance Hierarchy

This analysis suggests that the issue of human rights is closely related to political freedom. Human rights, including freedom of person and property, freedom of speech and association, the right of democratic participation, the right to an attorney and a fair trial, as well as equal opportunity and nondiscrimination on the basis of gender, class, caste, or creed, are guarantees against despotism and hence are the cultural form of modern-day reverse dominance hierarchy.

As such, human rights will have almost universal support among the populace of virtually all countries. The enemies of human rights are the same as the champions of despotism—extremists who know that civil liberties and democratic participation cannot lead to the implementation of extremist social policies.

My analysis suggests why the classic arguments for freedom and democracy tend to garner widespread acceptance even in societies that have attempted strenuously to foster a culture sympathetic to autocratic or theocratic government, and egalitarian ends can be attained by supporting freedom fighters everywhere. Domestic, grassroots freedom movements are generally potent and effective because they strike a deep chord in the hearts of contemporaries that resonate with the emancipatory concerns humans have promoted deep into our evolutionary past.

VII. Strong Reciprocity

Strong reciprocity is a propensity, in the context of a shared social task, to cooperate with others similarly disposed, even at personal cost, and a willingness to punish those who violate cooperative norms, even when punishing is personally costly. This behavior involves "reciprocity" because it embraces an ethic of treating others as they treat us, bestowing favors on those who cooperate with us, and punishing those who take advantage of our largesse. This behavior is a "strong" version of reciprocity because it is not self-regarding in the long run, unlike more traditional forms of reciprocity, such as tit-for-tat (Axelrod and Hamilton, 1981) and reciprocal altruism (Trivers, 1971): strong reciprocators are altruistic cooperators and altruistic punishers who do not expect to be rewarded for their prosocial behavior.

Individuals treat moral values as ends in themselves, not merely means toward maintaining a valuable social reputation or otherwise advancing their self-regarding goals. This conclusion follows from observing that even in one-shot, anonymous interactions of the sort studied in our experimental work, presented below, individuals behave in ways that reflect the moral standards of their particular social group. This insight has helped us understand the social welfare systems of the advanced welfare states, as we discuss in section 12 (Gintis, Bowles, Boyd, and Fehr, 2005).

Altruistic punishment is critically important to both the health of egalitarian systems, as well as to their demise. On the one hand, a small fraction of altruistic punishers can induce self-interested individuals to cooperate, on threat of being punished for detecting. On the other hand, when the frequency of free riding is too high, altruistic punishers will withdraw their participation, thereby exacerbating the problem of low participation rates, leading to the complete unraveling of social cooperation. We now turn to this issue.

VIII. The Liberation of Cultural Evolution from Natural Selection

While human culture was shaped by the requirements of fitness enhancement in the evolution of Homo sapiens, the growth of material wealth in humans since the advent of settled agriculture and trade has created a phenomenon completely unique in the biological world, the so-called demographic transition. The demographic transition occurs when per capita material wealth achieves a certain high level and takes the form of a decline first in death and then in birth rates, so that families shift from producing many children to producing few children in which they invest a high level of physical and cultural resources. The demographic transition, exhibited only in our species, has occurred in every country that has passed through the industrial revolution stage of economic development.

Due to the demographic transition, "successful" cultural innovations are no longer fitness enhancing (i.e., they do not lead to more offspring), but rather follow a complex social dynamic that is only partially understood. Some cultural innovations are welfare enhancing, others are simply pleasure enhancing (the two are not the same because some cultural practices, such as tobacco use, are pleasurable but welfare reducing), and yet others are promulgated by religious and state authorities, as well as collective action movements for social change. These cultural forms nevertheless continue to evolve according to an evolutionary dynamic, more successful mutant cultural forms replacing less successful ones.

IX. Self- and Other-regarding Behavior in the Laboratory

We have not arrived at an understanding of the roots of human behavior even after decades of scientifically observing people in real-life settings. We can use attitude surveys to ask people about their preferences and motivations, but often people do not have a very good idea of the roots their own behavior, which mostly lie below the level of conscious thought. Moreover, respondents to attitude surveys have an incentive to portray themselves in a favorable light, thus inhibiting them from revealing true motivations. For these reasons, we must turn to experiments in controlled laboratory settings to assess regularities in human motivation.

In an experimental economics session, a number of subjects interact according to a set of social rules laid down by the experimenter and known to all the subjects. Each set of actions by the subjects is associated with a real monetary payoff for each subject, depending on the joint actions taken by all the subjects. Often subjects are college students, but many other subject pools have been studied. Subjects are anonymous to one another, are paid real money, are not deceived by the experimenters, and are instructed in the rules of play to the point where they fully understood these rules and the payoffs before playing for real.

Consider, for instance, the Ultimatum Game (Güth, Schmittberger, and Schwarze, 1982), in which, under conditions of anonymity, two players are shown a sum of money, say $10. One of the players, called the Proposer, is instructed to offer any number of dollars, from $1 to $10 to the second player, who is called the Responder. The Proposer can make only one offer, and the Responder can either accept or reject this offer. If the Responder accepts the offer, the money is shared accordingly. If the Responder rejects the offer, both players receive nothing. The two players do not face each other again.

This game is extremely simple. If the Responder is self-regarding, he will accept any offer, no matter how small. If the Proposer believes his Responder counterpart is self-regarding, and if he is himself self-regarding, the Proposer will offer the minimum possible amount, $1, and this will be accepted by the Responder.

However, when actually played in the laboratory, the self-regarding outcome is almost never attained or even approximated. In fact, as many replications of this experiment have documented, under varying conditions and with varying amounts of money, Proposers routinely offer Responders very substantial amounts (50% of the total generally being the modal offer), and Responders frequently reject offers below 30% (Camerer and Thaler, 1995; Güth and Tietz, 1990).

Are these results culturally dependent? Do they have a strong genetic component, or do all successful cultures transmit similar values of reciprocity to individuals? Roth, Prasnikar, Okuno-Fujiwara, and Zamir (1991) conducted the Ultimatum Game in four different countries (United States, Yugoslavia, Japan, and Israel) and found that while the level of offers differed a small but significant amount in different countries, the probability of an offer being rejected did not. This indicates that both Proposers and Responders share the same notion of what is considered fair in that society, and that Proposers adjust their offers to reflect this common notion. The differences in level of offers across countries, by the way, were relatively small. When a much greater degree of cultural diversity is studied, however, large differences in behavior are found, reflecting different standards of what it means to be fair in different types of societies (Henrich, Boyd, Bowles, Camerer, Fehr, and Gintis, 2004).

Behavior in the Ultimatum Game thus conforms to the strong reciprocity model: fair behavior in the Ultimatum Game for college students is a 50–50 split. Responders reject offers under 40% as a form of altruistic punishment of the norm-violating Proposer. Proposers offer 50% because they are altruistic cooperators, or 40% because they fear rejection. To support this interpretation, we note that if the offers in an Ultimatum Game are generated by a computer rather than by the Proposer, and if Responders know this, low offers are rarely rejected (Blount, 1995). This suggests that players are motivated by reciprocity, reacting to a violation of behavioral norms (Greenberg and Frisch, 1972). Moreover, in a variant of the game in which a Responder rejection leads to the Responder getting nothing but allows the Proposer to keep the share he suggested for himself, Responders never reject offers, and proposers make considerably smaller (but still positive) offers (Bolton and Zwick, 1995). As a final indication that strong reciprocity motives are operative in this game, after the game is over, when asked why they offered more than the lowest possible amount, Proposers commonly said that they were afraid that Responders will consider low offers unfair and reject them. When Responders rejected offers, they usually claimed they want to punish unfair behavior. In all of the above experiments, a significant fraction of subjects (about a quarter, typically) conformed to self-regarding preferences.

X. Cooperation and Punishment in the Public Goods Game

Another experimental game played in the laboratory is known as the public goods game. A typical public goods game consists of a number of rounds, say 10. In each round, each subject is grouped with several other subjects—say 3 others. Each subject is then given a certain number of points, say 20, redeemable at the end of the experimental session for real money. Each subject then places some fraction of his points in a "common account" and the remainder in the subject's "private account." The experimenter then tells the subjects how many points were contributed to the common account and adds to the private account of each subject some fraction, say 40%, of the total amount in the common account. So if a subject contributes his whole 20 points to the common account, each of the 4 group members will receive 8 points at the end of the round. In effect, by putting the whole endowment into the common account, a player loses 12 points, but the other 3 group members gain in total 24 (8 times 3) points. The players keep whatever is in their private accounts at the end of the round.

A self-regarding player contributes nothing to the common account. However, only a fraction of the subjects in fact conform to the self-regarding model. Subjects begin by contributing on average about half of their endowments to the public account. The level of contributions decays over the course of the 10 rounds until in the final rounds, most players are behaving in a self-regarding manner. This is, of course, exactly what is predicted by the strong reciprocity model. Because they are altruistic contributors, strong reciprocators start out by contributing to the common pool, but in response to the norm violation of the self-regarding types, they begin to refrain from contributing themselves.

How do we know that the decay of cooperation in the public goods game is due to cooperators punishing free riders by refusing to contribute themselves? Subjects often report this behavior retrospectively. More compelling, however, is the fact that when subjects are given a more constructive way of punishing defectors, they use it in a way that helps sustain cooperation.

For instance, Fehr and Gächter (2000) set up an experimental situation in which the possibility of strategic punishment was removed. They used 6-and 10-round public goods games with groups of size 4, and with costly punishment allowed at the end of each round, employing three different methods of assigning members to groups. There were sufficient subjects to run between 10 and 18 groups simultaneously. Under the Partner treatment, the four subjects remained in the same group for all 10 periods. Under the Stranger treatment, the subjects were randomly reassigned after each round. Finally, under the Perfect Stranger treatment, the subjects were randomly reassigned but assured that they would never meet the same subject more than once.

Fehr and Gächter (2000) performed their experiment for 10 rounds with punishment and 10 rounds without. Their results are illustrated in Figure 6.1. We see that when costly punishment is permitted, cooperation does not deteriorate, and in the Partner game, despite strict anonymity, cooperation increases to almost full cooperation even in the final round. When punishment is not permitted, however, the same subjects experienced the deterioration of cooperation found in previous public goods games. The contrast in cooperation rates between the Partner treatment and the two Stranger treatments is worth noting because the strength of punishment is roughly the same across all treatments. This suggests that the credibility of the punishment threat is greater in the Partner treatment because in this treatment, the punished subjects are certain that once they have been punished in previous rounds, the punishing subjects are in their group. The pro-sociality impact of strong reciprocity on cooperation is thus more strongly manifested the more coherent and permanent the group in question.[1]

Many behavioral game theorists have found that while altruistic punishment increases participation, it often leads to such a high level of punishment that overall average payoffs, net of punishment, are low (Anderson and Putterman, 2006; Carpenter and Matthews, 2005; Casari and Luini, 2007; Nikiforakis, 2008; Page, Putterman, and Unel, 2005;). Some have interpreted this as showing

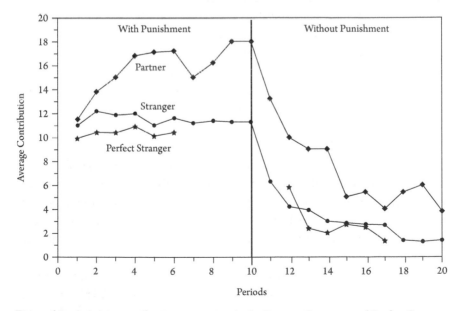

Figure 6.1 Average contributions over time in the Partner, Stranger, and Perfect Stranger Treatments when the punishment condition is played first (Fehr and Gächter, 2000).

that strong reciprocity "could not have evolved" or "is not an adaptation." It is more likely, however, that the problem is with the experiments themselves. These experiments attempt to refute the standard "homo economicus" model of the self-regarding actor and do not attempt to produce realistic punishment scenarios in the laboratory. In fact, the motive for punishing norm violators is sufficiently strong as to lower overall payoffs when not subject to some social regulation. In real societies, there tends to be collective control over the meting out of punishment, and the excessive zeal of individual punishers is frowned upon and socially punished. Indeed, in one of the rare studies that allowed groups to regulate punishment, Ertan, Page, and Putterman (2005) found that groups that voted to permit only punishment of below-average or of average and below-average contributors achieved significantly higher earnings than groups not using punishment.

XI. Altruistic Third Party Punishment

Pro-social behavior in human society occurs not only because those directly helped and harmed by an individual's actions are likely to reciprocate in kind, but also because there are general social norms that foster pro-social behavior, and many people are willing to bestow favors on those who conform to social norms and to punish those who do not, even if they are not personally helped or hurt by the acts involved. In everyday life, third parties who are not the beneficiaries of an individual's pro-social act will help the individual and his family in times of need, will preferentially trade favors with the individual, and otherwise will reward the individual in ways that are not costly but are nonetheless of great benefit to the cooperator. Similarly, third parties who have not been personally harmed by the antisocial behavior of an individual will refuse aid even when it is not costly to do so; will shun the offender; and approve of the offender's ostracism from beneficial group activities, again at low cost to the third party but highly costly to the offender.

It is hard to conceive of human societies operating at a high level of efficiency in the absence of such third party reward and punishment. Yet, self-regarding actors will never engage in such behavior if it is at all costly. An experiment conducted by Fehr and Fischbacher (2004) addresses this question by conducting a series of third party punishment experiments using prisoner's dilemma and dictator games.

In the prisoner's dilemma game, each of two players Alice and Bob must decide simultaneously either to cooperate (play C) or defect (play D). Typical payoffs are then the reward payoff $r = 3$ for each player if they both play C, the punish payoff $p = 1$ if they both play D, and the sucker payoff $s = 0$ if a player plays C and his partner plays D, the defecting partner receiving the temptation payoff $t = 4$. In general, the payoffs are chosen so that $t > r > p > s$, in which case no matter what Bob does, a self-regarding Alice will always defect (play D). Thus, if Bob also defects, both get $p = 3$, but if Bob cooperates (plays C), Alice gets $t = 4$ and Bob gets $s = 0$. Thus, the pro-social behavior in the prisoner's dilemma is to play C, even though this necessarily lowers your monetary payoff.

In the dictator game, which is even simpler, the experimenter gives Alice, who is called the Dictator, say, $10, and instructs her to give any portion of the money to Bob (whom she does not know and cannot see), who is called the Receiver. The Dictator keeps whatever she does not choose to give to the Receiver. Obviously, a self-regarding Dictator will give nothing to the Receiver.

The experimenters implemented four experimental treatments, in each of which subjects were grouped into threes. In each group, in stage one, subject A played a prisoner's dilemma or dictator game with subject B as the recipient, and subject C was an outsider whose payoff was not affected by A's decision. Then, in stage two, subject C was endowed with 50 points and allowed to deduct points from subject A, such that every 3 points deducted from A's score cost C 1 point. In the first treatment (TP-DG), the game was the dictator game, in which A was endowed with 100 points and could give 0, 10, 20, 30, 40, or 50 points to B, who had no endowment.

The second treatment (TP-PD) was the same, except that the game was the prisoner's dilemma. Subjects A and B were each endowed with 10 points, and each could either keep the 10points or transfer them to the other subject, in which case it was tripled by the experimenter. Thus, if both cooperated, each earned 30 points, and if both defected, each earned 10 points. If one cooperated and one defected, however, the cooperator earned 0 and the defector 40 points. In the second stage, C was given an endowment of 40 points and was allowed to deduct points from A and/or B, just as in the TP-DG treatment.

To compare the relative strengths of second and third party punishment in the dictator game, the experimenters implemented a third treatment, S&P-DG. In this treatment, subjects were randomly assigned to player A and player B, and A-B pairs were randomly formed. In the first stage of this treatment, each A was endowed with 100 points and each B with none, and the A's played the dictator game as before. In the second stage of each treatment, each player was given an additional 50 points, and the B players were permitted to deduct points from A players on the same terms as in the first two treatments. S&P-DG also had two conditions. In the S condition, a B player could only punish his own dictator, whereas in the T condition, a B player could only punish an A player from another pair, to which he was randomly assigned by the experimenters. In the

T condition, each B player was informed of the behavior of the A player to which he was assigned.

To compare the relative strengths of second and third party punishment in the prisoner's dilemma, the experimenters implemented a fourth treatment, S&P-PG. This was similar to the S&P-DG treatment, except that now they played a prisoner's dilemma.[2]

In the first two treatments, because subjects were randomly assigned to positions A, B, and C, the obvious fairness norm is that all should have equal payoffs (an equality norm). For instance, if A gave 50 points to B, and C deducted no points from A, each subject would end up with 50 points. In the dictator game treatment (TP-DG), 60% of third parties (C's) punish dictators (A's) who give less than 50% of the endowment to recipients (B's). Statistical analysis (ordinary least squares regression) showed that for every point an A kept for himself above the 50–50 split, he was punished an average 0.28 points by C's, leading to a total punishment of $3 \times 0.28 = 0.84$ points. Thus, a dictator who kept the whole 100 points would have $0.84 \times 50 = 42$ points deducted by C's, leaving a meager gain of 8 points over equal sharing.

The results for the prisoner's dilemma treatment (TP-PD) were similar, with an interesting twist. If one partner in the AB pair defected and the other cooperated, the defector would have on average 10.05 points deducted by C's, but if both defected, the punished player lost only an average of 1.75 points. This shows that third parties (C's) care not only about the intentions of defectors, but how much harm they caused and/or how unfair they turned out to be. Overall, 45.8% of third parties punished defectors whose partners cooperated, whereas only 20.8% of third parties punished defectors whose partners defected.

Turning to the third treatment (T&SP-DG), second party sanctions of selfish dictators are found to be considerably stronger than third party sanctions, although both were highly significant. On average, in the first condition, where recipients could punish their own dictators, they imposed a deduction of 1.36 points for each point the dictator kept above the 50–50 split, whereas they imposed a deduction of only 0.62 points per point kept on third party dictators. In the final treatment (T&SP-PD), defectors are severely punished by both second and third parties, but second party punishment is again found to be much more severe than third. Thus, cooperating subjects deducted on average 8.4 points from a defecting partner, but only 3.09 points from a defecting third party.

This study confirms the general principle that punishing norm violators is very common but not universal, and individuals are prone to be harsher in punishing those who hurt them personally, as opposed to violating a social norm that hurts others than themselves.

XII. Reciprocity and the Welfare State

The experimental evidence would be of little policy value if people were not mo-tivated in daily life as they are in the laboratory. However, strong reciprocity is well represented in real-world social dynamics. A case in point is the so-called welfare rebellion—a decline in support for income redistribution witnessed in the United States and some European countries in the last two decades of the twentieth century. According to the norms associated with strong reciprocity, we would expect egalitarian policies that reward people independent of whether and how much they contribute to society to be considered unfair, even if the intended recipients are otherwise considered worthy of support, and even if the incidence of noncontribution in the target population is rather low. This would explain the shift from support for opposition to welfare measures for the poor, since such measures are thought to have promoted various social pathologies that had become salient during that period. At the same time, it explains the con-tinuing support for Social Security and Medicare in the United States through-out this period, since the public perception is that the recipients are "deserving," and the policies do not support what are considered antisocial behaviors.

A striking fact about the decline in the support for the former Aid to Families with Dependent Children, Food Stamps, and other means-tested social support programs in the United States, however, is that overwhelming numbers of indi-viduals came to oppose these programs, whatever their income, race, or personal history with such programs. This pattern of public sentiment, I will show, can be accounted for in terms of strong reciprocity.

I rely mainly on two studies. The first (Farkas and Robinson, 1996) analyzes data collected in late 1995 by Public Agenda, a nonprofit, nonpartisan research organization. The authors conducted eight focus groups around the country, then did a national survey involving half-hour interviews, of 1000 randomly se-lected Americans, plus a national oversample of 200 African Americans. The second, political scientist Martin Gilens's Why Americans Hate Welfare, is an analysis and review of several polls executed during the 1990s and earlier by var-ious news organizations. A third study by Weaver, Shapiro, and Jacobs (1995), drawing in addition on NORC and General Social Survey data, comes to broadly similar conclusions.

In the Public Agenda survey, 63% of respondents thought the welfare system should be eliminated or "fundamentally overhauled" while another 34% thought it should be "adjusted somewhat." Only 3% approved of the system as is. Even among respondents from households receiving welfare, only 9% expressed basic approval of the system, while 42% wanted a fundamental overhaul, and an addi-tional 46% wanted some adjustments.

The cost of welfare programs cannot explain this opposition. While people generally overstate the share of the federal budget devoted to welfare, this cannot account for the observed opposition. Farkas and Robinson note the following conclusions.

> By more than four to one (65% to 14%), Americans say the most upsetting thing about welfare is that "it encourages people to adopt the wrong lifestyle and values," not that "it costs too much tax money." . . . Of nine possible reforms presented to respondents—ranging from requiring job training to paying surprise visits to make sure recipients deserve benefits—reducing benefits ranked last in popularity.
>
> The cost, apparently, is not the problem. In focus groups: participants invariably dismissed arguments about the limited financial costs of welfare in almost derisive terms as irrelevant and beside the point. (Farkas and Robinson, 1996: 9, 10).

The perception of fraud cannot account for this opposition. While 64% of respondents and 66% of respondents on welfare believe welfare fraud is a serious problem, most do not consider it more serious than in other government programs, and only 35% of survey respondents would be more "comfortable with welfare" if fraud were eliminated.

In the Public Agenda study, respondents overwhelmingly consider welfare to be unfair to working people and addictive to recipients. Indeed, 70% (71% of welfare recipients) say welfare makes it "financially better for people to stay on welfare than to get a job," while 57% (62% of welfare recipients) think welfare encourages "people to be lazy," and 60% (64% of welfare recipients) say the welfare system "encourages people to have kids out of wedlock." The truth of such assertions is beside the point. Whether or not, for example, welfare causes out-of-wedlock births or fosters an unwillingness to work, citizens object that the system provides financial support for those who undertake these socially disapproved behaviors. Their desire is to bear witness against the behavior and to disassociate themselves from it, whether or not their actions can change it.

This interpretation is supported by a careful study by Luttmer (2001), who matched U.S. General Social Survey (GSS) data with census tract information on the number and characteristics of the GSS subjects' neighbors who were on welfare. He found that the number of people in the surrounding area who were receiving public assistance predicted opposition to welfare spending if those on welfare were predominantly not working (or working very little) and if many of those on welfare were unmarried mothers; and the subject voiced disapproval of premarital sexual relations. The relevant fact for our interpretation is that opposition was conditioned on the nonworking and unmarried mother status of the recipients and the moral beliefs of the subjects.

On the other hand, surveys support basic needs generosity," a virtually unconditional willingness to share with others to assure them of some minimal standard, especially, as the survey data show, when this is implemented through provision of food, basic medical care, housing, and other essential goods. The interplay of basic needs generosity and strong reciprocity, I think, accounts for the salient facts about public opinion concerning the welfare state.

My analysis supports the notion that declining voter support for the welfare state, where it occurred, was due not to the selfishness of the electorate but rather to the failure of social welfare programs to tap powerful commitments to fairness and reciprocity. There is substantial support for generosity toward the less well off as long as they are "deserving" poor, who have provided or tried to provide a quid pro quo and are in good standing. Poverty is often the result of low returns to such socially admired behaviors as hard unskilled work, independent small-scale entrepreneurship, and studious behavior in poor educational environments. Policies designed to raise the returns to these activities might garner widespread support. Strong reciprocity sentiments might also support policies that insure individuals against the vagaries of the weather or the market without compensating them for losses to laziness or poor judgment.

XIII. Implications for Human Rights Policies

There is a simple reason why groups dedicated to advancing human rights around the world have enjoyed solid support from citizens of the advanced industrial democracies. Human rights are deeply political yet virtually nonpartisan. Human rights are deeply political because when they are observed, citizens control the deliberative and coercive branches of government, and thus have the capacity to turn the state from an instrument of repression to an instrument of emancipation. Human rights are nonpartisan because they are supported by all major political philosophies in the liberal democratic countries that must bear the brunt of support for human rights movements in less-privileged parts of the world. Such support is fostered by strong reciprocity sentiments, both because many people feel an obligation to help others achieve a state of political freedom that they enjoy by virtue of the sacrifices of their forbears, and because the politically oppressed are rarely blamed for their condition, which generally is due to no fault of their own.

Notes

I would like to thank the European Science Foundation for research support.
  1. In Fehr and Gächter (2002), the experimenters reverse the order of the rounds with and without punishment to be sure that the decay in the "without punishment" phase was not due to its occurring at the end rather than at the start of the game. It was not.
  2. The experimenters never use value-laden terms such as "punish" but rather neutral terms such as "deduct points."

CODA

Human Rights: An Evolutionary and Behavioral Perspective

RYAN GOODMAN, DEREK JINKS, AND ANDREW K. WOODS

Herbert Gintis's chapter summarizes the evolutionary and behavioral foundations of human society and political order. Human social behavior, he argues, exhibits certain fundamental, transcultural features. The conception of human nature that emerges is, in several important respects, at odds with the standard economic model of human motivation. Drawing on a broad range of materials in the behavioral sciences—including anthropology, game theory, and experimental economics—Gintis advances two central descriptive claims. First, humans evolved in a biological and social context that strongly disfavored the tendency toward hierarchical power. In this way, Gintis suggests that humans have a natural predisposition to support certain fundamental human rights and to oppose state despotism. Second, humans also have an evolved commitment to "strong reciprocity." Strong reciprocity is a propensity to cooperate with others similarly disposed, even when cooperation is costly, and a willingness to punish those who violate cooperative norms, even when punishing is costly to the punisher. Strong reciprocators are, in this way, "altruistic cooperators" and "altruistic punishers." We explore here several applications of Gintis's work. We should note, as we discussed in the Introduction, the implications of the claim that humans are predisposed to be "strong reciprocators" are staggering—implicating every aspect of human rights scholarship and practice founded on the standard economic model of human motivation. The scope and scale of the applications we detail here are representative of this much broader range of applications.

I. Target: Opponents/Critics of Universal Human Rights Standards

Gintis provides an important rejoinder to cultural relativism critiques of universal human rights standards. Gintis argues that certain important normative and behavioral predispositions are common across cultures. Indeed, in this view, culture itself is founded in evolutionary biology. These predispositions, when understood in a global historical context, suggest a transcultural commitment to a normative framework consistent with fundamental human rights standards. Notably, this normative framework, according to Gintis, causes predispositions favoring civil and political rights—the very category of international human rights most commonly subjected to claims of cultural relativism. Whether this research documents only a thin normative consensus or something more fulsome is debatable, of course. However, this empirically grounded, increasingly refined model of "humans" has clear and important implications for our understanding of the relationship between culture and human rights. This aspect of Gintis's chapter also may complement the work of John Mikhail. Specifically, Gintis's chapter offers further support for Mikhail's claim that, at least with regard to some bargaining patterns, there is enough evidence of a shared and innate morality to ground a conception of human rights in human nature.

II. Target: Proponents of Human Rights/ Regime Architects

A. The Substantive Content of Human Rights Law

The research canvassed by Gintis strongly suggests a minimum content for human rights law. Gintis explicitly identifies a strong evolutionary and behavioral basis for a minimum (and fairly robust) civil and political rights. The implications of the research, though, also extend to economic, social, and cultural rights. For Gintis, behavioral research suggests that people generally support "'basic needs generosity,' a virtually unconditional willingness" to distribute resources to ensure people receive "some minimal standard" such as "food, basic medical care, housing, and other essential goods." Notably, this narrow category corresponds with one conception of the proper scope of human rights law—one that relies propounds a "minimum core" of essential requirements. (U.N. Committee on Economic, Social and Cultural Rights, Gen. Comment 3.) Whether to adopt and emphasize this "minimum core" approach is a matter of some controversy (Circle of Rights: Economic, Social and Cultural Rights Activism).

B. Conceptual Ordering of Human Rights Norms

At first blush, the Gintis chapter seems to support a sharp distinction between civil and political rights on the one hand and economic, social, and cultural rights on the other. However, the evolutionary and behavioral basis for predispositions favoring civil and political rights—counter hegemonic resistance to despotism—strongly suggest a deeper unity between the ostensibly distinct categories of rights. The fundamental point is that some economic and social rights—or the minimum core of some economic and social rights—may help citizens resist state despotism. Indeed, a subset of economic and social rights may more directly serve that purpose than a subset of civil and political rights. Notably, this issue may more precisely turn on whether people *perceive* or can be *persuaded* that particular economic and social rights serve to counter despotism. Since some economic and social rights arguably have this (perceived) function or effect, Gintis's work carries important conceptual implications. It would call for overhauling the distinction between civil and political rights and economic and social rights. Advocacy groups and other international organizations might be more effective in promoting only those rights that most directly and most apparently counter hierarchy and political despotism. Alternatively and less radically, civil and political rights organizations might supplement their work by incorporating into their mandate those economic and social rights that serve this counter-hierarchical purpose.

Which economic and social rights might fit this framework? Interestingly, Gintis lists the right to property among those that offer a significant bulwark against despotism. One form of republican theory suggests that guaranteeing citizens sustenance-level entitlements (contemporary forms of property) also provides them a stake in society and less vulnerability to tyrannical rule (Amar, 1990). The right to education may also provide more direct and far-reaching guarantees against social and political hierarchy than some civil and political rights (e.g., the right to marry, freedom of movement, the right to an attorney). Finally, some economic rights might be prerequisites for the exercise of certain political freedoms: the right to a printing press is not sufficient if one can't afford the printer; starvation is an impediment to exercising the right to assemble and mobilize politically.

While economic and social rights have been criticized for being politically unrealistic, Gintis's work also provides an insight into one method for overcoming objections to their fulfillment: the innate and powerful desire for fairness. The standard story about economic and social rights suggests that welfare regimes are politically difficult to sustain because they appear costly to elites who do not reap their benefits (indeed, they are often decried by elites as "unfair"). Gintis's chapter may suggest one way to turn this logic on its head. The reciprocal altruism research suggests that parties are willing to undergo certain costs in order to correct what they perceive as unfair dealings. If welfare could be recast as a project to correct such unfair dealings, perhaps elites will be more willing to sign on.

C. The Scope of State Obligations under Human Rights Law

Gintis's research underscores the evolutionary and behavioral significance of the nature and scope of state obligations to implement human rights. As discussed in the chapter, strong reciprocity and third party punishment prompt adverse public reaction to governmental policies that are otherwise consistent with human predispositions favoring human rights. For example, certain welfare strategies might be more likely to prompt a political backlash. One implication for human rights law is that the obligations to fulfill, protect, and respect economic rights might yield different outcomes on the ground. An obligation to promote economic outcomes proactively risks the sort of social and political resistance described by Gintis—even though an obligation to respect and ensure might not. The point is that human rights law requires national governments to implement human rights standards within an increasingly well-defined behavioral and cognitive context. The specific features of this context ought to exert some influence on how we conceive of that obligation in the first instance.

D. Human Rights and Regime Influence in the International System

The international community may be described as a "societ[y] hav[ing] no centralized structure of governance (state, judicial system, church, Big Man), so the enforcement of norms depends on the voluntary participation of peers" (Gintis, 2009: 71). Accordingly, Gintis's research might inform regime design at the international level. For example, regime architects could learn from Gintis's research in calculating potential costs to hierarchically organized peer institutions (such as the U.N. Human Rights Council, which restricts membership based on human rights performance; proposals for a League of Democracies). Likewise, Gintis's research might suggest the prospect of cooperation among a loosely affiliated, large population of states. According to standard economic models of self-regarding (state) actors, such cooperation is not possible or exceedingly difficult to achieve. Gintis finds that strong reciprocators will eschew punishment when there is a large percentage of free riders. This finding may help explain the ineffectiveness of international human rights institutions in which violations are prevalent. It might also help build more effective international institutions in which strong reciprocity can facilitate social cooperation as long as the distribution of cooperators and deviant/noncooperating states is appropriately balanced. Along the same line, Gintis's scholarship might suggest such cooperation is more likely in multilateral organizations in which group membership is more coherent and permanent (Gintis, Bowles, Boyd, and Fehr, 2003: 162) Those factors would favor regional human rights organizations and would disfavor organizations in which participation fluctuates due to admission rules and limited tenures.

Note

This Coda, like the others in the book, offers some specific applications drawn from the insights in the contributor's chapter. It is not intended to be a list of fully developed policy prescriptions, but instead an example of the rich sorts of human rights policy applications that can be drawn from cutting-edge social science research. It does not question the insights offered in the chapter but instead asks what implications those insights might have for human rights law and policy. The Codas are the sole authorship of the editors of the volume.

7

Moral Grammar and Human Rights

Some Reflections on Cognitive Science and Enlightenment Rationalism

JOHN MIKHAIL

The moral sense is a distinct and original power of the human mind.... Our knowledge of moral philosophy, of natural jurisprudence, of the law of nations, must ultimately depend, for its first principles, on the evidence and information of the moral sense.

—James Wilson, *Lectures on Law*

Hobbes ... [believes] that justice is founded on contract solely, and does not result from the construction of man. I believe, on the contrary, that it is instinct, and innate, that the moral sense is as much a part of our constitution as that of feeling, seeing, or hearing. ... The moral sense, or conscience, is as much a part of man as his leg or arm.

—Thomas Jefferson, Letter to Peter Carr

Being men, they all have what Dr. Rush calls a *moral faculty;* Dr. Hutcheson a *moral sense;* and the Bible and the generality of the world, a *conscience.*

—John Adams, Letter to John Taylor

All human beings are born free and equal in dignity and rights. They are endowed with reason and conscience and should act towards one another in a spirit of brotherhood.

—Article 1, Universal Declaration of Human Rights

I. Human Rights and Human Nature

A striking feature of contemporary human rights scholarship is the extent to which it has turned its back on the idea that human rights can be grounded in a theory of human nature. Michael Ignatieff, former director of Harvard University's Carr Center for Human Rights Policy, illustrates a widespread tendency in the literature when he rejects the existence of any such foundation:

The Universal Declaration set out to reestablish the idea of human
rights at the precise historical moment in which they had been shown
to have had no foundation whatever in natural human attributes. All
that one can say about this paradox is that it defines the divided consciousness with which we have lived with the idea of human rights ever
since. We defend human rights as moral universals in full awareness
that they must counteract rather than reflect natural human propensities. . . . For the idea that these propensities are natural implies that
they are innate and universally distributed among individuals. The reality . . . is otherwise. (Ignatieff, 2001: 78–80)

Ignatieff's rejection of the traditional philosophical project of locating the
source of human rights in innate and universal features of human nature (see, e.g.,
Henkin, 1990; Hunt, 2007) is widely shared. Richard Rorty, for example, rejects
the Enlightenment premise—implicit in the Declaration of Independence (1776);
Declaration of the Rights of Man and Citizen (1789); Universal Declaration of
Human Rights (1948); and other human rights landmarks—that human rights
derive from a moral sense or conscience that "nature has made universal in the
whole species" (Hume, 1983/1751: 6; cf. Burlamaqui, 2006/1748; Hutcheson,
2007/1747; Kant, 1993/1788; Price, 1948/1758; Reid, 1969/1788; Rousseau,
1979/1762; Smith, 1976/1759; Wollstonecraft 1995/1792). In Rorty's view,
modern writers have justifiably abandoned the romantic eighteenth-century
belief in a universal moral faculty, possession of which constitutes a distinctively
human characteristic:

Contemporary intellectuals have given up the Enlightenment assumption that religion, myth and tradition can be opposed to something
ahistorical, something common to all human beings qua human. Anthropologists and historians of science have blurred the distinction
between innate rationality and the products of acculturation. Philosophers such as Heidegger and Gadamer have given us ways of seeing
human beings as historical all the way through. Other philosophers,
such as Quine and Davidson, have blurred the distinction between
permanent truths of reason and temporary truths of fact. Psychoanal-
ysis has blurred the distinction between conscience and the emotions
of love, hate, and fear, and thus the distinction between morality and
prudence. The result is to erase the picture of the self common to
Greek metaphysics, Christian theology, and Enlightenment rationalism: the picture of an ahistorical natural center, the locus of human
dignity, surrounded by an adventitious and inessential periphery.
(Rorty, 1993: 255)

Many prominent philosophers echo a similar refrain. Writing in 1949, one year after the Universal Declaration of Human Rights affirmed the proposition that all human beings are "endowed with reason and conscience," Gilbert Ryle poured scorn on this idea, labeling moral knowledge a "strained phrase" and insisting that folk beliefs about reason and conscience are a "nursery myth" (1949: 315–316). Two decades later, J. L. Mackie famously rejected the existence of a faculty of moral intuition on the grounds that such a faculty would be epistemologically and metaphysically "queer" (1977: 38–42). Another prominent mid-century philosopher, Kurt Baier, brusquely dismissed the idea of an innate moral sense in a few sentences: "The moral sense theory . . . claim[s] that we have a special moral sense . . . which enables us to see the rightness or wrongness of certain sorts of action. The absolutely fatal objection to this view is that there is no such moral sense. . . . There is no part of a man's body whose removal or injury would specifically affect his knowledge of the rightness or wrongness of certain types or courses of action" (1965/1958: 22–23). More recently, Bernard Williams wrote that the idea of a common moral faculty "has been demolished by a succession of critics, and the ruins of it that remain above ground are not impressive enough to invite much history of what happened to it" (1985: 94). Drawing out the implications of this history for the concept of human rights in his influential book, *After Virtue*, Alisdair MacIntyre asserts that the Enlightenment project of justifying human rights is dead: "there are no such rights," he observes, "and belief in them is one with belief in witches and unicorns" (1981: 67).

For more than a century, social scientists have also been generally hostile to the notion of an innate moral faculty or sense of justice that might supply a naturalistic foundation for human rights. Typical in this regard are the views of Emile Durkheim, who held that "society is the only source of morality" (Durkhiem, cited in Piaget 1932: 327); George Herbert Mead, who argued that "minds and selves are essentially social products" (1956: 16); and Ruth Benedict, who popularized the phrase "cultural relativism" and claimed that all standards of behavior, even those pertaining to violent crimes like homicide, are culturally relative (1934: 45). From this perspective, even one's deepest moral convictions are social constructs, which depend exclusively on culture, myth, or ideology; thus, they are fundamentally arbitrary. The concept of universal human rights therefore makes no sense; social norms "can make anything right and prevent condemnation of anything," as the early American sociologist William Graham Sumner observed (1906: 521). Behaviorist psychology, which criticized theoretical appeals to unobservable mental faculties on methodological grounds (see, e.g., Skinner, 1953; Watson, 1925), likewise left no room for the moral sense or conscience as it was traditionally conceived. For his part, Freud (1930) argued that conscience is simply the function of a super ego that originates from the internalization of instinctual aggression. Hence, every possible device must be used "to erect barriers against [these] aggressive instincts" and "hold their manifestations in check." Freud maintained that "men are not gentle, friendly creatures wishing for love, who simply defend themselves if they are attacked . . . [but] savage beasts to whom the thought of sparing their own kind is alien." The Golden Rule encourages people to love their neighbors, but a more realistic and unsentimental portrait of human nature reveals something quite different:

> "[T]heir neighbor is to them not only a possible helper or sexual object, but also a temptation to them to gratify their aggressiveness on him, to exploit his capacity for work without recompense, to use him sexually without his consent, to seize his possessions, to humiliate him, to cause him pain, to torture and kill him. *Homo homini lupus.*[1] Who has the courage to dispute it in the face of all the evidence in his own life and in history?" (Freud, 1930: 40)

Albeit with less dramatic flair than Freud, many judges and legal scholars also assume that human rights have no sound basis in science or logic. Judge Richard Posner, for instance, recently devoted an entire book to criticizing the "spurious" idea that there is "a moral order accessible to human intelligence and neither time-bound nor local, an order that furnishes objective criteria for praising or condemning the beliefs and behaviors of individuals and the design and operation of legal institutions" (1999: 3)—in short, to criticizing the very idea of universal human rights. Other prominent conservative jurists concur. In an influential critique of the Warren Court's due process and equal protection jurisprudence, which foreshadowed the subsequent development of much late twentieth-century conservative legal thought, Robert Bork argued that the moral value choices implicit in *Griswold v. Connecticut* and other landmark constitutional cases are essentially arbitrary: "there is no principled way to decide that one man's gratifications are more deserving of respect than another's. Why is sexual gratification more worthy than moral gratification? Why is sexual gratification nobler than economic gratification? There is no way of deciding these matters other than by reference to some system of moral or ethical values that has no objective or intrinsic validity of its own and about which men can and do differ" (Bork, 1971: 10; cf. Bork, 2003; Rehnquist, 1976; Scalia, 1997). Finally, a similar skepticism can often be found, at least implicitly, in the writings of influential *liberal* legal and political theorists, including Ronald Dworkin (1977), John Hart Ely (1980), Michael Perry (2005), and Charles Beitz (2009), along with other writers often associated with the defense of fundamental rights. They, too, appear to agree that human rights cannot be derived from a theory of human nature. As Albert Alschuler observes, all of these scholars on both the Right and

---

[1] Man is to man a wolf.

Left are effectively the heirs of Oliver Wendell Holmes Jr., who "sounded the principal theme of twentieth-century jurisprudence when he wrote that moral preferences are 'more or less arbitrary. . . . Do you like sugar in your coffee or don't you? . . . So as to truth'" (Alschuler, 2000: 1, quoting a 1902 letter from Holmes to Lady Pollock).

II. A New Paradigm

What is one to make of all this? Are Ignatieff and other skeptics correct to deny that human rights have any sound basis in a naturalistic worldview? Is the guiding idea of both Enlightenment Rationalism and the modern human rights movement— that human beings are moral creatures, who are endowed with a moral faculty or conscience—merely a religious fable or nursery myth?

The main purpose of this chapter is to defend a negative answer to these questions and thereby offer a new perspective on old and venerable arguments about the naturalistic foundation of human rights. This new approach begins from the observation that whether human rights can be given a secure foundation in "natural human attributes" (Ignatieff, 2001: 78) is not primarily a philosophical or theological question, but an empirical question that belongs in principle in the cognitive and brain sciences, broadly construed. The confident assertions of Ignatieff, Rorty, and other critics notwithstanding, one cannot therefore simply decide the matter from the armchair. On the contrary, probative evidence and sound scientific argument must be brought to bear.

This new paradigm also begins from the premise that two of the most significant intellectual and political developments of the past 50 years are the cognitive revolution in the sciences of mind, brain, and behavior and the human rights revolution in constitutional and international law (see, e.g., Gardner, 1985; Henkin, 1990). The former displaced the narrow forms of logical positivism and psychological behaviorism that dominated academic philosophy and psychology during the first half of the twentieth century and prevented researchers from formulating coherent theories of "the distinct and original power[s] of the human mind" (Wilson, 1967/1791: 378) that had formed the basis of much Enlightenment jurisprudence, moral philosophy, and political theory. Motivated by the unspeakable horrors of the Holocaust and other familiar atrocities, the human rights revolution in constitutional and international law, in turn, has dramatically extended the reach and application of basic moral and legal precepts to every corner of the globe. The central aim of the chapter is to bring these two movements into fruitful contact with one another by describing how researchers from a variety of disciplines have begun to converge on a scientific theory of human moral cognition that, at least in its broad contours, bears a striking resemblance to the classical accounts of moral philosophy, natural jurisprudence, and the law of nations that reverberate throughout the ages.

These classical accounts typically rest on the claim that an innate moral faculty or conscience and with it principles of justice, fairness, empathy, and solidarity are written into the very frame of human nature. They were particularly influential during the seventeenth and eighteenth centuries, when the modern human rights movement first emerged (see generally Haakonssen, 1996; Mikhail, 2007a; Schneewind, 1998). As I shall endeavor to explain, it is precisely this set of ideas that cognitive science, liberated from the crippling methodological restrictions of positivism, behaviorism, historicism, and other recent intellectual frameworks, has recently begun to explicate and to a substantial extent verify. This new trend in the science of human nature, I wish to suggest, has potentially profound implications for the theory and practice of human rights.

III. Universal Moral Grammar

A useful place to begin exploring these topics is to consider the hypothesis of a Universal Moral Grammar (UMG) that many writers have begun to discuss in recent years (see, e.g., Dubber, 2006; Dwyer, 1999, 2006, 2008; Harman, 2000, 2008; Hauser, 2006; Jackendoff, 2009; Kar, 2006; Mahlmann, 1999, 2005, 2007, 2009; Mikhail, 2000, 2007, 2009, 2011; Mikhail, Sorrentino, and Spelke, 1998; Robinson, Kurzban, and Jones, 2007; for criticisms and commentary, see, e.g., Dupoux and Jacob, 2007; Miller, 2008; Nichols, 2005; Patterson, 2008; Pinker, 2008; Prinz, 2007, 2008; Rai and Holyoak, 2009; Saxe, 2005). As a research program in cognitive science, UMG seeks to synthesize and distill many of the traditional arguments that were used to defend the claim that human beings possess an innate moral faculty and to reinterpret and investigate these claims within a modern empirical framework. The approach is modeled to some extent on Chomsky's theory of Universal Grammar (UG), and UMG thus draws inspiration and ideas from an analogy between rules of justice and rules of grammar that has been popular throughout the modern period (see Table 7.1). The parallels between these two research enterprises are often inexact, however, and should not be interpreted too rigidly.

Chomsky transformed linguistics and cognitive science by distinguishing at least five distinct problems that a scientific theory of human language must confront (Table 7.2). He also argued that certain observable aspects of linguistic behavior that bear on the first two problems can be studied mathematically, as a kind of input-output relationship. He therefore identified two models that an adequate linguistic theory must specify: a perceptual model and an acquisition model (see, e.g., Chomsky, 1964, 1965; Mikhail, 2007b, 2011; see Figure 7.1).

Table 7.1 **Some modern authors who draw a linguistic analogy (1625–2000)**

Grotius 1625	Cover 1975
Hale 1668	Donagan 1977
Pufendorf 1682	Chomsky 1978
Hutcheson 1730	Much and Shweder 1978
Hume 1740	Quine 1978
Rousseau 1754	Smith 1979
Smith 1759	Perrot 1980
Ferguson 1767	Kohlberg 1981
Reid 1785	Shweder, Turiel, and Much 1981
Bentham 1789	Gruter and Bohannan 1983
Paine 1792	Hampshire 1983
Von Savigny 1814	Grey 1983
Feuerbach 1833	Friedman 1985
Mill 1861	Kagan 1987
Bain 1868	Posner 1990
Von Jhering 1869	Tienson 1990
Darwin 1871	Ellickson 1991
Holland 1880	Flanagan 1991
Pollock 1882	Neale 1992
Nietzsche 1887	Fischer and Ravizza 1992
Gray 1909	Goldman 1993
Cohen 1916	Quinn 1993
Pareto 1935	Stich 1993
Ross 1939	Pinker 1994
Ladd 1957	Cosmides & Tooby 1994
Ryle 1958	McKie 1994
Brandt 1959	De Waal 1996
Oakeshott 1962	Fletcher 1998
Frankena 1963	Gert 1998
Fuller 1964	Harman 1998
Nozick 1968	Mikhail, Sorrentino, and Spelke 1998
Rawls 1971	Dwyer 1999
Kroy 1973	Jackendoff 1999
Simpson 1973	Mahlmann 1999
Gilmore 1974	Mikhail 2000

Table 7.2   **Five main problems of Universal Grammar and Universal Moral Grammar**

Problem	Universal Grammar	Universal Moral Grammar
Descriptive Adequacy	What constitutes knowledge of language?	What constitutes moral knowledge?
Explanatory Adequacy	How is knowledge of language acquired?	How is moral knowledge acquired?
Behavioral Adequacy	How is knowledge of language put to use?	How is moral knowledge put to use?
Neurocognitive Adequacy	How is knowledge of language physically realized in the brain?	How is moral knowledge physically realized in the brain?
Evolutionary Adequacy	How did knowledge of language evolve in the species?	How did moral knowledge evolve in the species?

UMG likewise begins by identifying five distinct questions that a science of human morality might answer (Table 7.2), and it seeks to clarify its research objectives by distinguishing two models, a perceptual model and an acquisition one, that an adequate moral theory must specify (Figure 7.1).

Simplifying somewhat for the purposes of this exposition, the initial goal in the theory of language is to determine how people can intuitively recognize the properties of novel expressions in their language, such as whether or not they are syntactically acceptable. This behavior can be usefully compared to the ability to determine whether or not a given action is morally permissible. The question that motivated Chomsky's famous book, *Syntactic Structures*, is "On what basis do people actually go about distinguishing grammatical from ungrammatical sentences?" (1957: 15). The related question that motivates UMG is "On what basis do people actually go about distinguishing permissible from impermissible acts?"

In Figure 7.1, provisional answers to this pair of questions are given by a linguistic grammar (LG) and moral grammar (MG), respectively. This perceptual level of analysis, however, is not the most significant part of either research program. In both cases, the research enterprise becomes more interesting and more difficult when one considers how each individual's linguistic or moral grammar is acquired. As Chomsky (1959: 574–578) famously predicted in his blistering review of B. F. Skinner's

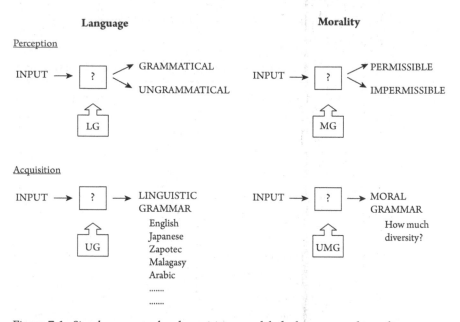

Figure 7.1 Simple perceptual and acquisition models for language and morality.

behaviorist manifesto, *Verbal Behavior* (1957), linguists and cognitive scientists have discovered that certain properties of the linguistic grammars that children acquire under normal social circumstances are dramatically underdetermined by the available evidence; there is a compelling basis, therefore, to assume that the human mind/brain is somehow specifically designed to acquire language by the natural development of the principles and parameters of a specific language faculty or Universal Grammar. Although this argument from the poverty of the stimulus (Chomsky, 1986) implies that some linguistic knowledge is innate, the variety of human languages provides an upper bound on this hypothesis; what is innate must be consistent with the observed diversity of human languages. Consequently, while UG must be rich and specific enough to get each child over the learning hump, it must also be flexible and accommodating enough to enable him or her to acquire different linguistic grammars in different cultural contexts.

In the case of moral cognition and moral development, it remains unclear whether models that incorporate parametric variation will likewise enter into the best explanation of UMG, the innate function or acquisition mechanism that presumably maps each child's early experience onto the mature state of his or her moral competence. Indeed, it remains unclear whether a comparable argument from the poverty of stimulus is plausible in the moral domain. What researchers need are answers to at least two questions: (1) What are the properties of the moral grammars that children do in fact acquire? (2) How diverse are these acquired moral grammars? Although it seems clear that cultural factors can have a dramatic influence, the available evidence suggests that at least some aspects of moral cognition may be innate, as I will explain in section IV.

Many significant objections can be raised about the UMG framework, of course, even on the basis of the fragmentary sketch offered thus far. Two of these objections are worth highlighting here because they bear directly on the topic of human rights and enable us to clarify and the scope and limits of this research program. First, there is the apparent existence of widespread moral disagreement, not only among but within diverse human societies and cultures. How can it be reconciled with the idea of a universal moral grammar? Second, there is the dismal historical record to which Freud refers, which clearly demonstrates that human beings are capable of committing the most horrible crimes imaginable and inflicting enormous suffering on one another. How is this history compatible with the idea of an inborn moral capacity in humans that distinguishes good and evil? For that matter, how can such a naïve and romantic idea be reconciled with countless acts of aggression, dehumanization, and exploitation that are still prevalent and indeed ubiquitous throughout the world today?

These are familiar objections, but the response is that they misunderstand the scope and limits of UMG and thereby rest on a mistake. The first objection mistakenly assumes that UMG denies or is otherwise incompatible with the existence of widespread moral disagreement. It also tacitly conflates at least two distinct types of disagreement: disagreement about the moral character of specific acts, practices, or institutional arrangements; and disagreement about the abstract moral theories or moral principles that best explain those particular moral judgments. The second objection likewise mistakenly assumes that UMG is a theory of voluntary human behavior that seeks to explain why humans often commit acts of aggression, dehumanization, exploitation, or other crimes and atrocities—rather than why humans often intuitively know or perceive that such acts are wrong. Both errors are easy to make, but they ultimately rest on an overblown and inaccurate conception of the features and operation of a mental grammar and, at a deeper level, the innate cognitive capacities that help to explain how that grammar is acquired by each individual on the basis of restricted and impoverished evidence.

To elaborate, there are at least three characteristics of UMG that deserve special emphasis in this context and help to clarify the nature of these misunderstandings. First, following Chomsky and in line with the fundamental methodological shift from behaviorism to mentalism, UMG distinguishes sharply between *moral competence* and *moral performance;* that is, between a person's intuitive moral knowledge (competence) and her actual voluntary behavior in concrete circumstances (performance) (see, e.g., Dwyer, 1999; Mikhail, 2000). The initial focus of this research program is thus the moral counterpart to what linguists sometimes call the *perception problem* (how people manage to recognize the properties of form and meaning in the linguistic stimuli they encounter) rather than the *production problem* (how people manage to use their linguistic knowledge in actual communication with one another in specific circumstances). Put differently, UMG is primarily concerned with the relatively simple problem of explaining the properties of people's rapid and spontaneous intuitive moral judgments and of the cognitive systems that generate and support these judgments (i.e., the problem of moral perception), not the more complex problem of explaining how people choose to act on the basis of these moral intuitions and multiple other factors, such as self-interest, false beliefs, prejudice, or ideology (i.e., the production problem). UMG thus recognizes and takes for granted that humans are complex creatures who are motivated by many interests, beliefs, and desires other than intuitions of justice and the impulse to pursue good and avoid evil. The scientist who seeks to discover what constitutes intuitive moral knowledge is studying one key factor involved in actual behavior, but not the only such factor, and perhaps not even the most important one. This distinction must be kept in mind when one is considering the scope and limits of this research program.

Second, adopting a traditional philosophical perspective (see, e.g., Bradley, 1962/1876; Brentano, 1969/1889; Hutcheson, 1971/1728; Leibniz, 1981/1705; Whewell, 1845), but departing sharply from the dominant trend in twentieth-century moral psychology (see, e.g., Kohlberg, 1981, 1984; Piaget, 1932), UMG draws a fundamental distinction between an individual's *operative* moral principles—the principles she actually uses in making her considered moral judgments—and her *express* principles—those statements she makes when she attempts to explain or justify those judgments (see, e.g., Mikhail et al., 1998). It makes no assumption that normal individuals are aware of the operative principles that constitute their intuitive moral knowledge or that they can become aware of them through introspection, or that their statements about them are necessarily accurate. On the contrary, it assumes that just as individuals are often unaware of or mistaken about the principles that guide their linguistic intuitions, so too they are often unaware of or mistaken about the principles that guide their moral intuitions. Searching for the seeds of a collective conscience in human nature is not the same thing as attempting to produce "a set of principles that all competent adults always and everywhere recognize as duties" (Posner, 1999: 18–19). The latter is too ambitious, but there is no reason why either the cognitive scientist or human rights theorist must be saddled with such an extravagant objective.

Finally, far from denying the existence of moral diversity, UMG is largely predicated on the existence of diversity and is directed to understanding and explaining it, much like UG itself. The key concept in both cases, however, is *constrained diversity*; that is, the recognition that there are identifiable limits within which normal human development unfolds in each case (see, e.g., Dwyer, 1999, 2007; Mikhail, 2000). In the case of language, for example, it is well known that some invented systems of communication (e.g., Esperanto, propositional calculus) are incompatible with UG and thus cannot be learned or acquired by the human language faculty in the same effortless way in which children acquire their native language (see, e.g., Baker, 2001; Pinker, 1994). Universal grammar is thus held to be "a theory of innate mechanisms, an underlying biological matrix that provides a framework in which growth of language proceeds," which provides structure and limits to normal language acquisition. Proposed principles of UG may thus be regarded "as an abstract partial specification of the genetic program that enables the child to interpret certain events as linguistic experience and to construct a system of rules and principles on the basis of that experience" (Chomsky, 1980: 187). Likewise, in the case of morality, universal moral grammar may be regarded as a theory of innate mechanisms that provides the basic framework and constraints within which human moral competence unfolds, and specific principles of UMG may be thought of as a partial characterization of the innate function or "morality acquisition device" that maps the developing child's relevant moral experience (her "moral data") into the mature state of her acquired moral competence (i.e., her moral grammar). Just as with language, moreover, some invented normative systems—for example, a completely strict liability moral system in which neither fault nor culpable mental states matter, or a system in which negligent homicide is judged to be systematically worse than intentional homicide—appear virtually "unlearnable" because they violate principles of UMG. One could perhaps deliberately acquire or internalize such a norm system, of course, but not simply by allowing one's natural moral sentiments to unfold.

A further point is that cultural differences are not always as extensive as they are made out to be, particularly in the domain of morality. For example, both human languages and human moralities are evidently quite diverse in many respects. Still, notwithstanding the more extreme claims of moral relativism, even the most superficial comparison of morality and language suggests that the development of moral competence is *more* constrained than the development of linguistic competence. Every normal human child can and will acquire any of the world's natural languages, merely by being exposed to them and growing up in an environment in which they are spoken. Nevertheless, the languages that children in diverse cultures acquire are not only remarkably different, but often mutually unintelligible. For example, a child who grows up speaking English is typically unable to locate the word boundaries of languages like Arabic, Hebrew, or Japanese—let alone to decide whether novel expressions in these languages are grammatical or ungrammatical. No comparable diversity exists in the moral domain, where the same event—say, a prison guard forcing a prisoner to stand naked and shackled in a painful position for hours on end—often triggers shared moral intuitions in persons from culturally divergent backgrounds. Further-more, individuals from diverse cultures frequently agree on how to analyze human actions into their main morally relevant components, such as act, intent, motive, cause and effect, foreseeable consequences, and other material and im-material circumstances. If the claims of extreme moral relativism were correct, then international human rights norms would be impossible, because the moral intuitions they embody and their conceptual building blocks would admit too much variation. Yet the Universal Declaration of Human Rights, International Criminal Court, and other familiar human rights instruments are real phe-nomena, which our best scientific theories of moral psychology must be consis-tent with, if not explain. Collectively, these international agreements appear to exhibit a degree of shared moral intuition that goes well beyond anything com-parable in the case of language.

Returning to the main theme, the simple point I wish to make is that in light of these qualifications, all of the foregoing distinctions can help to explain many familiar observations and to resolve many familiar quandaries in the domain of human rights policy and advocacy. For example, the distinction between operative and express principles helps to explain a familiar phenom-enon of human rights advocacy, which is that the "locus of moral certitude" (Jonsen and Toulmin, 1988: 16) in cases involving the concrete application of human rights norms is often located in the practical judgment of *whether* a given action, practice, or institutional arrangement is impermissible or unjust, rather than in the abstract or theoretical question of *why* this is so. The latter, more abstract question often admits of widespread disagreement, but the former practical question does so much less frequently. A famous episode in the drafting of the Universal Declaration of Human Rights, related by the French philosopher Jacques Maritain, illustrates the point. In 1947, while the United Nations Human Rights Commission was engaged in the preparation of the UDHR, the United Nations Educational, Scientific and Cultural Orga-nization (UNESCO) convened a series of meetings of writers and philoso-phers from around the world to discuss the philosophical foundation of human rights. To the surprise of many observers, these diverse thinkers were able to reach agreement on a highly specific list of fundamental human rights. Maritain (1949: 9) writes that at one of the UNESCO meetings, "someone expressed astonishment that certain champions of violently opposed ideolo-gies had agreed on a list of those rights. 'Yes,' they said, 'we agree about the rights *but on condition that no one asks us why.*' That 'why' is where the argument begins."

From a scientific perspective, the general phenomenon Maritain describes is entirely predictable, and it is in line with a substantial and growing body of evi-dence suggesting that much of what people do, they do unconsciously and for reasons that are inaccessible to them (Greene 2008; see also Gopnik, 1993; Nisbett and Wilson, 1977; White, 1988). The explanation of Maritain's specific observation thus appears relatively simple: considered moral judgments typically involve unconscious inferences, that is, mental operations that are not consciously accessible. In this respect, moral cognition may be compared not only to language perception but also to numerous other cognitive capacities such as vision, depth perception, musical cognition, and face recognition, all of which also depend on unconscious mental operations. The central challenge facing cognitive scientists in all of these domains is to extract and understand the operation of the mind's hidden rules of intuitive judgment. Moral psychology is no different from other domains in this regard. Even in the case of a higher mental faculty as diverse as language, moreover, it makes sense from a scientific point of view to assume that there is a single human language, as Chomsky (1975, 1995), Steven Pinker (1994), and other leading commentators have often observed. If there is a "single mental design" (Pinker, 1994: 430) underlying all known human languages, then it is not clear on what *empirical* grounds Ignatieff, Rorty, and other skeptics can so confidently deny the hypothesis that human beings share a common moral faculty, one rich enough to provide the foundation of a system of human rights and obligations.

IV. Converging Evidence

The foregoing remarks are highly abstract and comprise merely the skeleton of the research program based on an analogy between ethics and linguistics that has resurfaced and generated considerable public attention in recent years (see, e.g., Miller, 2008; Pinker, 2008; Saxe, 2005). It remains to be shown that the linguistic analogy is plausible, that the hypothesis of innate moral knowledge it implies is supported by a substantial body of empirical evidence, and that the conception of moral psychology it advances has something important to say about the foundation of human rights.

In keeping with the focus of this volume, the following discussion along these lines is selective and emphasizes those ideas and research findings that bear most directly on an interpretation of UMG that implies that human beings possess tacit or implicit knowledge of specific, human rights-related norms, together with a natural ability to compute mental representations of human acts and their morally salient components. The evidence that humans possess this knowledge and set of associated mental and behavioral capacities comes from multiple disciplines: developmental and social psychology, experimental philosophy, ethology, cognitive neuroscience, comparative linguistics, deontic logic, legal anthropology, and comparative law are just some of the fields that

supply grounds for affirming the plausibility of this hypothesis. None of this evidence is conclusive, and all of it is open to competing interpretations. Collectively, however, this evidence provides considerable support for the innate and
universal moral capacities presupposed by many leading human rights instruments (see, e.g., Glendon, 2001; Hunt, 2007; Meron, 2000; Wills, 1978).

A. Behavioral Studies of Children

In his masterpiece, *De Jure Belli et Pacis* (*On the Law of War and Peace*), the Dutch
jurist and philosopher Hugo Grotius defended the reality and universality of
moral distinctions and their foundation in human conscience with a poverty of
the stimulus argument of his own, observing that "some disposition to do good
to others appears" in infants "even before their training has begun"; consequently, "compassion breaks out spontaneously at that age" (1925/1625: 91). A
growing body of behavioral research suggests that Grotius's perceptive observations were correct. Scientists have documented that feelings of compassion and
impulses to assist others emerge early and apparently universally in human development. Moreover, these empathic responses appear to have deep evolutionary roots. Rats experience distress when exposed to the screams of other
rats (Church, 1959); likewise, chimpanzees and other great apes seek to console
the victim of an attack (De Waal, 2006). For their part, human babies cry more
in response to the cries of other babies than to tape recordings of their *own*
crying, implying that "they are responding to their awareness of someone else's
pain, not merely to a certain pitch of sound" (Bloom, 2010). Human children
also appear biologically predisposed to comfort others who are experiencing
emotional distress and, more broadly, to help others achieve their goals, to share
valuable resources with them, and to provide them with helpful information
(Batson, 1991; Warneken and Tomasello, 2009). Summarizing this research,
psychologists Felix Warneken and Michael Tomasello write that "from an early
age human infants are naturally empathetic, helpful, generous, and informative"
(Warkenen and Tomasello, 2009: 401). Simply put, Grotius apparently was
right and Freud was wrong or at least severely one sided in his bleak conception
of human nature.

In defending the existence of a common law of nations derived from principles of justice rather than express agreement or positive enactment, Grotius also
affirmed the traditional distinction between *mala in se* and *mala prohibita*: acts
that are inherently wrong, and thus imply inherent or natural rights; and those
that are merely authoritatively prohibited. Along the same lines, he held that
"the source of *Jus*, or Natural Law, properly called" could be found in "the nature
of the human intellect" and that the human faculty of moral judgment was
engraved with basic rules of criminal and civil liability: for example, "the rule of

abstaining from that which belongs to other persons; and if we have in our possession anything of another's, the restitution of it, or of any gain which we have made from it; the fulfilling of promises, and the reparation of damage done by fault; and the recognition of certain things as meriting . . . punishment" (1925/1625: 8).

Surprising as it may seem, Grotius's ambitious defense of a natural jurisprudence in these passages has begun to receive considerable empirical support in the past few decades. Researchers have discovered that the untutored moral intuitions of both adults and children are surprisingly complex and exhibit many characteristics of a well-developed legal code, including abstract theories of crime, tort, contract, and agency. For example, children as young as three and four years of age appear to utilize what is, in effect, a *mala in se/mala prohibita* distinction when making moral judgments, distinguishing "genuine" moral violations (e.g., battery, theft) from violations of social conventions (e.g., wearing pajamas to school) (Smetana, 1983; Turiel, 1983). Three- and four-year-olds also use information about an actor's intent or purpose to distinguish two acts with same result (Baird, 2001; Nelson, 1980)—just as the laws of war and all highly developed legal systems typically do (see, e.g., *Morissette v. United States*, 342 U.S. 246 (1952)). Four- and five-year-olds use a proportionality principle to determine the correct level of punishment for principals and accessories (Finkel, Liss, and Moran, 1997). Likewise, five-year-olds display a nuanced understanding of negligence and restitution (Shultz, Wright, and Schleifer, 1986).

One man shoots and kills his victim on the mistaken belief that he is aiming at a tree stump. A second man shoots and kills his victim on the mistaken belief that killing is not wrong. Just as adults and mature legal systems typically do, five- and six-year old children distinguish cases like these in conformity with the distinction between mistake of law and mistake of fact, recognizing that false factual beliefs can often exculpate, but false moral beliefs typically do not (see, e.g., Chandler, Sokal, and Wainryb, 2000). Five- and six-year-olds also calibrate the punishment they assign to harmful acts on the basis of mitigating factors, such as provocation, necessity, and public duty (Darley, Klossen, and Zanna, 1978). Six- and seven-year-olds exhibit a keen sense of procedural fairness, reacting negatively when punishment is inflicted without affording the parties notice and the right to be heard (Gold, Darley, Hilton, and Zanna, 1984). In more complex cases of necessity, such as the trolley problems (Foot, 1967; Thomson, 1985; see Table 7.3), children as young as three are willing to permit harming one to save five, but only if the chosen means is not wrong, the bad effects are not disproportionate to the good effects, and no morally preferable alternative is available; that is, only in accord with the principle of double effect (Pellizzoni et al., 2010; cf. Mikhail, 2002; Mikhail and Sorrentino, 1999).

In all of these cases and others like them, to explain the observable data scientists must be willing to attribute unconscious knowledge and complex mental operations to the child that go well beyond anything she has been taught. Indeed, as difficult to accept as it may seem, they must be prepared to assume that children possess an elaborate system of natural jurisprudence and an ability to compute mental representations of human acts and omissions in legally cognizable terms. In the case of trolley problems, for example, it seems clear that children must represent and evaluate these novel fact patterns in terms of properties like ends, means, side effects, and prima facie wrongs, such as battery, even where the stimulus contains no direct evidence of these properties. These concepts and the principles which underlie them are as far removed from experience as the hierarchical tree structures and recursive rules of linguistic grammars. It seems implausible to think that they are acquired by means of explicit instruction; examples in the surrounding environment; or any known processes of imitation, internalization, socialization, and the like. This conclusion becomes particularly compelling once one realizes that the moral intuitions in question cannot be explained by appeal to tacit or implicit knowledge of even the most sophisticated adult codifications of common legal norms, such as the Model Penal Code or the Restatement of Torts. Neither of these codifications recognizes a principle of necessity that is sensitive to the intended or causal *means* by which the greater harm or evil is avoided in cases where a choice of harms or evils is unavoidable. Yet ordinary individuals, including young children, appear to utilize a means-sensitive principle, such as the categorical imperative or the principle of double effect, to grasp the moral status of the acts in question. Hence, there are plausible grounds for assuming that at least some aspects of moral grammar and intuitive jurisprudence are innate, in the same dispositional sense in which puberty and other aspects of human biological development are innate (see generally Mikhail, 2000, 2002, 2007b, 2011; Mikhail et al., 1998; see also Chomsky, 1986; Descartes, 1986; Dwyer, 1999, 2004; Harman, 2000; Pellizzoni et al. 2010; Solum, 2006). This argument is not conclusive, however, and more research is needed to clarify the relevant conceptual and evidentiary issues.

B. Adult Judgment and Decision Making

Recent experimental research of adult judgment and decision making has likewise tended to reinforce and amplify the traditional rationalist argument that ordinary individuals are intuitive lawyers who possess a sophisticated natural jurisprudence. For example, Wilkinson-Ryan and Baron (2009) have documented that ordinary adults are acutely sensitive to the moral dimensions of breach of contract, especially the perceived intentions of the breaching party. Likewise, Cushman and colleagues (2006: 1082) found that adults make moral judgments in conformity with central doctrines of tort and criminal law, relying in particular on three key principles that distill the essence of purposeful battery: "(a) Harm caused by action is worse than harm caused by omission, (b) harm intended as a means to a goal is worse than harm foreseen as the side effect of a goal, and (c) harm involving physical contact with the victim is worse than harm involving no physical contact." In another important paper, Alter, Kernochan, and Darley (2007) found that adults apply the mistake of law defense differently depending on the perceived morality of the defendant's behavior at the time of the illegal act. The authors conclude that laypeople adopt a sophisticated just deserts approach to criminal law, which influences their responsiveness to a criminal defendant's claim of mistake or ignorance.

In perhaps the most dramatic recent behavioral experiment of this type, which targeted moral intuitions of proportionality, Robinson and Kurzban (2007) asked a demographically diverse group of adults to rank order 24 crime scenario descriptions according to the amount of punishment each act deserved. The results revealed an astonishing level of agreement in participants' ordinal ranking of these scenarios. Utilizing a common statistical measure of concordance, Kendall's coefficient of concordance ("Kendall's W"), in which 1.0 indicates perfect agreement and 0.0 indicates no agreement, the authors found a Kendall's W of 0.95 (with $p < .001$) for these intuitions. As the authors observe, "This is a striking level of agreement. One might expect a similarly high Kendall's W if subjects were asked to judge the relative brightness of different groupings of spots, for example." The authors further note that "[i]n the context of more subjective or complex comparisons, such as asking travel magazine readers to rank the attractiveness of eight different destinations, a Kendall's W of 0.52 is typical. When asking economists to rank the top twenty economics journals according to quality, one gets a Kendall's W of 0.095" (Robinson, Kurzban, and Jones, 2007: 1637–38). In short, the available evidence that can be gleaned from behavioral studies like that of Robinson and colleagues suggests that, as a general matter, many lay intuitions of justice are surprisingly nuanced, complex, and widely shared. The moral grammar hypothesis according to which ordinary individuals possess unconscious moral and legal knowledge (Mikhail, 2011) thus appears to have considerable empirical support. By contrast, the extreme relativist claim that cultural differences necessarily result in irreconcilable moral disagreements appears to be overstated, if not altogether untenable.

Perhaps the strongest evidence of the prevalence and indeed apparent universality of human rights-related norms comes from the experimental study of trolley problems and other cases of necessity (Table 7.3). In a series of experiments that began in the mid-1990s, my colleagues, Cristina Sorrentino and Elizabeth Spelke, and I began testing these problems on hundreds of individuals from diverse backgrounds, including both adults and children. The participants

Table 7.3 **Six Trolley Problems**

---

1. Bystander: Hank is taking his daily walk near the train tracks when he notices that the train that is approaching is out of control. Hank sees what has happened: the driver of the train saw five men walking across the tracks and slammed on the brakes, but the brakes failed and the driver fainted. The train is now rushing toward the five men. It is moving so fast that they will not be able to get off the track in time. Hank is standing next to a switch, which he can throw, that will turn the train onto a side track, thereby preventing it from killing the men. There is a man standing on the side track with his back turned. Hank can throw the switch, killing him; or he can refrain from doing this, letting the five die. Is it morally permissible for Hank to throw the switch?

---

2. Footbridge: Ian is taking his daily walk near the train tracks when he notices that the train that is approaching is out of control. Ian sees what has happened: the driver of the train saw five men walking across the tracks and slammed on the brakes, but the brakes failed and the driver fainted. The train is now rushing toward the five men. It is moving so fast that they will not be able to get off the track in time. Ian is standing next to a *heavy object*, which he can throw *onto the track in the path of the train*, thereby preventing it from killing the men. *The heavy object* is a man, standing *next to Ian* with his back turned. Ian can throw the *man*, killing him; or he can refrain from doing this, letting the five die. Is it morally permissible for Ian to throw the *man*?

---

3. Loop Track: Ned is taking his daily walk near the train tracks when he notices that the train that is approaching is out of control. Ned sees what has happened: the driver of the train saw five men walking across the tracks and slammed on the brakes, but the brakes failed and the driver fainted. The train is now rushing toward the five men. It is moving so fast that they will not be able to get off the track in time. Ned is standing next to a switch, which he can throw, that will *temporarily* turn the train onto a side track. *There is a heavy object on the side track. If the train hits the object, the object will slow the train down, giving the men time to escape. The heavy object* is a man, standing on the side track with his back turned. Ned can throw the switch, preventing the train from killing the men, but killing the man. Or he can refrain from doing this, letting the five die. Is it morally permissible for Ned to throw the switch?

---

4. Man-in-Front: Oscar is taking his daily walk near the train tracks when he notices that the train that is approaching is out of control. Oscar sees what has happened: the driver of the train saw five men walking across the tracks and slammed on the brakes, but the brakes failed and the driver fainted. The train is now rushing toward the five men. It is moving so fast that they will not be able to get off the track in time. Oscar is standing next to a switch, which he can throw, that will temporarily turn the train onto a side track. There is a heavy object on the side track. If the train hits the object, the object will slow the train down, giving the men time to escape. *There* is a man standing on the side track *in front of the heavy object* with his back turned. Oscar can throw the switch, preventing the train from killing the men, but killing the man; or he can refrain from doing this, letting the five die. Is it morally permissible for Oscar to throw the switch?

Table 7.3 (*continued*)

---

5. Drop Man: Victor is taking his daily walk near the train tracks when he notices that the train that is approaching is out of control. Victor sees what has happened: the driver of the train saw five men walking across the tracks and slammed on the brakes, but the brakes failed and the driver fainted. The train is now rushing toward the five men. It is moving so fast that they will not be able to get off the track in time. Victor is standing next to a switch, which he can throw, that will drop a heavy object into the path of the train, thereby preventing it from killing the men. The heavy object is a man, who is standing on a footbridge overlooking the tracks. Victor can throw the switch, killing him; or he can refrain from doing this, letting the five die. Is it morally permissible for Victor to throw the switch?

---

6. Collapse Bridge: Walter is taking his daily walk near the train tracks when he notices that the train that is approaching is out of control. Walter sees what has happened: the driver of the train saw five men walking across the tracks and slammed on the brakes, but the brakes failed and the driver fainted. The train is now rushing toward the five men. It is moving so fast that they will not be able to get off the track in time. Walter is standing next to a switch, which he can throw, that will *collapse a footbridge overlooking the tracks* into the path of the train, thereby preventing it from killing the men. *There* is a man standing on a footbridge. Walter can throw the switch, killing him; or he can refrain from doing this, letting the five die. Is it morally permissible for Walter to throw the switch?

---

in our initial experiments included several groups of American adults, several groups of American children, one group of recent Chinese immigrants to the United States, and two groups of master's students at Harvard University's Kennedy School of Government. Collectively, the participants hailed from a diverse set of countries and regions, including Belgium, Canada, China, Columbia, Denmark, Egypt, Finland, France, Germany, India, Iran, Israel, Italy, Japan, Lebanon, Mexico, Puerto Rico, South Africa, and South Korea. Our central aim was to pursue the central ideas of UMG and to begin to investigate a variety of empirical questions that arise within this framework. Our basic prediction was that the moral intuitions elicited by two of the most familiar trolley problems (Bystander and Footbridge) would be widely shared, irrespective of demographic variables such as race, sex, age, religion, national origin, or level of formal education (see generally Mikhail, 2000, 2002; Mikhail, Sorrentino, and Spelke, 1998). This prediction was confirmed, and our initial findings have now been replicated and extended with over 200,000 individuals from over 120 countries (Pinker, 2008; see also Miller, 2008; Saxe, 2005). The result is perhaps the first qualitatively new data set in the history of the discipline, which has transformed the science of moral psychology and opened up many new and promising avenues of investigation (see, e.g., Bartels, 2008; Bucciarelli, Khemlani, and Johnson-Laird, 2008;

Cushman, Young, and Hauser, 2006; Dupoux and Jacob, 2007; Greene, Lindsell, Clarke, Nystrom, and Cohen, submitted; Koenigs, Young, Adolphs, Tranel, Cushman, Hauser, and Damasio, 2007; Lombrozo, 2008; Machery, 2007; Moore, Clark, and Kane, 2008; Nichols and Mallon, 2006; Sinnott-Armstrong, Mallon, McCoy, and Hull, 2008; Waldmann and Dieterich, 2007; Young, Cushman, Hauser, and Saxe, 2007).

Depending on one's philosophical commitments, the fact that trolley problems elicit "complex, instinctive, and worldwide moral intuitions" (Pinker, 2008) could be looked upon with dismay or regret. After all, there is no apparent difference between any of these problems in terms of the final outcome and number of lives saved. Perhaps it follows that these intuitions cannot be given a principled explanation, and the data are simply another indication of widespread bias, irrationality, or incoherence in commonsense intuitive judgments, similar to familiar heuristics and biases in other domains (see, e.g., Sunstein, 2005). In a number of publications (Mikhail, 2005, 2007, 2009, 2011), I have resisted this conclusion and have argued not only that there is a principled explanation of these intuitions, but also that it is one that progressive human rights advocates should *welcome* because it suggests that certain basic moral principles that are already reflected in international humanitarian law may be innate and universal, as many philosophers, jurists, and cognitive scientists have often assumed.

Several interrelated observations support this line of argument. First, trolley problems can be given a simple and elegant solution by assuming that Grotius and other Enlightenment figures were essentially correct: ordinary individuals are intuitive lawyers, who possess implicit knowledge of basic rules of criminal and civil law, along with a natural readiness to compute the specific mental representations presupposed by these rules. In particular, an indefinitely large class of these problems and other familiar cases of necessity can be explained by postulating tacit or unconscious knowledge of a small set of rules and principles, including the prohibition of intentional battery, the prohibition of intentional homicide, the rescue principle, and the principle of double effect. The prohibition of intentional battery forbids purposefully or knowingly causing harmful or offensive contact with another individual or otherwise invading her physical integrity without his or her consent (see, e.g., Prosser, 1941). The prohibition of intentional homicide likewise forbids purposely or knowingly killing another individual without her consent (see, e.g., LaFave, 2003). The rescue principle is a familiar principle of common morality—but not the common law—that forbids one from failing to prevent an easily preventable death or other serious misfortune, where this can be accomplished without risking one's own life or safety, or without violating other fundamental moral precepts (see, e.g., Bentham, 1948/1789; Scanlon, 1998; Singer, 1972; Weinrib, 1980). Finally, the principle of double effect is a complex principle of justification, narrower in scope than the traditional necessity defense, which holds that an otherwise prohibited action, such as battery, that has both good and bad effects may be permissible if the prohibited act itself is not directly intended, the good but not the bad effects are directly intended, the good effects outweigh the bad effects, and no morally preferable alternative is available (see, e.g., Fischer and Ravizza, 1992).

All of these norms require further clarification, of course, but, taken together and suitably formalized (Mikhail, 2009), they can be used to explain the relevant pattern of intuitions in a relatively straightforward manner. For example, the key distinction that that explains the standard cases in the literature is that the agent commits one or more distinct batteries prior to and as a means of achieving his good end in the impermissible conditions (e.g., Footbridge, Loop Track, Drop Man), whereas these violations are subsequent and foreseen side effects in the permissible conditions (e.g., Bystander, Man-in-Front, Collapse Bridge). The structural descriptions implied by this explanation can be exhibited in a two-dimensional tree diagram, or act tree, successive nodes of which bear a generation relation to one another that is asymmetric, irreflexive, and transitive. Further, a variety of independent experimental tests can be used to verify the structural properties of these unconscious act trees (Goldman, 1970; Mikhail, 2005, 2009; see Figure 7.2).

Second, the moral grammar hypothesis illustrates how the poverty of the stimulus argument operates at the level of perceptual processes themselves. It thereby provides an important window into the unconscious inferences that support and generate considered moral judgments. For example, the main scientific problem implied by the foregoing explanation is how people manage to

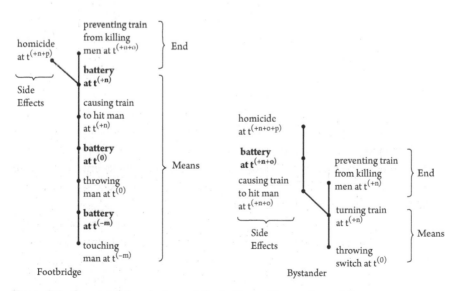

Figure 7.2 Structural descriptions of footbridge and bystander problems.

compute a full structural description of the relevant action that incorporates properties like ends, means, side effects, and prima facie wrongs like battery, even when the stimulus contains no direct evidence for these properties. This is a distinct poverty of stimulus problem, involving perception rather than acquisition (Fodor, 1985), similar in principle to determining how people manage to recover a three-dimensional representation from a two-dimensional stimulus in the theory of vision (e.g., Marr, 1982) or to recognize the word boundaries in unmarked auditory patterns in the theory of language (e.g., Chomsky and Halle, 1968; Jackendoff, 1994). In our case, the question is how, and why, individuals make the particular inferences they do about the various agents and actions in our examples, even when we deliberately deprive them of direct evidence of those agents' mental states and other morally salient properties.

Elsewhere (see, e.g., Mikhail, 2007, 2009), I have shown how these properties can be recovered from the stimulus by a sequence of operations that are largely mechanical. The main steps in this process include (i) identifying the various action descriptions in the stimulus; (ii) placing them in an appropriate temporal order; (iii) decomposing them into their underlying causative and semantic structures; (iv) applying certain moral and logical principles to these underlying structures to generate representations of good and bad effects; (v) computing the intentional structure of the relevant acts and omissions by inferring in the absence of conflicting evidence that agents intend good effects and avoid bad effects—that is, by extending a presumption of innocence and good intentions to these agents; and (vi) deriving representations of morally salient acts like battery and situating them in the correct location of one's act tree. Although each of these operations is relatively simple in its own right, the overall length, complexity, and abstract nature of these computations, along with their rapid, intuitive, and at least partially inaccessible character lends at least modest support to the hypothesis that they depend on innate, domain-specific algorithms.

Third, when properly constructed, action plan diagrams not only enable one to predict moral intuitions with surprising accuracy, but also to see at a glance a variety of structural relationships, including those that might have been overlooked or ignored. For example, act trees can be used not only to identify the basic differences between the Footbridge and Bystander problems, but also to explain the *variance* one finds in highly refined manipulations of these cases, such as the Loop Track, Man-In-Front, Drop Man, and Collapse Bridge problems. As Figure 7.3a reveals, the intuitive data in these six cases form a remarkably consistent pattern, with permissibility judgments increasing linearly across the six conditions. Moreover, as Figure 7.3b illustrates, these results can be tentatively explained as a function of the properties of each problem's structural description. Other things equal, acts are more likely to be judged permissible as counts of battery committed as a means decrease from three (Footbridge) to two (Drop

Man) to one (Loop Track), and as these violations become side effects and additional structural features come into play. In Man-In-Front, the agent's goal presumably is to save the men by causing the train to hit the object but not the man, yet the actual result (not shown) is likely to involve hitting the man before hitting the object and slowing the train down; hence from an ex post perspective, the agent will have committed a battery prior to and as a means of achieving his good end. Likewise, in Collapse Bridge, one or more counts of battery must necessarily occur before the good end is achieved. By contrast, in Bystander, battery and homicide are side effects that occur only after the good end has been secured by turning the train onto the side track. In short, not only the modal data but also the statistical variance at issue in various trolley problems can be explained with reference to the implicit geometry of their corresponding act trees.

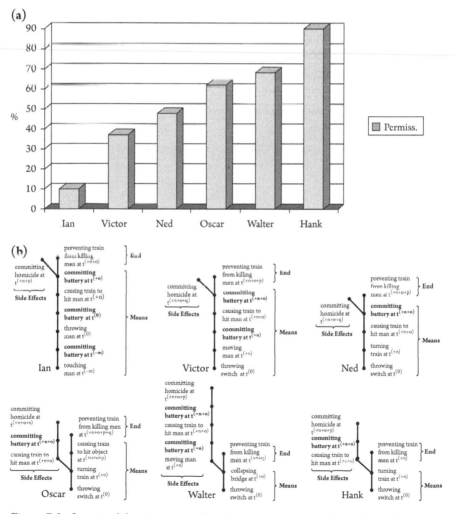

Figure 7.3 Structural descriptions explain the variance in six trolley problems. Data in (a) from Mikhail, 2002, 2007, 2011.

Finally, and most important for our purposes, it is vital to recognize that many of the rules and representations implicit in the moral grammar hypothesis and in particular concepts like ends, means, side effects, and prima facie wrongs such as battery and homicide already play a critical role in many common legal doctrines (Figure 7.4). Of particular significance, these doctrines include laws of war pertaining to noncombatant immunity, proportionality, and military necessity; the prohibition against torture and extrajudicial killing; the general protections extended to both civilian populations and belligerents; and other elements of international law. For example, the principle of double effect's implied norm of noncombatant immunity—that is, its prohibition against directly targeting civilians, together with its tightly qualified acceptance of harming civilians as a necessary side effect of an otherwise justifiable military operation—has long been part of customary international law and is codified in Article 48 of the First Protocol (1977) to the 1949 Geneva Conventions (see, e.g., Henkin, Pugh, Schacter, and Smit, 1992: 364–365). Likewise, the principle's implied norm of proportionality is also part of customary international law and is codified in Articles 22–23 of the Hague Convention of 1907 (see, e.g., Henkin et al., 1992: 368). The prohibitions of intentional battery and homicide, of course, are lesser included offenses of a wide range of human rights abuses, including murder, extermination, deportation, torture, rape, genocide, and other crimes against humanity. Finally, the rescue principle is a familiar motivation for international humanitarian relief efforts in Darfur, Gaza, Haiti, and other troubled regions throughout the world.

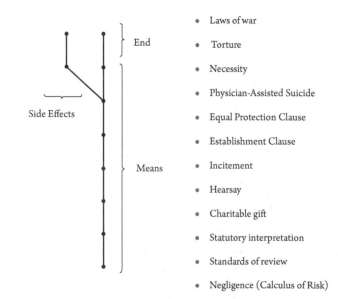

Figure 7.4 Common legal analysis: Ends, means, and side effects.

This list of potential applications presumably could be expanded, moreover, for even on a narrow interpretation, the moral grammar hypothesis also implicates many other fundamental rights protected by the laws of war, Universal Declaration, International Criminal Court, and a number of other important human treaties and instruments, including but not limited to freedom from enslavement, false imprisonment, or sexual slavery (ICC, Article 7); the right to equality and nondiscrimination (UDHR, Article 2); the right to life, liberty, and the security of one's person (UDHR, Article 3); freedom from torture or cruel, inhuman, or degrading treatment (UDHR, Article 5); and the presumption of innocence (UDHR, Article 11). The existence of these and other plausible links between cognitive science and human rights further reinforces a central thesis of this chapter: Grotius and other Enlightenment authors were correct to assume that a common law of nations can be derived from a common moral faculty or conscience with which the human mind is naturally endowed, quite apart from any positive law, consent, or customary practice (cf. Hutcheson, 2007/1747; Smith, 1976/1759).

C. Animal Studies

In *The Descent of Man*, Charles Darwin affirmed his belief in an innate moral faculty, explaining that he fully agreed with "the judgment of those writers who maintain that of all the differences between man and the lower animals, the moral sense or conscience is by far the most important" (Darwin, 1981/1871: 70). Darwin insisted that the moral sense was not a mysterious gift of unknown origin, however, but the natural result of human evolution, with identifiable antecedents in the social instincts of other animals. He thus famously argued that "any animal whatever, endowed with well-marked social instincts, would inevitably acquire a moral sense or conscience, as soon as its intellectual powers had become as well developed, or as nearly developed, as in man" (id. at 71–72). And he laid the foundation of subsequent research on the evolution of morality and cooperation by examining a range of related animal instincts and behaviors, including their sociability, desire for companionship, and the misery they feel when they are abandoned; their love, sympathy, and compassion for one another; and their mutual willingness to sacrifice themselves and to render services to one another when hunting or defending against attack.

Darwin held that the social instincts of nonhuman animals developed "for the general good of the community," which he defined as "the means by which the greatest possible number of individuals can be reared in full vigor and health, with all their faculties perfect, under the conditions to which they are exposed" (id. at 97–98). The same was true of Homo sapiens, he inferred; therefore, neither egoism nor a universalistic hedonism (the "Greatest Happiness Principle") was descriptively adequate: "When a man risks his life to save that of a fellow-creature, it seems more appropriate to say that he acts for the general good or welfare, rather than for the general happiness of mankind" (id. at 98). Darwin endorsed Herbert Spencer's conclusion that "'the experiences of utility organized and consolidated through all past generations of the human race, have been producing corresponding modifications, which, by continued transmission and accumulation, have become in us certain faculties of moral intuition—certain emotions responding to right and wrong conduct, which have no apparent basis in the individual experiences of utility'" (id. at 101–102). Finally, Darwin held that the combination of social instincts, active intellectual powers, and the effects of habit would "naturally lead to the golden rule: 'As ye would that men should do to you, do ye to them likewise.'" This rule, he wrote, "lies at the foundation of morality" (id. at 106).

After a period of relative misunderstanding and neglect that was dominated by "social Darwinism" and other perversions of ethical naturalism, researchers have recently begun to return to and build upon Darwin's pioneering attempt to understand the origin of the moral sense from the side of natural history. A wide range of animal studies has helped to improve our knowledge of the behavioral, cognitive, and emotional capacities of nonhuman animals and thereby to dismantle many of the perceived boundaries between human social and moral instincts and those of other animals. For example, building on important late nineteenth- and early twentieth-century studies of the natural origins of human conscience (see, e.g., Kropotkin, 1993/1924; Spencer, 1978/1897; Westermarck, 1908), a number of scientists have recently investigated the evolutionary foundations of unselfish giving (e.g., de Waal, Leimgruber, and Greenberg, 2008) and reciprocal altruism (e.g., Gintis, Bowles, Boyd, and Fehr, 2003; Hamilton, 1964; Trivers, 1971). Other researchers, focusing specifically on notions of unfairness and retributive justice, have argued that nonhuman animals possess at least rudimentary counterparts to core human intuitions about what constitutes serious wrongdoing and how it should be punished. For example, several species of nonhuman primates respond negatively to perceived inequity (see, e.g., Brosnan et al., 2010; De Waal, 2009). Wolves and other canines apparently refuse to associate with those who violate social rules against injury (Bekoff, 2004), and behavior akin to theft is punished in a range of species (see, e.g., Clutton-Brock and Parker, 1995; see generally Robinson and Kurzban, 2007). Summarizing these findings and the overall picture emerging in animal studies, two commentators write:

> Mammals living in tight social groups appear to live according to codes of conduct, including both prohibitions against certain kinds of behavior and expectations for other kinds of behavior. They live by a set of

rules that fosters a relatively harmonious and peaceful coexistence. They're naturally cooperative, will offer aid to their fellows, sometimes in return for like aid, sometimes with no expectation of immediate reward. They build relationships of trust. What's more, they appear to feel for other members of their communities, especially relatives, but also neighbors and sometimes even strangers—often showing signs of what looks very much like compassion and empathy. (Bekoff and Pierce, 2009: 5)

The fundamental insight driving this ongoing research as it relates to human evolution is Aristotle's as well as Darwin's, reinforced and amplified by later naturalists such as Peter Kropotkin (1993/1924) and Frans de Waal (2006, 2010): humans are inherently social and normative creatures, and complex animal societies appeared on earth long before the appearance of human beings.

D. Cognitive Neuroscience

Many readers will be familiar with the famous case of Phineas Gage, a nineteenth-century railroad worker in Vermont whose moral capacities were significantly impaired after an accidental explosion which caused a large tamping iron to be driven completely through his cheek and out the top of his head, destroying much of his ventromedial prefrontal cortex in the process. Amazingly, Gage not only survived the incident but also emerged with his cognitive capacities virtually intact. Nevertheless, thereafter he frequently exhibited irresponsible and antisocial behaviors, compromised moral decision making, and various emotional deficits. His case was an early indication that at least some of the processes and components of moral cognition may be dissociable from other cognitive capacities (Harlow, 1848, 1868; see also MacMillan, 2000; Young, 1970).

In the past few years, numerous clinical and experimental studies have confirmed that distinct cortical regions are involved in moral judgment and that damage to various parts of the brain can lead to specific deficits in moral judgment while leaving other social, linguistic, and cognitive abilities unimpaired (see, e.g., Blair, 2009; Damasio et al., 1994; Moll et al., 2005; Prehn and Heekeren, 2009). For example, damage to prefrontal cortex impairs moral cognition but leaves other forms of cognition intact (Damasio et al., 1994). Likewise, psychopaths have difficulty distinguishing moral and conventional violations, apparently regarding moral rules as if they were conventional (Blair, 1995, 2002).

More recently, Greene and colleagues (2001, 2004) identified a set of brain regions associated with judging actions involving an actor's use of battery, homicide, and rape or sexual assault as a means to achieve his objectives, including the medial prefrontal cortex (mPFC), posterior cingulum cortex (PCC), posterior superior temporal sulcus (pSTS), and amygdala (see generally Mikhail, 2011). They also gathered reaction-time data that suggest that people are slow to approve of these violations but quick to condemn them; by contrast, approvals and disapprovals are equally fast for judgments that are broadly consequentialist or morally indifferent (Greene et al., 2001). Subsequently, Mendez et al. (2005) found that patients with frontotemporal dementia, who are known for their "emotional blunting," were disproportionally likely to approve of committing battery or homicide as a means to save others in cases of necessity like the Footbridge Problem. Koenigs et al. (2007) and Ciaremelli et al. (2007) observed similar results in patients with emotional deficits due to lesions in the ventromedial prefrontal cortex (VMPFC). Heekeren and colleagues (2003, 2005) discovered no effects in the amygdala when they used narratives devoid of violence, but they found increased activity in the amygdala in response to stimuli involving bodily harm. Jena Schaich-Borg and her colleagues (2006) found that the anterior superior temporal sulcus (aSTS) and VMPFC exhibit increased activity in response to moral dilemmas in which the harm is an intended means, as opposed to a foreseen side effect. Finally, Liane Young, Rebecca Saxe, and their colleagues (Young and Saxe, 2008; Young et al., 2007) compared the neural responses to intended harms, accidental harms, failed attempted harms, and ordinary harmless actions in a 2 × 2 design that crossed mental state information (the agent did/did not intend the harm) and outcome information (the harm did/did not result). They found that the mPFC, PCC, and especially the right temporal parietal junction (RTPJ) were selectively recruited for intended harms and failed attempts, indicating that processes for ascribing morally salient beliefs and intentions to individuals are localized in these regions.

In sum, a variety of functional imaging and patient studies have led researchers to conclude that a fairly consistent network of brain regions is involved in moral judgment tasks, including those judgments that implicate human rights-related norms. These regions include the anterior prefrontal cortex, medial and lateral orbitofrontal cortex, dorsolateral and ventromedial prefrontal cortex, anterior temporal lobes, superior temporal sulcus, and posterior cingulate/precuneus region (Moll et al., 2005; see also Greene and Haidt, 2002; Prehn and Heekeren, 2009). The picture emerging from these studies is complex, but at a minimum these findings flatly contradict the breezy armchair theorizing of moral philosophers like Kurt Baier, who as we have seen held that the "absolutely fatal objection" to the moral sense theory "is that there is no part of a man's body whose removal or injury would specifically affect his knowledge of the rightness or wrongness of certain types or courses of action" (Baier, 1965/1958: 22–23). Fortunately, this type of philosophical dogmatism has given way in recent years to a more empirically grounded approach to moral psychology by philosophers and psychologists alike (see, e.g., Haidt, 2010; Knobe and Nichols, 2008).

E. Comparative Linguistics and Deontic Logic

In *A Dissertation Upon the Nature of Virtue,* another classic Enlightenment text, Joseph Butler threw down the gauntlet against any extreme form of moral relativism that would deny the existence of a common moral faculty. Along the way he made some penetrating observations about moral cognition that many subsequent British and American writers understood had to be explained by any adequate moral philosophy (see, e.g., Meyer, 1972; Schneewind, 1977):

> That we have this moral approving and disapproving faculty is certain from our experiencing it in ourselves, and recognizing it in each other. It appears from our exercising it unavoidably, in the approbation and disapprobation even of feigned characters; from the words "right" and "wrong," "odious" and "amiable," "base" and "worthy," with many others of like signification in all languages applied to actions and characters; from the many written systems of morals which suppose it, since it cannot be imagined that all these authors, throughout all these treatises, had absolutely no meaning at all to their words, or a meaning merely chimerical; from our natural sense of gratitude, which implies a distinction between merely being the instrument of good and intending it; from the like distinction everyone makes between injury and mere harm, which Hobbes says is peculiar to mankind, and between injury and just punishment, a distinction plainly natural, prior to the consideration of human laws. It is manifest [that a] great part of common language, and of common behavior over the world, is formed upon the supposition of such a moral faculty, whether called conscience, moral reason, moral sense, or divine reason; whether considered as a sentiment of the understanding or as a perception of the heart, or, which seems the truth, as including both (Butler, 1983/1726: 69)

Butler's contention that certain basic moral distinctions are manifested in human languages throughout the world is controversial. Yet in recent years it, too, has begun to be supported by a considerable body of empirical evidence. For example, every natural human language appears to have words or devices to express basic deontic concepts such as *may, must, must not,* or their equivalents (see, e.g., Bybee and Fleischman, 1995; see Figure 7.5). These concepts comprise the basic categorization scheme of most human moral, legal, and religious systems, and their natural domain of application consists of the voluntary actions of moral agents (as Butler averred; see supra at 70). Furthermore, it is well known that the branch of logic known as deontic logic—the logical study of obligation, permission, and other deontic modalities—can be formalized. In particular, the three primary deontic operators can be placed in the traditional *square of opposition and equipollence,* similar to those for quantified and modal forms (see, e.g., Prior, 1955, 1958; Von Wright, 1951, 1963; see Figure 7.6).

From a scientific perspective, the fact that ordinary moral cognition appears to rely on deontic concepts in making moral judgments, as opposed to countless other ways to conceptualize a system of moral or social norms, appears to be a nontrivial human universal. In addition, at least three further points about Figure 7.6 bear emphasis in this context. First, this diagram reveals that an accurate description of the deontic component of human moral competence can be extremely simple, orderly, and algorithmic. In fact, as the equipollence relations (i.e., logical equivalences) expressed in the four corners of this figure imply, the moral theorist needs to select only one of the three principal deontic concepts—for example, the

Forbidden	Permissible	Obligatory
"must not"	"may"	"must"
haram	mubah	wajib
verboten	zulassig	obligat
ne...pas	pouvoir	devoir/il faut
(neg)	poder	deber
interdictum	licitus	debitum
far inte	matte	bora
myen a tway	to tway	ya hay/tway
swanelo	sibaka	mwilla
....	....	....

Figure 7.5 Deontic modalities in natural languages.

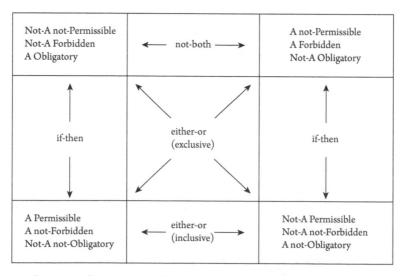

Figure 7.6 Deontic logic: Square of opposition and equipollence.

concept *forbidden*—and assume it to be a deontic primitive. Then with the aid of just two logical connectives and the concepts of *act* ("A") and *omission* ("not-A"), the remaining expressions at issue can be mechanically defined.

Second, Figure 7.6 enables one to grasp how the basic principles of deontic logic interface with two other bodies of information: (1) substantive legal rules that seek to delineate what it means for one person to wrong another; and (2) linguistic and logical rules that enable statements of rights to be generated on that basis, including the bridge principles and linguistic transformation rules that formalize Hohfeld's (1913, 1917) influential analysis of fundamental legal conceptions (Figure 7.7). By combining these different sets of rules with the "complex, instinctive, worldwide moral intuitions" (Pinker, 2008) that cognitive scientists have begun to identify, specific statements about rights, duties, liberties, and so forth can be rigorously derived and, in effect, proven as theorems in a computational model of moral cognition. In this way, a rich generative system of ideas can be assembled in which "theorems of moral geometry" (Rawls, 1971: 126) can be shown to be strictly derivable from higher-order principles. In short, Figures 7.6 and 7.7 help to explain how certain propositions about fundamental human rights can be given a rational and even axiomatic foundation in ordinary human moral cognition.

Finally, Figures 7.6 and 7.7 also help to explain why the familiar claim, advanced by MacIntyre (1981: 67) and others—that human rights are nonexistent "fictions"—seems inapposite insofar as that claim is meant to restate and amplify Bentham's original criticisms in the same vein. Bentham's original indictment of the idea of natural rights was that it was "simple nonsense," and that

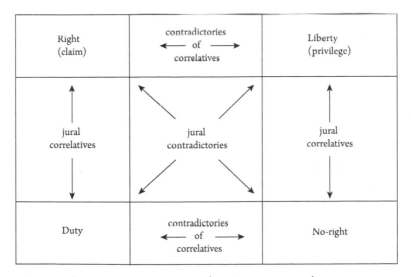

Figure 7.7　Fundamental legal conceptions (Hohfeld, 1913, 1917).

the further idea of natural and inalienable rights was even worse—"nonsense upon stilts" (Bentham, 1792/1843). His argument to this effect in *Anarchical Fallacies* was mainly rhetorical, however, and it is crucial to recognize that his deeper philosophical criticisms of natural rights were in large measure a consequence of his own theories of natural language, in particular his theory of fictions (see, e.g., Ogden, 1932). In fact, although the point has not been widely appreciated, the proper standpoint from which to understand Bentham's philosophical critique of natural rights is the computational and internalist theory of language and mind that Bentham shares with many contemporary philosophers, cognitive scientists, and linguists. From this naturalistic perspective, human rights are indeed "fictions" in more or less Bentham's sense—mental constructs that are indispensible for human thought and discourse, but which have no immediate referent in the mind-independent external world, as described by the natural sciences—but surely no worse off for that; for the same thing may be said of most concepts of folk psychology and ordinary discourse, and, as we have seen, the principles that generate these rights can be as much a part of a scientific theory of human nature as any other principles of cognitive science. In sum, contrary to a great deal of conventional wisdom, Bentham's original philosophical criticisms of natural rights are compatible with a robust modern conception of human rights, and neither of them is inconsistent with a contemporary scientific worldview.

F. Legal Anthropology and Comparative Law

Let us turn finally to legal anthropology and comparative law. Do these disciplines also reinforce the idea that human beings possess a shared, intuitive sense of justice that might support a robust system of universal human rights? Here again the answer appears to be a qualified yes. On the one hand, anthropologists have long argued that norms against murder, rape, and other forms of aggression appear to be universal or nearly so (Brown, 1991; Hoebel, 1954; Mead, 1961). The same has been said of distinctions based on causation, intent, and voluntary behavior (Fletcher, 1998; Green, 1998). Likewise, leading comparative scholars have argued that a small set of basic distinctions captures a "universal grammar" of the criminal law (see, e.g., Fletcher, 1998, 2007).

On the other hand, even with respect to bedrock norms like the homicide prohibition, it seems clear that not enough systematic research has been done to establish conclusively the universality of this fundamental principle. The leading social scientific studies of homicide, such as Martin Daly and Margo Wilson's *Homicide* (1988) or Dane Archer and Rosemary Gartner's *Violence and Crime in Cross-National Perspective* (1984), contain many valuable insights, but they do not squarely address the existence of this or any other substantive moral or legal universal or their codification in positive law. Daly and Wilson's study is mainly concerned with the behavioral profile and evolutionary psychology of homicide, of *who* kills and why, while Archer and Gartner's book is focused primarily on homicide *rates*; that is, on recorded patterns of homicide and other violent crimes in different cultural contexts. Neither volume seeks to describe a shared blueprint for considered judgments about homicide or their basis in human moral cognition. Although anthropologists, cognitive scientists, and other researchers have occasionally undertaken to study in general terms the role of intent, causation, and other elements of blame and responsibility in different cultural contexts, the ethnographic record is likewise largely devoid of the kind of detailed analysis of mens rea, actus reus, and available defenses or their civil law counterparts that might uncover the precise structure of a universal prohibition against homicide or its basis in human cognitive capacities. As a result, even answers to relatively simple questions, such as whether every known society utilizes an intent requirement or recognizes some kind of insanity, necessity, or mistake of fact defense, remain elusive and unavailable.

For their part, legal scholars have also generally failed to investigate the potential global reach of a specific, structured homicide prohibition. At least two major factors appear responsible for this puzzling state of affairs. First, as a general matter, comparative criminal law is a relatively neglected and underdeveloped discipline; those studies that do exist are mainly concerned with procedural rather than substantive law. Second, legal reform rather than accurate description has often been at the heart of comparative research (see generally Dubber, 2006). The monumental 16-volume "Comparative Depiction of German and Foreign Criminal Law" published under the direction of the German Justice Ministry from 1905 to 1909, for instance, was designed in connection with the reform of the German criminal code. Although it contains a great deal of useful information, it is not conceived or organized in a manner that is particularly helpful to those researchers in anthropology, cognitive science, experimental philosophy, or related fields who might seek to identify moral universals or to elaborate modern conceptions of universal jurisprudence (Dubber, 2006).

Other large-scale projects follow the same pattern. For example, *Homicide Law in Comparative Perspective* (Horder, 2007) is a collection of essays arising out of reform proposals of the Law Commission for England and Wales. Each contributor analyzes the law of homicide in his or her respective jurisdiction. Although the precise structure of the homicide prohibition and its various fault elements are given serious attention, the dominant orientation remains legislative reform. Further, only nine jurisdictions are represented. Once again, a sound basis for significant generalizations that might cut broadly across cultural, geographic, or historical boundaries appears to be lacking. More broadly, none of the existing

research endeavors in comparative criminal law has been so bold as to hypothesize and then systematically investigate the possible universal structure of the
homicide prohibition, let alone its potential reflection of innate moral capacities.

These remarks help to explain the novel research project in cognitive science
and comparative criminal law summarized in the remainder of this section.
Drawing on several years of research, my students and I have begun to fill this gap
in the literature and thereby help to advance our theoretical understanding of
moral and legal universals—and, ultimately, of the biological and cultural processes that generate and support them—by examining how the prohibition of
homicide is codified in several hundred jurisdictions throughout the world, including all of the member-states of the United Nations and the Rome Statute of the
International Criminal Court. Among other objectives, our study seeks to identify
the proportion of jurisdictions that criminalizes one or more forms of homicide
and that includes a mental state element in their definition of criminal homicide.
The study also seeks to examine the prevalence and substance of specific justifications and excuses, including eight of the most prominent legal defenses: (1)
self-defense, (2) necessity, (3) insanity or mental illness, (4) duress or compul-
sion, (5) provocation, (6) intoxication, (7) mistake of fact, and (8) mistake of law.

Although this research program is still unfolding, the main provisional finding
thus far is that the prohibition of homicide does appear to be both universal and
highly invariant, at least within the parameters of our investigation, which is restricted to codified law and excludes other sources of legal norms, such as custom or case law, and which is aimed primarily at uncovering broad generalizations
related to the foregoing categories rather than identifying other, more specific
differences. In particular, all of the jurisdictions investigated thus far do appear
to criminalize one or more forms of homicide. In addition, all of these jurisdictions do appear to include a mental state element in their definitions of unlawful
homicide. That is, none of the jurisdictions investigated thus far adopt a purely
strict liability approach to unlawful homicide.

In addition, the particular justifications and excuses identified thus far in our
research are remarkably similar and appear to consist of a relatively short list of
familiar categories, including the eight main defenses enumerated above. Among
other things, this suggests that the specific circumstances in which intentional
killing is held to be justified or excused may be far more constrained than many
commentators have implied. On the other hand, there does appear to be significant
diversity with respect to some of these defenses, at least at the level of codified law.
Specifically, although some of the most common defenses, such as self-defense
and insanity/mental illness, appear to be universal or nearly so, other categories,
such as necessity, duress, and provocation, appear somewhat less prevalent.

The main provisional results of the study are exhibited in Figure 7.8, which
supplies a representative sample of 164 of the 205 jurisdictions included thus

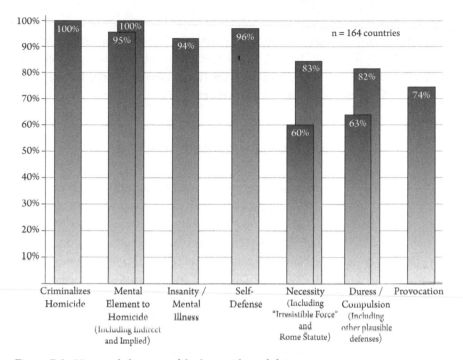

Figure 7.8   Universal elements of the homicide prohibition.

far in our research (over 80% of the member-states of the United Nations). Stated in its strongest form, the picture that emerges from this research is that legal systems and therefore individuals throughout the world recognize that intentional killing without justification or excuse is prohibited, and that self-defense and insanity; and to a lesser extent necessity, duress, and provocation, can sometimes be potentially valid justifications or excuses. These are noteworthy generalizations that go beyond anything comparable in the existing scientific or legal literature in uncovering or at least beginning to illuminate the properties of a specific universal or near-universal norm against homicide. They also directly challenge the conventional relativist assumption that "what counts as murder . . . varies enormously from society to society" (Posner, 1999: 6).

In addition, these findings imply that at least some technical legal definitions of prohibited acts and recognized defenses may indeed capture the structure of common moral intuitions (Mikhail, 2007b). To this extent, they lend support to moral grammar hypothesis and reinforce and extend many of the findings referred to above: that children utilize both a *mala in se/mala prohibita* distinction and a mistake of law/mistake of fact distinction when making moral judgments; that adults make such judgments in conformity with basic doctrines of civil and criminal law; that specific brain regions are selectively recruited during moral judgment tasks, particularly ones that require sensitivity to an agent's intentions; and other similar findings. In short, together with the other evidence presented in this chapter, these findings tend to corroborate and reinforce the guiding assumption that human beings possess a moral grammar that includes basic norms against homicide and other inherently wrongful acts.

V. Lessons and Implications

As the remarks by Ignatieff and Rorty with which I began amply illustrate, many contemporary academics have apparently given up on the possibility of discovering natural human capacities that might generate and reinforce a set of universal human rights. This chapter suggests that this abandonment may be premature. Surprising as it might seem, a significant body of scientific research has begun to transcend the modern denial of human nature and to reinvigorate two classical ideas about human beings that were powerful themes in both ancient philosophy and Enlightenment Rationalism: first, that a sense of justice and the gift of speech are two characteristics that distinguish humans from other animals (Aristotle); and second, that both of these capacities are "implanted in us, not by opinion, but by a kind of innate instinct (Cicero)." If these scientific developments are correct or at least on the right track, then the potential implications for the theory and practice of human rights would seem to be profound.

For our purposes, at least three major lessons can be tentatively drawn from this new set of research programs. First, although the matter clearly merits more attention, it seems reasonable to infer that a clear conceptual and empirical bridge between moral grammar and human rights can be built along the lines outlined in this chapter, as many jurists, philosophers, and cognitive scientists have often assumed. As we have seen, one key argument supporting this conclusion is relatively simple: many of the most obvious and significant human rights violations in the world today and throughout history involve acts of violence, aggression, or exploitation that rest at bottom on core human wrongs such as assault, battery, rape, homicide, theft, fraud, false imprisonment, torture, enslavement, and other familiar prohibited actions. Indeed, a handful of simple torts with well-defined content and widespread acceptance, such as assault, battery, false imprisonment, and intentional infliction of severe emotional distress, constitute lesser included offenses of a huge percentage of today's most pressing human rights violations—although they by no means exhaust these violations. These basic wrongs and, in particular, the tort of harmful battery likewise supply the basic perceptual and cognitive tasks of many influential research programs in the cognitive science of morality, including fMRI studies of emotional engagement in moral judgment (see, e.g., Greene et al., 2001; Koenigs et al., 2007);

neurocognitive and developmental studies of the role of intentional harm in moral judgment (see, e.g., Nelson, 1980; Young and Saxe, 2008); computational studies of adult moral judgment (see, e.g., Cushman et al., 2006; Mikhail, 2007); developmental, neurocognitive, and clinical studies of the moral-conventional distinction (see, e.g., Blair, 1995, 2002; Turiel, 1983); and behavioral research on infant moral cognition (see, e.g., Hamlin et al., 2007) (for further discussion, see Mikhail, 2011). Thus, collectively all of these considerations seem to point to the same dramatic conclusion, one with broad ramifications for the theory of human rights: our species may have evolved a special emotional sensitivity to assault, battery, and other core wrongs, and the intuitive aversion to them appears to be built into distinct regions of the human brain.

Second, although the foregoing observations are perhaps sufficiently provocative and important in their own right, the connection between cognitive science and human rights they exemplify would seem to run even deeper. For example, it seems reasonable to speculate on the basis of the arguments outlined in this chapter that many if not all of the specific human rights recognized in the Universal Declaration of Human Rights and other leading human rights instruments can likewise be shown to rest on a solid naturalistic foundation, insofar as they depend on more basic moral intuitions that can be discovered and explained within a moral grammar framework. Furthermore, this procedure need not be limited to civil and political rights, but presumably could be extended to include the full range of human rights already recognized by international lawyers; NGOs; and other human rights advocates, including social, economic, and cultural rights (such as those rights enumerated in Articles 22–27 of the UDHR) and the right to be free from all unjustified forms of authority, exploitation, subordination, and dependency. The fact that one can seriously contemplate this far-reaching possibility—that cognitive science and human rights can be linked in this manner—is significant and worth reflecting upon. In the final analysis, the progressive development of these ideas may turn out to be the most important application of the research outlined in this chapter.

Finally, and more modestly, the arguments and evidence outlined in this chapter suggest that a fundamental paradigm shift may be in order in the domain of legal policy. Contemporary legal doctrine in both the United States and most other jurisdictions generally favors positive law as a source of guidance for courts and generally eschews the notion that legally enforceable human rights can be grounded in universal moral values. As the new science of moral psychology continues to unfold, however, it seems likely that courts may begin to invoke this new research and its apparent implications in determining issues such as the boundaries of a norm, whether a norm is universal, or whether a norm is fundamental. Less directly, courts could perhaps begin to develop greater confidence in relying on particular sources of human rights law, such as the UDHR or the Martens clause of the 1899 and 1907 Hague Conventions, which refer without elaboration to laws of humanity and the dictates of a collective conscience. These sources might reasonably be held to have greater moral and legal authority in light of the research outlined in this chapter. Likewise, jurists might consider "general principles of law" to be a less indeterminate and more reliable source of international law than they currently are inclined to do. So, too, in identifying new customary norms, judges could presume the existence of universal moral values and ask whether positive legal enactments and state practices qualify or rebut that presumption with respect to a particular value or legal issue. This would be a sharp departure from the dominant interpretive theory today, which presumes the absence of human rights norms unless they are affirmatively expressed or ratified in positive law or customary state practice. In sum, contemporary research in the cognitive science of moral and legal judgment may have far-reaching implications for our understanding of constitutional and international law and the human rights they must protect. Only time will tell how strong and durable this foundation can be.

Notes

I wish to thank Ryan Goodman, Derek Jinks, and Andrew Woods for their suggestions and encouragement. Some parts of this chapter are drawn from previously published work, including *Elements of Moral Cognition: Rawls' Linguistic Analogy and the Cognitive Science of Moral and Legal Judgment* (Cambridge University Press, 2011); Is the Prohibition of Homicide Universal? Evidence from Comparative Criminal Law, 75 *Brooklyn Law Review* 497 (2009); and The Poverty of the Moral Stimulus, in *Moral Psychology, Vol. 1: The Evolution of Morality: Innateness and Adaption* (Walter Sinnott-Armstrong, ed., MIT Press, 2008).

CODA

Moral Grammar and Human Rights

RYAN GOODMAN, DEREK JINKS, AND ANDREW K. WOODS

I. Introduction

John Mikhail's chapter on moral intuitions applies cutting-edge research from the mind sciences to fundamental questions about human rights. Many human rights scholars and practitioners have abandoned questions of rights foundationalism as impractical; but as this chapter shows, such an inquiry offers numerous practical applications. Whether further evidence of a "moral organ" is forthcoming, Mikhail's chapter surveys an explosion of recent research about the biological basis for moral intuitions that could have significant implications for law and policy. If moral intuitions are as universal as the international human rights regime's norms claim to be, several benefits may obtain. We consider some of these briefly here, focusing in turn on two potential targets for policy.

Before discussing specific applications, it is worth noting the rich overlay possible when combining this work with that of many of the other chapters in this volume. Future research might address whether and to what extent the universality of moral intuitions explains or perhaps expands the psychic numbing effects discussed in Paul Slovic and David Zionts's chapter 2. First, research must address the question of why, if intuitions about morality are so widely shared, do people value lives so differently at the individual, small group, and large group levels. Similarly, the moral intuitions literature could form the backbone of a campaign aimed at outing pluralistic ignorance along the lines discussed in Prentice's chapter 2. Finally, one approach to the problem of naïve realism in Ross et al.'s chapter 10, might be to begin by noting the shared intuitions of both parties in a heated conflict. All of this is to say that a strength of the moral intuitions literature is its focus on the biology of the individual, a level of analysis that—whatever one thinks of the findings—has the benefit of eschewing interpersonal differences that so often lie at the root of conflict, including conflicts over human rights.

II. Target: Promoters of Human Rights

A. The Moral Dimension of Human Rights

One of the chief tools of human rights advocacy is "naming and shaming" rights violators. The efficacy of this method has been questioned (Hafner-Burton, 2008), but the moral intuitions literature explains the natural appeal of such an approach, and in some respects may justify its expansion. If audiences share intuitions about moral and immoral behavior, human rights campaigns to identify certain behaviors as falling along a moral/immoral axis could have certain significant benefits. This is not to say that human rights practitioners can—as some do—assume that human rights norms will be accepted as moral issues in and of themselves, or that they will be accepted with the same normative judgment (as an extreme example, genocidaires often use moralistic language to justify atrocities). Audiences may still need to be convinced of the moral dimension of human rights. But if rights violations can be framed in such a way so that they trigger universal moral intuitions, then this could aid practitioners along a number of dimensions.

First, if people can be persuaded that human rights issues are moral issues, they may be more inclined to see the wrongness of rights violations. This may affect not only how they behave personally but also how they raise their family; how they educate their students; and how they perceive and judge the actions of others, which in turn could affect social norms on a wide scale. Similarly, if rights talk can draw on the moral dimension of human nature, people may see the protection and defense of rights as a personal duty—a sense of duty that could be embedded into professional codes and the like. One could imagine, for example, a unit on "moral biology" as a standard unit in human rights education and training. This unit could start with facts about the biology of moral emotions and use this to ground a discussion of the importance of human rights. As technologies advance, the mind sciences may take on both a greater role in primary education but also a more interactive, hands-on role. Philosophers have already begun to wonder whether this shift will change, over the long term, lay perceptions about the law (Green and Cohen, 2004). We might wonder what the effect would be, for example, of Israeli and Palestinian children looking at images of each other's brains as they make moral judgments.

Related to professional duty is professional spirit. Practitioners suffering resource constraints and political opposition might take courage from the knowledge that their moral convictions are widely shared. In a line of work that can face intimidation and other attempts at dispiriting advocates, the knowledge that intuitions about justice are shared across the globe could embolden practitioners in nontrivial ways.

B. Harmonization Projects

The research surveyed in Mikhail's chapter also suggests that there may be a biological argument for attempts to harmonize the international human rights regime. The regime's global aspirations are regularly contested by critics who emphasize difference rather than similarity across peoples. The differences are partly reflected in the international regime, which some have noted is "fragmented" (Benvenisti and Downs, 2007). For example, sentencing practices in domestic human rights trials and across the international criminal tribunals differ widely (Drumbl, 2007). These differences can be defended on the grounds that they represent cultural diversity and locally tailored justice. But if moral intuitions about justice are shown to be in fact quite harmonized across the globe, then this could argue in favor of harmonized international sentencing practices. This is not to say that the universal nature of moral intuitions about sentencing has been conclusively shown; however, greater evidence along that dimension could aid harmonization efforts—which have suffered political challenges—in sentencing practices and beyond.

III. Target: Potential and Actual Perpetrators of Human Rights Violations

A. Communications Should Emphasize Shared Intuitions

Mass atrocity—of the sort that relies on high levels of civilian coordination—depends crucially on propaganda. One potential payoff of the moral intuitions research is material that emphasizes similarity rather than difference. That is, the moral intuitions literature may produce information which could serve as descriptive norms for advocacy campaigns along the lines of those outlined in the Prentice and Hornik chapters (2 and 3). This could be done not only as part of human rights education as discussed above, but also as part of a more aggressive attempt to stop incitements to atrocity. In the Rwandan civil war, for example, media played a crucial role in coordinating the killings and in spreading misinformation about Tutsis. In similar situations, human rights practitioners could conceivably draw on the moral intuitions literature to highlight the fact that attempts to emphasize difference stand on weak empirical ground.

B. The Utility of Desert

Finally, this research could be useful for regime design questions in international criminal justice. What, for example, should be the aim of human rights trials? Should they seek to prevent rights abuses going forward, or should they seek redress for past rights violations? The universal nature of some moral intuitions has been used by legal scholars to argue that domestic criminal regimes should be retributive in order to capitalize on shared intuitions of justice (Jones and Kurzban, 2010). The argument goes as follows: if intuitions about justice in a community are widely shared, and they include the retributive impulse, then the criminal regime could tap into that sense of moral outrage. If the regime fails to tap the retributive impulse, it will be viewed as illegitimate and obedience to the law will suffer. If this view is right—the so-called utility of desert argument—it could be extended to international human rights trials and international criminal tribunals on the ground that, as Mikhail's chapter shows, intuitions about justice are widely shared. There obviously are numerous normative concerns with such an approach, but the empirical evidence suggests how it would work. On the other hand, if the retributive impulse is not universally shared, such evidence could challenge global institutions that presume certain domestic criminal justice strategies will work in the international domain (Woods, 2011).

In fact, the evidence could affect not only the aim and emphasis of the regime—retributive versus consequential—but also its methods. For example, shaming sanctions could backfire terribly if a tribunal shames someone who the relevant community does not deem blameworthy. But perhaps the moral intuitions literature will show that in some cases, for some crimes, shaming would in fact increase the legitimacy (and perhaps therefore the efficacy) of a tribunal. (See Coda to Slovic and Zionts chapter 5).

Note

This Coda, like the others in this part of the book, offers some specific applications drawn from the insights in the contributor's chapter. It is not intended to be a list of fully developed policy prescriptions, but instead an example of the rich sorts of human rights policy applications that can be drawn from cutting-edge social science research. It does not question the insights offered in the chapter but instead asks what implications those insights might have for human rights law and policy. The Codas are the sole authorship of the editors of the volume.

8

Parochialism as a Result of Cognitive Biases

JONATHAN BARON

I. Introduction

The tendency of people to favor a group that includes them while underweighing or ignoring harm to outsiders has been called parochialism (Schwartz-Shea and Simmons, 1991). A prime example is nationalism, a value that goes almost unquestioned in many circles, just as racism and sexism went unquestioned in the past. Nationalists are concerned with their fellow citizens, regardless of the effect on outsiders. Nationalists are willing to sacrifice their own self-interest in order to harm outsiders (e.g., in war, for the benefit of conationals).

Nationalism is of course one example of a whole class of phenomena that led to ethnic and religious wars, which seem more common today than wars between nations as such. The in-group may consist of a tribe, a religious group, speakers of a common language, or, within nations, interest groups such as workers, gun owners, or farmers. Each person is typically a member of several groups that can potentially command this sort of loyalty. People often shift their loyalty, as happened in Sri Lanka, for example, where the current hostilities involve groups that became salient to people only recently.

Because parochialism can support such hostilities, it leads to violations of what might be called human rights, such as the right of noncombatants to live in peace without being killed or raped. Parochialism directly opposes a fundamental property or set of principles that constitute these rights—namely, that they are human: they apply to everyone (Risse, 2008). They are not just the rights of Americans or the rights of any other group. We do not need the concept of human rights, however, to regard killing and raping of noncombatants as horrendously awful.

As I shall discuss, parochialism also exerts itself in other forms that seem mild, until we consider the duration of its effects and the number of people affected. In particular, parochialism is almost always involved in "rent seeking" by groups that lobby governments for special privileges, to the general detriment of others. It is generally not in each individual's interest to contribute to this group effort, yet individuals end up acting against their self-interest and against the general interest in order to support their group's lobbying efforts.

An experiment by Bornstein and Ben-Yossef (1994) shows a parochialism effect in laboratory games similar to social dilemmas. (In a social dilemma, each of several people is faced with a choice between an option that is in her self-interest and an option that has much benefit for the group as a whole. Examples are things like recycling.) Subjects came in groups of six and were assigned at random to a red group and a green group, with three in each group. Each subject started with five Israeli Shekels (IS; about $2). If the subject contributed this endowment, each member of the subject's group would get three IS (including the subject). This amounts to a net loss of two for the subject but a total gain of four for the group. However, the contribution would also cause each member of the other group to lose three IS. Thus, taking both groups into account, the gains for one group matched the losses to the other, except that the contributor lost the five IS. The effect of this five IS loss was simply to move goods from the other group to the subject's group. Still, the average rate of contribution was 55%, and this was substantially higher than the rate of contribution in control conditions in which the contribution did not affect the other group (27%). Of course, the control condition was a real social dilemma in which the net benefit of the contribution was truly positive.

Similar results have been found by others (Schwartz-Shea and Simmons, 1990, 1991). Notice that the parochialism effect is found despite the fact that an overall analysis of costs and benefits would favor the opposite result. Specifically, cooperation is truly beneficial, overall, in the one-group condition but truly harmful in the two-group condition, because the contribution is lost and there is no net gain for others.

This kind of experiment might be a model for cases of real-world conflict, in which people sacrifice their own self-interest to help their group at the expense of some other group. We see this in strikes and in international, ethnic, and religious conflict, when people even put their lives on the line for the sake of their group, and at the expense of another group. We also see it in attempts to influence government policy in favor of one's own group at the expense of other groups, through voting and contributions of time and money. We can look at such behavior from three points of view: the individual, the group, and everyone (the world). Political action in favor of one's group is beneficial for the group but (in these cases) costly to both the individual and the world.

As I noted, parochialism underlies the concept of competing interest groups within nations, as described by Olson (1965, 1982) as well as competition among nations. In both cases, groups organize to promote their group interests against the interests of others, in a game that would be zero sum except for the effort expended in competition itself. "Public choice theory" and "rational choice theory" have incorporated the idea of interest groups to explain the function of democratic governments through the idea that people pursue their rational self-interest (Brennan and Buchanan, 1985; Green and Shapiro, 1994). Often hidden in such explanations, however, is the assumption that people go beyond their self-interest in order to act on behalf of their group (as pointed out by Brennan and Lomasky, 1993). If action on behalf of interest groups is as widespread as it seems to be, then we must explain why people are so willing to sacrifice on behalf of groups but apparently so much less willing to sacrifice on behalf of larger, more inclusive groups.

Parochialism also underlies some social-psychological theories of group conflict, such as realistic-conflict theory of group conflict (which grew out of the work of Sherif et al., 1961; see Sabini, 1992; other relevant work in social psychology is reviewed by Wildschut et al., 2003). According to this theory, people's own interests are mobilized when their group is in competition with another group for scarce resources. Thus, according to the theory, competitive behavior is rationally self-interested, even when it inflicts harm on the opposition. This argument assumes, however, that self-sacrifice on behalf of one's own group is in one's own self-interest. If this is an illusion, then such behavior is not, in fact, rationally self-interested.

In defining parochialism as neglect of the interests of outsiders, I do not mean to imply that group loyalty implies such neglect or that group loyalty itself has no benefits. People have many good reasons to cooperate with in-group members, reasons that do not apply to out-group members. Group loyalty provides emotional benefits, but these do not need to come at the expense of others to such an extent that the harms exceed them.

And it is not necessarily parochial when we refuse to do something to improve things for out-group members. Many groups (including nations) operate within a scheme of local responsibility, in which, for efficiency reasons, they are given local control. In such cases, interference with a group by outsiders, even for what appears to be the greater good, would have the negative effect of undermining local control and setting a precedent for outsiders coming in and making things worse (Baron, 1996).

Parochialism may be in part an inevitable side effect of group loyalty that exists for good reasons combined with thoughtlessness about outsiders. But some of it may result from fallacious—or "biased"—thinking, or particular ways of framing the situation. Fallacies can be corrected, and people can be encouraged to use other frames. Thus, the study of cognitive biases and framing effects can give us a way of correcting a small piece of a large problem. The problem is so large that even a small piece is worthy of our attention.

In this chapter, I present the results of several experiments, which are designed to probe how people think about parochialism. The study of people's conscious reasons can help us understand the phenomenon, even if these reasons are not the only determinant of behavior. First, I present some new evidence concerning the role of an illusion in which people see self-sacrifice for their group as really not sacrifice at all, an "illusion of morality as self-interest." Then I present evidence of two moderators of the effect. Parochialism is reduced when harm is seen as being caused by action rather than omission, and when people think in terms of individuals rather than the abstraction of groups (such as nations). Next I show that parochialism is sometimes very strong because it is moralistic—something that people want to impose on others whatever the consequences—and morally objective. And I argue that citizens see support of their nation as their moral duty even when this support does more harm than good.

I conclude with a discussion of implications. Arguments against parochialism might just work, and they might be most effective if they are directed at beliefs that people have been found to endorse, or ways of thinking that they follow. This is particularly true when the thinking involved can be seen as fallacious on more general grounds. I also discuss the benefits of approval voting. Although our efforts to affect parochialism may have small effects, we should note that it is always a matter of degree, and less of it is better. People are not always parochial: they do consider effects on outsiders. So we are not starting with an empty glass; it is half full.

II. Parochialism and the Self-Interest Illusion

Parochialism may result from all the various mechanisms that cause people to co-operate (see Baron, 2000). These include altruism; conformity; reciprocity; and various illusions, such as the voter's illusion (Quattrone and Tversky, 1984). In that illusion, people behave as if they thought their behavior would influence others, even though they know only that they and others are subject to common influence. Of course, this is true, in that a vote supports a social norm favoring voting, but the belief in question may go beyond that. Voters may reason, "If people on my side vote, I'll probably vote too. My voting will thus be linked with theirs. Hence, I'd better vote, because if I don't, they won't either."[1] The same reasoning could apply to any social dilemma, of course. The essential confusion here is between diagnostic and causal relationships. Their own voting is diagnostic of the overall turnout on their side, but it does not affect the turnout, except for their own vote.

A second type of illusion that causes cooperation is the "illusion of morality as self-interest" (Baron, 1997, 2001). In a social dilemma, people try to reduce the apparent self-other conflict by convincing themselves that it doesn't exist. They may do this by telling themselves that "cooperation doesn't do any good anyway, so I do not need to sacrifice my self-interest." They may also do the opposite and convince themselves that cooperation is in their self-interest after all. They may focus on the slight self-interested benefit that accrues to them indirectly from their own cooperation and ignore the fact that this benefit is less than the cost of cooperating. (If it were not less than the cost, then we would not have a social dilemma after all.) The tendency to conflate morality and self-interest may be exacerbated by the fact that moral behavior is often self-interested, too (because of effects on reputation and ties with others, for example). People tend to overgeneralize and act as though the two are correlated even when they are not.

The self-interest illusion is particularly relevant to cooperation with members of a group that is part of a larger group or one of two (or more) groups. People who sacrifice on behalf of others like themselves are more prone to the self-interest illusion, because they see the benefits as going to people who are like themselves in some salient way. They think, roughly, "My cooperation helps people who are X. I am X. Therefore it helps me." This kind of reasoning is easier to engage in when X represents a particular group rather than when it represents people in general.

Supporting this explanation, Baron (2001) did an experiment following the design of Bornstein and Ben-Yossef (1994) in comparing cooperation within a single group with cooperation within a group when that group's gain is another group's loss (the two-group condition). The main addition was that subjects answer questions about their self-interest, in order to test the hypothesis that the self-interest illusion is greater in the two-group condition.

Subjects did contribute more in the two-group condition than in the one-group condition (82% v. 73%), replicating the parochialism effect. More importantly, the parochialism effect for contributing was highly correlated across subjects with the parochialism effects for the self-interest questions, including a question about which option would make more money for the decision maker. In other words, those subjects who showed a greater parochialism effect for contributing showed a greater self-interest illusion when the gain for their group was a loss for the other group.

When subjects were forced to calculate the effects of their contribution on themselves and others, the parochialism effect was reduced. Thus, parochialism is somewhat labile. As suggested by Singer (1982), it may be possible, through reason, to understand the arbitrariness of group boundaries. The more that people think of boundaries as arbitrary, the more they can direct their non-self-interested concern at the greater good rather than the parochial interests of their group.

Of course the self-interest illusion can explain only part of the parochialism effect. Much of the rest of it may arise from a sort of limited altruism, in which people really do care about the good of the comembers more than about the good of outsiders.

More generally, parochialism can be analyzed into three components. One is limited altruism, of the sort that people extend to family members. Limited altruism beyond the family (e.g., for a nation) is arguably difficult to justify because it is arbitrary. But any altruism is better than no altruism, so we can hardly say that it is something we should discourage, if no altruism is the alternative.

The second is competition, the value we place on doing better, rather than just doing well. In games and sports, parties willingly agree to rules that allow competition. Even in a mild sport like tennis, a player may try to tire out his opponent by making him run from side to side repeatedly. In international affairs, however, Americans and Europeans cannot so easily justify hurting the Chinese out of fear that they will "beat us" by appeal to any sort of principle of consent, especially given the fact that many international trade agreements explicitly discourage such competitive behavior.

The third is the result of the self-interest illusion, which I have found to be exacerbated by the salience of an out-group.

The next section reports an experiment to examine further the role of the self-interest illusion. It asks whether this illusion is present when competition is the only available motive, as well as when in-group interest is present.

III. Experiment 1a: Self-Interest Illusion

The main purpose of this experiment was to ask whether the self-interest illusion applied to a motive favoring the in-group as distinct from a motive opposing the out-group (competition). The explanation I have given implies that the illusion would be limited in this way, because it is about the benefits of helping one's group. The experiment included a pure competition condition, in which an option would hurt the out-group without helping the in-group. The reasoning that "if something helps my group then it helps me" should apply to benefits, but not to harm to the out-group. It is theoretically possible that a person could reason, "if something hurts the other group then it helps me." If this second type of reasoning occurs, then we would find that the self-interest illusion occurs in competition as well as in the standard parochialism condition. The critical test is thus whether the illusion is greater when the self is actually helped.

A. Method

The questionnaire, called "Policy proposals," began:

> This study is about trade policies that affect the average income in different countries, and policies for allocation of U.S. government funds that affect income in different U.S. states.
>
> In each cases, suppose that the policy choice affects average income and has no other effects that matter to you. The effects on income are the same (in percent) for people with different income levels.
>
> In some cases, a proposed policy will cause changes in incomes. In other cases, it will prevent changes, leaving incomes as they are. In these cases, defeat of the proposal will lead to the changes in question.
>
> In each case, suppose there is a referendum that requires 50% of the registered voters, and polls suggest that the vote will be close.

In 6 of the 12 pages, the question concerned adoption of a proposal. In the other 6, it concerned prevention of the adoption of a proposal. The idea was to examine the effect of acts vs. omissions, but the wording was apparently difficult, with many subjects apparently responding in the opposite way from what was intended, so these questions are ignored henceforth. (If they are included in the data analysis, they do not change any conclusions reported here.) The 12 pages were presented in a random order chosen for each subject.

The 6 relevant pages differed in what the subjects was asked to imagine to be his or her country or state, and what the other country or state was. The pairs were: California and New York; California and Texas; California and Florida; the U.S. and Japan; the U.S. and China; the U.S. and India. Here is an example of the top of a page:

> Suppose you are a citizen of the U.S.A., which is holding a referendum about a policy proposal concerning allocation of U.S. government expenditures.
>
> The proposal will cause the following changes in average income: AN INCREASE OF 2% FOR THE U.S.A. AND AN INCREASE OF 2% FOR INDIA. What would you do about the proposal?
>
> contribute money opposing it
> oppose it without contributing
> not sure
> favor it without contributing
> contribute money favoring it

Would you personally have more money in the long run if you contribute money to your favored side?

more if I do not contribute money
not sure
more if I contribute money

The second question was designed to assess the self-interest illusion. Each page had four proposals, each followed by these two questions. In the other three proposals, the outcomes were, respectively: 4 for your nation (or state) and −4 for the other; 0 and −4; and −1 and 4. The order was reversed on every other page. The first pair (2, 2) represented a cooperative choice. The second could be chosen either out of self-interest or competition, but the third was pure competition. The fourth was altruistic.

Eighty-two subjects completed the study, but 5 were eliminated because they gave the same answer to the first question every time it was asked. Of the remaining 77, 21% were male, and ages ranged from 19 to 69 (median 42).

B. Results

Table 8.1 shows the summary results as a function of the type of allocation, the four proposals on each page. The "Mean" is on a scale from −2 to 2, where 2 is "contribute money favoring" the proposal, and 0 is "not sure." The column labeled "Favor" is the proportion of responses that favored the proposal (with or without contributing). It is apparent from the first two columns of numbers that subjects were interested in both their own group and the other group. "Both" responses exceeded "Self," indicating willingness to sacrifice, although the low agreement with "Help" suggests that the object of the sacrifice was equality (fairness) or avoidance of harm to the other group, rather than altruism.

The third column of numbers, "Illusion," is the proportion of "Favor" responses in which subjects thought they would "personally have more money" if they contributed to their side.

Table 8.1 **Mean responses, Experiment 1**

Allocation	Mean	Favor	Illusion
Both (2, 2)	.84	.79	.31
Self (4, −4)	.63	.63	.39
Compete (0, −4)	−.30	.20	.10
Help (−1, 4)	−.71	.11	.25

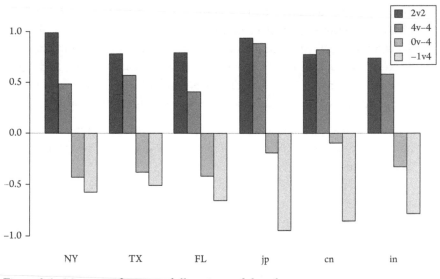

Figure 8.1 Means as a function of allocation and the other group.

The proportion was computed for each subject and averaged across subjects. (Hence, subjects who had no responses favoring a proposal did not contribute to these results.) Of greatest interest is the low proportion for Compete. Subjects did not often think that contributing money to hurt the other side would give them more money in the future. The Illusion measure was significantly lower for Compete than for Self ($t41 = 5.38$, $p = 0.0000$) and Both ($t40 = 4.00$, $p = 0.0003$), but not Help ($t13 = 1.06$), although only 14 subjects were available for the last comparison. In sum, it is clear that the self-interest illusion is present for proposals that benefit the subject's group, but it is not present in pure competition. People do not seem to think that they benefit from contributing to proposals that harm others, even though they engage in such competition.

Figure 8.1 shows the mean responses for the four allocation conditions (where "2v2" is "Both," and so on) as a function of the other group. The subject's group was the United States for the three countries (abbreviated by their country codes on the Internet) and California for the three states. In general, subjects were more competitive and less helpful toward other countries than toward states. Most subjects were from the United States, however, and not from California, so the country-state comparison is confounded.

C. Experiment 1b: More on the Illusion

It is possible that the illusion results from the belief that the subject is decisive in voting. To test this possibility, I did a follow-up experiment using only the Self and Compete conditions.

Twelve pages were presented in a random order chosen for each subject. Six involved two countries, and six involved two states. The pairs were: California and New York, California and Texas, California and Florida, New York and Texas, New York and Florida, Texas and Florida, the United States and Japan, the United States and China, the United States and India, Japan and China, Japan and India, and China and India. Here is an example of the top of a page:

> Suppose you are a citizen of the U.S.A., which is holding a referendum about a policy proposal concerning allocation of U.S. government expenditures.
>
> Suppose the proposal would lead to: an increase of 4% for the U.S.A. and a decrease of 4% for India.
>
> How would you vote on the proposal?
>
> against it   not sure (or wouldn't vote)   for it
>
> Would you be better off financially, in the long run, if the proposal passes than if it fails?
>
> no   yes
>
> If you vote for the proposal, would you be better off financially than if you vote against it? In other words, would your vote for it lead you to have more money in the long run?
>
> no   yes
>
> If you would be better off financially from voting for the proposal, is this because your vote would cause the proposal to be adopted?
>
> I would not be better off financially   no   yes

The third questions were designed to assess the self-interest illusion, and the fourth question was to assess the explanation in terms of influence on the outcome. A pure self-interest illusion is thus a yes answer to the third question and a no answer to the fourth. Items with a yes answer to the fourth question were thus eliminated from the main analysis.

Seventy-one subjects completed the study; 27% were male, and ages ranged from 21 to 72 (median 45). Five others were omitted because of very fast responses.

The mean proportion (across subjects) of uncorrected illusion responses was .60 for Self (yes answers to the third question about whether the subject would be better off from voting), and .16 for Compete. However, 89% of the uncorrected illusion responses to the Self items (yes to the third question) were associated with yes answers to the last question (and 81% of the uncorrected illusion responses to the Compete items). People thought they would (or might) affect the outcome. The pure illusion measure removed these cases with yes answers to the last question. The proportions of pure illusions for Self and Compete were, respectively, .19 and .05. This difference was significant (t48 = 3.19, p = 0.0025, across subjects; some subjects provided no relevant data).

In sum, although much of the illusion is associated with beliefs about an effect on the outcome, some of it is independent of these beliefs, as hypothesized by Baron (1997, 2001).

IV. Experiment 1c: Another Test of the Self-Interest Illusion

Experiment 1c distinguished parochialism from competition in a different way. It compared two proposals, one favoring the in-group, the "Self" proposal; and another that was almost as good for the in-group but much better for the outgroup, the "Best" proposal. It also included a third proposal that was worse than both of these (for reasons to be explained shortly). The main prediction is that the self-interest illusion is greater in those who support the Self proposal.

The experiment also compared approval voting with standard plurality voting. Baron, Altman, and Kroll (2005) found that approval voting reduced parochialism when both groups voted. Of interest here is whether this effect could also happen when only the in-group voted. It is possible that the Best proposal could win even in this case, if some voters approved only the Best proposal. Perhaps they would do this strategically, thinking that most others would approve both Self and Best, but a few would approve Self only. Such a situation might be more likely when the third proposal was much worse than Self and Best. If voters use a strategy of approving proposals that are much better than other proposals, then we, and other voters, would expect more approvals of both Self and Best, and the way would be open for strategic voters for Best only to carry the day.

The experiment also compared situations in which the out-group voted and in which only the in-group voted. The groups consisted either of nations or states of the United States. In the in-group-only condition, Best could win only if more voters approve only Best than those who approve only Self. This is unlikely, but possible if enough voters take a utilitarian perspective that includes both groups and vote only for their top choice.

A. Method

The introduction to the study began:

> This study is about trade policies that affect the average income in different countries, and policies for allocation of U.S. government funds that affect income in different U.S. states.

In each case, suppose that the policy choice affects average income and has no other effects that matter to you. The effects on income are the same (in percent) for people with different income levels.

This was followed by a short explanation of approval voting. An example of one of the 12 pages is as follows:

Suppose you are a citizen of the U.S.A., which is holding a referendum about a policy proposal concerning international trade. (The citizens of China are not voting.) Consider the following proposals:

A leads to: an increase of 4% for the U.S.A. and no change for China
   B leads to: an increase of 3% for the U.S.A. and an increase of 3% for China
   C leads to: an increase of 2% for the U.S.A. and an increase of 4% for China
   Which proposal(s) would you approve? (The proposal with the largest number of approvals will be chosen.)

   A   B   C   A and B   A and C   B and C

   If you could vote for only one, which would you vote for?

   A   B   C

Suppose that a voter must pay $5 to vote by approval. She pays $5 and approves just Proposal A. Is this decision a good bet? Is the $5 worth paying just because of its possible effect on her income? (Choose the answer that comes closest to what you think.)

   No.
   Yes. Proposal A is more likely to win if she votes.
   Yes. The money she pays will help the citizens of her nation, including her.
   Yes, for both of the last two reasons.

Suppose now that the citizens of China were voting at the same time on the same three proposals:

   A leads to: an increase of 4% for the U.S.A. and no change for China
   B leads to: an increase of 3% for the U.S.A. and an increase of 3% for China.
   C leads to: an increase of 2% for the U.S.A. and an increase of 4% for China (You are still a citizen of the U.S.A.)

Which proposal(s) would you approve? (The proposal with the largest number of approvals in both nations will win.)
   A   B   C   A and B   A and C   B and C

Table 8.2 **Percent of votes for each proposal in each voting condition**

Condition	Self	Best	Other	Self & Best	Self & Other	Best & Other
Plurality	44	45	11			
Approval	31	27	8	24	1	8
Both vote	19	46	10	13	1	10

The 12 pages differed in the two nations or states involved, as follows, with the first member of each pair being the one the subject was to consider as his own: California/New York, California/Florida, New York/Florida, United States/China, United States/India, China/India. Each of these 6 pairs appeared once with each of two versions of the third option: 2%/4% (as shown in the example above) or 0%/0%. The latter was the more distant option, hypothesized to increase the approvals for A (Self) and B (Both).

The 86 subjects ranged in age from 23 to 72 (median 45.5), and 26% were male.

B. Results

The manipulation of option C had no significant effects on any voting responses, and the nation v. state manipulation also had no significant effects on these responses.

Table 8.2 shows the votes for each proposal in the three voting conditions. Consistent with the findings of Baron et al. (2005), when both groups voted, Best tended to win (t85 = 5.69, p = 0.0000, comparing Best and Self across subjects). Even in the Approval condition with only the in-group voting, Best did better than Self, although not significantly so, in both approval and standard plurality voting. Best did better when both groups voted (t85 = 5.31, p = 0.0000).

IV. Experiment 2: Acts and Omissions

Parochialism may interact with the act/omission distinction. Many people seem to favor harm caused by omission over harm caused by action, an omission bias (Ritov and Baron, 1990; Spranca et al., 1991; see Baron and Ritov, 2004, for a recent summary). People may be unwilling to harm outsiders by action, although they may be willing to harm them through omission: through doing nothing to prevent them from being harmed. The distinction may apply less to insiders. Indeed, Haidt and Baron (1996) found that the omission bias was reduced when a decision maker had a close relationship with the affected person, or when the decision maker was responsible for the welfare of others. People may feel this sort of closeness or responsibility toward insiders. The present experiment looks for an interaction between act/omission and in-group/out-group harm.

A. Method

The scenario involved an opportunity to help or hurt other employees of a company. The hypothesis was that harm through action would be less parochial than harm through omission. The experiment had some conditions that are not of interest here, so these are deleted from the following description. The introduction read:

1. Contributions and profits

Imagine that you live in the U.S. You work for a company with one other branch in the U.S., nearby and in the same state, another branch in China, and one in India. Each of the four branches has 50 employees. All salaries are equivalent to $50,000 in purchasing power.

Sometimes the company gets opportunities to invest money in ways that will generate income immediately. When this happens, the management asks the employees to contribute $100 to an investment fund, and the $200 gains from the fund are returned to the employees.

Management is experimenting with different ways of distributing the gains.

- Sometimes they go to the branch that contributes, sometimes to another branch.
- Sometimes each employee decides whether to contribute or not, and sometimes a group votes on whether everyone in the group will contribute or not.
- Sometimes management makes the decision, and the question is whether to reverse it and withdraw a contribution.

In all cases, each employee must make a decision without consulting anyone else. These decisions may be repeated in the future. All employees know the rules.

Each branch has an list of employees. When the $200 gain goes to "next person in the list," we mean the person with the position on the list just below your position. (If you are the last, then the "next" person is the first.)

We also refer to your "counterpart." For this purpose, each employee is paired up with another employee, in the same branch or in a different branch. Counterparts can help each other as a pair.

The rules may seem strange, but strange things happen. Aside from these rules, imagine that these are typical workplaces and the employees are typical of Chinese Indian, or U.S. employees of medium-size companies.

The main conditions of interest involved omissions and acts. In the omission case, a typical question was:

If you contribute $100, the next person on the list in the Indian branch gains $200. Everyone in both branches has the same choice: if everyone in your branch contributes $100, you all gain $200.

Would you contribute?

yes no

From a moral point of view, how should someone in your position answer the last question?

yes no

If you contribute, how would that affect the monetary outcomes for you personally in the long run?

I would be more likely to gain than to lose.
I would be more likely to lose than to gain.
I would be no more likely to gain, or lose.

The last question was about the self-interest illusion. The corresponding question in the action condition was:

In this case the contributions have already been made for everyone and the choice is whether to withdraw them. (The recipients know this.)
If you withdraw $100, the next person on the list in the Indian branch loses $200. . . .

These questions were crossed with two other manipulations: One manipulation was the next-on-the-list versus counterpart versus voting. In the counterpart condition, "next person on the list" was replaced with "your counterpart." An example of the voting condition was: "Everyone in your branch votes on whether to contribute $100 or not. If a majority votes yes, then everyone in your branch contributes $100, and everyone in the Chinese branch gains $200. If the vote fails, then nobody contributes and nobody in the Chinese branch gains $200. They will have the same vote: if a majority in the Chinese branch votes yes, then everyone in that branch contributes $100, and everyone in your branch gains $200." A fourth condition also involved a complicated voting system, but subjects apparently did not understand it, so I do not discuss it here. I also do not discuss the effect of counterpart v. next-on-the-list and voting here. (The effect was not quite significant but is addressed in a more sensitive experiment later.)

The other manipulation was "your branch," "the other U.S. branch," "the Chinese branch," and "the Indian branch." The main comparisons were simply United States v. foreign. Parochialism is greater cooperation with the United States than with China or India.

Seventy-three subjects did this study.

Table 8.3 **Percent noncooperative responses in Experiment 2 (including list, counterpart, and vote conditions).**

	United States	*Foreign*
Noncooperation:		
Act (% withdraw)	10.3	11.9
Omit (% not contribute)	13.4	29.9
Morality of Noncooperation:		
Act (% withdraw)	8.4	11.9
Omit (% not contribute)	15.0	25.3
Self-Interest of Noncooperation:		
Act (% withdraw)	8.0	8.7
Omit (% not contribute)	13.2	22.8
Self-Interest of Cooperation:		
Act (% withdraw)	64.2	58.9
Omit (% not contribute)	69.2	52.1

B. Results

The main hypothesis was supported, as shown in Table 8.3. Subjects were quite willing to harm foreigners through omission (29.9%) but not through acts (11.9%). The act-omission distinction was very large for foreigners but barely present for Americans. The interaction was significant ($t72 = 3.49$, $p = 0.0008$).

Notice that, as shown in Table 8.3, the same interaction is found for judgments of the morality of noncooperation and for the extent to which this serves self-interest (both significant). On the whole, though, the self-interest illusion carried the day, and cooperation—the dominant response in all conditions—was generally seen as self-interested, even when the beneficiaries were foreign.

In sum, parochialism is reduced when people think of their behavior as harming others (as opposed to failing to help them). The next experiment looks at a different way to reduce parochialism, thinking in terms of effects on individuals.

V. Experiment 3a: One-to-One Relationship

Experiment 3a was mainly to test the hypothesis that parochial competition is reduced when people see themselves as having a one-to-one relationship with someone in the other group. When people are seen as individuals rather than as members of a group, the desire to hurt them for the sake of beating them may be reduced because of greater empathy or identification. People are much more real than abstractions like "nations" and "the enemy."[2] The experiment also manipulated other variables, mostly to increase the number of pages and collect more data.

A. Method

The questionnaire, called "Salary proposals," began:

> This study is about voting decisions that affect salaries of workers in a company that employs you, and another company that does business with your company. Your department has 10 workers, and so does the corresponding department in the other company. The other company is in another country.
>
> All workers make enough for a basic middle-class lifestyle, but, in some cases, the average income of those in the other company is half of that in your company.
>
> In each case, you and others vote, and the majority determines the outcome. If the vote is tied, one of the options is the default, and it goes into effect. In some cases, just one person votes (you), so you determine the outcome.
>
> In each cases, the choice affects only the annual bonus, not the base salary, so the change is just for one year.

Each page presented four choices, each in the following form:

OPTION A (DEFAULT): NO CHANGE.
OPTION B: AN INCREASE OF 2% FOR YOUR DEPARTMENT AND AN INCREASE OF 2% FOR THE OTHER DEPARTMENT.

In the other three choices, the outcomes for Option B were, respectively: 4 for your department and −4 for the other; 0 and −4; and −1 and 4. The order was reversed on every other page. As in Experiment 1, the first pair (2, 2) represented a cooperative choice. The second could be chosen either out of self-interest or competition, but the third was pure competition. The fourth was altruistic. Subjects were asked which they would vote for, and they were given the choice of abstaining. (There was also a test question about which option would be better in monetary terms. I shall ignore this here, except to say that it was answered correctly in 77% of the cases.)

The 16 pages of the experiment, presented in a random order chosen for each subject, varied in which option was the default (A or B). They also varied in the income of the other company. At the beginning of the page, the first statement was either "The workers in the other company's department make the same average income as workers in your department," or "half of the average income of."

Of primary interest, there were four voting conditions, also explained near the beginning of the page:

> Your department and the corresponding department in the other company will vote on the following options:
>
> Your department (and not the other department) will vote on the following options:
>
> You and one person in the other department will 'vote' on the following options, which affect only the two of you. If you both vote for the same option, you both will get it. Otherwise you will both get the default.
>
> You alone will vote (decide). Your choice will affect only you and one person in the other department. If you abstain, the default will take effect.

The last two conditions involve the (hypothetical) subject and a single other person, thus making the decision more personal. Whether the other group (or a member of it) voted or not was included without any particular hypothesis about its effect, largely to increase the number of pages.

The study was completed by 96 subjects, but 6 were omitted because they gave the same (or almost the same) answer to every question. Of the 90 remaining, 19% were male, and the median age was 40 (range 21 to 67).

B. Results

Table 8.4 summarizes the responses for the different allocation conditions, averaged across the other conditions. It is analogous to Table 8.1 except that the response had only 3 options, so that the range of the mean is from -1 to 1 instead of from -2 to 2. In general, competition responses were rare compared to Experiment 1a, and subjects were also less willing to hurt the other group in order to benefit in the "Self" condition.

The main results concern the responses to the competition item (0 for self, -4 for other) and the self-interest item (4, -4). Subjects voted for the competition

Table 8.4 **Mean responses, Experiment 3a**

Allocation	Mean	Favor
Both (2, 2)	.81	.89
Self (4, −4)	−.08	.35
Compete (0, −4)	−.76	.07
Help (−1, 4)	−.64	.12

item in very few cases, but they did so more in the group condition, 7.8%, than in the personal (one-to-one) condition, 5.3%. They also abstained slightly more often in the group condition (11.3% v. 10.1%). Coding the responses as 1 (compete), 0 (abstain), and −1 (reject competition), the mean responses were significantly different across subjects (−.73 v. −.79; t89 = 2.32, p = 0.0224). The results were similar, although not quite significant, for the self-interest item (36.9% favoring in the group condition and 32.9 in the personal condition, −.05 v. −.12 for the mean responses; t89 = 1.93, p = 0.0566), although more subjects voted for this response in both group and personal conditions. (The two results together, self-interest and competition, were significant—t89 = 2.50, p = 0.0142—and they did not differ significantly.) Although these results are small in magnitude, many subjects showed large effects, while other subjects behaved as if they were trying to be consistent, ignoring variables that they had decided were irrelevant. In sum, personal, one-to-one decisions reduce the parochialism effect.

When the income of the other group was lower, self-interest responses were reduced (means of −.13 v. −.03; t89 = 3.38, p = 0.0011), and helping responses, a sacrifice of 1% for a benefit of 4% increased (−.59 v. −.69; t89 = −2.90, p = 0.0047). Competition was unaffected, however, suggesting that the self interest and helping response were influenced by fairness considerations but competition was not.

VI. Experiment 3a: Group v. Personal

Experiment 3a tests the same general hypothesis in a different way, using the methods of Experiment 2.

A. Method

The instructions were as follows:

> Imagine that you live in the U.S. You work for a small company with one other office in the U.S., nearby and in the same state, another office in China, and one in India. Each of the four offices has 10 employees. You do not know anyone in any other office. All salaries are equivalent to $50,000 in purchasing power.
>
> Sometimes the company gets opportunities to invest money in ways that will generate income immediately. When this happens, the management asks the employees to contribute 100 or 50 to an investment fund, and the gains that result from each contribution are returned to the employees.

Management is experimenting with different ways of distributing the gains:

Sometimes they go to the office that contributes, sometimes to another office.

Sometimes each employee decides whether to contribute or not, and sometimes a group votes on whether everyone in the group will contribute or not.

Sometimes a contribution goes to a particular other person, and sometimes it is divided among everyone in an office.

In all cases, each employee must make a decision without consulting anyone else. These decisions may be repeated in the future. But the employees never know for sure who made the decision that caused them to gain (or not). Thus, employees cannot reciprocate directly.

The questions on each page were similar to those in Experiment 2. For example, "If you contribute $100, another person in **the other U.S. office nearby** [the **Chinese** office] gains $250. Each contributor is paired with a different recipient. If everyone in your office contributes, then each recipient gains $250." In the group condition, the wording of the parallel question was "If you contribute $100, a total gain of $250 is divided equally among those in **the other U.S. office nearby** [the **Chinese** office]. Everyone in your office can contribute."

Two additional questions were added to make a finer assessment of willingness to cooperate. The cooperation measure was the sum of the yes responses to the three questions.[3]

Suppose the contribution were $50 instead of $100 (and the gain still $250). Would you contribute?

Suppose the contribution were $50, and the gain were $500 instead of $250. Would you contribute?

To assess parochialism, the contributions affected either someone in your own office, the other U.S. office, China, or India. Because some subjects found "own office" confusing, I compared the "other U.S office" to China and India, thus ignoring the "own office" condition. All items were repeated using voting instead of individual decision making as the response. The order of the 16 resulting items (4 recipients, personal v. group, individual decision v. vote) was randomized for each subject. I ignore the voting conditions here.[4]

Seventy-five subjects did this study.

B. Results

On the three-point scale of cooperation, the means were 1.18 for the Other-U.S group condition and 0.81 for the foreign group condition, a difference of 0.37 (t75 = 2.77, p = 0.0070). The means were 1.37 for the Other-U.S personal condition and 1.17 for the foreign personal condition, a difference of 0.20 (n.s.). The second difference was significantly smaller than the first (i.e., the interaction was significant: t75 = 2.39, p = 0.0195). In sum, parochialism is again greater when people think in terms of groups: almost twice as great.

Similar results were found for the morality question and the self-interest question. The interaction was not quite significant for the morality question (t75 = 1.85, p = 0.0676), but it was significant for the self-interest question (t75 = 2.10, p = 0.0387). The interaction effect in the self-interest question was correlated with the interaction effect in the cooperation question (r = .51, p = .000). More interestingly, the interaction for the self-interest question correlated with the interaction for the morality question (r = .47, p = .000): when people think it is morally acceptable not to help foreigners as a group, they also think that this is in their self-interest, but they do not think this about failing to help individuals.

VII. Experiment 4a: Parochialism as a Moral Judgment

Parochialism, especially as expressed politically in the form of nationalism, may elicit strong judgments and emotions. In particular, it may take the form of a moralistic goal.

Moralistic goals are those that we try to exhort others to achieve, just as we do with moral goals (Baron, 2003). The distinction is that moral goals (as I define them) derive from the personal goals of people. We have reason to exhort each other to help each other achieve our respective personal goals. Moralistic goals have no such derivation, although people often try to supply it after the fact. For example, some people have moralistic goals against homosexual behavior between consenting adults. It is not clear how such behavior is bad for anyone, yet those who hold these goals often try to argue that it has bad side effects, such as "undermining the institution of marriage."

Nationalism, and parochialism in general, may be moralistic because nationalists want their conationals to pursue parochial goals even when these goals cannot be justified in terms of the overall good (including the good of outsiders). Nationalists typically want others in the group to be nationalist as well. Nationalism seems to dominate political behavior. The idea that one should vote for the good of humanity as a whole, regardless of the effect on one's own nation, would make total sense to a utilitarian (and it would require little self-sacrifice because voting has such a tiny effect on self-interest), but it is considered immoral by the nationalist.

Moralistic goals are often seen as moral absolutes. They are seen as "protected values"; they are protected from trade-offs with other values (Baron and Leshner, 2000; Baron and Spranca, 1997). They may also be seen as objective, not a matter of judgment, but true regardless of what anyone thinks (Goodwin and Darley, 2008).[5]

On the other hand, nationalism could be a social norm (Bicchieri, 2006). A social norm is seen as an obligation, which should be followed even when it requires some self-sacrifice, but it is a conditional obligation. It is a readiness to support the norm, both through one's own behavior and one's endorsement of the norm for others, given that others are supporting it. Thus, endorsement of the norm would depend on others' endorsements of it. In a way, nationalism with respect to a specific nation must be a social norm, although it may not be perceived as one. Specifically, nations themselves are defined by people's adherence to them.

The expression of a social norm cannot be moralistic exactly because it depends on the desires of others while moralistic values do not. This is a critical distinction between the two. The social norm itself, as distinct from its expression, could be moralistic only because people could think that others must be ready to follow a norm, once it is agreed on by a sufficient number of co-citizens.

In the present study, I asked subjects whether they saw nationalistic and other parochial policies as moral, as moralistic (i.e., to be imposed regardless of what anyone thought), as objective, and as dependent on the desires of others.

A. Method

Eighty-five subjects completed the study; 21% were male, and their median age was 41. One additional subject was removed because of apparent misunderstanding (a high negative correlation between the voting question and the question about morality, described below). The introduction began:

Each of 20 pages describes some action that may be controversial. We ask six questions about the action.

One question is whether the morality of the action is objective. This means that its truth or falsity does not depend on anybody's judgment. The opposite of "objective" is "subjective." Subjective judgments can differ from person to person.

Examples of objective statements are: "2 + 2 = 4," "2 + 2 = 5" (which is objectively false), "the earth orbits the sun," and "a Hummer gets 28 mpg."

Examples of subjective statements are: "hot pepper tastes good," "Brigitte Bardot was the most attractive movie star of all time," "rap music is annoying," and "Woody Allen is funny."

Each page described a public action favoring citizens over non-citizens. Table 8.5 shows the actions. Following each action, the subject answered the following questions, with the numbers in brackets indicating the percentage of answers in each category:

What do you think of this action?

1. It is not a moral issue. [25]
2. It is morally acceptable. [10]
3. It is a moral issue, but I cannot say in general whether it is wrong or not. [12]
4. It is morally wrong, but it should be allowed. [9]
5. It is morally wrong, and it should be banned in most cases. [20]
6. It is morally wrong, and it should be banned in all cases, regardless of the benefits to the outsiders. [13]
7. ... regardless of the benefits to the outsiders and citizens. [11]

Is the moral rightness or wrongness of this objective or subjective? Options were: subjective [58], objective [30], and not sure [12].

Suppose there were a referendum about whether to allow this action or not. This issue is the only one on the ballot, so you would have to make a special effort to vote. Allowing this action would provide a small benefit. How do you think you would probably vote?

Allow it [28], Ban it [53], Would not vote [19]

Suppose someone you know said s/he was not planning to vote. How would you respond?

Express disapproval [51], Express approval [8], Say nothing either way [41]

Suppose that polls showed that only 10% planned to vote in this referendum, and 90% of the citizens did not care one way or the other about it. How would this information affect your own decision about voting?

Table 8.5 **Experiment 4a actions and percent responses to ban in most or all cases or in all cases**

Item	Ban most	Ban all
Companies hire recent immigrants while some native citizens who are almost as qualified do not have jobs.	41	21
Companies hire foreigners, helping them immigrate, while some citizens who are almost as qualified do not have jobs.	46	31
Companies open new facilities in foreign countries rather than their own country, even though the foreign cost is only a little less.	33	21
Companies buy supplies from foreign countries rather than their own country, even though the foreign cost is only a little less.	35	18
Nongovernmental disaster-relief organizations send more help in response to a foreign disaster than to a domestic one, even though the domestic need is almost as great.	39	21
Governmental disaster-relief agencies send more help in response to a foreign disaster than to a domestic one, even though the domestic need is almost as great.	56	32
Investors put their money into foreign assets rather than domestic assets with slightly lower expected returns.	24	12
Private universities in the United States accept foreign students while rejecting some U.S. students who are almost as well qualified.	45	26
Private universities in the United States give financial assistance to foreign students while denying it to some U.S. students who are almost as needy.	46	16
Consumers buy imported clothing rather than domestic clothing that is almost as good in price and quality.	20	9
Local governments provide public housing for illegal immigrants while denying it to some citizens who are almost as needy.	65	40

Table 8.5 (*continued*)

Item	Ban most	Ban all
State universities in the United States (funded by state taxes) give financial assistance to foreign students while denying it to some U.S. students who are almost as needy.	64	34
Public schools (supported by local taxes) provide special education for learning-disabled children of illegal immigrants, while denying it to some citizens' children whose need is almost as great.	65	33
State universities in the United States (funded by state taxes) accept foreign students while rejecting some students from other U.S. states who are almost as well qualified.	53	31
The national government gives research grants to foreign scientists, while rejecting applications from domestic scientists that are almost as worthy.	38	20

Less likely to vote [5], More likely [44], No effect [51]

Suppose that polls showed that 80% planned to vote to ban the action, and 80% felt that other citizens should do the same in order to express the clearest possible disapproval of it. How would this information affect your own decision about voting?

More likely to vote to allow the action. [13] More likely to vote to ban the action. [35] No more likely to vote to allow the action or to vote to ban it. [53]

B. Results

The percent responses are shown above in the Method section, for all the questions. It is apparent that many subjects thought that many of these issues were moral.

Table 8.5 shows the percent of responses indicating that the act should be banned in most or all cases (answers greater than 4 to the first question) or in all cases (greater than 5).

Answers to the moral realism question (objectivity) seemed to depend largely on the subject. Coefficient alpha for the reliability of the 15-item "test" was .92 (with three levels of response). Thirty-three percent of the subjects thought that no actions were objective, with the rest spread out roughly uniformly from 1 to 15.

Thus, subjects differed substantially. One, in a comment on a pilot study, said that she saw herself as a "citizens of the world." Ten subjects (12%) never said that any act was morally wrong. Eleven subjects never said that any act should be banned. Parochialism in the form of nationalism is thus widespread and moralized, but it is not universal.

One purpose of this experiment was to distinguish social norms from moralistic values. Social norms would be indicated by disapproval of non-voting and sensitivity to the behavior of others, as indicated by the last two questions. We looked at just those cases in which the subject said the behavior should be banned in the first question (answers greater than 4) and found the average proportion of these cases, for each subject, in which the subject would be less likely to vote when few others were voting. (Only 74 subjects could be used for this analysis, as the rest had no relevant cases.) The mean across subjects was 5%, and 85% of the subjects never said they would vote less when others were not voting. The corresponding mean for the effect of voters planning to vote for the action and thinking that others should do the same was 51%. We discuss this result later.

Moralistic values, on the other hand, would be indicated by willingness to vote for a ban and continued willingness (equal or increased) even when others were not interested. By the same analysis, 87% of the relevant cases were moralistic, and 68% of the subjects showed this pattern in every relevant case.

VIII. Experiment 4b: Further Tests of Social Norms

Although Experiment 4 provided no support for the possibility that nationalism is a social norm, the question about voting when others were uninterested was worded in a way that could give subjects another reason to vote; specifically, they would have more voting power when fewer others were voting. We thus did another study with modified questions. The main modification was to say that the turnout would be high.

A. Method

The cases and the first two questions about each case (wrongness, objectivity) were the same as in Experiment 4. Here are the questions, with percent responses:

What do you think of this action?

1. It is not a moral issue. [25]
2. It is morally acceptable. [10]
3. It is a moral issue, but I cannot say in general whether it is wrong or not. [13]
4. It is morally wrong, but it should be allowed. [9]
5. It is morally wrong, and it should be banned in most cases. [22]
6. It is morally wrong, and it should be banned in all cases, regardless of the benefits to the outsiders. [11]
7. ... regardless of the benefits to the outsiders and citizens. [9]

Is the moral rightness or wrongness of this objective or subjective?

subjective [32], objective [33], not sure [34]

Suppose there were a referendum about whether to allow this action or ban it. The referendum is part of a general election with high turnout. How do you think you would probably vote on this issue?

Allow it [26], Ban it [50], Would not vote [23]

How do you think good citizens should vote?

Allow it [14], Ban it [39], Whatever they think best [47]

Suppose a poll found that 80% of the voters thought that good citizens should vote to ban the action. Would this information increase your obligation to vote for a ban?

Yes. This figure means that other citizens care, and that matters. [18] No. It would have no effect on my obligation to vote for a ban. [78] No. It would reduce my obligation to vote for a ban. [4]

Suppose a poll found that 80% of the voters thought that good citizens should vote to allow the action. Would this information reduce your obligation to vote for a ban?"

Yes. Other citizens do not care about their nation, and that matters. [6] No. It would have no effect on my obligation to vote for a ban. [78] No. It would increase my obligation to vote for a ban. [16]

Eighty-six subjects completed the study. None had completed Experiment 4. Their median age was 41, and 22% were male.

B. Results

The responses to the questions common to Experiments 4 and 5 were nearly identical. It is also apparent from the overall response rates that very few responses indicated that the opinions of others would matter.

Considering only the cases in which the subject would ban the action in the first question (answers greater than 4), subjects were again unresponsive to the situation in which others thought that they should oppose the ban. The mean across subjects was 3%, of thinking that this decreased the obligation to support a ban. On the other hand, the corresponding mean for the effect of others thinking that good citizens should vote for the ban was 26%.

In sum, it appears that many subjects think that their obligation is increased when others think they should support a ban, but it is not decreased by the apathy or antipathy of others. It is possible that the form of nationalism has elements of both a social norm and of a moralistic value.

IX. Experiment 5: Duty

Citizens could use their votes, and other potential actions, to advance the good of all people. Instead, many citizens seem to see their duty as advancing the good of their nation (or some other unit) even when the harm to outsiders outweighs the good to conationals (insiders), according to their own perception of harm. These parochial attitudes are often moralistic; that is, values that people have for others, without regard to whether honoring these values causes conflict with the values of those affected. And they are often seen as objective, not as social norms, and as absolute (protected from trade-offs). The present experiment looks for this concept of duty.

A. Method

In one experiment, subjects were told the following:

> ... imagine that you are voting in a referendum on proposals for tax reductions. Each reduction is specified as a percent of taxes now paid.
>
> The reductions are available because of a budget surplus, and they will help the economy. Assume that more tax reduction is always better. The proposals are all conservative; none will cause a deficit.
>
> Different groups of taxpayers are taxed according to somewhat different rules. In the United States, for example, the tax rates depend on whether you are married or single, whether you have dependents, whether you are a dependent yourself, and whether you are retired.
>
> The concern of this study is your obligation as a voter. Thus, it will not specify WHAT your group is, because we do not want you to think about the needs of particular groups.

Table 8.6 **Experiment 5: Duty**

Your group is 1/3 of the population.

	Reduction for your group	*Reduction for all others*
Proposal A:	2%	4%
Proposal B:	4%	2%
Group size	1/3	2/3

Notice that:

* Proposal A has more total benefits.

* Proposal B is better for your group.

How would you vote?

Assume that your group and other groups are treated fairly now.

Sometimes the vote will be close, and sometimes it will not be close. Predictions about the vote depend on predictions of turnout for the groups involved.

An example of a situation, and the questions used for all cases, are as follows. Each question could be answered yes or no, except the first (about voting).

Why would you vote this way? (More than one can be "yes.") [Subjects responded yes or no to each item.]

Because it is in my personal self-interest.

Because it is in my group's interest.

Because it is best on the whole.

Because it is my duty to vote this way.

Because it is my group's duty to vote this way.

Because it is everyone's duty to vote this way.

What is your duty in a case like this?

My duty is to vote what is in my personal self-interest.

My duty is to vote what is in my group's interest.

My duty is to vote what is best for everyone.

In a case like this, what would lead to the best overall outcome?

If everyone voted according to his or her self-interest.

If everyone voted according to his or her group's interest.

If everyone voted according to his or her view of what is best for everyone.

It doesn't matter because both proposals are equally good.

The 85 subjects ranged in age from 23 to 64 (median 41); 76% were female. The experiment had several conditions. Inadvertently, their order was not randomized, so I focus here on overall results rather than comparisons of the conditions, which were, in any case, varied largely in order to increase the number of pages presented without repeating any. The manipulations were the size of "your group" (1/3 or 2/3), whether the election was close, the size of the payoffs, and whether the two proposals were equal in total benefits or whether proposal A was greater. I report only the eight cases in which A had greater benefits. (Subjects were more likely to choose B when the benefits were equal.)

B. Results

For the most part, subjects consistently chose either the self-interested option (B) or the best option (A): 32% chose the self option every time, and 11% chose the best option every time. The other subjects had some mixture of the two, but, in general, subjects were consistent enough so that the reliability coefficient (α) was 0.88.

I examined correlations, across subjects, of the proportion of choice of the self-interested option. The highest correlations (0.25 or higher[6]) were with SelfInt (0.40, self-interest as a reason), GrpInt (0.57, group interest as a reason), Whole (−.50, what is best on the whole as a reason, negative because this is given as a reason for voting for the best proposal), AllDuty (−0.39, everyone's duty), DutySelf (0.36, duty to vote for self-interest), DutyGrp (0.41, duty to vote for group interest), DutyAll (−.60), and BestAll (−0.39, the best outcome would result from everyone voting for what they thought was best for all). In sum, people who vote on the basis of self- or group interest are those who think it is their duty to do so.

Figure 8.2 shows the proportions of endorsement of each item, broken down according to the answer to the first question, even though the main determinant of this response is the individual subject.

The main result is that the self voters (black) think that their duty is to themselves and their group (middle group of lines), yet they acknowledge that it would be best to vote for the benefit of all (bottom group). They see their duty as to support their group even when the overall outcome is worse as a result.

This result was tested statistically in several ways, and was highly significant.[7] The result held for the entire data set as well as for just the votes for self. In sum, people tend to see their duty as more parochial than what they themselves think is best overall.

C. Follow-Up

The results of the experiment just described could arise from the coincidence of group interest and self-interest. Subjects might have voted for their group's interest because they themselves would benefit. Self-interest is almost surely an insufficient

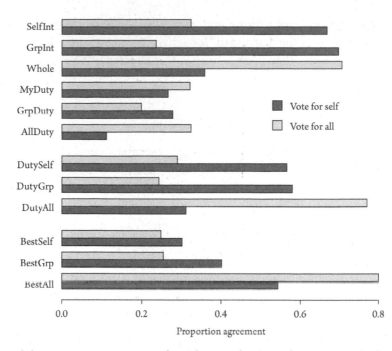

Figure 8.2 Responses to questions about duty as a function of responses to the first question about choice.

reason for voting for one's group because of the low probability of having an effect, but the subjects might have thought otherwise. In a follow-up experiment, self-interest and group interest were separated. This did not matter: People see a duty to their group even when self-interest does not coincide with group interest.

Baron (2010) presents data from a follow-up study, which included cases in which the subject did not benefit at all from helping her group (because of a quirk in the law). When self-interest was aligned with group interest (as in the last experiment), 64% of the votes favored the proposal that was best for the group. When self-interest was opposed to group interest, the new cases—40%—favored this proposal, still a substantial number. The difference between the two indicates that some voters do think that voting is justified by self-interest, and some even think that it is their duty to vote for their own interest. Again, in these cases, subjects felt they had a duty to support their group even when they thought that this would not have the best consequences.

X. Conclusion

Parochialism is one of the big problems in the world today. It is related even to such apparently unrelated problems as climate change (Baron, 2006): the burden of reducing global warming must fall on rich nations, yet the main beneficiaries will be poor nations; and, moreover, the nearly inevitable rise in sea level will increase the demand of "foreigners" to migrate into the same rich countries (and into other poor countries less affected). What can be done about it?

A. Approval Voting

The results I have reported, and others, suggest several approaches. First, widespread adoption of approval voting may help—possibly even across nations, as in international bodies that set rules.[8] The results indicate that people can take the opportunity to approve proposals that are somewhat less good for their own group but better on the whole. Approval voting can thus favor compromise among competing groups. For example, workers may fear that a trade agreement would threaten their jobs, but they may also care about increased access to goods and about benefits to other workers elsewhere. If they were offered enough options, they might approve a free trade agreement if they saw it as sufficiently beneficial for all.

In the studies I have described, voting had no personal consequences. This is somewhat like the real situation, since the perception that "one vote doesn't matter" is widespread, and people tend to perceive their voting more as a matter of expression than as action with real consequences (Brennan and Lomasky, 1993).

The experiments thus show that people are open to the kind of understanding that would lead to the reduction of parochialism.

The benefits of approval voting depend on which proposals are put to a vote. If only two proposals were available, then approval voting would have no advantage over standard voting. Addition of a second Self proposal, similar to the first, could also drive the self-interested utility of Best below the mean and reduce its rate of approval. In this case, approval voting might be just as subject to parochialism as standard voting. Approval voting could never be more sensitive to parochialism, however.

B. The Self-Interest Illusion

The illusion that cooperation promotes self-interest seems to be a beneficial one. It encourages people to sacrifice their true self-interest when doing so can increase the net benefits to all. Yet, in previous work, I have found that it operates even more strongly when membership in a group is salient. Moreover, the appearance of being beneficial may itself be an illusion, since the ultimate cause may be the desire to reduce perceived conflict between morality and self-interest, and the reduction could go the other way too: people could rationalize their selfishness by convincing themselves that their self-sacrifice does not really do anyone any good.

The experiments described here suggest that the self-interest illusion is not about competition between groups. On the other hand, the perception of competition may itself increase parochial attitudes. For example, many Americans think that the United States is competing with China for some sort of economic dominance of the world. Arguably, economic competition between the United States and China can benefit both countries. Only military competition poses a danger, and, if anything, the (low) risk of that is only exacerbated by the politics of economic competition.

Efforts to reduce the self-interest illusion may lead to a general decline in political participation. Yet, if such participation is motivated by parochial concerns rather than concerns for the good of all, do we need it? Moreover, if the reduction of the self-interest illusion were brought about by a general increase in the perception of conflict between morality and self-interest, then the opposite illusion could also decrease, so that public participation would increase.

Parochialism is, in a way, an intermediate state: between commitment to the self and commitment to humanity in general. Political action in favor of a group often hurts both the actor and humanity. If people understood this, self-interest might conspire with utilitarianism to keep parochial voters at home. The utilitarians would remain. However, the moralists would also remain, as I shall discuss shortly.

C. Acts and Omissions

As discussed by many writers (e.g., Singer, 1993), the harmful neglect of outsiders is an example of what I have called omission bias, a tendency to ignore the harms of omission. I have shown here how omission bias is greater for outgroups. Thus, parochialism is manifest largely in failure to help, rather than in active harm. (This asymmetry is consistent with the idea that competition plays a small role, since competition, as in sports, allows active harm ... within limits.)

It is encouraging that individual differences in omission bias are large (Baron and Ritov, 2004). It is thus possible to overcome this bias, and some people indeed find the failure to help others to be just as repugnant as active harm. The radicals of the 1960s had a slogan (attributed to Eldridge Cleaver in a 1968 speech), "If you're not part of the solution, you're part of the problem." Such an attitude could work to reduce parochialism, insofar as people came to see their neglect of outsiders as equivalent to harmful action. In the case of behavior of citizens, it could be especially useful, since little effort is require to support (or not oppose) policies that benefit outsiders. Often, simply voting for the better candidate is all that is required.

D. Groups v. Individuals

The distinction between groups and individuals examined here is almost a "framing effect," an effect of two different ways of describing the same situation. When we harm groups, we harm the individuals who comprise those groups, yet many people are less willing to harm the individuals than to harm the groups. It should not be difficult to find political opponents of more lenient treatment of illegal immigrants who, at the same time, respect and help particular illegal immigrants whom they know. Arguments against parochialism, in addition to emphasizing the equivalent effects of acts and omissions, should also emphasize the humanity of out-group members. I don't think this conclusion will surprise anyone, but we now have some experimental evidence for it.

E. Moralistic Values and Citizens' Duty

The results found here also suggest that parochialism, in the form of nationalism, is often moralistic, absolute, and seen as objectively required. It also has elements of a social norm, in that it is responsive to the opinions of others when they favor nationalism but not when they oppose it. And it is seen as part of a citizen's duty.

Arguably, it would not make sense for nationalism to have no element of social norms. This is because a nation is defined by what its people take it to be. We see the operation of shifting national norms both in history and in modern conflicts (Yugoslavian v. Croatian, Iraqi v. Kurd, Sri Lankan v. Tamil, and so on). It, however, could make sense to have a nation-relative value that was not a social norm; that is, "people should support their own nation, whatever they take it to be." The results here suggest, however, that parochial norms of nationalism are generally seen as fixed, independent of what others think. They tend to be moralistic.

In the long run, we might be able to de-bias moralistic values. Even now, these values are locked in a political struggle with various forms of altruism, including utilitarian altruism that considers outsiders as well as conationals. Many moralistic values might arise partly as errors based on false beliefs about the good of others. People may think that others are more like them than they are. People's good may really differ. If people could come to see moralistic values as possible errors, they would be more open to discussion about them, and more open to evidence about the true nature of other people's good, and about how they could use their power as citizens to advance the good of others.

In the meantime, we have one protection against the imposition of moralistic values: liberty as a general political commitment, limited necessarily by consideration of externalities (including those that result from the imposition of moralistic values themselves). When people make decisions for themselves, they are un-likely to be influenced much by the moralistic goals of others. When governments remove the power to make decisions, limiting choice, they open up the possibility that groups of people with moralistic goals can influence the law, usually in the guise of paternalism, in order to protect people protected from the consequences of their own decisions. To the extent that liberty is salient as a general political issue, however, those who are afraid of such intrusions will join together to defend liberty as such, even when they might agree with some particular moralistic effort.

Finally, it would be nice if it became more fashionable to see people's duty as citizens as the result of a (very small) power they have to influence events. If they step back from questions about the origin of that power and consider how they should best use it, now that they have it, they might conclude that it is best used for the good of all, and not as an obligation to return the favor of the nation that granted it.

Notes

1. Quattrone and Tversky (1984) told subjects about a hypothetical election in a country with 4 million supporters of party A, 4 million supporters of party B, and 4 million non-aligned voters. Subjects were told that they were supporters of party A. Some subjects were told that the election depended on whether more of the supporters of party A or the sup-porters of party B turned out to vote. These subjects thought that party A was substantially more likely to win if they voted than if they did not vote. They were also quite willing to vote. Other subjects were told that the election depended on whether more of the non-aligned voters voted for party A or for party B. These subjects thought that the probability of A winning was not much different whether they voted or not, and they were less willing to vote than subjects in the other condition. Of course, one vote is one vote.

2. Schick (1991, p. 1) tells the following story:

   > Writing about his experiences in the Spanish Civil War, George Orwell tells this story. He had gone out to a spot near the Fascist trenches from which he thought he might snipe at someone. He waited a long time without any luck. None of the enemy made an appearance. Then, at last, some disturbance took place, much shouting and blowing of whistles followed, and a man:
   > . . . jumped out of the trench and ran along the parapet in full view. He was half- dressed and was holding up his trousers with both hands as he ran. I refrained from shooting at him. . . . I did not shoot part because of that detail about the trousers. I had come here to shoot at 'Fascists'; but a man holding up his trousers isn't a 'Fascist,' he is visibly a fellow-creature, similar to yourself, and you don't feel like shooting at him.

3. In less than 1% of responses, subjects were inconsistent, saying that they would contribute in the first question but not in one of the others in which its contribution has less cost or more benefit. In these cases, I assumed that willingness to contribute in the first case implied willingness to contribute in the others, implying that the latter unwillingness was unintended.

4. The voting conditions yielded non-significant results. As a result of this failure, it would be appropriate to multiply all p values by 2. On the other hand, the hypothesis is one tailed, and I report two-tailed p's.

5. This sort of "moral realism" has recently been challenged (by Greene, 2002), although it is widely accepted.

6. The next highest was 0.19.

7. The most concise was the use of a multi-level (mixed effects) model with subject as the grouping variable and the difference between BestAll and DutyAll as the only dependent variable, which yield a t value greater than 4. But the effect held both within those subjects who made different choices and across subjects.

8. Note that approval voting is one type of alternative to simple plurality or majority voting. Another set of methods that has many of the same theoretical advantages as approval voting involves ranking. This set includes the "single transferable vote," the Hare method, and "instant runoff." The Borda count, in which ranks are summed, seems more subject to strategic voting than any of these other methods. The Wikipedia entry on voting provides excellent introductory material and citations.

CODA

Parochialism as a Result of Cognitive Biases

RYAN GOODMAN, DEREK JINKS, AND ANDREW K. WOODS

Jonathan Baron's chapter identifies cognitive biases whereby individuals sacrifice self-interest for the benefit of in-group members, especially in the presence of an affected out-group and especially when the effect on out-group members results from omission rather than action. People are also misled by a "self-interest illusion": fallaciously believing that their sacrifices for the group redound to their personal benefit even when their actions incur a net personal cost. Turning to applications, we consider strategies for overcoming the negative effects of these psychological dynamics. We also consider strategies for exploiting these psychological dynamics to promote human rights.

I. Target: Promoters of Human Rights

A. Overcoming Negative Effects of Cognitive Bias

The international human rights regime frequently suffers from a lack of will to address human rights abuses in foreign countries. Due to parochialism—and the omission bias—citizens and political leaders may be reluctant to direct their national resources to other countries. Baron's research suggests the value of precommitment strategies to overcome omission bias by international actors. Consider three such applications: (1) National governments could precommit to devoting a significant percentage of their annual budgets to foreign humanitarian assistance; this amount could be reduced or overridden by the legislature or an executive body, but an affirmative step would have to be taken to withdraw funding. (2) The Security Council could precommit to take action in the case of humanitarian disasters in which the target state is unwilling to let outsiders deliver aid (e.g., the 2008 Burma cyclone). The Security Council could also establish a mechanism to place the issue automatically on its agenda (China and South Africa blocked this step in the Burma situation). (3) The board or controlling executive body of international organizations such as the World Bank/IMF could preauthorize their institutions to employ sanctions against countries in the event of a genocide or similar atrocity. The organization could decide to override this precommitment, but that would also take an affirmative decision to act. All these measures could gain additional political traction on the understanding that they help overcome errors in decision making that preclude actors from realizing their true preferences.

Baron's research also suggests the importance of framing human rights away from groups and collective harms and toward individuals and personalized harm. Similar to Slovic and Zionts's chapter, these research insights suggest empowering individual victims in decision-making processes of international organizations. International institutions such as the Security Council and European Union have the power to levy sanctions against human rights violating states. These bodies could provide an opportunity for "victim impact statements"—whether in person, via video, or in writing—before deciding on a range of measures against a human rights violating state. Indeed, such devices could help counteract psychological dynamics that favor personal connections among diplomatic brethren. Additionally, international organizations could hold meetings "on location" in an affected country (e.g., in the DRC) to develop closer relations with community members and greater accessibility to individuals. The Security Council could hold a session in the affected country, international prosecutions of war criminals could take place on location or in a nearby country rather than in The Hague (consider a recent decision of a Finish court to interview witnesses on location in Rwanda and to hold the trial in Tanzania), and outreach programs could be better conceived as a "two-way" process whereby personal connections effectuate better decision making on the part of international bodies.

B. Exploiting Beneficial Effects of Cognitive Bias

Baron's research paradoxically might support strategies for harnessing parochialism to promote human rights activism and may also explain the mechanisms for past successes in human rights promotion. By framing a particular human rights cause around a group identity (e.g., mothers of the disappeared), a social movement can expect their members (and affiliates) to make greater personal sacrifices to promote the welfare of the group. Individuals may also be willing to vote for political leaders and to contribute to economic boycotts (even if against self-interest) to promote the human rights agenda of their group. Indeed, it may also prove effective to frame a human rights campaign around resource trade-offs with out-groups (e.g., if the out-group is multinational corporations). In short, a general lesson may be to link human rights to (group) identity (politics).

II. Target: Perpetrators of Human Rights Violations

A. Overcoming Negative Effects of Cognitive Bias

International legal institutions could use devices to compel actors to calculate the overall effect of their decisions.[1] Some existing international rules already perform this function, but they may be underappreciated and underenforced. Consider two examples.

(1) International humanitarian law requires decision makers planning military attacks to "do everything feasible to verify that the objectives to be attacked are neither civilians nor civilian objects and are not subject to special protection" and to "take all feasible precautions in the choice of means and methods of attack with a view to avoiding, and in any event to minimizing, incidental loss of civilian life, injury to civilians and damage to civilian objects."[2] Institutions should make it more likely that violations of these rules will incur liability. ICRC and military training programs may achieve more effective results by emphasizing (and devoting more of their scarce resources to) compliance with a procedural obligation—e.g., the *duty to consider* all precautions to minimize collateral damage—rather than the duty to refrain from attacks that cause disproportionate loss of life. That is, the *duty to consider* may prevent unnecessary loss of life more effectively than a rule directly prohibiting the infliction of unnecessary loss of life.

(2) A similar approach could be taken to ramp up protections of economic and social rights (e.g., the right to water, food, shelter). It may be critical to focus more on procedural requirements and encouraging officials to justify their decisions. Even relaxed substantive standards and heightened procedural rules might produce significant benefits by overcoming decision errors. Specifically, violations of economic and social rights generally involve acts of omission, and the victims generally consist of members of disempowered groups (out-groups) A debate in human rights practice is whether economic and social rights are "justiciable"; that is, whether they should be subject to review by courts and other tribunals. Baron's research suggests the value of judicial or administrative bodies requiring actors to justify their distributional decisions even if only to satisfy a de minimis standard of review or reporting requirement. The process of justification—compelling decision-makers to consider the consequences of their omissions in the context of social and economic rights—could yield considerable benefits. Additionally, review/reporting bodies could also require certain procedures (rather than outcomes) be fulfilled. For example, states could be required to have particular ministries of government participate in the policy formulation (to widen and deepen the impact of close consideration of policy omissions); governments could also be required to seek input in the legislative process from politically marginalized groups; courts could overturn laws if the legislature failed to consider the interests of the most marginalized groups in society (the South African Constitutional Court's jurisprudence serves as a model for the latter).

B. Exploiting Beneficial Effects of Cognitive Bias

Parochialism—and the self-interest illusion—might be employed in the service of influencing (potential) perpetrators of human rights abuses. For example, perpetrators might be encouraged to forego their personal interests in favor of group benefits. Indeed, the self-interest illusion suggests that even if actors are motivated purely by self-regarding interests, they may accept costly self-restraint to achieve benefits to in-group members. This mechanism is enhanced if their decision has an effect on particular out-groups (e.g., their relative standing among other nations).

Consider two types of relationships in which this dynamic might operate to promote human rights. First, a governmental official might refrain from committing a human rights violation that would serve her interest due to a potential negative impact on the nation/government (status of the nation in the international community affected by human rights violations; or economic sanctions/rewards for the state on the basis of its human rights compliance). If this scenario is a plausible application of Baron's research, it opens up the prospect of successfully directing incentives (including deterrence strategies) toward the state even though the potential perpetrators might not directly and personally benefit from compliance. Indeed, such strategies will prove even more powerful if the individual, operating under the self-interest illusion, falsely perceives the net effect to benefit her personally. The same approach may hold true for calibrating the preferences of non-state actors (e.g., rebel leaders) and the interests of their group (e.g., the insurgency or rebel organization).

Second, states may refrain from pursuing a course of action that violates human rights because of the negative impact on their regional group. Indeed, regional human rights regimes might be employed to amplify this effect. That is, regional human rights commissions, courts, and special rapporteurs could frame compliance with regional human rights standards in terms of the impact on the regional group in the global community of nations. Accordingly, explicit efforts to harmonize human rights standards to build an integrated regional community (e.g., Europe) could accordingly amplify the willingness of member states to sacrifice illiberal interests for group benefits.

III. Supporters of Human Rights Violations

Baron's chapter suggests that individuals may voluntarily consent to governmental restrictions on their personal freedoms in favor of perceived national interests and will do so to an even greater extent in the context of relationships with outgroups. In making this trade-off, individuals may also operate under a self-interest illusion—miscalculating the net benefits (overall security and rights) to themselves. Note an additional corollary of this insight: even if the risks (probability and impact) from attack by an enemy is equal to that of a natural disaster (e.g., climate change), individuals will be more willing to forego self-interest in the former situation (the existence of a well-defined out-group).

These insights are especially provocative because they identify citizens as willing agents in the (excessive) erosion of their own rights. Such insights can be important to human rights advocates in choosing which actors to target for persuasion in an illiberal regime, in considering potential perverse outcomes of democratic institutions, and in determining what persuasive messages might gain traction with particular audiences. These insights also suggest nations should, prior to the emergence of a threat from an out-group, develop devices to reduce the likelihood of excessive rights restrictions. For example, national legislatures might require supermajority votes and cooling-off periods before enacting rights restrictions, and they might require sunset clauses in particular categories of legislation. Such measures are not unusual in lawmaking. Baron's research, however, provides independent and strong reasons for their adoption. Indeed, such measures can now be justified on the basis that they foster individuals' ability to realize their "true preferences."

Notes

This Coda, like the others in the book, offers some specific applications drawn from the insights in the contributor's chapter. It is not intended to be a list of fully developed policy prescriptions, but instead an example of the rich sorts of human rights policy applications that can be drawn from cutting-edge social science research. It does not question the insights offered in the chapter but instead asks what implications those insights might have for human rights law and policy. The Codas are the sole authorship of the editors of the volume.

1. The editors thank David Zionts for first suggesting examples in this section.
2. The Geneva Conventions, Protocol I, Art. 57.

9

Networks and Politics

The Case of Human Rights

DAVID LAZER

Domestic practices related to human rights are in part a reflection of the international context within which a state resides. The international context provides models and information for human rights-related practices, instills norms, offers resources to domestic groups, and direct pressures from other governments. However, the "international context" is not a singular object. States differ in how they are situated. North Korea, Romania, and Zimbabwe are in dramatically different positions in the international system. Among other differences, they vary in their trade patterns, the movement of people to and from other locations in the world, and their access to the global informational commons. If the international context matters to human rights practice, this variability in connections will have implications for the human rights regimes of these countries. The objective of this chapter is to offer an introduction to one way to study the variability of connectedness within social systems: the structural approach to networks. Network science offers a family of theories and methods that might well offer understanding into the dynamics of human rights practices around the world.

The human rights regime of a country is, at its foundation, political, because it is about the definitive allocation of rights, resources, and responsibilities within a community. This chapter therefore places the discussion of networks and human rights into the broader intellectual foundation of how network ideas have been used to understand politics. What is the relational dimension of politics? Does it matter how people and organizations are connected to each other? Are opinions affected by who we talk to? Are legislators affected by lobbyists? Is the capacity of social movements to mobilize affected by the structure of societal networks? The objective of this chapter is to provide some sense of the intellectual history of the study of social networks, of political networks, and to conclude with a discussion of how the network lens might matter to understanding the diffusion of human rights-related policies.

I. The Governance and Structural Perspectives on Networks

The word "network" has multiplied in both academic and popular parlance in the last decade. As the word has proliferated, its meaning across different audiences has become murkier, evoking, at once, terrorist organizations and Facebook. In its academic identity, one may distinguish between two usages relevant to the study of human rights: one that focuses on the governance implications of how authority is distributed in a system (and, in particular, the implications for governance of the absence of a central authority); and the second one that examines the determinants and consequences of the pattern of relationships within a system.

While the literature on human rights and international relations has largely focused on the first usage of network, this paper focuses on the second. We therefore begin with a discussion of the relationship between these two understandings of the term. The first construction of "network" is often used to refer to a group of nonhierarchically arranged but heavily interdependent entities. Thus, one may refer to a "terrorist network" or a network of human rights organizations with shared goals and interests, in which there is no central authority. The contrasting case would be one where there is a central authority, with a clearly defined set of authority relationships, such as the U.S. Army. The key question that this framing of network evokes is what governance mechanism emerges (or not) to manage collective problems. Examples include management of the commons in the absence of a central government authority (Ostrom, 1990), and the mobilization of human rights movements globally (Keck and Sikkink, 1998). Such a network form is sometimes contrasted with hierarchical and market-based forms of organizing collective efforts (e.g., Powell, 2003; Williamson, 1973).

While the first notion of network focuses on the presence or absence of authority relationships within a system, the second construction of "network" is open with respect to the types of relationships that exist within the system. The necessary ingredient to the structural perspective on networks (cf. Wellman and Berkowitz, 1988) is the analytic focus on configuration of connections among the elements of a system. What is the association between promotion and the patterns of one's friendships within an organization (e.g., Ibarra, 1992)? How is position in the market related to profitability (e.g., Burt, 1995)?

If viewed as a Venn diagram, these two literatures on "network" appear as overlapping circles, neither encompassing the other. Most of the governance literature on networks does not examine the structure of connectedness within the systems studied; most of the network literature does not focus on governance issues. However, in the area of intersection, there is a substantial body of work emerging out of the literature on social capital, with a particular focus on how network structure regulates market exchange (for a useful synthesis, see Jones, Hesterly, and Borgatti, 1997). Some of the foundational work in social capital emphasizes how network closure (e.g., friends of friends know each other) facilitates exchange in immigrant communities because of possible reputational consequences from bad behavior (Bourdieu, 2001). The role of embeddedness in systems of relationships, in particular, has been explored in industries that require episodic collaboration among autonomous organizations or people—including such varied sectors as construction and Broadway. The conundrum this literature studies is the following: Given the lack of a central authority, the inadequacy of contracts to specify all contingencies, and the constant possibility of exploitation of one party by another, how does a set of organizations come together to work effectively on a particular project?

The answer, according to some economic sociologists, is that individual agency is constrained by the social structure in which individuals are embedded (Granovetter, 1985). Uzzi (1996), in particular, developed the ideas of relational and structural embeddedness. *Structural embeddedness* is, essentially, the tendency of one's exchange partners to know each other; and *relational embeddedness* is the tendency for individuals to have multiple types of relationships with exchange partners (e.g., business partners who are also family). The essential argument of Uzzi and others is that structural embeddedness limits bad behavior because of the possible ramifications for exchange opportunities with third parties; and relational embeddedness limits bad behavior because of spillover effects on one's other relationships with that particular exchange partner.

The primary objective of this chapter is to offer an overview of the second (structural) perspective on networks, with a particular focus on the potential applicability to human rights. We begin with a brief primer on the key concepts of the structural approach.[1]

II. The Structural Perspective on Networks: Key Concepts

In the structural perspective on networks, the core building blocks of a network are *nodes* and *edges*. Nodes are typically actors, and edges are relationships among actors. Exactly what constitutes a node and an edge depends on the application of the approach—for example, nodes may be people, organizations, countries; edges may be friendships, e-mail volume, or physical proximity. Edges may be *undirected* (A and B are connected) or *directed* (A sends B a tie), as well as *unvalued* (a tie exists or does not exist) or *valued* (there are a variety of values it might take). Here are some examples: whether countries touch each other is necessarily undirected and unvalued, the total volume of phone calls between two countries is valued and undirected, whether a country has an embassy in another country is directed and unvalued, and exports/imports between two countries is valued and directed.[2]

Most research within the social network field is on *whole network data*. Whole network data involves relational information on some closed set of actors. For example, one might ask everyone in an organization who their friends are, enabling a system-level picture of the entire network. In contrast, *egocentric network data* involves analysis of an individual's local network, typically by asking a set of focal individuals (each respondent is called "ego") about their discussion partners (the "alters"). Each type of data has particular limitations. Egocentric data, as noted above, allows application of scientific sampling to large populations from whom it is impractical to collect whole network data. It is not practical, for example, to conduct a network survey of every individual in the United States. However, through the collection of a sample of responses from just hundreds of individuals, it is possible to make statistically robust statements about some characteristics of the network connecting 300 million people. For example, it is possible to make statements about the extent to which friendships cross racial (Marsden, 1987) and political (Huckfeldt and Johnson, 2004; Mutz, 2006;) lines by asking respondents about the characteristics of their alters. Whole network methods, however, do enable statistical statements about certain important characteristics of the network that egocentric methods do not. It is not possible, for example, to state what is the maximum observed separation (the number of hops it takes to go from one node to another) between any two nodes in a given network based on egocentric data.

Any relational information might be construed as "network" data. This includes self-report data on relationships, transaction data, archival data, observational data, and so on. Historically, the bulk of research on social networks has relied on self-report data, which, in turn, has focused the development of analytic tools on single snapshots of small networks (since collecting self reports many times or on large-scale networks is not practical). Self-report relational data, as with other self-report data, are also subject to substantial reliability issues, as was the subject of a vigorous literature in the field in the 1980s (Bernard et al., 1984; Eagle, Pentland, and Lazer, 2009; Freeman, Romney, and Freeman, 1987). The reliance on self-report data has begun to change over the last decade, with the increased availability of large-scale archival data, such as call log and e-mail data (Lazer et al., 2009).

Network data can be *one mode* or *two mode* in nature. One mode data involves ties among a set of agents, and two mode ties between two different mutually exclusive sets of agents. For example, direct ties among nations, such as trade, would be one mode in nature. Ties from nations to international organizations would be two mode in nature, where two mode data might be converted to one mode by examining the number of overlapping affiliations that agents have (e.g., Hafner-Burton and Montgomery, 2006). Thus, for example, countries A and B might belong to five of the same international organizations, or two international organizations might share three members. Or, as in Figure 9.1b, one may view senators as being connected by shared contributors, where the graph reveals both some unsurprising structural features (the strong partisan divide, the strong tie between the Udall cousins), as well as notable (e.g., the especially strong tie between McConnell and Coleman). This figure also provides hints regarding the power of particular senators; the centrality of McConnell (the minority leader) suggests the possibility that a source of McConnell's power is in directing his contributors to other senators.

Network analysis might focus on any of a number of levels of analysis. At the *positional level*, one might look at the position of nodes in the overall network. *Centrality* is the positional variable that has received the most attention in the network literature, and for which a wide array of measures have been developed (Freeman, 1979). One of the major questions that has been the focus of social network analysis is on the positional correlates of success, where Burt (1995), among others, has argued that connecting actors that are otherwise disconnected provides actors substantial competitive advantage.

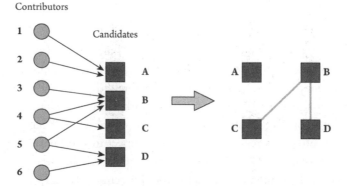

Figure 9.1a   Unipartite projection of bipartite data.

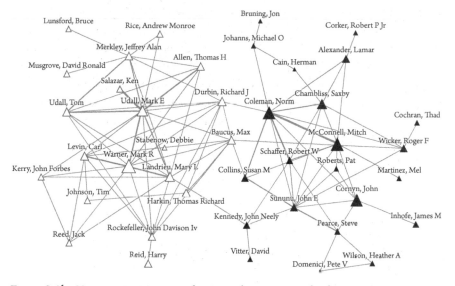

Figure 9.1b Unipartite projection of co-contribution network of 2008 Senate candidates.

Bipartite network represents financial contributions from individual contributors to political candidates.

Cut-off is at $50,000 both for nodes and links, white nodes represent Democratic candidates, and black nodes Republican; thickness of edges and size of nodes corresponds to amount of co-contribution. (Adapted from Onnela and Lazer, 2010).

At the *dyadic level*, one would look at the determinants and consequences of a tie between pairs of actors. Perhaps one of the most robust patterns found in the social sciences is that similar actors are relatively likely to have a tie (McPherson, Smith-Lovin, and Cook, 2001); see discussion below regarding homophily. Conversely, there is ample research on contagion and diffusion (Rogers, 1995) that suggests that actors that have a tie are likely to converge in behavior—for example, with respect to smoking (Christakis and Fowler, 2008) and political beliefs (Lazer et al., 2010).

At the triadic level, one of the key statistical questions is the extent to which a tie between two actors is statistically dependent on the presence or absence of ties to third parties, where the presence of a tie between third parties enhances the likelihood of the tie of a particular pair of individuals (Holland and Leinhardt, 1970). Between the triadic and systemic level, there have been various efforts over the years to detect cohesive subgroups (Freeman, 2003); with particular efforts in recent years to develop scalable algorithms for "community detection" (for review, see Porter, Onnela, and Mucha, 2009). Finally, the systemic level has received particular attention in recent years, following, especially, from

Watts and Strogatz's (1998) small world work, where the measure of interest is the typical degrees of separation between any two actors in the system, and the Barabasi and Albert (1999) work on degree distribution. Watts and Strogatz developed the mathematical undergirdings of the small world finding of Milgram (1967). In Milgram's classic experiment, a source individual in Nebraska was provided a package to forward to a target individual in Massachusetts, with the proviso that the package had to be sent only to someone the source knew by first name. That second person, in turn, could only send a package to someone they knew by first name, until, eventually, the package reached the target. While most of the packages did not reach their target, some did; and the average number of steps in completed chains was about six—yielding the famous "six degrees of separation." The key empirical puzzle raised by the experiment is the apparent inconsistency of this finding with the fact that most of our networks are quite parochial, circumscribed by geography, class, religion, and so on. That is, how can we be so few steps away from individuals so apparently disconnected from us? The insight of Watts and Strogatz was twofold: (1) that the tendency for networks to be "small world"—locally parochial but with small degrees of separation separating any two actors—is robust across dramatically different types of networks (human and nonhuman); and (2) the statistical reason for this is quite simple—that a small number of random linkages provides enough shortcuts in the network to yield the relatively small degrees of separation.

Barabasi and Albert examined a different dimension of the same data used by Watts and Strogatz—the distribution of connectedness of the nodes. If connectedness had a bell curve (Gaussian) type of distribution, there would be a relative scarcity of very poorly and very well-connected nodes. Instead, they found a scale-free distribution, where most nodes were poorly connected, but where there were a surprising number of extremely well-connected hubs. Such a distribution is consistent with a preferential attachment process, where the number of links a node creates at a given point in time is proportional to the number of links it already has (although, as later research shows, there are many processes that yield similar distributions—Clauset, Shalizi, and Newman, 2009).

III. A Short Intellectual History of the Study of Networks

The focus of the network paradigm is on the causes and consequences of the connections among the elements of a system. The genesis of the modern study of social networks is usually dated to the work of Moreno (Moreno, 1934) and the emergence of sociometry (the quantitative measurement of relations) in the 1930s.[3] The 1940s and 1950s witnessed an explosion of research on social networks, some of which is still required reading in many disciplines. Much of this work was in sociology and social psychology but with significant political themes: the Columbia studies on public opinion (Lazarsfeld, Berelson, and Gaudet, 1968); Festinger and his collaborators' work on social influence (Festinger, 1954; Festinger, Schachter, and Back, 1963); Bavelas's work on small group networks (Bavelas, 1950); and the Robbers Cave experiment (Sherif et al., 1961). By the 1960s, the work on networks had largely been consolidated into sociology and anthropology and, to some extent, communication. The one major exception during this period was Milgram's (Milgram, 1967) work on small worlds, discussed above. Important scholars in this area during this time were Harrison White (Boorman and White, 1976; White, Boorman, and Breiger, 1976), Linton Freeman Freeman, 1979), and Everett Rogers (Rogers, 1995) who wrote some of the foundational work during this period and mentored the generation of scholars who followed—most notably, Mark Granovetter, whose 1973 paper on the "strength of weak ties" is the most cited paper on social networks in the social sciences (Granovetter, 1973).

From the 1970s to the 1990s, the study of networks was fairly stable, with a consolidation in focus around the statistical characterization of the structure of networks; and with a steady niche presence in sociology, anthropology, communications, and related fields (e.g., organizational behavior). The 1990s witnessed an explosion of research on networks that has ricocheted across the academy. There were two veins of research, largely independent of one another, which were associated with this explosion. In the social sciences, there was the emergence of interest in social capital, in part fueled by research by Robert Putnam (Putnam, 2001; Putnam, Leonardi, and Nanetti, 1993) The general proposition of this literature is that just as physical and human capital are related to the productivity of individuals and collections of individuals, how people are connected also affects productivity (broadly viewed). To take a simple example, sometimes knowing someone with a lawnmower is just as valuable as owning a one. One's friends have resources, and friendship sometimes offers entrée to those resources. In the literature, the exact characterization of the relationship between social network ideas and social capital is ambiguous. Putnam's work emphasizes affiliations more than interpersonal ties—how many people belong to bowling leagues, civic associations, churches, boy scouts, and so on. His famous observation regarding the United States is that more people seem to be "bowling alone," not in bowling leagues. His argument is that the connections forged in these organized associations are essential to the smooth functioning of society because they facilitate collective action of various types.

The relationship between Putnam's construction of social capital and the structural perspective on networks is a bit fuzzy, because it is unclear whether the decline of bowling leagues and the like is necessarily associated with an overall decline of connectedness of individuals. It is possible, for example, that some of the decline in civic associations reflects the movement of women into the workforce, and thus a secular shift in the societal foci for relationship creation from civic associations to the workplace. In short, underlying Putnam's argument is the notion that there is a tectonic shift in where relationships are based in our society, but the data are not primarily focused on the structure of societal networks. There are other treatments of social capital, however, that emphasize the structural dimension of social networks (e.g., Lin, 2001).

The second vein of academic research, on the small world problem, emerged from physics, marked by the publication of the Watts and Strogatz (1998) and Barabasi and Albert (1999) papers discussed above. An enormous literature emerged almost overnight in physics on small world-related research, as well as in computer science, biology, and ecology, among other fields (these two papers, together, have a remarkable 27,000 citations in Google scholar).

It is almost certainly not a coincidence that this interest emerged in synchrony with the development of a network-based medium, the Internet,. Some of the network research caught popular attention, serving as part of motivation for Malcolm Gladwell's *Tipping Point* (Gladwell, 2002) and other popular books by many of the principals in this research, including Watts (2003, 2004), Strogatz (2003), Barabasi (2003), and Christakis and Fowler (Christakis and Fowler, 2009).

An exhaustive list of the themes explored in these literatures is well beyond the scope of this chapter, which will attempt to summarize a few of the major threads of this research, categorized into (1) the effects of networks, and (2) the origins and structure of networks.

IV. The Effects of Networks

The reason to study networks rests on the assertion that they are somehow consequential: being in a good position in the network increases the odds of success; being near someone with the flu increases your odds of becoming sick, and so on. A majority of the literature that studies the effects of networks can be categorized as focusing on the circulatory, regulatory, or control effects of networks, which are discussed in turn below.

Arguably, the biggest single category of network research rests on the metaphor of networks as a structure through which things circulate. The vast diffusion of innovation literature (Rogers, 1995), for example, in part examines the relational determinants of innovation adoption. Epidemiology studies how various contact patterns affect the spread of pathogens (Morris and Kretzschmar, 1997). Similarly, the literature on social influence (Christakis and Fowler, 2007; Festinger, Schachter, and Back, 1963; Marsden and Friedkin, 1994) asserts that convergence in behavior flows through ties. Much of the power of the small world research comes from the intuition that even in a world where most ties are local, a small number of ties connecting distant actors experiences vastly accelerated diffusion. Further, much of the positional analysis done on networks (see below) rests on the circulatory metaphor—for example, central people are more likely to get information first.

A second, large segment of the network literature focuses on how network structure regulates individual behavior. This is the point of intersection between the governance and structural perspectives on networks, as discussed above. Much of the social capital literature, following "network closure," argues that closed networks—where friends of friends tend to know each other—reduces opportunistic behavior. That is, a transaction between A and B has implications for the transaction between A and C (see discussion regarding structural embeddedness above). The network as regulator of markets has formed the basis for a whole subfield of sociology—economic sociology—following Granovetter's (1985) classic paper on embeddedness in markets.

A third stream of literature, particular relevant to the study of politics, examines how position in the network affects control. Exchange theory (Emerson, 1976) offers one paradigm in which this has been explored. In this vein, Padgett and Ansell (1993), offer a compelling examination of the rise of the Medici in medieval Florence, arguing that the position of the Medici in the marriage and exchange networks of Florence enabled effective control of their coalition.

Particular theories within the network field, of course, weave these streams together. Most prominently, Burt's structural hole (Burt, 1995) argument in part relies on the proposition that individuals who are tied to structurally diverse others are exposed to more information (the circulatory element), as well as on the assertion that being connected to individuals who are not connected enables greater control (e.g., resulting in greater rents through arbitrage).

V. The Origins and Structure of Networks

Perhaps one of the most robust findings in all of the social sciences is that of homophily: that individuals who are similar to one another are more likely to form ties—for a thorough review, see McPherson, Smith-Lovin, and Cook, 2001. This is almost certainly a pattern with many causes. In some cases, homophily may reflect a simple preference to be with those like oneself; in other cases, that revealed preference may reflect an instrumental need to be with similar others (e.g., because they are more likely to have useful information); and in yet other cases, homophily may be the result of who people have an opportunity to meet (only wealthy people live in expensive neighborhoods, and your neighborhood influences who you talk to). Certainly, the relevance of homophily to political discussion networks was demonstrated in the early Columbia studies and has continued to be the focus of research (Huckfeldt and Sprague 1995; Mutz 2004); although see Lazer et al., 2010). Schelling (Schelling, 1978) has explored the emergent properties of the preference for homophily, finding that mild preferences to be with similar others tend to be amplified. Physical proximity has been shown to be a particularly powerful predictor of tie formation, at scales large and small (Allen, 1970; Butts, 2003).

VI. Threads of Networks in the Study of Politics

There is an obvious match between politics and social network ideas. At a casual level, it is impossible to deny that friendship matters in the authoritative distribution of resources—whether we are talking about the banal politics of a university department, or the more consequential politics of the U.S. Congress. It is therefore unsurprising that from the early days of the study of networks, politics was there. In fact, at least one early study of legislative friendships that involved the collection of sociometric data was conducted at roughly the same time as Moreno's work on sociometry (Routt, 1938). However, political science has been fairly unfriendly territory for social network research until recent years. Arguably, this is because the dominant methodological paradigm in political science since the 1950s has been centered on public opinion research, which has relied on the assumption that observations in a sample are independently distributed of one another. Scientific sampling methods are not necessarily at odds with the network approach (e.g., see discussion of egocentric network data above), because the assumption that the observations in a sample are independent of one another does not rule that those observations are dependent on individuals not included in the sample. As a metaphor for human behavior, however, it excludes the social dimension of opinion formation. It is also a methodology that is inconsistent with whole network methods, which have dominated social network analysis. It is not surprising, therefore, that to the extent that social influence has been studied in political science, it has been with egocentric data (Huckfeldt and Sprague, 1995; although for an exception that uses whole network data, see Lazer et al., 2010), whereas in sociology, whole network methods have been utilized (Friedkin, 1998).

There have been several active strands of network-based research in political science. The most robust has been around public opinion, following the classic Columbia studies. The research on "breakage effects"—the tendency for minority partisans in an area to vote like the majority (Berelson, Lazarsfeld, and McPhee, 1986; also see Putnam, 1966, and critique by Prysby, 1976) – in political science followed in the 1950s; and in the last generation, the work by Huckfeldt and colleagues is particularly notable, as well as the recent work by Mutz (2006) on ties across partisan and ideological divides. There has also been a thin but steady stream of research on networks in the U.S. Congress, starting with Routt, 1938, as noted above, with Patterson and collaborators starting in the 1950s (Patterson, 1959). More recently, there has been an uptick of interest in utilizing the network dimension of data on the cosponsorship of bills by members of the U.S. Congress (Fowler, 2006).

There has also been research on political organization—for example, the role that connections within the political system matter. For example, in the U.S. context, research has been done on how elected officials, bureaucrats, and organized interests are tied together (Carpenter, Esterling, and Lazer, 2008; Heaney, 2006; Heinz, 1993; Laumann and Knoke, 1987), and in the medieval Florentine context, Padgett and Ansell (1993) study archival records to show how the Medici rose to power due to their unique bridging position in the Florentine marriage and trade network.

International relations has the ironic distinction of being the subfield of political science that has "relations" in its name and yet historically has rarely used the analytic tools of network methods. In fact, many of the canonical data sets in international relations are network in nature—typically where the nodes are nation-states; and the edges are some relational variable, such as trade, treaties, measures of conflict, etc. There has been a fair amount of research where dyads (or dyad years) have been the analytic focus, but until recent years this research has not incorporated broader structural variables, or dealt with known statistical dependencies that are endemic in network. In the last decade, this has changed substantially, with work by Hafner-Burton, Kahler, and Montgomery (2009); Maoz (2010); O'Loughlin et al. (1998); and Lazer (1999) explicitly using network ideas.

VII. Trends and Future Issues

Receiving (deservedly so) increased attention in recent years in the study of networks is the development of methods for making robust statements regarding the causal effects of networks. As is typical in the social sciences, observational data offer particular challenges for interpretation. The finding that two people who have a relationship are similar to one another may be the result of social influence, homophily, or some other process that pushes similar individuals together. A number of strategies have emerged to address causation. Laboratory experiments have a long tradition in the study of social networks (Bavelas, 1950; Kearns, Suri, and Montfort, 2006), although an intrinsic limitation is the simulation of psychologically meaningful relationships in the laboratory setting. Field experiments offer particular power, although there are only a few examples as applied to networks (Nickerson, 2008) being an innovative example from political science; and Mobius, Szeidl, and Center (2007) from economics. The importance of location in determining ties has also been utilized as an instrument of sorts for network ties—for example, this was used in Festinger, Schachter, and Back (1963); and more recently in studies of the influence of roommates on each other (Sacerdote, 2001). The applicability of any experimental or quasi-experimental research, of course, varies dramatically with subfield in political science—for example, field experiments are highly applicable in the study of political opinion and behavior but irrelevant in the study of international relations.

Longitudinal data also offer power in discerning causal direction, where the observation of temporal precedence may allow an inference of causal order (Snijders, 2005). The power of that logical leap depends on additional assumptions, however—for example, that there is not some unobserved process that affects both position in the network and outcome over time. For example, if skill causes network position at time t, and success at time t + 1, an inference that network position yielded success based on temporal precedence would be spurious.

The reliance on exogenous processes to push information through networks is another method that has been used to assist in causal inference. For example, the assumption that elections cause increased communication regarding politics was used both in the Columbia studies and more recent work following in that tradition (Huckfeldt and Sprague, 1995). A challenge in interpretation there is the assumption that other messages (such as media use, targeted messages from the campaign) are uncorrelated with network structure.

There has also been increased attention to network dynamics (Carley, 2003). Many relationships are intrinsically episodic. "Network dynamics" can reflect either the change in probability of those episodes over time or the specific temporal sequence of those episodes. Thus, the question, for example, "With whom do you talk to about politics" captures an overall tendency to talk about politics, but actually talking about politics with someone takes place at particular points in time. While more attention has been focused on the first notion of network dynamics, it turns out that the second can have pretty important implications for core constructs in the study of social networks such as centrality.

Closely related to the increased attention on network dynamics has been the increased availability of massive, passive data about human behavior (Lazer et al., 2009). For example, Onnela et al. (2007) offered an analysis of mobile phone call log data of millions of individuals based on months of observations, and the Internet offers a plethora of network data. These types of data clearly offer potentially extraordinary insights of the dynamics of relationships on a societal scale. They also offer significant challenges to the social sciences, from privacy/ human subjects issues, to bread and butter methodological concerns. (For example, as a social science construct, what does a phone call between two people mean? What statistical methods scale to data sets with millions of nodes and trillions of dyads?)

VIII. Applicability of Network Ideas to the Study of Human Rights

The essential premise that network ideas might be relevant to thinking about human rights and international relations is that how a nation is connected to others affects its policies as they relate to human rights. There are several levels at which network ideas might be relevant.

Nation-state: The essential building block of international relations theory is the nation-state. Variants of the realist approach to international relations focus on how the structure of the international system drives policy at the national level, with resulting patterns of behavior systemically (Waltz, 1979). In the classic, realist, construction of international relations, the domestic policy of other states is not a driver of foreign policy because the key interest of a state is security (Carr and Cox, 2001). In more mercantile models of realism, the goals of the state are broadened to include economic interests and development (Gilpin, 1983). The state might then have an interest in access to markets, which, in turn, might require harmonization of certain domestic (e.g., regulatory) policies (Lazer, 2001). However, in the traditional realist model of international relations, there is little room for human rights (and thus for networks to matter vis-à-vis human rights at the nation-state level).

A broader definition of interest might conceivably incorporate human rights. The constructivist literature in international relations suggests that the traditional realist view of the nation-state is itself endogenous (Wendt, 2009). A corollary to this is that the security based orientation of the state is not necessarily accurate. This perspective is further bolstered by the democratic peace literature, which suggests that there may, in fact, be legitimate security interests in the domestic (i.e., related to human rights) policies of another state.

A. Sub-Nation/Cross-National Networks

In a more disaggregated view of the state, state and society are made up of a variety of entities. These entities may be connected across national boundaries, where those connections may provide important resources. There may be connections among government agencies (Lazer, 2005) or of organized interests, where these transnational networks might be a critical source of resources for domestic groups pushing for particular human rights practices (Keck and Sikkink, 1998).

B. Flows of People

Individuals flow across national borders. This includes everything from semipermanent migration to tourism to attending university in another country and returning home. This movement of individuals, in turn, might be consequential for the policies of the countries involved, as discussed below.

C. Flows of Information

Even in the absence of flows of individuals across national borders, there is a flow of bits. People communicate by phone, surf the Internet, and watch satellite television. The access to information can and should be conceived in network terms. Not all individuals in the world have access to the same information, and those that do don't necessarily pay attention to the same sources of information.

At each of these levels, one might conceive of how different types of connections might affect diffusion/adoption/rejection of particular domestic practices related to human rights. Of potential relevance is the regulatory/control/circulatory framework above.

IX. The Regulatory and Control Dimensions of International Relations

Beginning with the assumption that states have preferences vis-à-vis human rights in other states, the structure of interdependence among states becomes critical. Per exchange theory, if focal state A is uniquely dependent on state B, then the preferences of state B will be especially important to state A. Alternatively, if state A has other potential partners that could substitute for state B, then the preferences of state A are less important. For example, historically, South America has had particularly strong ties and dependence on the United States. The preferences of the United States vis-à-vis human rights were, and are, more

consequential for Peru than they are for Burma. And as China rises in importance, an interesting question is whether this will have ramifications with respect
to human rights policies in its trading partners, given its preferences with respect
to human rights.

Further, international institutions play a potentially key role in the regulatory
effects of the network. To what extent are human rights values embedded within
particular multilateral institutions? For example, did the prospect of joining the
European Union affect human rights-related choices of former Eastern bloc
countries? Certainly, these values were institutionalized in the European Union
in the form of the Copenhagen criteria, which explicitly identified human rights
as a necessary but not sufficient criterion for membership. How this affected
prospective members, in turn, must have depended in part on the value of the
prospects of EU membership, which is something that should be conceived of in
network terms—for example, that there were no substitutes in terms of partners
that could provide the economic and security value of the European Union.

The examples of "flows" in the international system also carry with them the
possibility of international diffusion. Thus, for example, one might ask what are
the long-term consequences of the influx of Chinese graduate students into
Western universities? Are the values of these students affected by their experiences; and if so, does this have a long-term impact on Chinese society upon their
return (or their communication of their experiences to friends and family back
in China)? Similarly, what impact does access to information have on a society
such as China? Such free flow of information is intrinsically subversive, in the
sense that in hierarchic societies, the power of the state to mediate information
flows is undermined. The Internet, in particular, has a decentralized architecture
conceived and born in a liberal context, and one of the key narratives of the
twenty-first century will be the resolution of the tension between this decentralized architecture and the centralized architecture of power in states such as Iran
and China (Zittrain, 2009).

X. Conclusion

The connectionist—network—perspective on phenomena has gained tre-
mendous currency over the last decade, with research on everything from the
structure of the brain, to the relationship between genes and cancer, to the
structure of relationships among members of the U.S. Congress. The objective
of this chapter was to offer an overview of the structural view of networks, focusing on its application to political phenomena, and to evaluate what insights
network analysis might offer into the (non)spread of human rights globally.
The case to be made for the relevance of network methods to understanding

human rights-related policies is that these policies are, in part, a function of the international context. International context should be conceived of, in part, in network terms because every state has different connection to that broader context. Nations vary in their patterns of interdependencies, their migration patterns, and their communication patterns. These dependencies almost certainly have an impact on human rights practices.

Notes

1. This introduction is in part drawn from Lazer (2011).
2. Interestingly, the bulk of research on networks has been on unvalued (and usually undirected) data; although, arguably, the bulk of network phenomena involves valued relations. This reflects the challenges in analyzing (and sometimes collecting) valued relational data.
3. For useful discussions of the intellectual antecedents of social network analysis, see L. C. Freeman (2004) and Scott (1988).

CODA

Networks and Politics

RYAN GOODMAN, DEREK JINKS, AND ANDREW K. WOODS

David Lazer's chapter gives an overview of the fast-growing and interdisciplinary field of network analysis. The study of how relationships are structured as a set of nodes and ties has an intuitive appeal, given the dominance of the Internet in modern life. While a great deal of attention has been paid to the Internet as a communication medium that could help human rights advocates, Lazer's chapter suggests that this focus on the technology of social connections misses the real payoff of network analysis. Networks are a useful conceptual tool for mapping social arrangements, for understanding social phenomena, and for policy design. The discussion below shows that the implications of network analysis for human rights are broad—they cover state-to-state interactions, but also interpersonal and intercommunity linkages.

I. Target: Promoters of Human Rights

One way that network analysis might assist the human rights regime is to explain the network dynamics at play in social movements. Despite the proliferation of NGOs operating in support of human rights, there is little analytical work explaining how the various groups can or should interconnect. What tools and what social phenomena would be most useful to practitioners as they seek to expand their influence as a movement? Perhaps a better understanding of network dynamics would allow practitioners to both expand and mobilize supporters of human rights causes. Initially, this work may be purely descriptive: identifying the various players and their relationships to gain a more sophisticated understanding of how various actors contribute to the movement.

What is the relationship between non-state actors and the rights regime? Network analysis could play an enormous role in explicating this relationship, perhaps first by mapping the relationships among various non-state actors and establishing causal pathways between those actors and the individuals they seek to regulate (Bender-deMoll, 2008). For example, many funders call for cross-border; North-South; South-South collaboration, etc., as do the NGOs themselves; network analysis could chart these relationships and determine if and how they change over time. This same information could be useful in tracking the influence of how powerful donors shape human rights law and policy. Indeed, a better understanding of the relationship between various social and political networks could ultimately affect fundraising, strategic partnerships, and information campaigns.

Network analysis might assist NGOs in determining and shaping influence pathways. This information could be used in human rights training—to prepare practitioners to become more effective norm entrepreneurs by identifying relevant nodes in a network of normative influence. Similarly, if there are gross disparities or gaps in networks—for example, between non-state actors of a certain stripe or between NGOs and academics—specific linkages could be developed to erode these gaps. Or perhaps network analysis would demonstrate the benefits of certain gaps in the network and suggest that the gaps be widened. The point is that network analysis could provide a more refined, more systematic approach to managing successful relationships. Better information could, for example, enable weaker states with pro-human rights foreign policy agendas to know how they might employ networks in combination with soft power to compete with global or regional military powers (Bátora, 2005).

II. Target: Actual and Potential Perpetrators of Human Rights Violations

A. Networks of Illiberal Actors

The insights discussed in this chapter can also be used to understand the dynamics in illiberal movements. For example, network analysis has been used by the U.S. National Security Agency to map the connections between alleged terrorists to identify a coherent structure and hierarchy out of a decentralized group. The same network information can be used to understand the origins and structure of social support for illiberal groups more generally—for example, those supporting ethnic cleansing, violence against immigrants, and antigay and lesbian hate crimes.

Identifying the relationship among rights abusers can be useful in a number of ways. As a policy matter, it may be important to have a sense of just how close violence is to the surface. Does the presence of hate speech or incidents of abuse mean that wide-scale violence may occur tomorrow? In a year? On what scale? Network analysis may help to answer these questions. In the Rwandan genocide, there were many indicators of the coming violence, but perhaps there was no better indicator than the fact that the individual signs of impending genocide were linked to each other. The key early-stage organizers of the genocide not only coordinated funding, weapons, and messaging; they also organized several "networking" events with the specific purpose of creating more links between prospective genocidaires. Network analysis can reveal the significance of those explicit relationships as well as more implicit ones.

This discussion raises an important point: most, if not all, of the implications explored here can also be exploited by illiberal, rights-violating actors. Network analysis might be used by rights violators to build a web of support for their cause. Or it may be used by illiberal states to illuminate networks of political dissidents. But the hope is that a better understanding of network dynamics may also enable policy makers to better predict and respond to illiberal network dynamics. For example, if a particular node is central to an illiberal network—as the Hutu Power radio station in Kigale was to the Rwandan genocidaires—action to identify and, in turn, isolate that node may be the best way to disrupt the network. Additionally, if illiberal states use network analysis to repress dissidents, the latter would be aided by such insights in developing responses.

These same network dynamics may also help to clarify legal concepts that attempt to capture the structural nature of group crimes—especially offenses that otherwise may not fit well within existing legal paradigms. For example, the "incitement to genocide" standard could be developed considerably with network analysis concepts (Woods, 2010). Rather than merely looking for speech inciting people to violence, a rich understanding of network analysis might provide for superior legal doctrines to account for the knowing manipulation of information infrastructure. This behavior is not currently considered incitement to genocide, but perhaps it should be. In the case of the Rwandan genocide, the distribution of radios to checkpoints is considered by some to have been a necessary precursor to the coordinated killing. Network analysis may help prosecutors to better understand and convict the key players responsible for constructing hateful information pathways and genocidal networks.

B. Embeddedness

If the evidence is indeed overwhelming that, as Lazer puts it, "actors that have a tie are likely to converge in behavior" (Lazer, this volume citing Rogers, (1995), Christakis and Fowler (2008), and Lazer et al. (2010)), then perhaps human rights organizations will want to create greater embeddedness of parts of a national security apparatus within human rights institutions for purposes of contagion. For instance, the dominant trend in many countries is to maintain firewalls between law enforcement and the national human rights commission. But perhaps the networks would benefit from overlap. In India, for example, the national commission is composed of law enforcement officers secunded to the investigative branch of the institution, and this creates new networks that may promote or retard human rights—depending on the direction of the contagion. The mechanism for this effect could come either from structural or relational embeddedness, again depending here on the nature of the overlap.

The same analysis might inform ideas about integration among populations. Diversity and integration are liberal ideals—but the network analysis literature may help regime designers to understand the consequences of segregated versus integrated population patterns on homophily. The relationship between population distribution and homophily may affect how we seek to prevent intergroup conflict. This could have implications for city planning, architecture, and design—fields that are currently considered tangential to human rights, but which may become more central as we learn more about the role of connectedness in homophily.

These questions have been given some thought already in the international relations and legal literatures. There is some evidence that embeddedness, for example, has an effect between and among states (Goodman and Jinks, forthcoming; Goodman and Jinks, 2004; Meyer, 2011; Simmons, 2009). Network analysis may foster a more nuanced analysis of how embeddedness—and different kinds—affects rights practices. A better understanding of embedding effects would be especially useful for predicting and planning diffusion among actors who are connected to multiple communities—such as the transfer of global cultural norms among foreign service officers (Johnston, 2007), or among states embedded in multiple regional and international bodies (Beckfield, 2010; Torfason and Ingram, 2010).

Note

This Coda, like the others in the book, offers some specific applications drawn from the insights in the contributor's chapter. It is not intended to be a list of fully developed policy prescriptions, but instead an example of the rich sorts of human rights policy applications that can be drawn from cutting-edge social science research. It does not question the insights offered in the chapter but instead asks what implications those insights might have for human rights law and policy. The Codas are the sole authorship of the editors of the volume.

10

Barriers to Dispute Resolution

Reflections on Peacemaking and Relationships between Adversaries

BYRON BLAND, BRENNA POWELL, AND LEE ROSS

I. Introduction

What stands in the way of agreement? What prevents individuals and groups from reaching agreements that are not only in the best interests of the parties but respectful of the human rights of those affected by an ongoing conflict and likely to benefit from a just settlement of that conflict? More specifically, what prevents those with the power to make or block an agreement from opting for the latter? Addressing this simple question can help guide those trying to manage or resolve a protracted conflict. This question of "barriers" is especially relevant in cases where consideration of the objective interests of the conflicting parties makes it clear that there are possible agreements that, by any objective assessment, would constitute an advance over the status quo for both parties and welcome relief to the suffering of the most vulnerable. Indeed, in many cases (for example, in the conflict between Israel and Palestinians and the search for a "two-state" solution), even as the stalemate persists, costs mount, and suffering continues, the broad outlines of such an agreement may be apparent to all concerned. In rare cases, the main source of the stalemate may be personal stubbornness on the part of political leaders or lack of skill on the part of the negotiators. More typically, however, the barriers are less personal. Indeed, we believe that the level of analysis required is one that goes beyond the normal realms of political science and statecraft.

In 1995, an interdisciplinary group of social scientists associated with the Stanford Center on Conflict and Negotiation (now the Stanford Center on *International* Conflict and Negotiation or SCICN) provided the beginnings of such analysis in an edited volume entitled *Barriers to Conflict Resolution* (Arrow,

Mnookin, Ross, Tversky, and Wilson eds., 1995). In the introductory chapter of that volume, Mnookin and Ross began by noting some familiar conflicts, ranging from domestic labor strikes and lawsuits to intergroup and international disputes that subject many to gross violations of their human rights, which prove refractory to resolution even when both sides would seemingly have benefited from avoiding the struggle or from reaching an earlier settlement and saving the various costs of that struggle. At the time, the Cold War, which saw the United States and the Soviet Union spend vast sums and endure great risks in an ever-escalating arms race when their mutual interests would have been better served by mutual de-escalation, was much on the mind of the authors. But in the decades that followed that stalemate, which now seems a distant memory as the two sides continue a program of periodic mutual reductions in nuclear weapons, has been replaced with a number of ethnic and religious struggles that have proven to be no less costly to the parties, a source of even greater suffering, and similarly refractory to solution.

The authors of the SCICN volume distinguished three types of barriers that account for the failure of parties to do what negotiation theorists, including Homans (1961) and Fisher and Ury (1981) in their justly celebrated thin volume, *Getting to Yes*, prescribe as the recipe for successful negotiation. That is, each side is urged to yield what it values less than its counterpart in order to receive what it values more than its counterpart. In a sense, what this chapter addresses is the challenge of converting intergroup conflicts from unproductive and intractable exchanges of charges and countercharges into interest-based negotiations wherein such efficient trades of concessions, and ideally proposals to "expand the pie" to mutual advantage, become possible. In this chapter, we begin by briefly reviewing these three sets of barriers. We then proceed to discuss the "real-world" lessons that successive SCICN scholars and practitioners have learned in lending their services to ongoing peacemaking efforts: lessons that have led us increasingly to focus on the task of improving the relationship between the parties so that it ceases to exacerbate, and ideally begins to attenuate, the barriers in question. While our research has not dealt specifically with the issue of human rights, failures of leaders and elites to reach agreement inevitably exact a particularly heavy toll on the most disadvantaged and vulnerable members of the relevant communities. Furthermore, as will be apparent, some of the real-world lessons we have learned deal specifically with the thorny problem of balancing the pursuit of justice and the end to humiliating conditions against mere improvement of the status quo.

A. Structural Barriers

One set of barriers involves organizational, institutional, and/or situational constraints that prevent the parties from meeting and coordinating their interests. These barriers include constraints on the exchange of information required for the parties to discern and communicate relevant priorities and agency problems insofar as the interests of factional leaders or representatives and political or economic elites are served over the best interests of the principal parties. They also include bureaucratic practices that discourage the acceptance of political costs and risks and otherwise elevate short-term, special interests over longer-term, general concerns. An additional barrier in many conflicts is the fact that the necessary compromises and concessions must be made sequentially rather than simultaneously—so that one side has to "go first" with no certainty that the other side will follow suit, which requires political courage and the trust of the leader's constituency.

B. Tactical and Strategic Barriers

A second set of barriers arises from the dynamics of self-interested bargaining and negotiation. The parties seek to maximize their own share of any gains to be achieved from an agreement through secrecy, deception, bluffing, foot-dragging, and other "hardball" tactics. While these tactics may not be irrational in terms of the calculus of negotiation, they do impose costs and risks. Inevitably, they delay agreements and increase transaction costs. Typically, the relevant failures to co-operate in the task of joint problem solving also decrease the "efficiency" or joint value of any agreements that are reached. If we consider the familiar bargaining metaphor that involves the making and dividing of a pie, in employing such tactics to increase their share, the parties decrease the size (and value) of the pie they are dividing.

C. Psychological Barriers

The remaining set of barriers discussed by Mnookin and Ross are ones that the authors claimed had received insufficient attention from negotiation theorists and practitioners. These barriers, which we review below, involve psychological processes and biases that are rooted in the way that ordinary human beings perceive, understand, and interact with the actors and events they experience. The list of such barriers—some discussed in their seminal chapter, others suggested in subsequent work by SCICN researchers and their colleagues—include not only the failure to recognize the possibility of "win/win" agreements but also avoidance and reduction of cognitive dissonance; biased assimilation of relevant information about past events and bases for entitlements, and the assumption that one's own views are more objective or realistic than those of one's adversary; judgmental overconfidence about the future and relevant BATNAs; insistence on equity or justice instead of mutual gain; loss aversion that entails the overweighting of potential losses relative to potential gains; and "reactive devaluation."

1. Failure to recognize the potential for "win/win" agreements

Parties may assume that no mutually beneficial trades of concessions or efforts at creating joint value exist. Indeed, in extreme cases—cases in which the parties are convinced that the "other side" is an implacable enemy that seeks their destruction—they may assume that their struggle is a zero-sum game in which gains by the other side necessarily represent losses for their own side, and vice versa. At best, the two sides in such cases may agree to short-term truces or *hudnas* as they prepare for the next stage of the struggle. Insofar as such beliefs are incorrect, and moderate elements in both parties have overlapping interests but fail to realize that they have counterparts on the other side, "hardliners" will dictate policy to the detriment of all concerned. Moreover, those hardliners will brand people on their side of the conflict who are interested in dialogue and negotiation as traitors. While this portrait seems highly applicable to some on-going conflicts, it is worth noting cases in which dialogue and patient negotiation has overcome this barrier, and formerly implacable adversaries now are willing, albeit warily, to cooperate. Northern Ireland is perhaps the most obvious case in point. Maximalist demands that would be totally unacceptable to the other side have become rare, and those seeking somewhat different futures are obliged to pursue their aims at the ballot box and through the processes of persuasion rather than resort to car bombs and guns.

2. Dissonance reduction and avoidance

While the failure to recognize the existence of potential agreements that would be to the benefit of both sides in a conflict may be a source of mutually hurting stalemates, such is often not the case. It is certainly not the case in the Middle East. There, as in other protracted conflicts in which the parties fail to make the mutual compromises recognized by most to be necessary to end those conflicts, the role of *cognitive dissonance* (Festinger, 1957) is palpably apparent. In particular, the rationalizations and means of dissonance reduction that allowed the parties to justify their past sacrifices and suffering, and their past rejection of potential agreements that could have ended that suffering, make it difficult to accept a deal that is no better, and perhaps even worse, than one that might have been available in the past. The rallying calls of the rejectionists are all too familiar: *The other side is the devil incarnate. We can't deal with them because we can't trust them. God (or history) is on our side. We are more resolute than the other side because right makes might. We can't break faith with the martyrs who fell in service of the cause or who suffered the most at the hands of the other side. The rest of the world is bound to wake up one day and recognize the injustice we are suffering and the justice of our aspirations.* These calls, and the threats issued against those willing to pay the price required for peace, serve to perpetuate deadlocks even when circumstances favoring agreement have changed for the better, or when the folly of continuing the struggle has become more apparent to all concerned.

While the implications of dissonance reduction may be bleak in the context of protracted and costly stalemates, there is one optimistic note worth sounding before we continue our account of other barriers that stand in the way of achieving agreements. Once a settlement *has* been reached, the process of disso-nance reduction can play a rather constructive role—especially if the decision to settle has been freely reached, if effort has been expended, or sacrifices made that require rationalization to the self or public justification (Aronson, 1969; Brehm and Cohen, 1962). In the aftermath of agreements that represent dramatic changes in policy, leaders and followers alike may strive to find and exaggerate positive features and unanticipated benefits of the settlement and to minimize or disregard negative ones. We saw such processes occur in dramatic fashion early in 1972 when former President Richard Nixon suddenly and unexpectedly reached détente with China. And we have some optimism that the same pro-cesses would operate in the aftermath of agreements in the Middle East and in other troubled areas of the globe.

3. Biased assimilation and "naïve realism"

One of social psychology's most enduring contributions to the understanding of disagreement has been to highlight the importance of subjective interpretation. Long ago, Solomon Asch's classic text, Social Psychology (1952), cautioned us that differences in judgment might reflect differences not in values or prefer-ences but in the way the objects of judgments are being perceived or construed by the relevant individuals. In a paper that helped to launch the cognitive revolu-tion throughout all of psychology, Jerome Bruner (1957) observed that people go "beyond the information given." They fill in details of context and content, they infer linkages between events, and they use their existing dynamic scripts or schemes or adopt new ones to give events coherence and meaning. In short, they interpret events—both past and present—in light both of their expectations and of their needs, hopes, and fears (see Nisbett and Ross, 1980; also Fiske and Tay-lor, 2008; Ross, Lepper, and Ward, 2010).

In the context of ongoing conflict, parties disagree both about historical facts and the relationship between facts. They learn different histories in school and from their parents and from the media—about what happened and why it hap-pened, about who initiated acts of aggression and whose aggressive acts were justifiable retaliations, about who has been stubborn or untrustworthy in the past, and who has merely been realistic and principled. One needs only to read articles or hear speeches by opposing partisans, or to expose oneself to the media in the warring societies, to observe such divergent views of reality. Each side points to the violations of human rights they have suffered at the hands of their adversaries and dismisses their misdeeds as inevitable responses to the wrongs perpetrated by the other side, or as the responsibility of extremists acting without the blessing of their leaders.

Different understandings of the past and present add fuel to any conflict, giving rise to different claims and demands about the requirements for a satisfactory, much less just, resolution of the conflict. This barrier is exacerbated by the fact that opposing partisans not only disagree, they also make *attributions* about each other's claims and narratives offered in support of those claims. To some extent, those claims and narratives are apt to be dismissed as simple exercises in dishonest pleading that are designed to maintain passion and solidarity or to justify unreasonable actions and demands to parties outside the conflict who are urging resolutions. But to some extent, they are seen to be the actual views of the claimants. The latter attribution, in fact, can create even more of a barrier to fruitful negotiation than the former one.

Let us enlarge a bit on this contention. When people, whether laypeople or sophisticated policy makers, consider information, they do so with the conviction that a one-to-one relationship exists between their personal *perceptions* of the objects and events they are considering and the *real* nature of the objects and events themselves (see Ross and Ward, 1996). As "naïve realists" we believe that we see entities and events as they are in objective reality. This conviction applies not only to our basic perceptions, but to the attitudes, preferences, sentiments, and priorities that arise from those perceptions. We believe that our particular views reflect a relatively dispassionate, unbiased, and essentially "unmediated" or "bottom-up" apprehension of the information or evidence at hand. From this conviction, it follows that those who express *different* views about the real nature of things and about the implications that follow from "objective" are either dishonest or deluded. The inference is that insofar as the other side believes what it is claiming, their views are the product of self-interest, lies told by leaders, some pernicious ideology, or some other source of "top-down" bias to which those on their *own* side (or at least those on their own side who are just as reasonable and rational as themselves) have been immune.

The inference that others are seeing matters in an inaccurate, even systematically biased manner does not immediately produce enmity. On the contrary, it may well lead people of goodwill to assume that rational open-minded discourse, in which information and cogent arguments are freely exchanged, will lead to agreement (or at least to a marked narrowing of *dis*agreement). Such optimism, in my own experience and that of others who have conducted intergroup dialogue processes, however, generally proves to be short lived. While the dialogue participants' experience may be positive in many respects, neither side generally yields much to the other side's attempts at enlightenment. The conclusion reached by individuals on both sides of the issue, especially when it is clear that those on the other side are not lacking in interest or intellectual capacity, is that the ability of those on the other side to proceed from facts and evidence to conclusions continue to be distorted by some combination of self-interest, defensiveness, or mistaken ideology.

Attributions involving individual or collective self-interest made by partisans are, in fact, apt to be buttressed by observation and analysis. There generally *is* a nontrivial correlation between beliefs held or policies advocated and the individual or collective self-interest of the relevant advocates. Partisans thus rarely will find it difficult to detect that linkage in the positions advocated by those on the other side of the table. What they generally lack is recognition that a similar correlation exists between their *own* views and their *own* self-interests. This bleak account of the fate of many attempts at intergroup dialogue in the context of ongoing conflict can be linked to the message from ongoing laboratory research. In a series of studies dealing with perceived bias versus objectivity in judgments about political issues that typically divide Americans (e.g., Pronin, Kruger, Savitsky, and Ross, 2001; Pronin, Lin, and Ross, 2002), investigators have shown that people see themselves as less subject to a large number of specific biases (including wishful thinking, self-serving biases in interpreting data, and a variety of other psychological failings that both produce bad decisions and exacerbate conflict) than other individuals. Moreover, the tendency for people to see others as more susceptible than themselves to such bias appears to be a linear function of the size of the perceived discrepancy between their own views and the views of those "others" (Pronin, Gilovich, and Ross, 2004). In the context of conflict, the combination of biased assessment of facts and naïve realism leads to pessimism at best, and typically also to distrust and demonization of those on the other side.

4. Judgmental overconfidence

Overconfidence in judgment and undue optimism about one's ability to anticipate and control events is a ubiquitous and much-documented phenomenon. One source of that overconfidence particularly relevant to conflict situations involves asymmetries in information (see Kahneman and Tversky, 1995). In particular, parties know their own plans and information reflected in those plans better than they know the plans and bases for plans of the other side. The parties also know what they will do to thwart the plans of the other side better than they know what preventative or retaliatory measures the other side might take. Accordingly, both sides are apt to feel that their bargaining position, or even freedom to act in the absence of any agreement, will be better in the future than at the present. As such, they will adopt harder-line positions or show less willing-ness to sit down at the bargaining table than would be the case in the absence of such asymmetries in information.

Naïve realism of the sort described earlier may also play a role insofar as both sides are unduly optimistic that reasonable third parties will share their views about the requirements of an equitable resolution, if not immediately, then in the not-too-distant future after the "real" nature of the conflict and the relative merits of the two sides' arguments and demands have been explained. One side may be correct in the conviction that time is on its side, but each side would be advised to reflect on the fact that the other party seems to think that time is on *its* side. In our experience, both sides initially underestimate the price that con-tinuation of the conflict will exact. Indeed, it is only when at least one party comes to recognize that time is not on its side—that at best it will continue to pay a heavy price without improving its leverage, and at worst its position will deteriorate—that real progress becomes possible. Ideally, of course, what is needed is a combination of despair and hope, growing pessimism about the wis-dom of continuing to make maximalist demands and growing optimism that agreement is possible, and growing appreciation of the benefits that would ensue.

5. Insistence on equity or justice

Negotiating parties are customarily urged to engage in exchanges whereby each improves its situation by ceding things they value less than the other party in order to gain things it values more than the other party. But in the context of long-standing conflict, the parties typically seek more than a simple advance over the status quo—they demand and feel entitled to receive *fairness, equity*, or even *justice* (see Adams, 1965; Homans, 1961; also Berkowitz and Walster, 1976; and Walster, Walster, and Berscheid, 1978). The parties want an agreement that allocates gains and losses in a manner proportionate to the strength and le-gitimacy of the negotiating parties' respective claims—one that not only ends the other side's violation of human rights but offers fair compensation for the victims. Such demands for equity, and especially for justice, raise the bar for the negotiators, especially when the parties inevitably have different narratives about past events and thus what would be an equitable agreement differ.

Looking through the prism of naïve realism, both sides in the conflict feel that it is they who have acted more honorably in the past, they who have been more sinned against than sinning, and they who are seeking no more than that to which they are entitled. Both sides, moreover, are apt to feel that it is *their* inter-ests that most require protection in any negotiated agreement—for example, by avoiding ambiguities in language that could provide "loopholes" that could be exploited by the other side (while, at the same time, avoiding unrealistically rigid requirements for their own side that could compromise their ability to deal with unforeseen future developments). They also are bound to have divergent views about the future (i.e., who will grow stronger with the passage of time and whose assurances can be taken at face value and trusted).

Third party mediators may face a particularly difficult challenge in this regard, as both parties are apt to see evenhandedness as giving their side less than its due. Even if the parties recognize that the mediator is seeking an "efficient" agreement in light of the parties' interests and priorities, they are apt to resent the fact that the greater legitimacy of their side's aspirations has not been taken into account, and the parties disagree strongly about the "balance" of any proposal that seeks to give both parties what they feel they need and deserve. Moreover, the disputants are apt to misattribute each others' cool response to the mediator's proposal in a way that heightens enmity and mistrust. Each party is likely to feel that the other is being disingenuous in its public pronouncement of concern and disappointment—that the other side is engaging in "strategic" behavior designed to secure sympathy from third parties and win further concessions. And, of course, each party responds with anger and suspicion when it hears its own response characterized in such uncharitable terms.

6. Loss aversion

The work that Danny Kahneman and Amos Tversky (1979) pioneered on prospect theory, in general, and on the role of loss aversion, in particular, has profound relevance for our understanding of negotiation stalemates (Kahneman and Tversky, 1995). That is, research suggests that parties attach greater weight to prospective losses than prospective gains, especially when the former are certain and immediate, and the latter are uncertain and prospect more for the future than the present. One important consequence is that parties will take unwise risks to avoid certain and immediate losses. At the same time, the parties will prove unwilling to take risks—even risks with better prospects in terms of probable outcomes—in order to pursue gains. Another is that parties in negotiation will unwisely turn down proposed changes of concession that offer a mix of gains and losses, even when the former promise to be objectively greater than the latter.

Prospect theory also points toward a further complication for conflict resolution. Parties quickly assimilate gains as an entitlement but are slow to reconcile with losses. Thus, a concession received is likely to be viewed as an entitlement, while a concession granted is likely to remain an irritant. This asymmetry of assessment makes it likely that the parties will disagree about the worth of a concession in the negotiation process, and this disagreement fosters mistrust and suspicion. An obvious implication of prospect theory for practitioners involves the importance of "framing" potential risks and gains. In particular, it is important that parties recognize that maintenance of the status quo is itself a choice that entails potential losses and risks. The risks and losses of a particular course of action may seem more attractive, or at least be considered more rationally, when the risk and losses of doing nothing or forcefully preventing changes are also factored into the equation.

7. Reactive devaluation

Beyond the impediments to negotiated agreement posed by the motivational and cognitive biases discussed thus far, there is a further barrier resulting from the dynamics of the negotiation process itself that has been documented in research. That is, the evaluation of specific package deals and compromises may *change* as a consequence of their having been put on the table, especially if they have been offered or proposed by one's adversary. Evidence for such "reactive devaluation" has been provided in laboratory and field settings in which subjects evaluated a variety of actual or hypothetical dispute resolution contexts and proposals (see Ross and Ward, 1995).

Three findings emerge from this work. First, and perhaps least surprising, the terms of a compromise proposal for bilateral concessions are rated less positively when they have been put forward by the "other side" than when the same terms ostensibly have been put forward by a representative of one's own side. A Cold War era cartoon nicely anticipates the relevant phenomenon. It shows two men in a coffee shop. One man reading the paper says to the other, "You know, a total test ban on testing nuclear weapons could bring a halt to the arms race." The second man responds, "It sounds good, but the Soviets would never agree to it." The first replies, "They are the ones who proposed." The second retorts, "Then it's out of the question!" This was demonstrated convincingly in a study by Maoz, Ward, Katz and Ross (2002) in which Israeli Arabs and Jews rated actual proposals put forward by the two sides in the post-Oslo negotiations, with the putative authorship of these proposals manipulated by the experimenter. As predicted, putative authorship influences the relative attractiveness of these proposals to the two groups of participants. Indeed, when the Israeli proposal was attributed to the Palestinian side in the negotiation and vice versa, Israeli participants rated the actual proposal of their side to be less attractive than the actual proposal of the other side.

Our work in many conflict contexts has repeatedly prompted us to discuss this barrier with political leaders. One such occasion was a meeting with a Unionist official in Stormont just after the IRA had offered to allow third parties to inspect the relevant weapon caches and verify that they were safely stored and beyond use. He echoed the sentiment of his political party by insisting that the opportunity to inspect those caches of weapons was a positive step, but what really mattered was actually turning in the guns—and that the failure to agree to do so was a sign of bad faith and a cause for suspicion. We then asked him how he would have responded had the IRA offered to turn in guns but refused to allow inspection of weapon caches. Remarkably, he got the point immediately. He smiled and said that such an offer would have been met with similar skepticism—that it would have prompted him to say that it was easy to turn in some guns (that they could be bought by taking up a collection in a few Irish Republican bars in Belfast or Boston), and the failure to allow inspections would be a source of suspicion.

Reactive devaluation arises from many sources—some quite rational, others less so. But one source is the previously discussed phenomenon of loss aversion. When an offer is put on the table that proposes an exchange of concessions, the things to be given up count as losses, and are given great weight, while the things to be gained are given less weight, especially if the losses are reckoned to be certain and immediate, and gains merely future prospects that depend on the goodwill and trustworthiness of the other side.

II. Relational Processes and Barriers: Lessons Learned in the Field

In the aftermath of the *Barriers* volume, SCICN academicians continued to pursue and publish their work in the standard scholarly journals. But they also began to accept invitations to involve themselves in "real-world" peacemaking efforts. In particular, they addressed the question of how structural, strategic, and especially psychological barriers were making their influence felt in the context of two particular conflicts. One was the conflict between unionists and nationalists struggling to reach a final agreement in Northern Ireland. The other was the post-1967 conflict between the Israelis and Palestinians in the West Bank and Gaza. Beyond participating in some second-track diplomacy efforts, SCICN investigators also worked with community leaders and peace activists engaged in intercommunity and intracommunity dialogue processes, and hosted or attended conferences with practitioners. The agenda of those conferences included two questions: What would practitioners do differently if they knew what academic researchers and theorists knew; and what would academicians concerned with conflict do differently, in particular, how would they refocus their work if they knew what practitioners knew? The SCICN investigators also made it a point to engage in discussions with a different class of "practitioners"—those who had engaged in violent confrontation. Work with ex-prisoners who had embraced political means, rather than violence, proved especially enlightening.

Perhaps the most important benefit from these activities has been a growing appreciation of the central role played by processes and issues that can exacerbate the barriers discussed above or point out the steps required to help overcome them. To some extent, the real-world lessons we learned have sharpened our previous analyses. But, to some extent, they also have provided insights about limitations in our earlier analyses—lacunae that must be addressed as we move from investigating barriers to considering strategies for overcoming such barriers. We offer a brief summary of five of those real-world lessons below and then turn our attention to the central role of relationships and relationship-building, which we increasing recognized to be the key requirement for real progress. (For an account of lessons learned and applied by members of the Harvard Negotiation Project in the year following the publication of *Getting to Yes*, which sounds some of the same themes offered in this chapter, we refer our readers to *Coping with International Conflict* (Fisher, Schneider, Borgwardt, and Ganson, 1997)).

A. The Importance of Trust

For real progress in moving beyond conflict, the parties must feel that their counterparts have both the motivation and capacity to follow through on any agreements. A key element of trust involves the task of dealing with spoilers who seek to undermine agreement by engaging in acts of violence or by making political demands that violate the letter or spirit of interim agreements along the road to peace and reconciliation. All too often the parties treat the other side's failure to completely curb spoilers as evidence of bad faith while insisting that the other side recognizes the delicacy of the political problem their side has in curbing spoilers. Patience and realism are required, but they in turn depend on trust about long-term intentions. Building such trust, as we shall discuss in more detail a bit later in this chapter, generally hinges on the development and communication of a shared view of (and shared commitment to) a *mutually bearable future*. Only when the two sides not only see a tolerable future for themselves but also see a tolerable future for the other side will they trust each other's expressed willingness to embrace an agreement and show the required patience in the face of short-term challenges by would-be spoilers.

B. The Importance of *Intragroup* Conflict

When there are no important divergences of goals or interests *within* the two sides in a conflict, resolution of the intergroup conflict is apt either to be easy or impossible. An important job for the practitioner is balancing the objective of fostering cooperation between the "moderates" on the opposing sides of the conflict with that of building support for realistic agreements in the two publics at large and easing opposition from hardliners.

C. The Futility of Trying to Convince People What They Can't Afford to Understand

People remain closed to arguments whose acceptance would expose them to intolerable uncertainty, threat, or humiliation. This is especially true in the case of acknowledging misdeeds and violations of human rights. Explaining why one's own side is right and entitled to what it seeks and why the other side is at fault, without addressing the other side's fears about the future, is futile. Again, only when the parties are confident that agreement will result in a tolerable future for them, for their families, and their communities, are people willing to hear each other's narratives and pleas.

D. The Importance of "Tipping Points"

It is important to recognize that conversion from militant to peacemaker need not involve any "blinding light" conversion. Sometimes, it is merely a matter of giving new hope, of shifting the calculations in question only slightly (from 51% to 49% in favor of violence to 51% to 49% in favor of negotiation, politics, and other nonviolent means) so that the path of peacemaking seems marginally more promising than the path of violent confrontation. In a sense, the lesson involves recognition that the choice of nonviolent tactics and strategies versus violent ones may be a function of the situation at hand, and the way that situation is interpreted or construed, rather than a simple reflection of the personal dispositions of the relevant actors. Testimony from ex-prisoners who became peace activists after their release from prison attested to such tipping points.

E. The Corrosive Effects of Humiliation

Every negotiated peace agreement imposes losses and injustices on the parties. The real question, therefore, is not whether a peace is just or generous but whether the losses and injustices it imposes are bearable and *non-humiliating*. In the face of asymmetric power, the weaker party is likely to feel humiliated by circumstances it experiences, including denial of rights and arbitrary treatment at the hands of the stronger party, and by its inability to change those circumstances. It will therefore be especially unwilling to accept any agreement that perpetuates circumstances it deems humiliating and/or one that is reached through a process it deems humiliating. Thus, unilateral "concessions" by the stronger party and trades of concessions proposed by powerful third parties are apt be received coolly even when objectively they offer an improvement over the status quo. Exchanges of concessions reached by agreement rather than unilateral concessions made with an accompanying demand for reciprocation can do more harm than good because the recipient of the unilateral concession is apt to feel that it is only getting a portion of what it is due, and it is being asked to give up something to which the other side is not, or at least not *yet*, entitled.

III. Four Questions to Be Addressed in any Fruitful Dialogue between Conflicting Parties

Both our barriers analysis and our experience in the field have led us to recognize that improving the relationship between parties who have been involved in struggle is essential if barriers are to be overcome. Dialogue is obviously required for repair and rebuilding of relationship, but, as we have outlined earlier, it is often highly frustrating and disappointing for participants who assume the candor and goodwill are sufficient to overcome all barriers. Although dialogue typically helps parties to individuate and humanize those on the other side and to gain a better understanding of each other's history, positions, and priorities, progress in moving toward concrete agreements and the willingness to defend those agreements to the participants' communities requires more than candor and goodwill. It is our experience, however, that the fruitfulness of dialogue will be enhanced if the parties at some point in the discussion address four specific questions.

Each of these questions calls upon the parties to undertake the familiar task of considering each other's perceptions and feelings. Typically, parties in conflict are implored to walk in each other's shoes or wear each other's eyeglasses. But such footwear and eyeglass metaphors ignore the problem of naïve realism described earlier. That is, the participants treat their "take" on matters, including the history of their conflict and the outlines of a just settlement, to be veridical and assume the views of the other side to be distorted by self-interest, ideological blinders, and other biases. Accordingly, they come to the dialogue with misplaced confidence about their ability to persuade. Neither party, in our experience, comes to such dialogue with the hope or expectation that they, rather than their counterparts, will be the parties who become more enlightened and, hence, more open to compromise. With this cautionary note regarding naïve realism in mind, let us now turn to the four questions that we have found fruitful to pose at the outset of a dialogue process and to periodically return to in the course of that process. We not only suggest the relevant question but reflect a bit on conflicts and negotiations that have succeeded or failed in addressing them.

A. The Question of a Shared Future

The first question introduces what we have come to believe is the sine qua non for ending a stalemate and advancing the peace process. *Are the parties able and willing to articulate a future for the **other** side that it would find bearable?* No agreement, or at least no agreement that the two sides would abide by when fortunes shift, is possible unless both parties feel that they would enjoy a reasonably tolerable existence, one acknowledging their basic human rights, if the other side's basic aspirations were to be realized. The parties do not need to share a single view of the future. Indeed, the future that one side seeks may be far from what the opposing side wants or would deem fair. Both sides may even be intent on thwarting each other's aspirations and on moving events in a direction more to their liking. But ultimately both sides must be reasonably confident that not only their own lives but also the lives of the other side would prove to be bearable, not just economically but in terms of human dignity and preservations of the rights and self-expression of their communities, in the aftermath of agreement. So fundamental is the presence or absence of a commitment to a mutually bearable shared future that we are inclined to call it *the peace question.*

The long struggle in South Africa that culminated in an end to apartheid and majority black rule is instructive in this regard. During the last years of his imprisonment, Nelson Mandela had come to recognize that the only way to avoid continuing bloodshed and uncertain prospects for the end of apartheid was to offer white South Africans the vision of a shared future. That vision had three components: "a unitary state without homelands; nonracial elections for the central Parliament; and one-person-one-vote." While he steadfastly refused to consider proposals that would have maintained the apartheid power structure enforced by his one-time jailors, he never let pass an opportunity to talk about the place of white South Africans in the new South Africa. Time and again, he made it clear, sometimes to the dismay of many ANC followers, that majority rule would not entail a new racial hierarchy wherein the white minority would be dominated by a black majority, and denied human rights in a manner akin to that suffered by that black majority in the preceding decades (see Mandela, 2005).

White South Africans who heard him, even those who sought to maintain as much of their former social and economic advantage as possible, had reason to feel that they, their families, and their community would enjoy a satisfying and secure life in the shared future he was proposing. Mandela understood that there would be no peace unless white South Africans heard and believed his recipe for the future, and the unfolding of events proved that belief to be correct.

In working with Israeli supporters of the peace process, we often hear wistful remarks about the need for a "Palestinian Mandela." If the wish is for a leader on the other side who is popular and perceived to be legitimate, but who is willing to make concessions that no other leader has been willing to offer, the reference to Mandela is misguided. Mandela made no such concessions. What he did accomplish was to offer a view of the future that made white South Africans willing to make concessions that they had previously claimed that they would *never* make. A reasonable goal for our Israeli colleagues, therefore, would be to urge their *own* government and society to adopt policies that make the emergence of such a "Mandela" possible.

This notion of a bearable shared future is clearly minimalist in at least one important respect. As noted above, it does not require the parties to endorse a shared *vision* of the future, one that entails agreement about the details of a new political arrangement and the institutions and policies that would exist in that arrangement. It merely requires that each party be committed to a political process that guarantees a range of outcomes—all of which the other side could live with, rejecting the use of violence in favor of normal political processes to achieve desired adjustments. Normal and stable political processes take root only when the whole range of possible futures is at least minimally acceptable to all that might have the capacity to threaten the peace. In such a context, parties become willing to accept political losses without abandoning the political processes of persuasion, consensus-building, and compromise. Of course, as we noted earlier, this desirable scenario depends upon *trust*—trust by the parties both that no outcome will emerge from the political process that it would find unbearable, and also that no outcome will occur that will move the other party to violent rejection of the political process.

Working to develop acknowledgment of the need for a mutually bearable shared future entails the creation of mutual recognition that each side's interests are encapsulated within those of the other side. Both parties can anticipate that its welfare will be advanced (or at least not subject to deterioration) even as both sides pursues their own stated political goals. In short, both sides come to believe that there is a shared interest in achieving a normal functioning society, one in which the benefits of peace will be greater than any losses suffered in the political process.

Initial steps in pursuing the goal of shared future are apt to be tentative and incomplete. Agreements on broad principles (such as "land for peace" or "respect for territorial integrity") often mask deeper disagreements. Typically, at least in the short run, the parties may "agree to disagree" or, more specifically, agree to postpone discussion of some disagreements.[1] This may be a useful strategy when those disagreements are likely to become less important as other issues are resolved, and the prospective fruits of peace become more tangible. But there is a disadvantage in such a strategy if the issue is an important one that may not be amenable to mutual compromise. When a single zero-sum issue remains, the possibility of including it in a broader agreement whereby the party that yields on the issue in question receives major concessions on other issues no longer exists. In other words, "logrolling" is no longer possible.

Short-term or interim agreements that conceal a continuing disagreement about long-term arrangements provide a relevant example. Indeed, such agreements may be possible precisely because the parties have *different* expectations about the future course of events. Each side's commitment to the interim agreement is tactical and predicated upon the calculation that it is a step toward some long-term advantage. If their calculations prove faulty, and events do not unfold as they had envisioned, they will have little compunction about violating the terms of the agreement or terminating it.

Cease-fire agreements are often predicated on just such a disagreement about the likely course of future events and, as such, can provide the fuel for future enmity and mistrust. Each side feels entitled to demand that the other side honor the cease-fire "come what may." At the same time, each side implicitly reserves the right to return to violence if and when new developments so warrant. The problem is compounded because each party may feel that it has made the more significant concession in agreeing to a cease-fire. The more powerful party, or at least the party faring best in the conflict at the moment, will feel that in agreeing to a cease-fire, it has forfeited the possibility of dictating favorable terms or punishing the other side with use of force. The less powerful or less successful party will feel that in agreeing to a cease-fire, it is enduring a degree of humiliation and perhaps putting itself at a continuing disadvantage.

This observation about the asymmetry of views and objectives pertains also to the issue of "open" versus "closed" agreements. The party with greater resources and coercive power will typically want the terms of any agreement that is reached to be irrevocable. In striking a deal, it will be reducing its ability to use future coercive tactics in return of peace, normalcy, and the ability of its constituency to go on with their lives—lives that were unbearable only because tranquility and personal security had been lacking. The party with fewer resources and less coercive power, especially if it acquiesced to terms that gained them little in the way of immediate change in the quality of their lives, will want the agreement to be more "open." In particular, they will want license to revisit those terms at a future date—perhaps when political circumstances, the support of third parties, or other sources of power, have shifted in their favor and issues of justice and compensation can at last be addressed.

In light of this analysis, it is not surprising that cease-fires and other interim agreements tend to break down when one or perhaps both of the parties discover that things are not unfolding as had been hoped and anticipated. For such agreements to create momentum toward a more stable peace, the parties must address the ultimate question of a bearable shared future to each other's satisfaction. The immediate challenge that arises, therefore, is for each party to do and say things to cause the other to believe that they share a commitment to find a mutually acceptable shared future and are prepared to take the difficult steps required to reach that future.

B. The Question of Trustworthiness

A second question follows directly from our analysis of the shared future question, and it is the one that has dominated our discussions with activists on both sides in the Middle East conflict. *Can the two sides trust each other to honor their commitments?* In particular, can each party trust the other to take the intermediate steps that will be required to create and sustain the necessary momentum toward that shared future? In the context of a long-standing stalemate, each side is all too aware of occasions when the other has aggravated the conflict to gain some immediate goal, not responded to initiatives, failed to honor implicit or even explicit commitments, or otherwise proven unable or unwilling to make the types of difficult compromises necessary for progress toward a settlement.

Both sides are apt to ask of the other: "What has changed that will make things different this time?" "What makes it possible, indeed prudent, to trust you to follow through and freely take the steps and make the compromises that you were previously unwilling to make even in face of the threat of force?" "Why, despite your past broken promises, should we trust you *now*?" Moreover, both sides must believe that the other will not return to force when its goals are thwarted or when violent means promise to be more fruitful, at least in the short run, than nonviolent ones.

Ideally, the parties can demonstrate their own trustworthiness through concrete deeds. Failing that, they can at least articulate the shift that has occurred in objective circumstances or in their calculations, and that now makes it reasonable for the other side to trust that they will follow through on their commitments. Each side must be given reason to believe that the other side will continue, in the face of political opposition and costs, to take the intermediate steps necessary to reach that mutually bearable future. It is worth noting that interim steps on the road to a final settlement often leave one of the parties in a disadvantaged position with regard to the other. In such instances, the less advantaged party may rightly fear that its concessions (and/or losses) will prove to be permanent and will not be compensated by concessions on the part of the other side. They may fear, perhaps justifiably, that their adversaries will drag their feet indefinitely rather than take the further steps needed to reach a longer-term, more satisfactory settlement. If their adversaries are the more powerful party in the conflict, and the later steps called for would jeopardize the privileges and security that their dominance affords them, this fear may well be warranted.

Political leaders signaling the desire for a change in relationship with the other side may also need to assure their own constituency that they are not "selling out" or leaving them vulnerable to exploitation at the hands of an adversary that is untrustworthy. In short, leaders must signal an increased willingness to move forward toward agreement in a way that encourages the other side to move forward as well. However, they must do so in a manner that does not appear rash and threatening to their supporters. More than a few peace processes have stumbled because leaders could not meet this challenge.

Perhaps no one has navigated these perilous straits more adroitly than Sinn Fein and Protestant loyalist leaders in Northern Ireland. Gerry Adams and Martin McGuiness, Sinn Fein's leading spokespersons, needed to convince the British government that their political goals had changed in such a way that a settlement was possible. This led Adams and McGuiness to pledge to stabilize politics in Northern Ireland by entering into government and a legislative assembly they had previously foresworn. But to reassure the grassroots that they had not betrayed the Republican movement, they insisted that their goal was to launch a process of social and political transformation. They argued that this new tactic, seen in a proper light, was a shrewd political step that would hasten the realization of Sinn Fein's ultimate goals. At the same time, Adams and McGuiness sought to reassure skeptical British and Unionist audiences that their shift to peaceful politics was fundamental. So successful were they in the latter effort that some commentators dubbed the apparent shift as the "decommissioning" of Republican ideology.

Implementation of the peace deal became possible as Unionist leaders undertook parallel steps. David Trimble's Ulster Unionist Party entered into peace talks with Sinn Fein and other parts, signaling a willingness to form a government with their former enemies and even to allow them to continue their struggle for political and social transformation—provided that they did so at the ballot box rather than through the gun or bomb. Loyalist leaders such as David Ervine and Gusty Spence made the same argument to grassroots Protestant communities, arguing that an end to sectarian violence would come about only through honest dialogue with their Republican counterparts.

However, Ian Paisley's more hardline Democratic Unionist Party accused Unionist and Loyalist leaders who participated in the peace talks with Sinn Fein of selling Protestants down the river. Paisley's party walked out of the talks, and refused to sign a deal. DUP intransigence undermined Trimble's efforts to convince the Protestant community that engaging Republicans in politics was the most effective way to thwart Republican extremism, and the new power-sharing government collapsed. Despite the political impasse, the British military continued to engage the IRA through reciprocal acts of demilitarization in exchange for decommissioning. The crisis was finally resolved when Paisley's party came to the conclusion that their own ability to exercise political power was tied up in sharing that power with Sinn Fein. The DUP shifted their stance to advocate engagement and persuaded their constituents that power-sharing was the key to political normalization and Sinn Fein's electoral mandate was as legitimate as their own.

These were bold strategies on the part of Republicans and Loyalists alike, and the key to maintaining their somewhat contradictory messages was a set of initiatives that not only communicated a commitment to a shared future but held the promise of improvement in the daily lives of their respective constituencies. The strategy adopted by both sides was essentially one of *reciprocal unilateral action*. The parties sought to identify and take actions that could be undertaken without the assistance of the other side, actions that furthered their own interests and bettered the everyday lives of their constituents and at the same time, communicated a commitment to bring about a future that the other side would find bearable, even if not particularly attractive. What the parties said and did throughout this process might have seemed unexceptional to outsiders. Nevertheless, the words and deeds were things that both sides thought they would never hear or see from their long-time adversary.

An even more dramatic example of signaling a change in position and the desire for a changed relationship was Anwar Sadat's visit to the Israeli Knesset in 1977. The journey undertaken by Sadat was one that most Israelis and even most outsiders would have characterized as inconceivable. It is worth noting that in his actual speech Sadat made few, if any, concessions to the Israelis. For the most part, he reaffirmed prior positions. Nevertheless, Israelis saw his willingness to come to Jerusalem to personally address the Knesset as evidence that Sadat was someone with whom they could make peace. The Egyptian prime minister's brave act led to a breakthrough that none had foreseen. Unfortunately, it also led to his death at the hands of spoilers who fully recognized the role he could play in making peace.

C. The Question of "Loss Acceptance"

Negotiated agreements are bound to result in a sense of loss because the terms of such agreements pale in comparison to the hopes and dreams that fueled the parties' steadfastness during the struggle and helped them to justify their sacrifices. As we noted earlier, the problem is exacerbated by the phenomenon of "loss aversion" noted by Kahneman and Tversky (1979, 1984), whereby the combination of uncertain prospective gains and certain losses are evaluated less positively than an objective assessment of their respective magnitudes would merit.

The challenge of getting the parties to accept their losses cannot be met head-on. Both sides feel that the losses they are being asked to accept are not matched by the losses that the other side is being asked to accept. They feel that a truly equitable agreement would require the other side to give up more and their own side less. Moreover, when they hear the other side complain about the balance of gains and losses in the agreement, they regard those complaints as tactical posturing, and they harden their resolve not to succumb to such tactics. They feel that, given the balance of concessions made by the two sides thus far, it should be up to the other side to make the *next* accommodation. Because both sides have the same conviction in this regard, they both stand back waiting for the other side to make a move and interpret their delay in doing so as a sign of insincerity.

It may not be possible to make either party (much less *both* parties) feel the terms of agreement that presently must be accepted to achieve peace are truly equitable. However, there is a more modest goal that can be pursued. The members of the two communities can be led to a greater appreciation of the magnitude and painfulness of the losses, both material and psychological, that the other side will be accepting. It is in pursuit of this objective that inter community dialogue and other citizen-based initiatives may prove most useful. In our experiences working with groups that bring together influential citizens on the two sides of a conflict, we have found that all too often attempts to formulate detailed peace plans merely recreate the stalemates that exist among leaders. But we have also found that something important takes place as dialogue participants share stories about the prices that they and others in their community have paid, and as they recount the process by which they have come to abandon previous hopes and dreams in favor of more pragmatic and potentially achievable agreements. What they come to appreciate is the *authenticity* of the sacrifices and lost hopes that the other side will be bearing. This, in turn, lessens their sense that peace will come at a heavier price for their side than the other side, and increases their willingness to pay that price.

Often, negotiators and mediators try to hide losses by formulating complicated terms in which so much trading or "logrolling" of gains and losses is going on that the parties are less inclined to focus on their losses. While such tactics may be effective in the context of certain commercial negotiations, in the pursuit of agreements to end conflicts between long-time adversaries, we have found it to useful to make losses *more* transparent, not less. Terms of agreement that unambiguously acknowledge what each side will be losing have two advantages. First, each side makes clear to the other side the painful losses it is now willing to accept. Second, each side can have more confidence that the other side will not balk at paying the full price of peace.

In this regard, it is instructive to compare two peace proposals that were circulated during the Second (or *al-Aqsa*) Intifada. One, the so-called *Geneva Accord* was 39 pages long, had 16 articles, contained almost 10,000 words, and spelled out the mechanisms for resolving contentious issues in great detail and with numerous qualifications. For example, with respect to the Palestinian refugee issue (which was described in over 2000 words and in 14 subsections), the Palestinians were offered five options to consider. Only two of the options, however, could be exercised by the unhindered choice of the Palestinians. The remaining three options were circumscribed by the discretion of Israel or third parties. Moreover, it was possible to read some of the provisions in more than one way. Most importantly, the highly complex document did not allow ordinary citizens to see exactly what their side and perhaps, more importantly, what the other side would be giving up.

By contrast, the other proposal, termed the *Nusseibeh-Ayalon Agreement* was just a page long. The 465-word agreement specified that Israel would keep little if any of the land it conquered in 1967 (except for mutually acceptable land swaps) and that the Jewish state would allow Palestinians to fulfill their cherished dream of an independent state with East Jerusalem as its capitol. Palestinians, in turn, would give up on all demands for a collective "right of return" to their former homeland in Israel, and the new Palestinian state would be demilitarized. Most important, the document makes it clear that no additional claims would be pursued, and that upon full implementation of the agreement the Israel-Palestinian conflict would at last be over.

Neither plan ultimately made much political headway in the face of weakened leadership on both sides. Some peace activists championed the Geneva Accord; others favored the Nusseibeh-Ayalon Agreement. However, virtually all the activists and dialogue participants with whom we worked welcomed the greater transparency of loss in the latter plan. In particular, they welcomed the fact that the other side would have no "wiggle room" allowing it to renege on its commitment to make the painful concessions called for in the agreement. The basic quid pro quo linking each side's prospective gains and losses was unambiguous and not amenable to haggling about details. Neither side, it was clear, would be able to "pocket" the gains offered to it by the plan without paying the full costs. The advantage of such transparency in a document intended to signify the wishes of ordinary citizens for a mutually acceptable shared future, as opposed to the inevitably complex provisions crafted by diplomats in a formal agreement, was apparent. Hearing both ordinary citizens and prominent ones on the other side openly and publicly—perhaps for the first time—acknowledge its willingness to accept the most painful of the losses it would have to endure to reach a settlement promised to build needed trust, as those on both sides would see that their adversaries were at last willing to pay the full price of peace.

D. The Question of Just Entitlements

The search for an agreement to end a costly and protracted conflict faces an additional obstacle. One or both sides is apt to feel that proposed terms of settlement, while perhaps bearable and clearly better than the status quo, are *inequitable* and therefore *unjust*. The antagonists feel that the proposed terms of agreement call upon them to make important and painful concessions without requiring the other side to concede anything of consequence—certainly not anything to which they had any entitlement in the first place. Insofar as the parties can make symmetric concessions (trading land for land or agreeing to a mutual rejection of violence), the problem of perceived inequity may be solved relatively easily, although this may be less true when one or both of the parties feel that the status quo before the flare up of conflict was itself inequitable. But when the relevant concessions will necessarily be asymmetric, loss aversion makes the problem of perceived inequity particularly intractable.

In the long run, assuming that the quality of everyday life sufficiently improves, the parties will come to hold more positive views about the "inequitable" deal they made and the value of the peace it achieved. They may even come to reduce their dissonance about the losses imposed by that deal by deciding that what they gave up wasn't so important after all. Indeed, they may come to feel that it was folly to have continued the struggle so long and at such cost. But, during the negotiation process and even in the immediate aftermath of agreement, the relevant terms are apt to leave both sides feeling dissatisfied and diminished, with a sense that the losses they are being obliged to accept are not being appropriately acknowledged and respected by their adversary and by third parties.

At a critical point in the South African negotiations, the ANC faced just such a decision involving tradeoffs between expediency to achieve agreement and what its members thought to be the demands of justice. Joe Slovo, hardline Marxist and long-time white member of the ANC, addressed the issue head-on in a now famous article entitled "Negotiations: What Room for Compromise?" Slovo reminded ANC supporters that they hadn't won a military victory and, therefore, they could not impose their maximalist demands on the Nationalist Afrikaner government. In such a context, he argued, the goal must be the creation of a political context in which a just nonracial democracy could be pursued under favorable conditions rather than any state of affairs whereby that goal would be blocked if not permanently then for the foreseeable future. All else—in particular, the replacement of white public officials in the state bureaucracy—were matters subject to compromise and tradeoffs. In other words, Slovo was advising the ANC to tolerate, at least temporarily, the perpetuation of what was perceived to be a remnant of the old unjust order as a means to achieve the main

goal of a just society, one in which secondary goals such as bureaucratic restruc-
turing could be pursued through normal political means.

While discussions of just entitlements can undermine the task of relationship-
building, the issue of justice cannot simply be ignored. More often than not, conflict, particularly violent political conflict, is foremost a struggle between
competing views of justice. When justice is understood by the parties to be getting that to which they are entitled, the other side—the party whose claims and
objections thwart that goal—become the embodiment of *injustice*. The mantra,
particularly for the party that has suffered most during the ongoing struggle,
becomes *no peace without justice*. The louder and more often that mantra is
sounded, the more likely it is that the result will simply be no peace.

The paradox is a familiar one for the peacemaker. While a minimal sense of
justice is an indispensable aspect of any durable peace, the headlong pursuit of
justice by one or both sides is apt to be counterproductive. Indeed, if the parties
did not disagree about what a just agreement would entail, there would not be a
conflict. In our experience, it is best to direct initial attention away from conflicting claims about history and the entitlements that arise from past losses and violations of human rights that had been endured.[2] Instead, the focus of discussion
should be two-fold. The parties should seek to rectify the most serious injustices
that are currently being endured. People of goodwill who cannot agree about the
requirements of justice can often recognize suffering that is undeserved and
unjust and can then agree on provisions to reduce such suffering. The parties
also should acknowledge the losses that a mutually acceptable settlement would
necessarily impose on at least some members of the other community as well as
their own.

We have also found it useful to note that the relationship between peace-seeking
and justice-seeking relates to a question that all of us face daily in our lives and with
our dealings within our own families and communities. Few of us feel that the
workings of our families are entirely fair and just. Fewer still would claim that our
workplaces and communities offer anything approximating complete fairness and
justice. The question we confront therefore is whether the particular departures
from what we deem fair and just are so egregious that we are not willing to bear
them in the interests of decent working relationships and the pursuit of important
life goals. The critical question that participants in conflict similarly must ask
themselves is not whether peace—at least, any *achievable* peace—is fully just.
Rather, it is whether the fruits of peaceful relationships are not, in fact, worth the
feelings of imperfect justice that they, and others, will have to bear if they are to
reap those fruits.

Is there a limit to the amount of injustice that can legitimately be accepted in
order to achieve various material benefits? Are there some circumstances in
which the very notion of "give-and-take" dealmaking is a moral affront? The

answer, which has political as well as moral significance, is obviously yes. Sometimes, it may be necessary to make a deal with the devil (see Mnookin, 2010) but not at the price of one's soul, or worse still, when it is *other people* who will have to pay the terrible price.

The Holocaust posed that dilemma for many leaders and, even today, people continue to debate the morality of deals with the Nazi regime that saved some, but in so doing, doomed others and served the interests of that evil regime. The philosopher Avishai Margalit draws the line between legitimate and illegitimate deals by focusing on the issue of humiliation, which Margalit suggests arises when human beings are treated as nonhuman—when they are denied the minimal rights and capacities that are owed to all people regardless of their status (Margalit, 1996). Margalit, in fact, sets a very high bar for rejecting a peace proposal because of its apparent injustice. Unless the proposed terms of settlement would treat one of the parties as less than human, or perpetuate such a state of affairs, he insists that those terms merit consideration. Negotiated agreements that would require the parties to forego some of the entitlements they feel they deserve in order to achieve peace and better the everyday lives of the people affected by the agreement are generally the best that can be achieved.

IV. Summary and Concluding Observations

Perhaps the chief lesson to be drawn from the reflections offered here is that in the context of many protracted conflicts treating conflict resolution as merely a matter of realigning or reconciling interests in search of "win-win" advances over the status quo is likely to be unsuccessful and perhaps even counterproductive. All conflicts, to some degree, pit the objective interests of one party against those of another party. However, conflicts differ in the extent to which the parties see their prospects in zero-sum terms. Some conflicts appear—at least to one party but often to both parties—to put at risk not only its future well-being but its very existence. The adversaries appear to each other not as rivals with whom business can be done where interests converge but as *enemies*. In these instances, the conflict is seen as a zero-sum struggle in which any potential gain by an enemy constitutes a threat and a loss to oneself, and to one's own side; and any loss that can be imposed on that enemy is seen as a gain.

Beyond the structural, strategic, and psychological barriers that must be overcome in any negotiation between parties with divergent interests, in many intergroup conflicts unaddressed feelings of injustice, humiliation, and powerlessness pose a particular problem. Such feelings can make it impossible for the weaker party to enter into seemingly beneficial agreements because it perceives such agreements as an affront to its dignity. Moreover, in the face of such feelings, even minor confrontations give offense and rub salt into existing wounds by reminding the weaker party of its limited means of redress. Conflicts such as these are sustained and exacerbated by feelings of humiliation and cannot be satisfactorily resolved until the relations in question are repaired to the point where considerations of material interest loom larger than such affective considerations.

In short, the nature of the relationship that exists between the conflicting parties makes the relevant barriers more difficult to overcome and can itself act as a barrier to the management or resolution of the conflict. Improving that relationship, providing a basis for trust to replace mistrust, and creating the sense that a shared future is possible, is generally the starting point for amelioration of a conflict that appears intractable, and for lightening the burden it imposes on the participants. From a barriers perspective, the two specific issues to be addressed are (1) What prevents a conflict that is currently intractable because of enemy relationships from becoming an ordinary conflict of interest, one in which mutually beneficial trades of concessions become possible? (2) What prevents a demeaning and degrading relationship from becoming a relationship in which both sides accept each other's humanity and right to a secure and dignified future? The peacemaker's task, accordingly, is to address these relational issues, so that "normal" interest-based negotiation in service of a mutually acceptable future can ensue.

In this essay, we shared a number of observations that come from our experiences in working with would-be peacemakers and bridge-builders between warring communities—some of which have reinforced ideas tested in experimental research and some of which have forced us to change our emphases and expand the domain of our concerns. We have also identified four questions—the question of a shared future, the question of trustworthiness, the question of loss acceptance, and the question of just entitlements that we believe provide a useful starting point for real-world efforts at conflict management and resolution. We have found that dialogue between the parties, not only at the level of diplomats and leaders but also at the level of factional representatives, opinion leaders, and even ordinary citizens, can be useful. But such dialogue must do more than allow the parties to reiterate long-held positions, air grievances, and offer arguments whose acceptance would threaten or humiliate the other side by continuing denial of basic human rights. It must begin to deal with these questions in a forthright manner, with each party trying its best to appreciate not only the other party's legitimate concerns but also its other understandable fears, frustrations, and feelings of prospective loss.

Notes

1. The example of the status of Jerusalem in any future peace agreement is a case in point. The moderates on both sides endorse the principle that East Jerusalem will be the capitol of the new Palestinian state. However, in our experience, having the parties discuss the details of a plan that would provide universal access to the Haram al Sharif by West Bank Palestinians without reducing security against terrorism for Israeli Jerusalemites quickly reveals the remaining distance between the parties.

2. It is a cliché to state that in protracted conflicts and deadlocked negotiation, "both sides are wrong." In our view, the real problem in most historical conflicts is that both sides are actually *right*—at least in the bill of particulars they offer in support of the injustice they claim to have suffered. No negotiated settlement will rectify all such injustice to the satisfaction of the aggrieved parties. On the contrary, in rectifying some injustices, it will impose new ones.

CODA

Barriers to Dispute Resolution

RYAN GOODMAN, DEREK JINKS, AND ANDREW K. WOODS

The Bland, Powell, and Ross chapter identifies several persistent barriers to conflict resolution. The chapter provides evidence of, and sustained reflection on, several psychological barriers including dissonance reduction, "naïve realism," judgmental overconfidence, insistence on equity or justice, loss aversion, and reactive devaluation. These barriers involve fundamental psychological processes and biases that shape the ways in which relevant actors interpret and understand both the dispute itself as well as the disputants. The intensity and durability of these barriers turn on the degree of trust between the parties, the nature and extent of intragroup conflicts, the availability and achievability of "tipping points," and the avoidance of humiliation.

At bottom, these barriers suggest that meaningful resolution of deep political disputes will often prove much more difficult than any objective assessment might otherwise predict. As a consequence, dispute resolution often requires much more than the realignment or reconciliation of interests. Bland, Powell, and Ross suggest that effective dispute resolution requires (1) awareness by the parties and any mediators of these psychological barriers, and (2) a concerted effort by the parties to consider carefully the subjective interpretations of the opposing party. As the authors acknowledge, this second step is an imperfectly understood, exceedingly complex process. The chapter maintains that this process can be impelled forward if structured around generating forthright answers to four questions: the question of a bearable shared future, the question of trustworthiness, the question of "loss acceptance," and the question of just entitlements.

At one level of generality, the research canvassed in this chapter has clear and, indeed, crucial application to human rights. Intractable political conflict—including, most important, situations of armed conflict—constitutes one of the most severe threats to the promotion and protection of human rights. Therefore, this chapter, in a very straightforward sense, provides useful guidance to human rights advocates and human rights institutions on how best to participate (and how not to participate) in the dispute resolution process arising out of such conflicts. In addition to these more direct lessons, we suggest here several collateral lines of application to human rights.

I. Target: Proponents of Any Peace Settlement

The chapter repeatedly emphasizes the importance of building trust and the corrosive effects of humiliation for conflict resolution. This finding strongly suggests that human rights commitments should be included in formal peace settlements—including the charters of transitional authorities in the context of any peacebuilding effort (Bell, 2004). This research also underscores the importance of protecting human rights during the conflict itself—precisely because the failure to do so would frustrate any attempt to conclude a viable peace settlement. This finding has obvious implications for the debate about the formal applicability of human rights law in time of armed conflict (Ben-Naftali, 2011). It also favors the promotion of human rights norms—for example, a concern for the dignity of prisoners above and beyond whatever is required by the letter of the law—as a matter of policy in those circumstances where neither human rights law nor international humanitarian law accord substantial protection against all forms of "humiliation."

The point here is not simply that human rights should be respected and protected in such circumstances, but also that formal reaffirmation of the human rights of relevant actors might yield some discrete, nontrivial benefit. These formal reaffirmations would be far less likely to capture this benefit, of course, if they diminish the level of rights protections otherwise afforded the relevant population. Such a "reaffirmation" is more likely to be perceived, at best, as the withdrawal of an entitlement and, at worst, as the imposition of a humiliating punishment. Conversely, rights protections that exceed the relevant baseline might capture a substantial benefit.

II. Target: Promoters of Human Rights—Human Rights Law as Negotiated Settlement

The psychological barriers to conflict resolution are especially relevant in the context of traditional armed conflicts—or other intractable conflicts in which the disputants do not consider themselves part of a viable, shared political process. Nevertheless, this research offers several valuable insights regarding a more mundane, but nevertheless important, family of political conflicts: the political disputes surrounding efforts to generate, elaborate, and administer and enforce human rights regimes. Of particular importance, in our view, are conflicts in these contexts between promoters of human rights and violators (or would-be violators) of human rights. These promoters include rights-regarding governments, nongovernmental organizations, intergovernmental organizations, members of the media, and even individuals. These violators (or would-be violators) include governments and non-state actors—whether they are resistant to the recognition or observance of human rights generally, of only some specific right or rights, or of some particular interpretation of a right. The fundamental point is that these encounters involve, in some irreducible sense, the process of conflict resolution. Once this analytical move is made, innumerable applications to human rights become readily apparent. We highlight here several examples that, we hope, are suggestive of further lines of application.

A. Dissonance Reduction or Avoidance

The chapter points out that predisposition toward dissonance reduction or avoidance often impedes dispute settlement. This occurs precisely because settlement of almost any sort will require the parties to abandon, or otherwise act in a manner inconsistent with, the justifications and rationales that initially motivated or later sustained the conflict. Human rights advocates and regime architects might address this concern by minimizing the imposition of reputational (and other) costs on target actors prior to securing some meaningful commitment from those actors. Shaming or economic coercion designed to secure an initial commitment will, unless immediately successful, generate social psychological processes that will ultimately make it more difficult to secure that commitment. As Bland, Powell, and Ross make clear, the predisposition toward dissonance reduction can become a positive force once the target actor has made some meaningful commitment—since the justifications for making the commitment generate pressure to endorse and abide by it. Nevertheless, these same processes exert a negative force on efforts to obtain commitments and concessions in the first place.

B. Loss Aversion and Prospect Theory

Loss aversion and prospect theory suggest that parties quickly assimilate gains as entitlements but are slow to accept losses. The core problem here is that the parties might have fundamentally different assessments of the value of any particular concession in the negotiation process. As a consequence, rights-disregarding actors are likely to view certain permissive features of human rights as broad, fundamental entitlements and the restrictive features as losses. This suggests caution in the drafting, interpretation, and enforcement of human rights agreements. One common strategy in human rights is to secure broad initial agreement to an abstract, exception-laden set of principles in order to establish an institutional framework within which ever more concrete, nonderogable norms might be elaborated and legitimated. That strategy may lead state actors to exaggerate the importance of the exceptions and loathe to bolster human rights once such exceptions are in place.

Human rights agreements do not merely entail costs ("losses") for states. They also confer legitimacy and may create political opportunity structures that provide cover for social reforms that would otherwise have been difficult for a state to enact. One implication of the loss aversion research—which suggests that people are overly optimistic about gains and pessimistic about losses—is that human right "obligations" be framed instead as entitlements. Rather than emphasize the significant affirmative responsibilities that states have under human rights agreements (which rights promoters hail in order to prove that rights agreements have teeth), promoters might do well, in the context of negotiations, to frame rights agreements as conferring significant credibility benefits at very low cost.

Loss aversion and prospect theory underscores an important complication associated with this approach. Recalcitrant states and other relevant actors are likely to view the concretization of human rights norms or the narrowing of excusing conditions as the turn away from an entitlement paradigm—and, as a consequence, are likely to resist any such moves. That this trajectory might be necessary to promote the larger substantive ambitions of human rights will be less compelling than proponents would expect because rights-disregarding actors might refuse to fully reconcile these "losses." It is also important for human rights advocates and regime architects to understand that their own view of the negotiation process and its product are likely to be influenced by the same psychological bias. Consider one example. For human rights proponents, derogation provisions and other limitations clauses are often perceived as unacceptably high "losses" in the treaty-making process. For these actors, broad derogation schemes are founded on the normatively indefensible notion that threats to sovereign authority trump the need to protect fundamental human rights. For proponents of human rights, rights restrictions ought not be excused except where absolutely necessary to protect human rights more broadly. That human rights treaties explicitly authorize states to disregard some fundamental rights protections in time of national emergency is, in theory and in practice, a travesty according to these actors. This view, though, arguably frustrates the ongoing negotiation between rights promoters and rights violators because it fails to acknowledge the degree to which legitimate state interests might warrant rights restrictions in some circumstances.

C. "Naïve Realism"

The chapter summarizes some of the evidence suggesting the prevalence of "naïve realism." The general idea is that partisans are systematically biased in favor of the accuracy and moral superiority of their sides' claims—and are likewise biased against the claims of their opponents. This psychological bias inhibits conflict resolution because it simultaneously accentuates the other psychological biases; instills in both sides the sense that they are systematically less susceptible to any such biases than the other side; and perhaps most important, generates or entrenches distrust and enmity between the parties. This insight has profound consequences for human rights scholarship and practice. We highlight three illustrative lines of potential application—each pitched at a different level of abstraction: (1) reflexive application (recognition that we are all naïve realists), (2) minimizing partisan factual and theoretical distortion (resolving disputes between naïve realists), and (3) minimizing naïve realism itself (negotiating disputes so as not to deepen conflict). Consider each example.

First, naïve realism no doubt pervades the political exchange between human rights advocates and rights violators/would-be rights violators. The chapter suggests caution—and introspection—by human rights advocates before imputing systematic biases and illicit motives to rights violators and would-be rights violators. It also suggests that human rights advocates likely systematically underestimate their own susceptibility to psychological (and other) forms of bias. This might entail developing metrics for systematically evaluating bias susceptibility. Even if such metrics are not determined to be useful in the short term, the mere effort to detect and minimize bias may enhance credibility in negotiation settings. As social psychological research on naïve realism becomes more fine grained, bias detection tools will likely improve accordingly.

Second, naïve realism strongly suggests that independent, third-party dispute resolution should take account of this bias. In this view, international courts, human rights treaty bodies, and international arbitration panels should not embrace robust forms of factual or interpretive deference. For example, this research counsels against according national authorities a "margin of appreciation" in interpreting human rights law. It also demonstrates one reason to disfavor robust exhaustion of national remedies requirements. Ultimately, the extent to which third-party bodies should defer to local parties may depend on the ability to assess the strength of the bias in any relevant situation. Where no bias is detected, greater deference may be warranted and vice versa; such metrics, if developed, could be especially helpful for designers of "hybrid" domestic-international bodies seeking to make trade-offs between (and harness the best of) local and international expertise.

Third, the chapter—and this line of research more generally—strongly suggests that human rights advocates might minimize naïve realism by minimizing moral realist language. Moral realist language—such as rights talk about absolute wrongs—encourages naïve realist thinking (Ross and Ward, 1996). Recent research demonstrates that this scenario often produces an escalatory spiral— further entrenching perception bias, deepening the conflict, and even converting simple disagreement into full-blown conflict (Kennedy and Pronin, forthcoming; Kennedy and Pronin, 2008). This line of research underscores an important, and underappreciated, downside to the conventional blame-and-shame model of human rights advocacy. In addition, it counsels against the formal or informal embrace of moral realist rationales for human rights institutions. For example, the reliance on retributivist rationales for international criminal law risks increasing naïve realist thinking—and the escalation of conflict (Woods, 2011). This also calls into question the interesting applications suggested by the Mikhail and Gintis chapters (7 and 6), where behavioral evidence suggested an even stronger argument for grounding human rights norms in universal moral intuitions. The naïve realism research suggests reasons to avoid treating rights violations as absolute moral wrongs—even if such claims could be grounded in a shared human morality.

None of this is to say that moral realist language and naïve realism are necessarily counterproductive in the human rights context. For instance, moral realist language and naïve realism no doubt foster the mobilization of public consciousness in many circumstances. The research canvassed in this chapter makes clear, though, that the psychosocial context that makes this mobilization possible also risks entrenching assimilation and perception biases in human rights violators— perhaps making any ultimate resolution of the issue less likely.

Note

This Coda, like the others in the book, offers some specific applications drawn from the insights in the contributor's chapter. It is not intended to be a list of fully developed policy prescriptions, but instead an example of the rich sorts of human rights policy applications that can be drawn from cutting-edge social science research. It does not question the insights offered in the chapter but instead asks what implications those insights might have for human rights law and policy. The Codas are the sole authorship of the editors of the volume.

11

The Difference It Makes

WILLIAM F. SCHULZ

I. Introduction

My father was a professor of law, specializing in criminal and administrative law. As far as I know, he was a very good teacher. But he had never been in private practice, never represented a plaintiff, never prosecuted an alleged criminal or defended someone accused of a crime, and never served in an administrative position in government. Similarly, when I went to theological school, the person who taught practical arts of ministry had never served as a minister in a parish. What he knew, he knew either from observing others or reading a book. Such a dearth of hands-on experience may not be catastrophic in the fields of law and theology, but I would hate to think what might happen if architecture was taught solely by people who had never designed a building or structural engineering by those who had never put up a dam.

Paradoxically, this disconnect between theory and practice can generate considerable envy in both camps. One of my oldest friends, a highly lauded professor of history at a fine university, remarked, upon learning of my work as executive director of Amnesty International USA, "Oh, what I would give to be actually making a difference in the world!" I had just been about to tell him that I yearned for the time and opportunity his profession afforded him to contemplate the larger picture and see how our daily human toil might be contributing to the long-term march of change.

The simple truth is, of course, that at their best, theory and practice reinforce one another; they are two halves of a whole. After all, the illumination of God denoted by the Greek word *theoria* came not through abstract philosophizing but through ascetic practice and conformity to God's commandments. But in much of academia, rarely the twain do meet. Fortunately, this volume disproves that "rule."

II. Why Activism Needs Academia

Understanding Social Action, Promoting Human Rights has been designed to bridge the gap between knowing and doing, study and service, research and rescue in the field of human rights. Such an enterprise is particularly welcome in this field for at least four reasons: first, because human rights needs all the help it can get; second, because it is a field that has traditionally been dominated by lawyers; third, because its practitioners often operate from the seat of their pants; and fourth, because some of the most important breakthroughs in the field are occurring at the intersection of the sciences and human rights advocacy.

While the impact of human rights on international politics and U.S. foreign policy has increased steadily since World War II, human rights is still often the forgotten stepchild of international relations, particularly when it is perceived to be at odds with other, more allegedly hard-nosed, strategic interests. Moreover, human rights advocacy remains the purview of a far more limited number of actors than, say, development, health care, or environmental activism—this despite the leap in the number of indigenous human rights groups around the globe over the past decade. As a result, human rights needs allies and resources in every community and from every sector, not least the academic, research, and technological.

The one sector from which there has been no dearth of human rights support or resources, however, has been the legal. On the one hand, much of the progress that can be charted in the creation of a human rights regimen recognized, if not always respected, by governments far and wide, is a result of the codification and enforcement of human rights law at both the national and international levels. Human rights norms absent human rights laws are so much chaff blowing in the wind. On the other hand, the identification of human rights advocacy as primarily a legal enterprise requiring legal training and expertise has tended to limit its appeal and narrow the terms and concepts employed in its pursuit. The law may be majestic, but it is inherently conservative and rarely given to embracing the kind of research into human behavior represented in the essays in this volume. For that reason alone, the introduction of fields other than the legal may broaden and energize what sometimes threatens to be a stultifying discipline.

Then, too, the human rights field is not exactly "disciplined" in the sense that assumptions about theories of change or decisions about priorities and strategies are often made by human rights organizations in a less-than-systematic way. In part, that is because they are often forced to react quickly to breaking events, but it is also because, like many movements for change, they rely more upon intuitive judgments than finely tuned conclusions to set direction. Resources from the academic and research communities cannot help but add refinement to that decision making.

Among the resources that have most prominently been brought to bear in recent years on the struggle for human rights are the technological and, though they are little represented in this book, they certainly reflect an amalgamation of research and action that holds enormous promise. The most obvious example are the ways in which cell phones; text messaging; social networks like Twitter, My Space and Facebook; and blogs and other evolving forms of information and communications technology are changing the human rights landscape—both helping activists organize, as we have seen most recently in the Middle East—and making it more and more difficult for governments to mistreat their citizens without the whole world knowing about it. Data sourcing applications are being used to process reams of information, such as the historical archives of the Guatemalan National Police or 17,000 victim and witness statements related to Charles Taylor's notorious escapades in Liberia, which can then be used before courts, tribunals, and truth commissions to bring perpetrators of crimes to justice. Medical forensics and DNA fact-finding, particularly as applied in the exhumation of mass graves, are making important contributions to the search for accountability. Perhaps most groundbreaking of all, satellite imaging is both tracking human rights crimes on the ground and, in some cases, offering a measure of protection to vulnerable populations. Satellite images of the Porta Farm settlement in Zimbabwe, for example, taken before and after reports in 2006 of a campaign against government opponents revealed the destruction of 850 homes; satellite tracking of changes in vegetation in Darfur, Sudan, between 2003–2007 documented a dramatic return of natural vegetation to an area that had been farming land prior to the systematic destruction of the farming population and their grazing livestock; and Amnesty International's "Eyes on Darfur" project focused commercial satellites on a dozen at-risk villages in Darfur seeking to protect them from marauding *janjaweed* militia. Growing recognition of the relationship between mass atrocities, on the one hand, and climate change, overpopulation, and economic scarcity on the other mean that an interdisciplinary approach to the prevention of human rights crimes is long overdue.

For all these reasons, the effort to meld academic reflection to human rights activism is a welcome one. But the crucial question about this volume for this essay is, "How well did we do?" What follows is not an attempt to evaluate the intellectual accuracy or academic rigor of the essays under consideration. That is for others with expertise in the various disciplines represented here to judge. My task is to ask a relatively simple question of each essay: "How useful are its insights for the real, on-the-ground work of human rights?"

III. Where Do Human Rights Come From?

The questions as to whether or not human rights are truly universal and, if they are, by what means we can persuade people to act as if those universal claims trump narrower ones are at the heart of the human rights enterprise. The first of these two baseline questions is addressed by Gintis and Mikhail; the second in one form or another by Baron, Prentice, Hornik, Lazer, and Slovic. Levi, Tyler, and Sacks tackle a somewhat different, if related, question regarding government legitimacy and compliance with law.

Gintis argues that human rights have their origin in the evolutionary development of a "reverse dominance hierarchy" that resists the natural disposition of societies to be controlled by "the hierarchical authority of a dominant individual." The result, he says, is that "human rights will have almost universal support among the populace of virtually all countries" and that "freedom and democracy tend to garner widespread acceptance even in societies that have attempted strenuously to foster a culture sympathetic to autocratic or theocratic government."

Natural law arguments for human rights like this one are appealing because they appear to lend solidity to human rights claims that they might otherwise lack. The American Declaration of Independence, covering all bases, invoked "the Laws of Nature and Nature's God" as the justificatory grounds for the rights to be asserted. The Universal Declaration of Human Rights, its drafters having been unable to agree on a religious basis for human rights, refers in its Preamble to "the *inherent* dignity" and "*inalienable* rights of all members of the human family," both of which phrases imply that the 30 articles that follow are sanctioned by something sacred or automatically inviolable in human nature (Morsink, 2000: 248).

The dangers of natural law arguments are manifold, however. In the first place, they are notoriously subject to the whims of the age and predispositions of their authors. John Locke famously discerned universal rights in Nature as long as the claimant was male and propertied. The Declaration of Independence's stirring affirmation that "all men are created equal" did not mean literally *all* men until Abraham Lincoln, rewriting history, said that it did. As Henry Louis Gates has observed, "Thomas Jefferson most certainly was not thinking of black men and women when he wrote the Declaration of Independence and no amount of romantic historical wishful thinking can alter that fact" (Wills, 2009).

The neoconservative political philosopher Francis Fukuyama, a keen advocate of natural law, wants to base human rights on "some common understanding of human ends or purposes" and assures us that "what gives [humans] dignity and a moral status higher than that of other living creatures" is the combination of moral choice, reason, language, sociability, sentience, emotions, and consciousness that characterizes the human species. Then comes the breath-taking leap: "This explains," Fukuyama says, "why there are a lot of capitalist liberal democracies around the world at the beginning of the twenty-first century but very few socialist dictatorships" (Fukuyama, 2002: 173).

Rights may be grounded in the vagaries of human evolution as Gintis asserts, but looking forward, that may be of scant interest to those who contend that an anthropocentric theory of rights is preposterously narrow not only because it ignores the rights of animals but because it has no relevance to the emerging notion that Nature itself may claim a set of rights (Tuhus, 2009).

Similarly, rights that purport to be grounded in the latest scientific theory are by definition put in jeopardy when that theory changes, as the history of science virtually guarantees us it will. What shall we do if future theorists of evolution discard the notion of a reverse dominance hierarchy? Throw out all the rights we have so confidently rested upon that putative notion? (And this is to say nothing about the difficulty of reaching universal scientific consensus on such a thing as a reverse dominance hierarchy in the first place.)

Finally, the problem with natural law theories of rights is that they generally only undergird a select set of rights. Gintis claims that that number includes "freedom of person and property, freedom of speech and association, the right of democratic participation, the right to an attorney and a fair trial, as well as equal opportunity and non-discrimination"—all well and good and quite a lot in and of themselves to be derived from an evolutionary disposition. But can we plausibly make the case that resistance to the "hierarchical authority of a dominant individual" accounts for such rights as that to a nationality or such economic rights as an adequate living standard[1] or an education?[2] Mikhail's essay, too, suffers from such implausibility, as we shall see in a moment.

To his credit, Gintis recognizes that if rights are evolutionarily grounded, they ought to be affirmed in every culture. But, to the contrary, his assertion that "human rights will have almost universal support among the populace of virtually all countries" is manifestly untrue. One need only look at that country that represents one-fifth of the world's population to see that far from being dissatisfied with the authoritarian nature of their national government, a majority of Chinese seem quite content with rulers who regularly flout human rights norms and are far less supportive of Western-style democracy than most other populations in Asia (Nathan, 2008: 25–43). One would be hard-pressed to contend that the subjugation of women in countries such as Saudi Arabia is perversely being foisted upon the population by the Saudi government and clerics despite "almost universal support among the populace" for women's rights! But then the psychoanalyst Erich Fromm argued almost 70 years ago in his classic work *Escape from Freedom* that, as the title page said, "Freedom can be frightening; totalitarianism can be tempting" (Fromm, 1941).

Mikhail's essay, in contrast to Gintis's, is grounded in a far more sophisticated approach. Citing evidence from fields as diverse as behavioral studies of children and animals to deontic logic and legal anthropology, Mikhail wants to refute the positivist notion that rights are merely the current collective perception of utility and assert instead that they are grounded in a Universal Moral Grammar (UMG), what used to be called an "innate moral conscience." This is, as I say, a felicitous notion for human rights advocates who often enough feel like describing human rights abusers as "monsters" and would surely like to be able to accuse them of violating not only law, custom, or God's commandments but of betraying something even more basic that makes us human.

Mikhail is suitably guarded in his claims for UMG, noting that "none of this evidence is conclusive and all of it is open to competing interpretations." His own research, for example, in comparative law designed to undergird UMG with the finding that 80% of the member states of the United Nations outlaw intentional killing without justification while codifying certain ameliorative justifications hardly proves that such strictures are inherent in the nature of being human. After all, to be a member of the U.N. requires de jure affirmation of certain fundamental principles, and it is certainly possible that some basic cultural norms have spread so widely, both because of their usefulness and because of global reinforcement, that virtually everyone pretends at least formally to affirm them. This is the case with torture, for example. But, given the almost universal persistence of its use throughout history, one could just as readily argue that it is the impulse to torture that is "natural" and that laws and norms against it have been adopted to stave off the inherent cruelty in our hearts. Mikhail argues that the fact that we don't always practice UMG doesn't mean that we don't know deep down ("intuitively") that we *should*. But that is a pretty convenient escape clause to explain away discrepancies between alleged universal norms and irrefutable evidence of universal practices.

Nonetheless, Mikhail is surely right to reject cultural relativism—though relativism stumbles even without his help, foist on the petard of its own oft-noted internal contradiction; namely, that if all truth is relative, then so is the truth that all truth is relative. But even if Mikhail's description of UMG is correct, where I think he misses the proverbial beat is in his understanding of its application to human rights.

Human rights, morality, and crimes are not the same things. If I commit adultery or gamble away my children's savings, I may be said to have committed immoral acts, but I am not guilty of a human rights violation. If I have a personal grudge against my neighbor and shoot him, I am guilty of a crime but not a human rights violation. That is because human rights violations must (1) be acts of commission or omission recognized as such by a significant portion of the international human rights regimen (courts, treaties, U.N. bodies, regional bodies, human rights NGOs, etc.) that (2) are the ultimate responsibility of some corporate entity—usually governments but also such things as businesses and armed opposition groups.

Moreover, human rights both set boundaries to that corporate behavior beyond which a government or other corporate actor may not go if they wish to be regarded as reputable members of the international community (what Isaiah Berlin famously called "negative liberties"), but they also describe a vision of the "Good Society," of what a truly civilized society or nation would look like ("positive liberties"). The former of these two tasks is often identified with civil and political rights and the latter with economic, social, and cultural, though the truth is that both sets of rights imply both positive and negative liberties.

Mikhail summarizes his conclusion about UMG this way: "All of these studies point to the same dramatic conclusion . . . : [that] human beings evolved a special emotional sensitivity to assault, battery and other core wrongs, and the intuitive aversion to them appears to be built into distinct regions of the human brain." But even if this claim can be substantiated, it speaks to only a very limited number of immoral acts, much less human rights violations.

Do we really believe that we can derive the right of every child "to be registered immediately after birth"[3] or the right of any person "to be free to leave any country, including his own"[4] from UMG? And aver as Mikhail does in his penultimate paragraph that UMG's justification of rights "presumably could be extended to include . . . social, economic and cultural rights," he offers no evidence for this, and it is even harder to imagine that it is "distinct regions of the human brain" that lead us inexorably to know deep inside our souls that the Good Society is one that allows for the formation of trade unions[5] or practices "industrial hygiene."[6]

The point is, then, that the findings from diverse fields of study that Mikhail cites may (or may not) convince us that certain elements of morality are grounded in an innate moral conscience, but those elements are too broad to tell us much about human rights and too narrow to mandate imperatives for governments and other corporate actors at whom human rights obligations are aimed. For my money, philosophical pragmatism, sometimes called consensualism, is a far more useful tool for substantiating human rights claims.

Yet regardless of the grounding of those claims, how do we enforce them? Gintis cites studies that describe how third parties (or "bystanders") may choose to punish norm violators, especially if they themselves have been the victims of the violation. Certainly finding ways to motivate outsiders to intervene on behalf of victims of human rights atrocities is a fundamental challenge for human rights practitioners—a challenge many of our authors have chosen to take up.

IV. Getting People to Do What Is Right

Baron defines parochialism as favoring "a group that includes [me] while under-weighing or ignoring harm to outsiders," and he identifies nationalism as a prime—and by implication, malevolent—example. What he means by nation-alism is not of course just identity with a nation since we have already noted that being deprived of a nationality is a human rights violation or even, presumably, being proud of one's nation since many nations embody or "stand for" values, in-cluding opposition to oppressors and hospitality to strangers, which we would no doubt like to affirm. The parochialism/nationalism Baron describes is that which is willing to advance what one perceives to be one's own interests at the expense of outsiders *even if* harming those outsiders is in fact *not* in one's self-interest. This is a very particular kind of behavior—almost a kind of group sadism—since the vast majority of actors perceive their parochial behavior as in fact benefiting themselves and/or because it is so difficult to predict ahead of time what will be in our own interests in the long run and what will not.

Moreover, as the philosopher Richard Rorty pointed out, parochialism   at least in the sense of caring first and most for the welfare of those who are most like us—may well be the starting point for a robust commitment to human rights. It is almost impossible, in Rorty's view, to identify with the abstraction called "humanity." We first identify with those who are most like us and then, through hearing stories and learning of the travails of others outside our group, gradually "see more and more traditional differences (of tribe, religion, race, customs and the like) as unimportant when compared with similarities with respect to pain and humiliation—the ability to think of people wildly different from ourselves as included in the range of 'us'" (Rorty, 1989). I emphasize this point because I have seen so many people come to the human rights movement—first because they cared foremost about Ethiopians or Uighurs or women or lesbian and gay people, often because they themselves fell into one of those categories, but who then came to extend their caring to others whose rights were being denied.

Nonetheless, parochialism/nationalism in the sense Baron means it can of course be a precursor to human rights violations—in fact, very serious human rights violations, like ethnic cleansing and genocide—and it is important to know how to combat it. Baron suggests, among other things, that we promote the "illusion" that "cooperation promotes self-interest"; that we emphasize the individual humanity of outsiders; and that we discourage what he calls "moral-istic values," the imposition of our values on others "whatever the conse-quences." We would be hard-pressed to argue with any of these recommendations, especially since cooperation (and respect for human rights) often *are* in one's own self-interest; "putting a human face" on human rights victims does indeed motivate others to help them (as Amnesty International's many successful campaigns for the release of individual Prisoners of Conscience so well illustrate); and imposing one's moral views on others can of course be enormously damaging, depending on what those moral views are. (I am far less sanguine about Baron's conclusion that "parochialism is manifest largely in failure to help, rather than in active harm" because, even if this is true from a strictly numerical point of view, the instances in which parochialism fosters "active harm" have such devastating consequences.)

The question that really needs to be addressed, however, is *how* we accomplish any of these ends. Levi, Tyler, and Sacks tell us that governments that are competent and, more important, treat people fairly and equitably are more likely to be perceived as legitimate and, when this is so, "voluntary cooperation with laws increases." This makes sense of course and may well be a useful argument to make to governments that are inclined to discriminate—though one is hard-pressed to imagine it would persuade Robert Mugabe to stop the murders of white farmers or the Burmese generals to hold truly free elections if Aung San Suu Kyi were a candidate—but what do we do when the government is itself the problem, as it often is?

The example of China is again instructive. There is little reason to believe that large numbers of Han Chinese (who constitute 92% of the population of the People's Republic) regard their national government (in contrast to their local governments) as illegitimate. This is no doubt at least in part, as Levi, Tyler, and Sacks hypothesize, because they regard it as fundamentally competent—certainly as long as it keeps the economy growing at around 10% per year—and because what discrimination exists is largely targeted at minorities, such as Tibetans, Uighurs, house church members, or Falun Gong practitioners. But from a human rights point of view, ceding legitimacy to a government that regularly resorts to torture, imprisonment without trial, the death penalty, etc., is hardly slated to advance human rights.

V. The Virtuous Circle: Changing Hearts, Norms, and Laws

What we need to do is to shift norms at the local, national, and international levels, among both grassroots and leadership, and here the remaining essays have much to tell us. Changing norms are particularly important at the international level because so much of international human rights law, unlike local and national, is largely self-enforcing. There is rarely a local sheriff to arrest the head of government who authorizes torture or genocide, even if he *has* been indicted by the International Criminal Court!

How, then, do norms change, and what is the relationship between that change, changes in individual hearts, and changes in law? As Prentice cogently points out, the three are intimately connected.

Consider, for example, how changes came about in the use of seat belts. Why is it that a significant majority of Americans—68%[7]—wear their seat belts when they drive or ride in a car even though there is virtually no chance that they will be arrested should they violate the seat belt laws?[8] The obvious answer is because they know they are less likely to be injured or lose their lives. But the truth is far more complicated than that.

In 1954, the American Medical Association (AMA) first called for the installation of lap belts in all automobiles. It was not until 1961, however, that New York State became the first state to require cars sold in the state to feature lap belts. Over the next two years, 22 states followed suit, and by 1965 all U.S. auto manufacturers, recognizing that a huge swath of their market would be off limits if they failed to install lap belts, had complied,[9] though not without stiff resistance, as Ralph Nader's groundbreaking work *Unsafe At Any Speed,* also published in 1965, made clear (Nader, 1965). But featuring seat belts in cars and getting people to wear them were two quite different things. The first mandatory seat belt law was not adopted until New York State did so in 1984, almost two decades after manufacturers had begun to carry the device as a matter of course. Did Americans really fail to understand for 19 years that wearing a seat belt increased their odds of surviving an auto accident unscathed?

The truth is that it took almost two decades for the norms about seat belt use to change sufficiently to overcome the resistance offered by the image of seat belt wearers as sissies, by plain old bad habits, and by a misplaced defense of personal liberty.[10] That change came about through a combination of dramatic advertisements and educational campaigns sponsored by citizens' groups, the Ad Council, and others about the ghastly consequences of failing to use seat belts; a growing chorus of advice offered by opinion leaders, health professionals, drivers' education teachers, insurance companies, and parents that using seat belts was the wise thing to do; and legislation pushed by advocacy groups that both reinforced that wisdom and made seat belt use a mark of a law-abiding citizen.

The result today is that a majority of Americans use their seat belts not because they fear the long arm of the law but because they don't want to be thought of either as stupid or as scofflaws. This point is reinforced by the fact that, though 68% of Americans actually wear their belts, 80% *say* that they do! (Phelps and Cennage, 2003).

In this case, as in so many other cases of social change, adjustments in people's personal habits and biases—in their hearts, if you will—were reinforced by changes in law, and those changes in law in turn fostered more changes in heart until new norms were well established—a virtuous circle. Contrary to the rallying cry of the old Southern segregationists, you really *can* legislate morality. This is one reason those who resist rights for gay and lesbian people are so exorcised about the growing number of states that sanction marriage equality: because they know that with codification of such same-sex marriages in law (as opposed to voluntary services of union not recognized by the state) will come growing numbers of people who are more and more comfortable with the extension of full equal rights to gays and lesbians. As Harold Hongju Koh, former dean of Yale Law School, puts it in his seminal essay, "How Is International Human Rights Law Enforced?"

> . . . the best way to enforce legal norms is not to coerce action, not to impose sanctions, but to change the way people think about themselves . . . In short, our prime way to enforce [international human rights] law is to encourage people to bring rules home, to internalize rules inside themselves, to transform themselves from lawless to law-abiding . . . (Koh, 2006: 311)

And, I would add, the same is true of nations. Prentice's work reinforces this notion. "Shaming rarely works in isolation," she says. "Rather, strengthening injunctive norms is an important part of a multifaceted strategy . . . that typically combines . . . directional social pressure"—what I am calling the changing of hearts—"with material and legal incentives." Her citation of studies that show that change can sometimes be induced by educating people about where they fall in relationship to their peers (and hence to prevailing norms) in such things as energy consumption or binge drinking is instructive. Just as most people don't want to think of themselves as outliers, so most nations want to think of themselves as abiding by international law and standards (norms) and hence as good citizens of the international community. (Large numbers of Americans reported strong discomfort with the United States' own defiance of those standards during the later years of the George W. Bush administration.[11]) One implication of Prentice's work therefore is that, even though international law can rarely be as robustly enforced as domestic, it is terribly important to have large numbers of states ratifying international human rights treaties and recognizing the authority of international human rights institutions in order to strengthen those norms against which nations may judge their own performances.

But, says Prentice, laws can change norms "only if people want to be liberated from the norms"—if, in other words, there has been some degree of change in hearts. How in the world do we stimulate that?

VI. "Selling" Human Rights

In the broadest terms, the answer is that we educate people. Hornik offers us advice as to how to do that, and Lazer describes ways in which networking can contribute to that process. "Keep it Simple, Stupid," Hornik advises us. Don't use advertising and communications campaigns to try to create generic human rights activists. Tie your "ask" of people into something concrete they can do. Link it to resources in the community. And, paraphrasing Spinoza, always take the view from eternity, the long view, recognizing that, in Theodore Parker and Martin Luther King Jr.'s oft-quoted words, "the arc of the universe is long but it bends toward justice." Sensible recommendations to a human rights community that often trucks with problems that feel overwhelming to people, incurable, beyond reach of rectification. The success of Amnesty International has been in part because it has given its members a sense that they actually *can* make a difference in the world.

On the other hand, many human rights dilemmas, especially the most serious, take place on a stage well beyond the arenas in which most of us function day to day and require action by large entities—governments, militaries, corporations, international financial institutions—over which we feel we have little control. Lazer suggests that network theory can help us understand how those large entities can be influenced—through other nations who have relations with the miscreant or through flows of people across borders or of information across firewalls.

Much of what Lazer treats as still speculative has by now been established. There is no question that states have different degrees of influence with other states and hence could theoretically have correspondingly greater impact on those states' human rights practices than states with less leverage. China certainly has greater potential to influence North Korea or Sudan than the United States does, and the same is true of South Africa in relation to Zimbabwe.

The fact that a networked relation exists, however, is in no way predictive of whether that will be a benefit to human rights or a threat. The European Union has pretty consistently used the promise of entry into the "network" as an incentive to countries like Croatia or Turkey to improve their human rights records. By explicitly refusing to link investments in the developing world to human rights benchmarks, on the other hand, China has undermined efforts to advance human rights. And, though everyone from former President Bill Clinton to the heads of information technology companies interested in snaring their share of the Chinese market have assured us, as Lazer does, that the "free flow of information is intrinsically subversive," that has by no means proven to be the case in all instances.

But what if our failure to "sell" human rights, to motivate people to speak up and act out against the most serious human rights crimes, like genocide, is not in the stars or in the shape of the world's power structures but in ourselves? That is the fascinating question Slovic explores in his description of how humans tend to emotionally discount or numb ourselves against the fates of a large number of victims in contrast to our generally compassionate reaction to "the identified individual victim, with a face and a name." Slovic offers a host of suggestions for infusing our problematic intuitive reactions with more of our deliberative and reflective natures. We should, for example, he says, use "powerful affective imagery such as that associated with Hurricane Katrina and the South Asian tsunami," something that human rights groups have tried hard to do with mixed results.[12] He offers an interesting proposal that governments commit, in the face of genocide, to engage in deliberations aimed at "producing a detailed action plan, factoring in the likely costs and benefits of different types of intervention." It is easy to criticize such a proposal, and I personally believe that what is most likely to diminish the appeal of crimes against humanity is an effective International Criminal Court bringing *genocidiares* to justice, and that our efforts would therefore best be spent in convincing the United States to join the court and the rest of the world to exert maximum pressure on countries to yield up those indicted. But, short of that, the kind of creative thinking in which Slovic engages is most welcome.

VII. Looking Forward

It goes without saying that one volume could not hope to touch upon all areas in which academic research can yield dividends to the human rights struggle. At first blush I can think of three areas right away in which more work (and probably a few PhD dissertations) would be useful: (1) Many countries have made the transition from authoritarian regimes to democratic—one thinks of Eastern Europe and many Latin American countries, to say nothing of South Africa, Taiwan, South Korea, and the Philippines. We have excellent studies of these individual cases but to my knowledge no systematic, cross-cultural study of the role that outsiders played in those transformations—what they did that helped and what hindered or had no impact on the change. (2) Economic sanctions are a popular but deeply flawed vehicle for bringing about changes in regimes or companies, and they have been utilized frequently enough by now that we could muster some pretty impressive empirical evidence to guide us in the future as to when they have and have not worked. (3) Predictive modeling has been used to forecast everything from how a new product will be received by consumers to whether Iran will build a nuclear bomb (Thompson, 2009).

Joshua Epstein has done some important work with computer modeling of circumstances that tend to promote inter-ethnic civil violence, but the application of such tools to human rights is in its infancy (Epstein, 2002).

About these and any number of other topics, one can only hope that academics and activists will tie their fortunes to one another more closely than they have in the past. If they do, this volume will have played an important role in that bonding.

Notes

1. Universal Declaration of Human Rights 1948, Art. 25.
2. Universal Declaration of Human Rights 1948, Art. 26.
3. International Covenant on Civil and Political Rights (UN) 1966, Art. 24.
4. International Covenant on Civil and Political Rights (UN) 1966, Art.12.
5. International Covenant on Economic, Social and Cultural Rights (UN) 1966, Art. 8.
6. International Covenant on Economic, Social and Cultural Rights (UN) 1966, Art. 12.
7. Facts about Automobile Safety from NHTSA. http://www.bhsbees.com/safety_stats.htm. Accessed March 8, 2011.
8. All states except New Hampshire make it illegal to drive or ride in a moving vehicle without wearing seat belts.
9. Highway Safety Research & Communications. http://www.iihs.org/laws/safetybeltuse.aspx.
10. This latter took the form of the contention that failure to use seat belts was a victimless crime and hence that mandating such use was an infringement upon Americans' liberty, an argument that failed to take into account both the fact that drivers who used seat belts tended to have fewer accidents, and that higher injury rates increased health insurance premiums for everybody.
11. Comprehensive Analysis of Polls Reveals Americans' Attitudes on U.S. Role in the World. *World Public Opinion.* 2007. http://www.worldpublicopinion.org/pipa/articles/brunitedstatescanadara/383.php?lb=brusc&pnt=383&nid=&id=. Accessed March 8, 2011
12. Interestingly enough, response to such imagery appears to be culturally influenced. Amnesty International Great Britain had been very successful in direct mail fundraising that included dramatic snapshots of torture victims after they had been abused. When this technique was tried in the United States, the results were disastrous—many recipients having objected to being exposed to such visual unpleasantness.

BIBLIOGRAPHY

Abbott, R. J., J. K. James, R. I. Milne, and A. C. M. Gillies. "Plant Introductions, Hybridization and Gene Flow." *Philosophical Transactions of the Royal Society* B 358 (2003): 1123–32. 2003.

Adamic, L. A., and N. Glance. "The Political Blogosphere and the 2004 U.S. Election: Divided They Blog." In *Proceedings of the 3rd International Workshop on Link Discovery*, 36–43. 2005.

Adams, J. S. "Inequity in Social Exchange." In *Advances in Experimental Social Psychology 2*, edited by L. Berkowitz. New York: Academic Press, 1965.

Akerlof, G. A. "Labor Contracts as Partial Gift Exchange." *The Quarterly Journal of Economics* 97 (1982): 543–69.

Alexander, R. D. *The Biology of Moral Systems*. New York: Aldine, 1987.

Allen, T. J. "Communication Networks in R and D Laboratories." *R and D Management* 1/1 (1970): 14–21.

Allman, J., A. Hakeem, and K. Watson. "Two Phylogenetic Specializations in the Human Brain." *Neuroscientist* 8 (2002): 335–46.

Alschuler, A. *Law without Values: The Life, Work, and Legacy of Justice Holmes*. Chicago: University of Chicago Press, 2000.

Alston, P., and F. Mégret, eds. *The United Nations and Human Rights: A Critical Appraisal*. Oxford: Oxford University Press, 2007.

Alter, A. L., J. Kernochan, and J. M. Darley. "Morality Influences How People Apply the Ignorance of the Law Defense." *Law and Society Review* 41 (2007): 819–64.

Amar, A. R. "Forty Acres and a Mule: A Republican Theory of Minimal Entitlements." *Harvard Journal of Law and Public Policy* 37/13 (1990).

Anderson, C., and L. Putterman. "Do Non-strategic Sanctions Obey the Law of Demand? The Demand for Punishment in the Voluntary Contribution Mechanism." *Games and Economic Behavior* 54/1 (2006): 1–24.

Archer, D., and R. Gartner. *Violence and Crime in Cross-National Perspective*. New Haven, CT: Yale University Press, 1984.

Aronson, E. A. "Theory of Cognitive Dissonance." In *Advances in Experimental Social Psychology 4*, edited by L. Berkowitz. New York: Academic Press, 1969.

Arrow, K., R. Mnookin, L. Ross, A. Tversky, and R. Wilson. *Barriers to Conflict Resolution*. New York: W. W. Norton and Company, 1995.

Asch, S. E. *Social Psychology*. Englewood Cliffs, NJ: Prentice-Hall, 1952.

Associated Press. "38,000 Shoes Stand for Loss in Lethal Year." *The Register-Guard* (2009): 6A.

Axelrod, R., and W. D. Hamilton. "The Evolution of Cooperation." *Science* 211 (1981): 1390–96.

Baier, K. *The Moral Point of View: A Rational Basis of Ethics*. New York: Random House, 1965/1958.

Bain, A. *Mental and Moral Science: A Compendium of Psychology and Ethics*. London: Longmans, Green, and Co., 1868.

Baird, J. "Motivations and Morality: Do Children Use Mental State Information to Evaluate Identical Actions Differently?" Paper presented at the Biennial Meeting for the Society for Research in Child Development, Minneapolis, MN, 2001.

Baker, M. *The Atoms of Language: The Mind's Hidden Rules of Grammar.* New York: Basic Books, 2001.

Banerjee, A., and S. Mullainathan. "Limited Attention and Income Distribution." *American Economic Review* 98, no. 2 (2008): 489–93.

Barabasi, A. L., and R. Albert. "Emergence of Scaling in Random Networks." *Science* 286/5439 (1999): 509.

Barabasi, A. L., and R. E. Crandall. "Linked: The New Science of Networks." *American Journal of Physics* 71 (2003): 409.

Baron, J. "Cognitive Biases in Moral Judgments that Affect Political Behavior." *Synthese* 172 (2010): 7–35.

Baron, J. "Confusion of Group-interest and Self-interest in Parochial Cooperation on Behalf of a Group." *Journal of Conflict Resolution* 45 (2001): 283–96.

Baron, J. "Confusion of Relative and Absolute Risk in Valuation." *Journal of Risk and Uncertainty* 14 (1997): 301–9.

Baron, J. "Do No Harm." *Codes of Conduct: Behavioral Research into Business Ethics,* edited by D. M. Messick and A. E. Tenbrunsel. New York: Russell Sage Foundation, 1996.

Baron, J. "The Illusion of Morality as Self-interest: A Reason to Cooperate in Social Dilemmas." *Psychological Science* 8 (1997): 330–35.

Baron, J. "Thinking about Global Warming." In *Climatic Change "The Psychology of Long Term Risk,"* special issue edited by A. Todorov and M. Oppenheimer 77 (2006): 137–50.

Baron, J. "Value Analysis of Political Behavior—Self-interested: Moralistic: Altruistic: Moral." *University of Pennsylvania Law Review* 151 (2003): 1135–67.

Baron, J., and S. Leshner. "How Serious are Expressions of Protected Values?" *Journal of Experimental Psychology: Applied* 6 (2000): 183–94.

Baron, J., and I. Ritov. "Omission Bias, Individual Differences, and Normality." *Organizational Behavior and Human Decision Processes* 94 (2004): 74–85.

Baron, J., and M. Spranca. "Protected Values." *Organizational Behavior and Human Decision Processes* 70 (1997): 1–16.

Baron, J., N. Y. Altman, and S. Kroll. "Parochialism and Approval Voting." *Journal of Conflict Resolution* 49 (2005): 895–907.

Barrett, L. F., and P. Salovey, eds. *The Wisdom in Feeling.* New York: Guildford, 2002.

Bartels, D. "Principled Moral Sentiment and the Flexibility of Moral Judgment and Decision Making." *Cognition* 108 (2008): 381–417.

Bartels, D. M., and R. C. Burnett. "Proportion Dominance and Mental Representation: Construal of Resources Affects Sensitivity to Relative Risk Reduction." Unpublished manuscript: Northwestern University, 2006.

Barzel, Y. *A Theory of the State.* New York: Cambridge University Press, 2001.

Bátora, J. "Public Diplomacy in Small and Medium-Sized States: Norway and Canada." *Discussion Papers in Diplomacy.* Clingendael, Netherlands: March 2005. Accessed March 8, 2011. http://www.clingendael.nl/publications/2005/20050300_cli_paper_dip_issue97.pdf.

Batson, C. D. *The Altruism Question: Toward a Social-Psychological Answer.* Hillsdale, NJ: Erlbaum, 1991.

Batson, C. D. "How Social an Animal? The Human Capacity for Caring." *American Psychologist* 45 (1990): 336–46.

Batson, C. D., K. O'Quin, J. Fultz, M. Vanderplas, and A. Isen. "Self-reported Distress and Empathy and Egoistic Versus Altruistic Motivation for Helping." *Journal of Personality and Social Psychology* 45 (1983): 706–18.

Bavelas, A. "Communication Patterns in Task-oriented Groups." *Journal of the Acoustical Society of America* 22 (1950): 725–30.

Bayefsky, Anne F. *The UN Human Rights Treaty System: Universality at the Crossroads.* Ardsley, NY: Transnational Publications, 2001.

Beckfield, J. "The Social Structure of the World Polity." *American Journal of Sociology* 115 (2010): 1018–68.

Beer, J. S., E. A. Heerey, D. Keltner, D. Skabini, and R. T. Knight. "The Regulatory Function of Self-conscious Emotion: Insights from Patients with Orbitofrontal Damage." *Journal of Personality and Social Psychology* 65 (2003): 594–604.

Beitz, C. *The Idea of Human Rights*. Oxford: Oxford University Press, 2009.

Bekoff, M. "Wild Justice, Cooperation, and Fair Play." In *The Origins and Nature of Sociality*, edited by R. Sussman and A. Chapmen, 2004, 53–80.

Bekoff, M., and Pierce, J. (2009). *Wild Justice: The Moral Lives of Animals*. Chicago: University of Chicago Press, 2009.

Bender-deMoll, S. "Potential Human Rights Uses of Network Analysis and Mapping." A Report of the American Association for the Advancement of Science (2008). http://shr.aaas.org/networkmapping/Net_Mapping_Report.pdf.

Benedict, R. *Patterns of Culture*. Boston: Houghton Mifflin, 1934.

Benkler, Y. "Technology, Policy, Cooperation, and Human Systems Design." In *The New Economics of Technology Policy*, edited by D. Foray. Northampton, MA: Edward Elgar Publishing, 2009.

Bentham, J. *An Introduction to the Principles of Morals and Legislation*. New York: Halfner Press, 1948/1789.

Benvenisti, E., and G. W. Downs. "The Empire's New Clothes: Political Economy and the Fragmentation of International Law." *Stanford Law Review* 60 (2007): 595–631.

Berelson, B., P. F. Lazarsfeld, and W. N. McPhee. *Voting: A Study of Opinion Formation in a Presidential Campaign*. Chicago: University of Chicago Press, 1986.

Berkowitz, L., and E. Walster., eds. *Equity Theory: Toward a General Theory of Social Interaction, Advances in Experimental Social Psychology* 9 New York: Academic Press, 1976.

Bernard, H. R., P. Killworth, D. Kronenfeld, and L. Sailer. "The Problem of Informant Accuracy: The Validity of Retrospective Data." *Annual Review of Anthropology* 13/1 (1984): 495–517.

Bicchieri, C. *The Grammar of Society: The Nature and Dynamics of Social Norms*. New York: Cambridge University Press, 2006.

Bicchieri, C. "Words and Deeds: A Focus Theory of Norms." In *Practical Rationality, Rules, and Structure*, edited by J. Nida-Rumelin and W. Spohn, London: Kluwer, 2000: 153–84.

Blair, J. A. "Cognitive Developmental Approach to Morality: Investigating the Psychopath." *Cognitio* 57 (1995): 1–29.

Blair, R. J. R., and U. Frith. "Neuro-Cognitive Models of Acquired Sociopathy and Developmental Psychopathy." In *The Neurobiology of Criminal Behavior: Neurobiological Foundation of Aberrant Behaviors*, edited by J. Glicksohn. Dordrecht, Netherlands: Kluwer Academic, 2002: 157–86.

Bloom, P. "The Moral Life of Babies." *The New York Times Magazine*, May 5, 2010, 8.

Blount, S. "When Social Outcomes Aren't Fair: The Effect of Causal Attributions on Preferences." *Organizational Behavior and Human Decision Processes* 63/2 (1995): 131–44.

Boehm, C. *Hierarchy in the Forest: The Evolution of Egalitarian Behavior*. Cambridge, MA: Harvard University Press, 2000.

Bolton, G. E., and R. Zwick. "Anonymity versus Punishment in Ultimatum Games." *Games and Economic Behavior* 10 (1995): 95–121.

Boorman, S. A, and H. C White. "Social Structure from Multiple Networks. II. Role Structures." *The American Journal of Sociology* 81/6 (1976): 1384–446.

Bork, R. "Neutral Principles and Some First Amendment Problems." *Indiana Law Journal* 47 (1971): 1–35.

Bork, R. H. *Coercing Virtue: The Worldwide Rule of Judges*. Washington, DC: AEI Press, 2003.

Bornstein, G., and M. Ben-Yossef. "Cooperation in Intergroup and Single-Group Social Dilemmas." *Journal of Experimental Social Psychology* 30 (1994): 52–67.

Bourdieu, P. "The Forms of Capital." *The Sociology of Economic Life* (2001): 96–111.

Bowles, S. "Policies Designed for Self-interested Citizens May Undermine 'The Moral Sentiments:' Evidence from Economic Experiments." *Science* 320 (2008):1605–9.

Bowles, S., and H. Gintis. *Democracy and Capitalism: Property, Community, and the Contradictions of Modern Social Thought.* New York: Basic Books, 1986.

Boyd, R., and P. J. Richerson. *Culture and the Evolutionary Process.* Chicago: University of Chicago Press, 1985.

Bradley, F. H. *Ethical Studies.* Oxford: Oxford University Press, 1962/1876.

Braman, D., D. Kahan, and D. A. Hoffman. "Some Realism about Punishment Naturalism." *University of Chicago Law Review* 77 (2010): 1531.

Brams, S. J., and P. C. Fishburn. *Approval Voting.* Boston: Birkhauser, 1983.

Brandt, A. M. *The Cigarette Century.* New York: Basic Books, 2007.

Brandt, R. *Ethical Theory: The Problems of Normative and Critical Ethics.* Englewood Cliffs, NJ: Prentice Hall, 1959.

Brehm, J. W., and A. R. Cohen. *Explorations in Cognitive Dissonance.* New York: John Wiley and Sons, Inc., 1962.

Brennan, G., and L. Lomasky. *Democracy and Decision: The Pure Theory of Electoral Politics.* Cambridge: Cambridge University Press, 1993.

Brennan, G., and J. M. Buchanan. *The Reason of Rules: Constitutional Political Economy.* Cambridge: Cambridge University Press, 1985.

Brentano, F. *The Origin of Our Knowledge of Right and Wrong.* New York: Humanities Press, Inc., 1969/1889.

Brown, D. E. *Human Universals.* New York: McGraw-Hill, 1991.

Brown, J. H., and M. V. Lomolino. *Biogeography.* Sunderland, MA: Sinauer, 1998.

Bruner, J. S. "Going Beyond the Information Given." In *Contemporary Approaches to Cognition,* edited by H. Gruber, K. R. Hammond and R. Jesser. Symposium held at the University of Colorado. Cambridge, MA: Harvard University Press, 1957.

Bucciarelli, M., S. Khemlani, and P. N. Johnson-Laird. "The Psychology of Moral Reasoning." *Judgment and Decision Making* 3/2 (2008): 121–39.

Burt, R. S. *Structural Holes: The Social Structure of Competition.* Cambridge, MA: Harvard University Press, 1995.

Burlamaqui, J. *The Principles of Natural and Politic Law.* Indianapolis, IN: Liberty Classics, 2006/1748.

Burrows, A. M. "The Facial Expression Musculature in Primates and its Evolutionary Significance." *BioEssays* 30/3 (2008): 212–25.

Butler, J. "A Dissertation upon the Nature of Virtue." In *Five Sermons,* edited by S. Darwall. Indianapolis, IN: Hackett, 1983/1736: 69–75.

Butts, C. T. "Predictability of Large-scale Spatially Embedded Networks." In *Dynamic Social Network Modeling and Analysis: Workshop Summary and Papers* (2003): 313–23.

Bybee, J., and S. Fleischman, eds. *Modality in Grammar and Discourse.* Amsterdam: John Benjamins, 1995.

Camerer, C., and T. Richard. "Ultimatums, Dictators, and Manners." *Journal of Economic Perspectives* 9/2 (1995): 209–19.

Camille, N. "The Involvement of the Orbitofrontal Cortex in the Experience of Regret." *Science* 304 (2004): 1167–70.

Campbell, B. G., J. D. Loy, and K. Cruz-Uribe. *Humankind Emerging.* New York: Allyn and Bacon, 2005.

Cardenas, S. "Norm Collision: Explaining the Effects of International Human Rights Pressure on State Behavior." *International Studies Review* 6/2 (2004): 213–32.

Carley, K. M. "Dynamic Network Analysis." *Dynamic Social Network Modeling and Analysis: Workshop Summary and Papers,* edited by R. Breiger, K. Carley, and P. Pattison. National Research Council of the National Academies: The National Academies Press, 2003: 133–45.

Carpenter, D. P., K. M. Esterling, and D. M. J. Lazer. "Friends, Brokers, and Transitivity: Who Informs Whom in Washington Politics?" *The Journal of Politics* 66/01 (2008): 224–46.

Carpenter, J., and Matthews, P. "Norm Enforcement: Anger, Indignation, or Reciprocity." Department of Economics, Working Paper 0503. Middlebury College, 2005.

Carr, E. H., and M. Cox. *The Twenty Years' Crisis, 1919–1939: An Introduction to the Study of International Relations*. New York: Palgrave Macmillan, 2001.

Casari, M., and L. Luini. "Group Cooperation Under Alternative Peer Punishment Technologies: An Experiment." Department of Economics, University of Siena, 2007.

Cavalli-Sforza, L. L., and M. W. Feldman. "Theory and Observation in Cultural Transmission." *Science* 218 (1982):19–27.

Chandler, M., B. Sokol, and C. Wainryb. "Beliefs about Truth and Beliefs about Rightness." *Child Development* 71 (2000): 91–97.

Chayes, A., and A. H. Chayes. *The New Sovereignty: Compliance with International Regulatory Agreements*. Cambridge, MA: Harvard University Press, 1996.

Checkel, J. T. "Norms, Institutions and National Identity in Contemporary Europe." *International Studies Quarterly* 43/1(1999): 84–114.

Chomsky, N. *Aspects of the Theory of Syntax*. Cambridge, MA: MIT Press, 1965.

Chomsky, N. *Current Issues in Linguistic Theory*. The Hague: Mouton, 1964.

Chomsky, N. "Interview with Noam Chomsky." *Linguistic Analysis* 4/4 (1978): 301–19. Reprinted in *Language and Politics*, ed. C. P. Otero. Montreal: Black Rose, 1988.

Chomsky, N. *Knowledge of Language: Its Nature, Origin, and Use*. Westport, CT: Praeger, 1986.

Chomsky, N. *The Minimalist Program*. Cambridge, MA: MIT Press, 1995.

Chomsky, N. "A Review of B. F. Skinner's *Verbal Behavior*" In *The Structure of Language: Readings in the Philosophy of Language*, edited by J. Fodor and J. Katz, Englewood Cliffs, NJ: Prentice-Hall, 1964: 547–78.

Chomsky, N. *Rules and Representations*. New York: Columbia University Press, 1980.

Chomsky, N. *Syntactic Structures*. The Hague: Mouton, 1957.

Chomsky, N. and M. Halle. *The Sound Pattern of Modern English*. New York: Harper and Row, 1968.

Christakis, N. A., and J. H. Fowler. "The Collective Dynamics of Smoking in a Large Social Network." *New England Journal of Medicine* 358/21 (2008): 2249.

Christakis, N. A., and J. H. Fowler. *Connected: The Surprising Power of Our Social Networks and How They Shape Our Lives*. New York: Little, Brown and Company, 2009.

Christakis, N. A., and J. H. Fowler. "The Spread of Obesity in a Large Social Network over 32 Years." *New England Journal of Medicine* 357/4 (2007): 370.

Church, R. M. "Emotional Reactions of Rats to the Pain of Others." *Journal of Comparative and Physiological Psychology* 52 (1959): 132–34.

Cialdini, R. B. "Crafting Normative Messages to Protect the Environment." *Current Directions in Psychological Science* 12/4(2003): 105–9.

Cialdini, R. B., C. A. Kallgren, and R. R. Reno. "A Focus Theory of Normative Conduct: A Theoretical Refinement and Reevaluation of the Role of Norms in Human Behavior." In *Advances in Experimental Social Psychology* 24, edited by M. P. Zanna, 201–34. San Diego, CA: Academic Press, 1991.

"Circle of Rights: Economic, Social and Cultural Rights Activism: Section 4 Training Module 8." Accessed March 9, 2011. http://www1.umn.edu/humanrts/edumat/IHRIP/circle/modules/module8.htm.

Clark, A. M. *Diplomacy of Conscience: Amnesty International and Changing Human Rights Norms*. Princeton, NJ: Princeton University Press, 2001.

Clark, M. S., and S. T. Fiske, eds. *Affect and Cognition*. Hillsdale, MI: Erlbaum, 1982.

Clutton-Brock, T. H. and G. A. Parker. "Punishment in Animal Societies." *Nature* 373 (1995): 209–12.

Cohen, B. *The Press and Foreign Policy*. Princeton, NJ: Princeton University Press, 1963.

Cohen, M. R. "The Place of Logic in Law." *Harvard Law Review* (1916). Reprinted in *Law and the Social Order: Essays in Legal Philosophy* by Cohen, M.R. Hamden. Archon Books, 1967/1933.

Coke, J. S., C. D. Batson, and K. McDavis. "Empathic Mediation of Helping: A Two-stage Model." *Journal of Personality and Social Psychology* 36 (1978): 752–66.

"Comprehensive Analysis of Polls Reveals Americans' Attitudes on U.S. Role in the World." *World Public Opinion*. Accessed March 8, 2011. http://www.worldpublicopinion.org/pipa/articles/brunitedstatescanadara/383.php?lb=bruscandpnt=383andnid=andid=.

Cook, K. S., R. Hardin, and M. Levi. *Cooperation Without Trust?* New York: Russell Sage Foundation, 2005.

Cortell, A. P., and J. W. Davis. "How Do International Institutions Matter? The Domestic Impact of International Rules and Norms." *International Studies Quarterly* 40/4 (1996): 451–78.

Cosmides, L., and J. Tooby. "Beyond Intuition and Instinct Blindness: Toward an Evolutionary Rigorous Cognitive Science." *Cognition* 50 (1994): 41–77.

Cover, R. *Justice Accused: Antislavery and the Judicial Process*. New Haven, CT: Yale University Press, 1975.

Cushman, F., L. Young, and M. Hauser. "The Role of Reasoning and Intuition in Moral Judgments: Testing Three Principles of Harm." *Psychological Science* 17/2(2006): 1082–89.

Dallaire, R. *Shake Hands with the Devil: The Failure of Humanity in Rwanda*. New York: Carrol and Graf, 2005.

Damasio, H., et al. "The Return of Phineas Gage: Clues about the Brain from the Skull of a Famous Patient." *Science* 264 (1994): 1102–5.

Darley, J., E. Klossen, and M. Zanna. "Intentions and their Contexts in the Moral Judgments of Children and Adults." *Child Development* 49 (1978): 66–74.

Darwin, C. *The Descent of Man, and Selection in Relation to Sex*. Princeton, NJ: Princeton University Press, 1981/1871.

Dawkins, R. *The Selfish Gene*. Oxford: Oxford University Press, 1976.

De Waal, F., K. Leimgruber, and A. Greenberg. "Giving is Self-rewarding for Monkeys." *Proceedings of National Academy of Sciences* 105/36 (2008): 13685–89.

De Waal, F. *Good Natured: The Origin of Right and Wrong in Humans and Other Animals*. Cambridge, MA: Harvard University Press, 1996.

De Waal, F. *Primates and Philosophers: How Morality Evolved*. Princeton, NJ: Princeton University Press, 2006.

Dearing, J., and E. Rogers. *Agenda-Setting*. Newbury Park, CA: Sage, 1996.

Dehaene, S. *The Number Sense: How the Mind Creates Mathematics*. New York: Oxford University Press, 1997.

Descartes, R. "Comments on a Certain Broadsheet." In *The Philosophical Writings of Descartes, 1*, edited by J. Cottingham, R. Stoothoff, and D. Murdoch. Cambridge: Cambridge University Press, 1985/1647.

Dickert, S. and P. Slovic. "Attentional Mechanisms in the Generation of Sympathy." *Judgment and Decision Making* 4 (2009): 297–306.

Dillard, A. *For the Time Being*. New York: Alfred A. Knopf, 1999.

Donogan, A. *The Theory of Morality*. Chicago: University of Chicago Press, 1977.

Drumbl, M. A. *Atrocity, Punishment and International Law*. Cambridge: Cambridge University Press. 2007.

Dubber, M. D. *The Sense of Justice: Empathy in Law and Punishment*. New York: NYU Press, 2007.

Dubinsky, Z. "The Lessons of Genocide [Review of the book *Conspiracy to Murder: The Rwandan Genocide*]." *Essex Human Rights Review* 2/1 (2005): 112–17.

Duflo, E. et al. "Powerful Women: Does Exposure Reduce Bias?" *Quarterly Journal of Economics* Vol. 124(4) (2009): 1497–540.

Dunbar, R. I. M. "Coevolution of Neocortical Size, Group Size and Language in Humans." *Behavioral and Brain Sciences* 16/4 (1993): 681–735.

Dupoux, E. and P. Jacob. "Universal Moral Grammar: A Critical Appraisal." *Trends in Cognitive Science* 11 (2007): 373–78.

Dworkin, R. *Taking Rights Seriously*. Cambridge, MA: Harvard University Press, 1977.

Dwyer, S. "How Good is the Linguistic Analogy?" In *The Innate Mind, Vol. 2: Culture and Cognition*, edited by P. Carruthers, S. Laurence, and S. Stich. Oxford: Oxford University Press, 2006.

Dwyer, S. "How Not to Argue that Morality Isn't Innate: Comments on Prinz." In *Moral Psychology, Vol. 1: The Evolution of Morality: Adaptation and Innateness*, edited by W. Sinnott-Armstrong. Cambridge: MIT Press, 2008.

Dwyer, S. "Moral Competence." In *Philosophy and Linguistics*, edited by K. Murasugi and R. Stainton, 169–90. Boulder, CO: Westview Press, 1999.

Eagle, N., Pentland, A. S., and Lazer, D. "Inferring Friendship Network Structure by Using Mobile Phone Data." *Proceedings of the National Academy of Sciences* 106/36 (2009): 15274.

Edgeworth, F. Y. *Papers Relating to Political Economy I*. London: Macmillan, 1925.

Eisenberg, N., and Miller, P. "Empathy and Prosocial Behavior." *Psychological Bulletin* 101 (1987): 91–119.

Elster, J. "Norms of Revenge." *Ethics* 100/4 (1990): 862–85.

Ely, J. *Democracy and Distrust: A Theory of Judicial Review*. Cambridge, MA: Harvard University Press, 1980.

Emerson, R. M. "Social Exchange Theory." *Annual Review of Sociology* 2/1 (1976): 335–62.

Epstein, J. M. "Modeling Civil Violence: An Agent-based Computational Approach." *Proceedings of the National Academy of Science* 99/3 (2002): 7243–50.

Epstein, S. "Integration of the Cognitive and the Psychodynamic Unconscious." *American Psychologist* 49/8 (1994): 709–24.

Ertan, A., T. Page, and L. Putterman. "Can Endogenously Chosen Institutions Mitigate the Free-Rider Problem and Reduce Perverse Punishments?" In *Working Paper 2005 13*. Department of Economics: Brown University, 2005.

Ewick, P., and S. S. Silbey. *The Common Place of Law: Stories from Everyday Life*. Chicago: University of Chicago Press, 1998.

Facts About Automobile Safety from NHTSA. Accessed March 8, 2011. http://www.bhsbees.com/safety_stats.htm.

Farkas, S., and J. Robinson. *The Values We Live By: What Americans Want from Welfare Reform*. New York: Public Agenda, 1996.

Farmer, P. "Never Again? Reflections on Human Values and Human Rights." *The Tanner Lectures on Human Values*. Salt Lake City: University of Utah, 2005. Accessed August 22, 2008. http://www.tannerlectures.utah.edu/lectures/documents/Farmer_2006.pdf.

Farrelly, M. C., K. C. Davis, M. L. Haviland, P. Messeri, and C. G. Healton. "Evidence of a Dose-Response Relationship Between 'Truth' Antismoking Ads and Youth Smoking Prevalence." *American Journal of Public Health* 95/3 (2005): 425–31.

Fechner, G. T. "Elements of Psychophysics." *Classics in the History of Psychology* (1860/1912). Accessed August 22, 2008. http://psychclassics.yorku.ca/Fechner/.

Fehr, E., and S. Gächter. "Altruistic Punishment in Humans." *Nature* 415 (2002): 137–40.

Fehr, E., and S. Gächter. "Cooperation and Punishment." *American Economic Review* 90/4 (2000): 980–94.

Fehr, E., and S. Gächter, and U. Fischbacher. "Third Party Punishment and Social Norms." *Evolution and Human Behavior* 25 (2004): 63–87.

Fehr, E., E. Kirchler, S. Gachter, and A. Weichbold. "When Social Norms Overpower Competition: Gift Exchange in Experimental Labor Markets." *Journal of Labor Economics* 16 (1998): 324–51.

Festinger, L. *Conflict, Decision, and Dissonance*. Stanford, CA: Stanford University Press, 1964.

Festinger, L. *A Theory of Cognitive Dissonance*. Stanford, CA: Stanford University Press, 1957.

Festinger, L. "A Theory of Social Comparison Processes." *Human Relations* 7/2 (1954): 117–40.

Festinger, L., S. Schachter, and K. Back. *Social Pressures in Informal Groups*. Stanford, CA: Stanford University Press, 1963.

Fetherstonhaugh, D., P. Slovic, S. M. Johnson, and J. Friedrich. "Insensitivity to the Value of Human Life: A Study of Psychophysical Numbing." *Journal of Risk and Uncertainty* 14/3 (1997): 283–300.

Fields, J. M., and H. Schuman. "Public Beliefs about the Beliefs of the Public." *Public Opinion Quarterly* 40/4 (1976): 427–48.

Finkel, N., M. Liss, and V. Moran. "Equal or Proportionate Justice for Accessories? Children's Pearls of Proportionate Wisdom." *Journal of Applied Developmental Psychology* 18 (1997): 229–44.

Fischer, J. M., and M. Ravizza. *Ethics: Problems and Principles.* Fort Worth, TX: Harcourt Brace Jovanovich, 1992.

Fishbein, M., and I. Ajzen. *Predicting and Changing Behavior: The Reasoned Action Approach.* New York: Taylor & Francis, 2009.

Fisher, R., A. K. Schneider, E. Borgwardt, and B. Ganson. *Coping with International Conflict.* Upper Saddle River, NJ: Prentice Hall, 1996.

Fisher, R., and W. Ury. *Getting to Yes.* Boston: Houghton Mifflin, 1981.

Fiske, A. P., and P. E. Tetlock. "Taboo Trade-offs: Reactions to Transactions that Transgress Spheres of Justice." *Political Psychology* 18 (1997): 255–97.

Fiske, S. T., and S. E. Taylor. *Social Cognition: From Brains to Culture.* Boston: McGraw-Hill, 2008.

Flanagan, O. *Varieties of Moral Personality: Ethics and Psychological Realism.* Cambridge, MA: Harvard University Press, 1991.

Fletcher, G. *Basic Concepts of Criminal Law.* Oxford: Oxford University Press, 1998.

Fletcher, G. *The Grammar of Criminal Law.* Oxford: Oxford University Press, 2007.

Fodor, J. "Précis of Modularity of Mind." *Behavioral and Brain Sciences* 8 (1985): 1–42.

Foot, P. "The Problem of Abortion and the Doctrine of Double Effect." *Oxford Review* 5(1967): 5–15. Reprinted in *Ethics: Problems and Principles,* edited by Fisher and Ravizza. Fort Worth, TX: Harcourt Brace Jovanovich (1992): S 60–67.

Forgas, J. P., ed. *Feeling and Thinking: The Role of Affect in Social Cognition.* Cambridge: Cambridge University Press, 2000.

Fowler, J. H. "Connecting the Congress: A Study of Cosponsorship Networks." *Political Analysis* 14/4 (2006): 456.

Franck, T. M. *The Power of Legitimacy among Nations.* New York: Oxford University Press, 1990.

Frankena, W. *Ethics.* Englewood Cliffs, NJ: Prentice Hall, 1963.

Freeman, L. C. "Centrality in Social Networks Conceptual Clarification." *Social Networks* 1/3 (1979): 215–39.

Freeman, L. C. *The Development of Social Network Analysis.* Vancouver: Empirical Press, 2004.

Freeman, L. C. "Finding Social Groups: A Meta-Analysis of the Southern Women Data." *Dynamic Social Network Modeling and Analysis: Workshop Summary and Papers* (2003): 39.

Freeman, L. C., A. K. Romney, and S. C. Freeman. "Cognitive Structure and Informant Accuracy." *American Anthropologist* 89/2 (1987): 310–25.

Freud, S. *Civilization and Its Discontents.* New York: Dover, 1994/1930.

Friedkin, N. E. *A Structural Theory of Social Influence.* Cambridge: Cambridge University Press, 1998.

Friedman, L. *A History of American Law,* 2nd ed. New York: Simon and Schuster, 1985.

Friedrich, J., P. Barnes, K. Chapin, I. Dawson, V. Garst, and D. Kerr. "Psychophysical Numbing: When Lives are Valued Less as the Lives at Risk Increase." *Journal of Consumer Psychology* 8 (1999): 277–99.

Fromm, E. *Escape from Freedom.* New York: Avon Books, 1941.

Fukuyama, F. *Our Posthuman Future: Consequences of the Biotechnology Revolution.* New York: Farrar, Straus and Giroux, 2002.

Fuller, L. *The Morality of Law.* New Haven, CT: Yale University Press, 1969/1964.

Galanter, E. "The Direct Measurement of Utility and Subjective Probability." *American Journal of Psychology* 75 (1962): 208–20.

Gardner, H. *The Mind's New Science: A History of the Cognitive Revolution.* New York: Basic Books, 1985.

Gazzaniga, M. *The Ethical Brain.* New York: Dana Press, 2005.

Geneva Conventions, Protocol I, Article 57.

Gerbner, G., and L. Gross. "Living with Television: The Violence Profile." *Journal of Communication* 26/2 (1976): 172–94.

Gert, B. *Morality: Its Nature and Justification.* New York: Oxford University Press, 1998.

Ghiselin, Michael T. *The Economy of Nature and the Evolution of Sex.* Berkeley: University of California Press, 1974.

Gilbert, D. T. "Ordinary Personology." In *The Handbook of Social Psychology,* 4th ed. 2, edited by D. T. Gilbert, S. T. Fiske, and G. Lindzey, 89–150. New York: McGraw Hill, 1998.

Gilens, M. *Why Americans Hate Welfare.* Chicago: University of Chicago Press, 1999.

Gilpin, R. *War and Change in World Politics.* Cambridge: Cambridge University Press, 1983.

Gintis, H. *The Bounds of Reason: Game Theory and the Unification of the Behavioral Sciences.* Princeton, NJ: Princeton University Press, 2009.

Gintis, H. "Strong Reciprocity and Human Sociality." *Journal of Theoretical Biology* 206 (2002): 169–79.

Gintis, H., S. Bowles, R. Boyd, and E. Fehr. "Explaining Altruistic Behavior in Humans." *Evolution and Human Behavior* 24 (2003): 153–72.

Gintis, H., Bowles, S., R. Boyd, and E. Fehr. *Moral Sentiments and Material Interests.* Cambridge, MA: MIT Press, 2005.

Gladwell, M. *The Tipping Point: How Little Things Can Make a Big Difference.* Boston: Back Bay Books, 2002.

Glendon, M. A. *World Made New: Eleanor Roosevelt and the Universal Declaration of Human Rights.* New York: Random House, 2001.

Glover, J. *Humanity: A Moral History of the Twentieth Century.* New Haven, CT: Yale University Press, 2001.

Glynn, C. J., A. F. Hayes, and J. Shanahan. "Perceived Support for One's Opinions and Willingness to Speak Out: A Meta-Analysis of Survey Studies on the 'Spiral of Silence.'" *Public Opinion Quarterly* 61 (1997): 452–63.

Gneezy, U., and A. Rustichini. "A Fine is a Price." *Journal of Legal Studies* 22 (2000): 1–17.

Gold, L., J. Darley, J. Hilton, and M. Zanna. "Children's Perceptions of Procedural Justice." *Child Development* 55 (1984): 1752–59.

Goldin, C., and L. F. Katz. *The Race between Education and Technology.* Cambridge, MA: Harvard University Press, 2008.

Goldman, A. "Ethics and Cognitive Science." *Ethics* 103 (1993): 337–60.

Goldman, A. *A Theory of Human Action.* Princeton, NJ: Princeton University Press, 1970.

Goldsmith, J. L., and E. A. Posner. *The Limits of International Law.* New York: Oxford University Press, 2005.

Goldstein, J., M. Kahler, R. O. Keohane, and A. M. Slaughter. *Legalization and World Politics.* Boston: MIT Press, 2001.

Goodman, R., and D. Jinks. "How to Influence States: Socialization and International Law." *Duke Law Journal* 54 (2004): 621–703.

Goodman, R., and D. Jinks. "Incomplete Internalization and Compliance with Human Rights Law." *European Journal of International Law* 19 (2008): 725.

Goodman, R., and D. Jinks. "International Law and State Socialization: Conceptual, Empirical, and Normative Challenges." *Duke Law Journal* 54 (2005): 983.

Goodman, R., and D. Jinks. "Socializing States: Promoting Human Rights Through International Law." New York: Oxford University Press, forthcoming.

Goodwin, G. P., and J. M. Darley. "The Psychology of meta-ethics: Exploring Objectivism." *Cognition* 106 (2008): 1339–66.

Gopnik, A. "How We Know Our Minds: The Illusion of first-person Knowledge of Intentionality." *Behavioral and Brain Sciences* 16 (1993): 1–14.

Granovetter, M. "Economic Action and Social Structure: The Problem of Embeddedness." *American Journal of Sociology* 91/3 (1985): 481.

Granovetter, M. S. "The Strength of Weak Ties." *American Journal of Sociology* 78/6 (1973): 1360.

Green, D. P. and Shapiro, I. *Pathologies of Rational Choice Theory: A Critique of Applications in Political Science.* New Haven, CT: Yale University Press, 1994.

Green, S. "The Universal Grammar of the Criminal Law." *Michigan Law Review* 98 (1998): 2104–25.

Green, J. and Cohen, J. "For the Law, Neuroscience Changes Nothing and Everything." *Philos Trans Royal Society of London B Biol Sci.* 359 (2004): 1775–85.

Greenberg, M. S., and D. M. Frisch. "Effect of Intentionality on Willingness to Reciprocate a Favor." *Journal of Experimental Social Psychology* 8 (1972): 99–111.

Greene, J. D. "Cognitive Neuroscience and the Structure of the Moral Mind." In *The Innate Mind, Vol. 1: Structure and Contents*, edited by S. Laurence, P. Carruthers, and S. Stich. New York: Oxford University Press, 2005.

Greene, J. D. "The Terrible, Horrible, No Good, Very Bad, Truth about Morality and What to Do about It." PhD diss., Princeton, 2002.

Greene, J., and J. Haidt. "How (and Where) Does Moral Judgment Work?" *Trends in Cognitive Sciences* 6/12 (2002): 517–23.

Greene, J. D., D. Lindsell, A. C. Clarke, L. E. Nystrom, and J. D. Cohen. *Pushing Moral Buttons: The Interaction between Personal Force and Intention in Moral Judgment* (submitted).

Greene, J. D., R. B. Sommerville, L. E. Nystrom, J. M. Darley, and J. D. Cohen. "An fMRI Investigation of Emotional Engagement in Moral Judgment." *Science* 293 (2001): 2105–8.

Grey, T. "Langdell's Orthodoxy." *University of Pittsburgh Law Review* 45 (1983): 1–53.

Grotius, H. *On the Law of War and Peace*, translated by F. W. Kelsey. Oxford: Clarendon Press, 1925/1625.

Gruter, M., and P. Bohannan, eds. *Law, Biology and Culture: The Evolution of Law*. Santa Barbara, CA: Ross-Erikson, 1983.

Guth, W., and R. Tietz. "Ultimatum Bargaining Behavior: A Survey and Comparison of Experimental Results." *Journal of Economic Psychology* 11 (1990): 417–49.

Guth, W., R. Schmittberger, and B. Schwarze. "An Experimental Analysis of Ultimatum Bargaining." *Journal of Economic Behavior and Organization* 3 (1982): 367–88.

Guzman, A. T. *How International Law Works: A Rational Choice Theory*. Oxford: Oxford University Press, 2008.

Haakonssenn, K. *Natural Law and Moral Philosophy: From Grotius to the Scottish Enlightenment*. Cambridge: Cambridge University Press, 1996.

Hafner-Burton, E. M. *Forced to be Good: Why Trade Agreements Boost Human Rights*. Ithaca, NY: Cornell University Press, 2009.

Hafner-Burton, E. M. "Sticks and Stones: Naming and Shaming the Human Rights Enforcement Problem." *International Organization* 62 (2008): 689–716.

Hafner-Burton, E. M., and A. H. Montgomery. "Power Positions: International Organizations, Social Networks, and conflict." *Journal of Conflict Resolution* 50/1 (2006): 3.

Hafner-Burton, E. M., M. Kahler, and A. H. Montgomery. "Network Analysis for International Relations." *International Organization* 63/3 (2009): 559–92.

Hahn, R., and C. Sunstein. "A New Executive Order for Improving Federal Regulation? Deeper and Wider Cost-benefit Analysis." *University of Pennsylvania Law Review* 150 (2002): 1489–552.

Haidt, J. "The Emotional Dog and Its Rational Tail: A Social Intuitionist Approach to Moral Judgment." *Psychological Review* 108/4 (2001): 814–34.

Haidt, J. "The New Synthesis in Moral Psychology." *Science* 316 (2007): 998–1002.

Haidt, J., and J. Baron. "Social Roles and the Moral Judgment of Acts and Omissions." *European Journal of Social Psychology* 26 (1996): 201–18.

Haidt, J., and C. Joseph. "Intuitive Ethics: How Innately Prepared Intuitions Generate Culturally Variable Virtues." *Daedalus* 133/4 (2004): 55–66.

Hale, M. "Preface to Rolle's Abridgement." In *Readings in Jurisprudence*, edited by J. Hall. Indianapolis, IN: Bobbs-Merrill, 1938/1668.

Hamburg, D. A. *Preventing Genocide: Practical Steps Toward Early Detection and Effective Action*. Boulder, CO: Paradigm, 2008.

Hamilton, D. L., and Sherman. "S.J., Perceiving Persons and Groups." *Psychological Review* 103/2 (1996): 336–55.

Hamilton, W. D. "The Genetical Evolution of Social Behaviour." *Journal of Theoretical Biology* 7 (1964): 1–52.

Hamlin, J. K., K. Wynn, and P. Bloom. "Social Evaluation by Preverbal Infants." *Nature* 450 (2007): 557–59.

Hampshire, S. *Morality and Conflict*. Cambridge, MA: Harvard University Press, 1983.

Hardin, R. *Trust and Trustworthiness*. New York: Russell Sage Foundation, 2002.

Harff, B. "No Lessons Learned from the Holocaust? Assessing Risks of Genocide and Political Mass Murder Since 1955." *American Political Science Review* 97 (2003): 57–73.

Harman, G. *Explaining Value: And Other Essays in Moral Philosophy*. Oxford: Oxford University Press, 2000.

Harman, G. "Moral Philosophy and Linguistics." Paper presented at the Twentieth Annual World Philosophy Congress, Boston, 1998.

Harman, G. "Using a Linguistic Analogy to Study Morality." In *Moral Psychology, Vol. 1: The Evolution of Morality: Adaptation and Innateness*, edited by W. Sinnott-Armstrong. Cambridge: MIT Press, 2008: 345–51.

Hathaway, O. "Do Human Rights Treaties Make a Difference?" *The Yale Law Journal* 111 (2002): 1935–2042.

Hauser, M. *Moral Minds: How Nature Designed Our Universal Sense of Right and Wrong*. New York: Harper Collins, 2006.

Hauser, M., F. Cushman, L. Young, R. Jin, and J. Mikhail. "A Dissociation between Moral Judgments and Justifications." *Mind and Language* 22 (2007): 1–22.

Heaney, M. T. "Brokering Health Policy: Coalitions, Parties, and Interest Group Influence." *Journal of Health Politics, Policy and Law* 31/5 (2006): 887.

Heinz, J. P. *The Hollow Core: Private Interests in National Policy Making*. Cambridge, MA: Harvard University Press, 1993.

Henkin, L. *The Age of Rights*. New York: Columbia University Press, 1990.

Henkin, L., R. C. Pugh, O. Schacter, and H. Smit. *Basic Documents Supplement to International Law: Cases and Materials*. St. Paul: West Publishing, 1992.

Henrich, J., R. Boyd, S. Bowles, C. Camerer, E. Fehr, and H. Gintis. *Foundations of Human Sociality: Economic Experiments and Ethnographic Evidence from Fifteen Small-scale Societies*. Oxford: Oxford University Press, 2004.

Highway Safety Research and Communications. http://www.iihs.org/laws/safetybeltuse.aspx

Hoebel, E. A. *The Law of Primitive Man: A Study in Comparative Legal Dynamics*. Cambridge, MA: Harvard University Press, 1954.

Hohfeld, W. *Fundamental Legal Conceptions*. New Haven, CT: Yale University Press, 1917.

Holden, C. J. "Bantu Language Trees Reflect the Spread of Farming Across Sub-Saharan Africa: A Maximum-parsimony Analysis." *Proceedings of the Royal Society of London B* 269 (2002): 793–99.

Holden, C. J., and R. Mace. "Spread of Cattle Led to the Loss of Matrilineal Descent in Africa: A Coevolutionary Analysis." *Proceedings of the Royal Society of London B* 270 (2003): 2425–33.

Holland, P. W., and S. Leinhardt. "A Method for Detecting Structure in Sociometric Data." The *American Journal of Sociology* 76/3 (1970): 492–513.

Holland, T. E. *The Elements of Jurisprudence*, 10th ed. New York: Oxford University Press, 1906/1880.

Homans, G. C. *Social Behavior in Elementary Forms*. New York: Harcourt, Brace, and World, 1961.

Homans, G. C. "Social Behavior as Exchange." *American Journal of Sociology* 65 (1958): 597–606.

Hong, M. L. K. "A Genocide by Any Other Name: Language, Law, and the Response to Darfur." *Virginia Journal of Environmental Law* 48 (2008): 238–72.

Horder, J. *Homicide Law in Comparative Perspective*. Portland: Hart Publishing, 2007.

Hornik, R., ed. *Public Health Communication: Evidence for Behavior Change*. Mahwah: Lawrence Erlbaum, 2002.

Hornik, R., L. Jacobsohn, R. Orwin, A. Piesse, and G. Kalton. "Effects of the National Youth Anti-Drug Media Campaign on Youth." *American Journal of Public Health* 98/12 (2008): 2229–36.

Hovland, C. I., I. L. Janis, and H. H. Kelley. *Communication and Persuasion*. New Haven, CT: Yale University Press, 1953.

Huckfeldt, R., and P. E. Johnson. *Political Disagreement: The Survival of Diverse Opinions within Communication Networks.* New York: Cambridge University Press, 2004.

Huckfeldt, R., and J. Sprague. *Citizens, Politics, and Social Communication: Information and Influence in an Election Campaign.* New York: Cambridge University Press, 1995.

Hume, D. *An Enquiry Concerning the Principles of Morals,* edited by J. B. Schneewind. Indianapolis, IN: Hackett, 1983/1751.

Hume, D. *A Treatise of Human Nature.* Analytical Index, L. A. Selby-Bigge, edited by P. H. Nidditch. Oxford: Clarendon Press, 1978/1740.

Hunt, L. *Inventing Human Rights: A History.* New York: Norton, 2007.

Hutcheson, F. *Illustrations on the Moral Sense.* Cambridge, MA: Harvard University Press, 1971/1728.

Hutcheson, F. "Innaugural Lecture on the Social Nature of Man." *Two Texts on Human Nature,* edited by Thomas Mantner. Cambridge: Cambridge University Press, 1993/1730.

Hutcheson, F. *Philosophiae Moralis Institutio Compendis; with A Short Introduction to Moral Philosophy.* Indianapolis, IN: Liberty Fund, 2007/1747.

Huxley, J. S. "Evolution, Cultural and Biological." *Yearbook of Anthropology* (1955): 2–25.

Ibarra, H. "Homophily and Differential Returns: Sex Differences in Network Structure and Access in an Advertising Firm." *Administrative Science Quarterly* 37/3 (1992): 422–47.

Ignatieff, M. *Human Rights as Politics and Idolatry.* Princeton, NJ: Princeton University Press, 2001.

Inkeles, A., and D. H. Smith. *Becoming Modern.* Cambridge, MA: Harvard University Press, 1974.

"International Commission on Intervention and State Sovereignty." *The Responsibility to Protect.* Ottawa: International Development Research Centre, 2001.

International Covenant on Civil and Political Rights, G.A. res. 2200A(XXI), 21 U.N. GAOR Supp. (No. 16) at 52, U.N. Doc. A/6316(1966), 999 U.N.T.S. 171, entered into force March 23, 1976.

International Covenant on Economic, Social and Cultural Rights, G.A. res. 2200A(XXI), 21 U.N.GAOR Supp. (No. 16) at 49, U.N. Doc. A/6316(1966), 993 U.N.T.S. 3, entered into force January 3, 1976.

Jablonka, E., and M. J. Lamb. *Epigenetic Inheritance and Evolution: The Lamarckian Case.* Oxford: Oxford University Press, 1995.

Jackendoff, R. *Language, Consciousness, Culture: Essays on Mental Structure.* Cambridge, MA: MIT Press, 2007.

Jackendoff, R. "The Natural Logic of Rights and Obligations." In *Language, Logic and Concepts: Essays in Memory of John Macnamara,* edited by R. Jackendoff, P. Bloom and K. Wynn. Cambridge, MA: MIT Press, 1999.

Jackendoff, R. *Patterns in the Mind: Language and Human Nature.* New York: Basic Books, 1994.

Jenni, K. E., and G. Loewenstein. "Explaining the 'Identifiable Victim Effect.'" *Journal of Risk and Uncertainty* 14 (1997): 235–57.

Johnston, A. I. *Social States: China in International Institutions, 1980–2000 (Princeton Studies in International History and Politics).* Princeton, NJ: Princeton University Press, 2007.

Jones, C., W. S. Hesterly, and S. P. Borgatti. "A General Theory of Network Governance: Exchange Conditions and Social Mechanisms." *Academy of Management Review* 22/4 (1997): 911–45.

Jones, O. D., and R. Kurzban. "Intuitions of Punishment." *Chicago Law Review* 77 (2010): 1633–41.

Jonsen, A. R., and S. Toulmin. *The Abuse of Casuistry: A History of Moral Reasoning.* Berkeley: University of California Press, 1988.

Jurmain, R., H. Nelson, L. Kilgore, and W. Travathan. *Introduction to Physical Anthropology.* Cincinatti, OH: Wadsworth Publishing Company, 1997.

Just, R. "The Truth Will Not Set You Free: Everything We Know about Darfur, and Everything We're Not Doing about It." *The New Republic,* August 27, 2008, 36–47.

Kagan, J. 'Introduction', In *The Emergence of Morality in Young Children,* edited by J. Kagan and S. Lamb. Chicago: University of Chicago Press, 1987.

Kahan, D. M. "Gentle Nudges vs. Hard Shoves: Solving the Sticky Norms Problem." *The University of Chicago Law Review* 67/3 (2000): 607–45.

Kahneman, D. "A Perspective on Judgment and Choice: Mapping Bounded Rationality." *American Psychologist* 58 (2003): 697–720.

Kahneman, D., and S. Frederick. "Representativeness Revisited: Attribute Substitution in Intuitive Judgment." In *Heuristics and Biases*, edited by T. Gilovich, D. Griffin and D. Kahneman, Cambridge: Cambridge University Press, 2002: 49–81.

Kahneman, D., and A. Tversky. "Choices, Values, and Frames." *American Psychologist* 39 (1984): 341–50.

Kahneman, D., and A. Tversky. "Conflict Resolution." In *Barriers to Conflict Resolution*, edited by K. Arrow, R. Mnookin, L. Ross, A. Tversky, and R. Wilson. New York: Norton, Pronin, Kruger, Savitsky & Ross, 2001.

Kahneman, D., and A. Tversky. "Prospect Theory: An Analysis of Decision Under Risk." *Econometrica* 47/2 (1979): 263–91.

Kant, I. *Critique of Practical Reason*, translated by L. W. Beck. New York: Macmillan, 1993/1788.

Kar, R. B. "The Deep Structure of Law and Morality." *Texas Law Review* 84 (2006): 877.

Karlan, D., M. Mobius, T. Rosenblat, and A. Szeidl. "Trust and Social Collateral." *The Quarterly Journal of Economics* 124 (2009): 1307-61.

Katz, D., and R. L. Schanck. *Social Psychology*. New York: Wiley, 1938.

Katz, E., and P. Lazarsfeld. *Personal Influence: The Part Played by People in the Flow of Mass Communication*, 2nd ed. London: New Brunswick and London Transaction Publishers, 2006.

Kauffman, K. "Prison Officers' Attitudes and Perceptions of Attitudes: A Case of Pluralistic Ignorance." *Journal of Research in Crime and Delinquency* 18/2 (1981): 272-94.

Kaufman, L. "Utilities Turn Their Customers Green, with Envy." *The New York Times*, January 31, 2009, sec. A1.

Kearns, M., S. Suri, and N. Montfort. "An Experimental Study of the Coloring Problem on Human Subject Networks." *Science* 313/5788 (2006): 824.

Keck, M. E., and K. Sikkink. *Activists Beyond Borders: Advocacy Networks in International Politics*. Ithaca, NY: Cornell University Press, 1998.

Kitts, J. A. "Egocentric Bias or Information Management? Selective Disclosure and the Social Roots of Norm Misperception." *Social Psychology Quarterly* 66/3 (2003): 222–37.

Klofas, J., and H. Toch. "The Guard Subculture Myth." *Journal of Research in Crime and Delinquency* 19/3 (1982): 238–54.

Knobe, J., and S. Nichols, eds. *Experimental Philosophy*. New York: Oxford University Press, 2008.

Koenigs, M., L. Young, R. Adolphs, D. Tranel, F. A. Cushman, M. D. Hauser, and T. Damasio. "Damage to Ventromedial Prefrontal Cortex Increases Utilitarian Moral Judgments." *Nature* 446 (2007): 908–11.

Kogut, T., and I. Ritov. "The "Identified Victim" Effect: An Identified Group, or Just a Single Individual?" *Journal of Behavioral Decision Making* 18 (2005): 157–67.

Kogut, T., and I. Ritov. "The Singularity of Identified Victims in Separate and Joint Evaluations." *Organizational Behavior and Human Decision Processes* 97 (2005): 106–16.

Koh, H. H. "How Is International Human Rights Law Enforced?" 3rd ed. In *Human Rights in the World Community: Issues and Action*, edited by Richard Pierre Claude and Burns H. Weston, 311. Philadelphia, University of Pennsylvania Press, 2006.

Koh, H. H. "Why Do Nations Obey International Law?" *The Yale Law Journal* 106 (1997): 2599–659.

Kohlberg, L. *Essays on Moral Development. Volume 1: The Philosophy of Moral Development*. New York: Harper and Row, 1981.

Korte, C. "Pluralistic Ignorance about Student Radicalism." *Sociometry* 35/4 (1972): 576–87.

Kristof, N. D. "Save the Darfur Puppy." *New York Times*, 2007. Accessed August 22, 2008. http://select.nytimes.com/2007/05/10/opinion/10kristof.html.

Kropotkin, P. *Ethics: Origin and Development*. Bristol: Thoemmes Press, 1993/1924.

Kroy, M. "Ethics and Conscience: A Program." *Philosophia* 3 (1973): 265–94.

Kuran, T. *Private Truths, Public Lies: The Social Consequences of Preference Falsification*. Cambridge, MA: Harvard University Press, 1995.

Ladd, J. *The Structure of a Moral Code: A Philosophical Analysis of Ethical Discourse Applied to the Ethics of the Navaho Indians.* Cambridge, MA: Harvard University Press, 1957.

LaFave, W. R. *Principles of Criminal Law.* St. Paul, MN: West Group, 2003.

Landman, T. *Protecting Human Rights: A Comparative Study.* Washington, DC: Georgetown University Press, 2005.

Latané, B., and J. M. Darley. *The Unresponsive Bystander: Why Doesn't He Help?* Englewood Cliffs, NJ: Prentice Hall, 1970.

Laumann, E. O., and D. Knoke. *The Organizational State: Social Choice in National Policy Domains.* Madison: University of Wisconsin Press, 1987.

Lazarsfeld, P. F., B. Berelson, and H. Gaudet. *The People's Choice.* New York: Columbia University Press, 1968.

Lazer, D. "The Free Trade Epidemic of the 1860s and Other Outbreaks of Economic Discrimination." *World Politics* (1999): 447–83.

Lazer, D. "Regulatory Capitalism as a Networked Order: The International System as an Informational Network." *The Annals of the American Academy of Political and Social Science* 598/1 (2005): 52–66.

Lazer, D. "Regulatory Interdependence and International Governance." *Journal of European Public Policy* 8/3 (2001): 474–92.

Lazer, D. et al. "Life in the Network: the Coming Age of Computational Social Science." *Science* 323/5915 (2009): 721–723.

Lazer, D. "Networks in Political Science: Back to the Future." *PS: Political Science and Politics* 44(1) (2011): 61–68.

Le Doux, J. *The Emotional Brain.* New York: Simon & Schuster, 1996.

Leibniz, G. W. *New Essays on Human Understanding,* edited by P. Remnant and J. Bennet. Cambridge: Cambridge University Press, 1981/1705.

Lessig, L. "The New Chicago School." *The Journal of Legal Studies* 27/2 (1998): 661–91.

Lessig, L. "The Regulation of Social Meaning." *The University of Chicago Law Review* 62/3 (1995): 943–1045.

Levi, M. *Consent, Dissent and Patriotism.* New York: Cambridge University Press, 1997.

Levi, M. *Of Rule and Revenue.* Berkeley: University of California Press, 1988.

Levi, M. "A State of Trust." In *Trust and Governance,* edited by V. Braithwaite and M. Levi. New York: Russell Sage Foundation, 1998.

Levi, M., and A. Sacks. "Achieving Good Government—and Maybe Legitimacy." In *Citizenship and Social Integration,* edited by A. Dani, and A. Varshney. Forthcoming.

Levi, M., and A. Sacks. "Legitimating Beliefs: Concepts and Indicators." *Afrobarometer Working Paper.* East Lansing: Michigan State University, 2007.

Levi, M., and L. Stoker. "Political Trust and Trustworthiness." *Annual Review of Political Science* 3 (2000): 475–507.

Levi, M., A. Sacks, and T. R. Tyler. "Conceptualizing Legitimacy, Measuring Legitimating Beliefs." *American Behavioral Scientist* 53 (2009): 354–75.

Levy Paluck, E., and Laurie Ball, "Social Norms Marketing Aimed at Gender Based Violence: A Literature Review and Critical Assessment." Report for the International Rescue Committee: 2010, available at: http://betsylevypaluck.com/Paluck%20Ball%20IRC%20Social%20 Norms%20Marketing%20Long.pdf.

Lewin, K., and D. Cartwright, eds. *Field Theory in Social Science.* New York: Harper, 1951.

Liebling, A. J. "Do You Belong in Journalism?" *New Yorker* 5 (1960): 109.

Lienhard, J. *No. 879: Babbage and Tennyson.* Accessed March 8, 2011. http://www.uh.edu/ engines/epi879.htm.

Lifton, R. J. *Death in Life: Survivors of Hiroshima.* New York: Random House, 1967.

Lin, N. *Social Capital: A Theory of Social Structure and Action.* Cambridge: Cambridge University Press, 2001.

Loewenstein, G., E. U. Weber, C. K. Hsee, E. S. and Welch. "Risk as Feelings." *Psychological Bulletin* 127 (2001): 267–86.

Lombrozo, T. "The Role of Moral Theories in Moral Judgment." Poster Presented to the 34th Annual Meeting of the Society of Philosophy and Psychology, Philadelphia, 2008.

Luttmer, E. F. P. "Group Loyalty and the Taste for Redistribution." *Journal of Political Economy* 109/3 (2001): 500–28.

Mace, R., and M. Pagel. "The Comparative Method in Anthropology." *Current Anthropology* 35 (1994): 549–64.

Machiavelli, N. *The Prince and the Discourses*. New York: The Modern Library, 1950.

Machery, E. "The Folk Concept of Intentional Action: Philosophical and Experimental Issues." *Mind and Language* 23 (2007): 165–89.

MacIntyre, A. *After Virtue*. Notre Dame, IN: University of Notre Dame Press, 1981.

Mackie, J. *Ethics: Inventing Right and Wrong*. New York. Penguin, 1977.

Mahlmann, M. "The Cognitive Foundations of Law." In *Foundations of Law* Volume 2, by H. Rottleuthner. Edited by E. Pattaro. *A Treatise of Legal Philosophy and General Jurisprudence.* Dordrecht, Netherlands: Springer, 2005.

Mahlmann, M. "Ethics, Law, and the Challenge of Cognitive Science." *German Law Journal* 8 (2007): 577–615.

Mahlmann, M. *Rationalismus in der praktishen Theorie: Normentheoric und praktische kampetenz.* Baden Baden: Nomos Verlagsgesellschaft, 1999.

Mahlmann, M. "Theorizing Transnational Law: Varieties of Transnational Law and the Universalistic Stance." *German Law Journal* 10/10 (2009): 1325–36.

Mandela, N. *Long Walk to Freedom*. Boston: Little, Brown and Company, 1995.

Maoz I., A.Ward, M. Katz, and L. Ross. "Reactive Devaluation of an 'Israeli' vs. a 'Palestinian' Peace Proposal," *Journal of Conflict Resolution* 46 (2002): 515–46.

Maoz, Z. *Networks of Nations: The Evolution, Structure, and Impact of International Networks, 1816–2001.* New York: Cambridge University Press, 2010.

Margalit, A. *The Decent Society.* Cambridge, MA: Harvard University Press, 1996.

Maritain, J. *Introduction to Human Rights: Comments and Interpretations.* UNESCO, Ed. New York: Allan Wingate, 1949.

Marr, D, *Vision.* San Francisco: Freeman, 1982.

Marsden, P. V. "Core Discussion Networks of Americans." *American Sociological Review* 52/1 (1987): 122–31.

Marsden, P. V., and N. E. Friedkin. "Network Studies of Social Influence." *Advances in Social Network Analysis: Research in the Social and Behavioral Sciences.* (1994): 3–25.

Matza, D. *Delinquency and Drift.* New York: Wiley, 1964.

McKie, J. R. "Linguistic Competence and Moral Development: Some Parallels." *Philosophical Inquiry* 26 (1994): 20–31.

McPherson, M., L. Smith-Lovin, and J. M. Cook. "Birds of a Feather: Homophily in Social Networks." *Annual Review of Sociology* 27/1 (2001): 415–44.

Mead, G. H. *The Social Psychology of George Herbert Mead.* Edited by A. Strauss. Chicago: University of Chicago Press, 1956.

Mead, M. "Some Anthropological Considerations Concerning Natural Law." *Natural Law Forum* 6 (1961): 51–64.

Mednick, S. A., L. Kirkegaard-Sorenson, B. Hutchings, J. Knop, R. Rosenberg, and F. Schulsinger. "An Example of Bio-social Interaction Research: The Interplay of Socio-environmental and Individual Factors in the Etiology of Criminal Behavior." In *Biosocial Bases of Criminal Behavior,* edited by S. A. Mednick and K. O. Christiansen, 9–24. New York: Gardner Press, 1977.

Mellstrom, C., and M. Johannesson. "Crowding Out in Blood Donation: Was Titmuss Right?" *Journal of European Economic Association* 4 (2008): 845–63.

Melvern, L. *Conspiracy to Murder: The Rwandan Genocide.* London: Verso, 2004.

Meron, T. "The Martens Clause, Principles of Humanity, and Dictates of Public Conscience." *American Journal of International Law* 94/1 (2000): 78–89.

Mesoudi, A., A.Whiten, and K. N. Laland. "Towards a Unified Science of Cultural Evolution." *Behavioral and Brain Sciences* 29 (2006): 329–47.

Meyer, D. H. *The Instructed Conscience: The Shaping of the American National Ethic.* Philadelphia: University of Pennsylvania Press, 1972.

Mikhail, J. *Elements of Moral Cognition: Rawls' Linguistic Analogy and the Cognitive Science of Moral and Legal Judgment.* Cambridge: Cambridge University Press, 2011.

Mikhail, J. "Law, Science, and Morality: A Review of Richard Posner's 'The Problematics of Moral and Legal Theory.'" *Stanford Law Review* 54 (2002): 1057–127.

Mikhail, J. "Moral Grammar and Intuitive Jurisprudence: A Formal Model of Unconscious Moral and Legal Knowledge." In *Psychology of Learning and Motivation, Vol. 50: Moral Judgment and Decision Making, series* edited by B. H. Ross and issue edited by D. M. Bartels, C. W. Bauman, L. J. Skitka, and D. L. Medin. San Diego: Academic Press, 2009.

Mikhail, J. "Moral Heuristics or Moral Competence? Reflections on Sunstein." *Behavioral and Brain Science*, 28/4 (2005): 557–58.

Mikhail, J. "'Plucking the Mask of Mystery from Its Face:' Jurisprudence and H.L.A. Hart." *Georgetown Law Journal* 95 (2007): 733–79.

Mikhail, J. "Rawls' Linguistic Analogy: A Study of the Generative Grammar Model of Moral Theory Described by John Rawls in *A Theory of Justice.*" PhD diss., Cornell University, 2000.

Mikhail, J. "Universal Moral Grammar: Theory, Evidence, and the Future." *Trends in Cognitive Sciences* 11 (2007): 143–52.

Mikhail, J., C. Sorrentino, and E. Spelke. "Toward a Universal Moral Grammar." In *Proceedings, Twentieth Annual Conference of the Cognitive Science Society,* edited by M. A. Gernsbacher and S. J. Derry, 1250. Mahwah, NJ: Lawrence Erlbaum Associates, 1998.

Milgram, S. "The Small World Problem." *Psychology Today* 2/1 (1967): 60–67.

Mill, J. S. *Utilitarianism,* edited by H.B. Action. London: Guernsey Press, 1972/1861.

Miller, B. L., A. Darby, D. F. Benson, J. L. Cummings, and M. H. Miller. "Aggressive, Socially Disruptive and Antisocial Behaviour Associated with Frontotemporal Dementia." *British Journal of Psychiatry* 170 (1997): 150–54.

Miller, D. T., and K. R. Morrison. "Expressing Deviant Opinions: Believing You are in the Majority Helps." *Journal of Experimental Social Psychology* 45 (2009): 740–47.

Miller, D. T., and D. A. Prentice. "Collective Errors and Errors about the Collective." *Personality and Social Psychology Bulletin* 20/4 (1994): 541–50.

Miller, D. T., and D. A. Prentice. "The Construction of Social Norms and Standards." In *Social Psychology: Handbook of Basic Principles,* edited by E. T. Higgins and A. W. Kruglanski, 799–829. New York: Guilford, 1996.

Miller, G. "The Roots of Morality." *Science* 320 (2008): 734–37.

Mnookin, R. *Bargaining with the Devil: When to Negotiate and When to Fight.* New York: Simon & Schuster, 2010.

Mnookin, R., and L. Ross. "Introduction." In *Barriers to Conflict Resolution,* edited by K. Arrow, R. Mnookin, L. Ross, A. Tversky, and R. Wilson, 2–25. New York: Norton, 1995.

Moll, J., R. de Oliveira-Sousa, and P. Eslinger. "Morals and the Human Brain: A Working Model." *NeuroReport* 14 (2003): 299–305.

Moll, J., R. Zahn, R. di Oliveira-Souza, F. Krueger, and J. Grafman. "The Neural Basis of Human Moral Cognition." *Nature Neuroscience* 6 (2005):799–809.

Moore, A., B. Clark, and M. Kane. "Who Shall Not Kill? Individual Differences in Working Memory Capacity, Executive Control, and Moral Judgment." *Psychological Science* 19 (2008): 549–57.

Moreno, J. L. *Who Shall Survive?* New York: Beacon House, 1934.

Morris, M., and M. Kretzschmar. "Concurrent Partnerships and the Spread of HIV." *Aids* 11/5 (1997): 641.

Morrison, K. R., and D. T. Miller. "Distinguishing between Silent and Vocal Minorities: Not All Deviants Feel Marginal." *Journal of Personality and Social Psychology* 94/5 (2008): 871–82.

Morsink, J. *The Universal Declaration of Human Rights: Origins, Drafting and Intent.* Philadelphia: University of Pennsylvania Press, 2000.

Mowrer, O. H. *Learning Theory and Behavior.* New York: John Wiley & Sons, 1960.

Mutz, D. C. "Cross-cutting Social Networks: Testing Democratic Theory in Practice." *American Political Science Review* 96/01 (2004): 111–26.

Mutz, D. C. *Hearing the Other Side: Deliberative versus Participatory Democracy.* Cambridge: Cambridge University Press, 2006.

Nader, R. *Unsafe at Any Speed: The Designed-In Dangers of the American Automobile.* New York: Grossman Publishers, 1965.

Nathan, A. J. "China's Political Trajectory: What are the Chinese Saying?" In *China's Changing Political Landscape; Prospects for Democracy,* edited by Cheng Li. Washington, DC: Brookings, 2008.

NCI (National Cancer Institute). "The Role of the Media in Promoting and Reducing Tobacco Use." *Tobacco Control Monograph* 19 (2008). (Bethesda, MD: NIH Pub. No. 07-6242).

Neale, S. "Paul Grice and the Philosophy of Language." *Linguistics and Philosophy* 15/5 (1992): 509–59.

Nelson, S. "Factors Influencing Young Children's Use of Motives and Outcomes as Moral Criteria." *Child Development* 51 (1980): 823–29.

Nichols, S. "Innateness and Moral Psychology." In *The Innate Mind, Vol. 1: Structure and Contents,* edited by S. Laurence, P. Carruthers, and S. Stich. New York: Oxford University Press, 2005.

Nichols, S. *Sentimental Rules: On the Natural Foundations of Moral Judgment.* Oxford: Oxford University Press, 2004.

Nichols, S., and R. Mallon. "Moral Dilemmas and Moral Rules." *Cognition* 100/3 (2006): 530–42.

Nickerson, D. W. "Is Voting Contagious? Evidence from Two Field Experiments." *American Political Science Review* 102/1 (2008): 49–57.

Nikiforakis, N. S. "Punishment and Counter-punishment in Public Goods Games: Can We Still Govern Ourselves?" *Journal of Public Economics* 92/1–2 (2008): 91–112.

Nisbett, R. E., and T. D. Wilson. "Telling More than We Can Know: Verbal Reports on Mental Processes." *Psychological Review* 84/3 (1977): 231–59.

Noelle-Neumann, E. *The Spiral of Silence.* Chicago: University of Chicago Press, 1984.

Noelle-Neumann, E. "The Spiral of Silence: A Theory of Public Opinion." *Journal of Communication* 24/2 (1974): 43–51.

Nozick, R. "Moral Complications and Moral Structures." *Natural Law Forum* 13 (1968): 1–50.

O'Brian, M. J., and R. L. Lyman. *Applying Evolutionary Archaeology.* New York: Kluwer Academic, 2000.

O'Gorman, H. J. "Pluralistic Ignorance and White Estimates of White Support for Racial Segregation." *Public Opinion Quarterly* 39/3 (1975): 313–30.

O'Loughlin, J. et al. "The Diffusion of Democracy, 1946–1994." *Annals of the Association of American Geographers* 88/4 (1998): 545–74.

Oakeshott, M. *Rationalism in Politics and Other Essays.* London: Methuen, 1962.

Odling-Smee, F. J., K. N. Laland, and M. W. Feldman. *Niche Construction: The Neglected Process in Evolution.* Princeton, NJ: Princeton University Press, 2003.

Ogden, C. K. *Bentham's Theory of Fictions.* London: Kegan Paul, 1932.

Olson, M. *The Logic of Collective Action: Public Goods and the Theory of Groups.* Cambridge, MA: Harvard University Press, 1965.

Olson, M. *The Rise and Decline of Nations: Economic Growth, Stagflation, and Social Rigidities.* New Haven, CT: Yale University Press, 1982.

Onnela, J. P., "Structure and Tie Strengths in Mobile Communication Networks." *Proceedings of the National Academy of Sciences* 104/18 (2007): 7332.

Ostrom, E. *Governing the Commons: The Evolution of Institutions for Collective Action.* Cambridge: Cambridge University Press, 1990.

Padgett, J. F., and C. K. Ansell. "Robust Action and the Rise of the Medici, 1400–1434." *American Journal of Sociology* 98/6 (1993): 1259.

Page, T., L. Putterman, and B. Unel. "Voluntary Association in Public Goods Experiments: Reciprocity, Mimicry, and Efficiency." *Economic Journal* 115 (2005): 1032–53.

Pareto, W. *The Mind and Society.* New York: Harcourt, Brace and Co., 1935.

Parsons, T. "Evolutionary Universals in Society." *American Sociological Review* 29/3 (1964): 339–57.

Patterson, D. "On the Conceptual and the Empirical (A Critique of John Mikhail's Cognitivism.)" *Brooklyn Law Review* 73 (2008): 611–23.

Patterson, S. C. "Patterns of Interpersonal Relations in a State Legislative Group: The Wisconsin Assembly." *Public Opinion Quarterly* 23/1 (1959): 101.

Pellizoni, S., M. Siegal, and L. Surian. "The Contact Principle and Utilitarian Moral Judgments in Young Children." *Developmental Science* 13, 2 (2010): 265–70.

Perrot, D. L. "Has Law a Deep Structure?—The Origin of Fundamental Duties." In *Fundamental Duties: A Volume of Essays by Present and Former Members of the Law Faculty of the University of Exeter to Commemorate the Silver Jubilee of the University*, edited by Lasok, D. et al. Oxford: Pergamon Press, 1980.

Perry, M. "The Morality of Human Rights: A Nonreligious Ground?" *Emory Law Journal* 54 (2005): 97–150.

Phelps, E. S. *Rewarding Work: How to Restore Participation and Self-support to Free Enterprise*. Cambridge, MA: Harvard University Press, 1997.

Phelps, S., and G. Cengage, eds. "Seat Belt Usage 2003." eNotes.com. Accessed March 8, 2011. http://www.enotes.com/everyday-law-encyclopedia/seat-belt-usage.

Piaget, J. *The Moral Judgment of the Child*. New York: Free Press, 1965/1932.

Pinker, S. *The Blank Slate: The Modern Denial of Human Nature*. New York: Viking, 2002.

Pinker, S. *The Language Instinct: How the Mind Creates Language*. New York: Harper-Collins, 1994.

Pinker, S. "The Moral Instinct" *The New York Times Magazine*, January 13, 2008, 32.

Popper, K. *Objective Knowledge: An Evolutionary Approach*. Oxford: Clarendon Press, 1979.

Porter, M. A., Onnela, J. P., and Mucha, P. J., 'Communities in Networks.' *ArXiv* 902/6 (2009).

Posner, R., *The Problematics of Moral and Legal Theory*. Cambridge, MA: Harvard University Press, 1999.

Powell, C. L. "The Crisis in Darfur [Testimony before the Senate Foreign Relations Committee.]" Washington, DC: U.S. Department of State, 2004. Accessed August 21, 2008 http://www.state.gov/secretary/former/powell/remarks/36042.htm.

Powell, W. W. "Neither Market nor Hierarchy: Network Forms of Organization Critique." In *The Sociology of Organizations: Classic, Contemporary, and Critical Readings*, edited by M. J. Handel. Thousand Oaks, CA: Sage,2003, 315–328.

Power, S. *A Problem from Hell: America and the Age of Genocide*. New York: Harper Perennial, 2003.

Prentice, D. A. "On the Distinction between Acting Like an Individual and Feeling Like an Individual." In *Individuality and the Group: Advances in Social Identity*, edited by T. Postmes and J. Jetten,. London: Sage Publications, 2006, 37–55.

Prentice, D. A., and D. T. Miller. "Pluralistic Ignorance and Alcohol Use on Campus: Some Consequences of Misperceiving the Social Norm." *Journal of Personality and Social Psychology* 64/2 (1993): 243–56.

Prentice, D. A., and D. T. Miller. "Pluralistic Ignorance and the Perpetuation of Social Norms by Unwitting Actors." In *Advances in Experimental Social Psychology*, edited by M. Zanna. San Diego, CA: Academic Press 28 (1996): 161–209.

Price, R. *A Review of the Principal Questions in Morals*, edited by D. D. Raphael. Oxford: Clarendon Press, 1948/1758.

Prinz, J. *The Emotional Construction of Morals*. Oxford: Oxford University Press, 2007.

Prinz, J. "Is Morality Innate?" In *Moral Psychology, Vol. 1: The Evolution of Morality: Adaptation and Innateness*, edited by W. Sinnott-Armstrong. Cambridge, MA: MIT Press, 2008: 367–406.

Prior, A. N. "Escapism: The Logical Basis of Ethics." In *Essays in Moral Philosophy*, edited by A. I. Meldon, 135–46. Seattle: University of Washington Press, 1958.

Prior, A. N. *Formal Logic*. Oxford: Clarendon Press, 1955.

Pronin, E., T. Gilovich, and L. Ross. "Objectivity in the Eye of the Beholder: Divergent Perceptions of Bias and Self Versus Others." *Psychological Review* 111 (2004): 781–99.

Pronin, E. J., J. Kruger, K. Savitsky, and L. Ross. "You Don't Know Me, but I Know You: The Illusion of Asymmetric Insight." *Journal of Personality and Social Psychology* 81 (2001): 639–56.

Pronin, E. J., D. Y. Lin, and L. Ross. "The Bias Blindspot: Perceptions of Bias in Self and Others." *Personality and Social Psychology Bulletin* 28 (2002): 369–81.

Prosser, W. *Casebook on Torts.* Minneapolis: University of Minnesota Press, 1941.

Prysby, C. L. "Community Partisanship and Individual Voting Behavior: Methodological Problems of Contextual Analysis." *Political Methodology* 3 (1976): 183–98.

Pufendorf, S. *De Officio Hominis Et Civic Juxta Legem Naturalem Libri Duo,* edited by James Scott Brown. New York: Oxford University Press, 1927/1682.

Putnam, R. D. *Bowling Alone: The Collapse and Revival of American Community.* New York: Touchstone Books, 2001.

Putnam, R. D. "Political Attitudes and the Local Community." *The American Political Science Review* 60/3 (1966): 640–54.

Putnam, R. D. Leonardi, R. and Nanetti R. Y. *Making Democracy Work: Civic Traditions in Modern Italy.* Princeton, NJ: Princeton University Press, 1993.

Pye, L., ed. *Communications and Political Development.* Princeton, NJ: Princeton University Press, 1963.

Quine, W. V. O. "On the Nature of Moral Values." In *Values and Morals,* edited by Goldman, A. and Kim, J. Dordrecht, Netherlands: D. Reidel Publishing Co, 1978.

Quinn, W. S. *Morality and Action.* Cambridge: Cambridge University Press, 1993.

Rai, T. S., and K. J. Holyoak. "Moral Principles or Consumer Preferences? Alternative Framings of the Trolley Problem." *Cognitive Science* 34/2 (2009): 311–21.

Raudenbush, S. W., and A. S. Bryk. *Hierarchical Linear Models: Applications and Data Analysis Methods.* Thousand Oaks, CA: Sage Publications, 2002.

Rawls, J. *A Theory of Justice.* Cambridge, MA: Harvard University Press, 1971.

Reeves, E. "Genocide Prevention: 60 Years of Abject Failure." *The Christian Science Monitor* January 30, 2008. Accessed August 21, 2008. http://www.csmonitor.com/2008/0130/p09s02-coop.html.

Reeves, E. "Secretary of State Colin Powell's Genocide Determination: What It Does, and Doesn't, Mean for Darfur." September 10, 2004. Accessed August 21, 2008. http://www.sudanreeves.org.

Rehnquist, W. "The Notion of a Living Constitution." *Texas Law Review* 54 (1976): 693–706.

Reid, T. *Essays on the Active Powers of the Human Mind.* Cambridge, MA: MIT Press, 1969/1788.

Reid, T. *Essays on the Intellectual Powers of Man.* Cambridge, MA: MIT Press, 1969/1785.

Relethford, J. H. *The Human Species: An Introduction to Biological Anthropology.* New York: McGraw-Hill, 2007.

Richerson, P. J., and R. Boyd. *Not By Genes Alone.* Chicago: University of Chicago Press, 2004.

Risse, M. "What are Human Rights? Human Rights as Membership Rights in the Global Order" Working paper RWP08-006. Boston: John F. Kennedy School of Government, Harvard University, 2008.

Risse, T., S. C. Ropp, and K. Sikkink, eds. *The Power of Human Rights: International Norms and Domestic Change.* New York: Cambridge University Press, 1999.

Ritov, I., and J. Baron. "Reluctance to Vaccinate: Omission Bias and Ambiguity." *Journal of Behavioral Decision Making* 3 (1990): 263–77.

Rivera, M. C., and J. A. Lake. "The Ring of Life Provides Evidence for a Genome Fusion Origin of Eukaryotes." *Nature* 431 (2004): 152–55.

Robinson, P., and R. Kurzban. "Concordance and Conflict in Intuitions of Justice." *Minnesota Law Review* 91 (2007): 1829.

Robinson, P., R. Kurzban, and O. Jones. "The Origins of Shared Intuitions of Justice." *Vanderbilt Law Review* 60 (2007): 1633–88.

Robinson, P., R. Kurzban, and O. Jones. "Realism, Punishment & Reform." 77 *University of Chicago Law Review* 1611 (2010).

Roccella, E. J. "The Contributions of Public Health Education Toward the Reduction of Cardiovascular Disease Mortality: Experiences from the National High Blood Pressure Education Program." In *Public Health Communication: Evidence for Behavior Change,* edited by R. Hornik, Mahwah, NJ: Lawrence Erlbaum, 2002: 73–84.

Roemer, J. "A Pragmatic Theory of Responsibility for the Egalitarian Planner." *Philosophy and Public Affairs* 22 (1993): 146–66.

Rogers, E. M. *Diffusion of Innovations*. New York: Free Press, 1995.

Rorty, R. "The Priority of Democracy to Philosophy." In *Prospects for a Common Morality*, edited by G. Outka and J. P. Reeder, Jr. 1993: 254–55.

Rorty, R. *Contingency, Irony, Solidarity*. Cambridge: Cambridge University Press, 1989.

Ross, L. "The Intuitive Psychologist and His Shortcomings." In *Advances in Experimental Social Psychology* 10, edited by L. Berkowitz. New York: Academic Press, 1977: 173–220.

Ross, L. "Reactive Devaluation Barrier to Dispute Resolution." In *Barriers to Conflict Resolution*, edited by K Arrow, R. Mnookin, L. Ross, A. Tversky, and R. Wilson. New York: Norton, 1995.

Ross, L., and R. E. Nisbett. *The Person and the Situation: Perspectives of Social Psychology*. New York: McGraw Hill, 1991.

Ross, L., and A. Ward. "Psychological Barriers to Dispute Resolution." In *Advances in Experimental Social Psychology* 27, edited by M. Zanna. New York: Academic Press, 1995.

Ross, L., M. Lepper, and A. Ward, "History of Social Psychology: Insights, Challenges, and Contributions to Theory and Application." In *Handbook of Social Psychology*, 5th edition, Volume 1, edited by S. T. Fiske, D. T. Gilbert, and G. Lindsey. Hoboken, NJ: Wiley, 2010, 3–50.

Ross, W. D. *Foundations of Ethics*. Oxford: Clarendon Press, 1939.

Roth, A. E., V. Prasnikar, M. Okuno-Fujiwara, and S. Zamir. "Bargaining and Market Behavior in Jerusalem, Ljubljana, Pittsburgh, and Tokyo: An Experimental Study." *American Economic Review* 81/5 (1991): 1068–95.

Rothstein, B. *Social Traps and the Problem of Trust*. New York: Cambridge University Press, 2005.

Rousseau, J. J. "Discourse on the Origin and Foundations of Inequality Among Men." In *Jean-Jacques Rousseau: The Basic Political Writings*, edited by D.A. Cress. Indianapolis, IN: Hackett Publishing Co., 1987/1754.

Rousseau, J. J. *Emile: Or, On Education*. Edited by A. Bloom. New York: Basic Books, 1979/1762.

Routt, G. C. "Interpersonal Relationships and the Legislative Process." *Annals of the American Academy of Political and Social Science* 195 (1938): 129–36.

Ryle, G. *The Concept of Mind*. Oxford: Oxford University Press, 1949.

Ryle, G. "On Forgetting the Difference Between Right and Wrong." In *Essays in Moral Philosophy*, edited by A. I. Meldon. Seattle: University of Washington Press, 1958.

Sabini, J. *Social Psychology*. New York: Norton, 1992.

Sacerdote, B. "Peer Effects with Random Assignment: Results for Dartmouth Roommates." *Quarterly Journal of Economics* 116/2 (2001): 681–704.

Sacks, A., and M. Levi. *Effective Government and its Consequences for Social Welfare*. Seattle, University of Washington, 2006.

Sampson, R. J., S. W. Raudenbush, and F. Earls. "Neighborhoods and Violent Crime: A Multilevel Study of Collective Efficacy." *Science* 277 (1997): 918–24.

Saxe, R. "Do the Right Thing: Cognitive Science's Search for a Common Morality." *Boston Review*, September/October, 2005.

Saxe, R., S. Carey, and N. Kanwisher. "Understanding Other Minds: Linking Developmental Psychology and Functional Neuroimaging." *Annual Review of Psychology* 55 (2004): 87–124.

Scalia, A. *A Matter of Interpretation: Federal Courts and the Law*. Princeton, NJ: Princeton University Press, 1997.

Scanlon, T. *What We Owe to Each Other*. Cambridge, MA: Harvard University Press, 1998.

Schelling, T. C. "*The Life You Save May Be Your Own*," edited by S.B. Chase, Jr. Washington, DC: Brookings Institute, 1968: 127–76.

Schelling, T. C. *Micromotives and Macrobehavior*. New York: W. W. Norton and Company, 1978.

Schick, F. *Understanding Action: An Essay on Reasons*. New York: Cambridge University Press, 1991.

Schneewind, J. *The Invention of Autonomy: A History of Modern Moral Philosophy*. Cambridge: Cambridge University Press, 1998.

Schneewind, J. *Sidgwick's Ethics and Victorian Moral Philosophy*. Oxford: Clarendon Press, 1977.

Schroeder, C. M., and D. A. Prentice. "Exposing Pluralistic Ignorance to Reduce Alcohol Use Among College Students." *Journal of Applied Social Psychology* 28/23 (1998): 2150–80.

Schroeder, P., and D. Schroeder-Hildebrand. *Six Million Paper Clips: The Making of a Children's Holocaust Museum*. Minneapolis, MN: Kar-Ben Publishing, 2004.

Schulkin, J. *Roots of Social Sensitivity and Neural Function*. Cambridge, MA: MIT Press, 2000.

Schultz, P. W., J. M. Nolan, R. B. Cialdini, N. J. Goldstein, and V. Griskevicious. "The Constructive, Destructive, and Reconstructive Power of Social Norms." *Psychological Science* 18/5 (2007): 429–34.

Schwartz-Shea, P., and R. T. Simmons. "Egoism, Parochialism, and Universalism." *Rationality and Society* 3 (1991): 106–32.

Schwartz-Shea, P., and R. T. Simmons. "The Layered Prisoners' Dilemma: Ingroup vs. Macro-efficiency." *Public Choice* 65 (1990): 61–83.

Scott, J. "Social Network Analysis." *Sociology* 22/1 (1988): 109.

Sen, A. "Democracy as a Universal Value." *Journal of Democracy* 10/3 (1999): 3–17.

Shelton, J. N., and J. A. Richeson. "Intergroup Contact and Pluralistic Ignorance." *Journal of Personality and Social Psychology* 88/1 (2005): 91–107.

Sherif, M., O. J. Harvey, B. J. White, W. R. Hood, and C. W. Sherif. *Intergroup Conflict and Cooperation: The Robbers Cave Experiment*. Norman, OK: University Book Exchange, 1961.

Shiller, R. J. *Macro Markets: Creating Institutions for Managing Society's Largest Economic Risks*. Oxford: Clarendon Press, 1993.

Shultz, T., K. Wright, and M. Schleifer. "Assignment of Moral Responsibility and Punishment." *Child Development* 57 (1986): 177–84.

Shweder, R. A. "Customs Control: Some Anthropological Reflections on Human Rights Crusades." *Virginia Journal of Social Policy and the Law* 14/1 (2006): 1–38.

Shweder, R., E. Turiel, and N. Much. "The Moral Intuitions of the Child." In *Social Cognitive Development*, edited by J.H. Flavell and L. Ross. Cambridge, MA: Harvard University Press, 1981.

Simmons, B. A. "International Law and State Behavior: Commitment and Compliance in International Monetary Affairs." *American Political Science Review* 94/4 (2000). 819–35.

Simmons, B. A. *Mobilizing for Human Rights: International Law in Domestic Politics*. Cambridge: Cambridge University Press, 2009.

Singer, P. *The Expanding Circle: Ethics and Sociobiology*. New York: Farrar, Strauss and Giroux, 1982.

Singer, P. "Famine, Affluence, and Morality." *Philosophy and Public Affairs* 1/3(1972): 229–43.

Singer, P. *Practical Ethics*, 2nd ed. Cambridge: Cambridge University Press, 1993.

Singer, P. "Should We Trust Our Moral Intuitions?" *Project Syndicate* (2007). Accessed August 22, 2008, http://www.utilitarian.net/singer/by/200703.htm.

Sinnott-Armstrong, W., R. Mallon, T. McCoy, and J. Hull. "Intention, Temporal Order, and Moral Judgments." *Mind and Language* 23/1 (2008): 90–106.

Sinnott-Armstrong, W., R. Mallon, T. McCoy, and J. Hull. *Verbal Behavior*. Acton, MA: Copley, 1957.

Skinner, B. F. *Science and Human Behavior*. New York: MacMillan, 1953.

Slaughter, A. M. *A New World Order*. Princeton, NJ: Princeton University Press, 2004.

Slovic, S., and P. Slovic. "Numbers and Nerves: Toward an Affective Apprehension of Environmental Risk." *Whole Terrain* 13 (2004): 14–18.

Slovic, P., M. L. Finucane, E. Peters, and D. G. MacGregor. "The Affect Heuristic." In *Heuristics and Biases: The Psychology of Intuitive Judgment*, edited by T. Gilovich, D. Griffin, and D. Kahneman. New York: Cambridge University Press, 2002: 397–420.

Slovic, P., M. L. Finucane, E. Peters, and D. G. MacGregor. "Risk as Analysis and Risk as Feelings: Some Thoughts about Affect, Reason, Risk, and Rationality." *Risk Analysis* 24 (2004): 1–12.

Small, D. A., G. Loewenstein, and P. Slovic. "Sympathy and Callousness: The Impact of Deliberative Thought on Donations to Identifiable and Statistical Victims." *Organizational Behavior and Human Decision Processes* 102 (2007): 143–53.

Smetana, J. "Social Cognitive Development: Domain Distinctions and Coordinations." *Developmental Review* 3 (1983): 131–47.

Smith, A. *The Theory of Moral Sentiments*. New York: Prometheus, 2000/1759.

Smith, E. A., and B. Winterhalder. *Evolutionary Ecology and Human Behavior*. New York: Aldine de Gruyter, 1992.

Snijders, T. A. B. "Models for Longitudinal Network Data." In *Models and Methods in Social Network Analysis*, edited by Carrington, P. J., Scott, J., and Wasserman, S. Cambridge: Cambridge University Press, 2005, 215–47.

Solum, L. "Natural Justice." *American Journal of Jurisprudence* 51 (2006): 65–105.

Spranca, M., E. Minsk, and J. Baron. "Omission and Commission in Judgment and Choice." *Journal of Experimental Social Psychology* 27 (1991):76–105.

Sreberny-Mohammadi, A. "Small Media for a Big Revolution: Iran" *International Journal of Politics, Culture and Society* 3/3 (1990) 341–72.

Stedman, S. "Spoiler Problems in Peace Processes." *International Security* 22/2 (1997): 17–35.

Steidle, B., and G. S.Wallace. *The Devil Came on Horseback: Bearing Witness to the Genocide in Darfur*. New York: Public Affairs, 2007.

Stevens, S. S. *Psychophysics*. New York: Wiley, 1975.

Stich, S. "Moral Philosophy and Mental Represenation." In *The Origin of Values*, edited by Hetcher, M. et al. New York: Aldine De Gruyter, 1993.

Stout, L., and M. Blair. "Trust, Trustworthiness, and the Behavioral Foundations of Corporate Law." 149 *University of Pennsylvania Law Review* 1735–1810 (2001).

Stover, E., and H. M.Weinstein, eds. *My Neighbor, My Enemy: Justice and Community in the Aftermath of Mass Atrocity*. Cambridge: Cambridge University Press, 2005.

Strogatz, S. H. *Sync: The Emerging Science of Spontaneous Order*. New York: Hyperion, 2003.

Sumner, W. G. *Folkways: A Study of the Sociological Importance of Usages, Manners, Customs, Mores, and Morals*. Boston: Ginn and Co., 1906.

Sunshine, J., and T. R. Tyler. "The Role of Procedural Justice and Legitimacy in Shaping Public Support for Policing." *Law and Society Review* 37 (2003): 513–48.

Sunstein, C. "Moral Heuristics." *Behavioral and Brain Sciences* 28 (2005): 531–73.

Sunstein, C. "Some Effects of Moral Indignation on Law." *Vermont Law Review* 33 (2009): 405, 433.

Sunstein, C. R., *Free Markets and Social Justice*. New York: Oxford University Press, 1997.

Susskind, J., K. Maurer, V. Thakkar, D. L. Hamilton, and J. W. Sherman. "Perceiving Individuals and Groups: Expectancies, Dispositional Inferences, and Causal Attributions." *Journal of Personality and Social Psychology* 76/2 (1999): 181–91.

Thaler, R. H., and C. R. Sunstein. *Nudge: Improving Decisions about Health, Wealth, and Happiness*. New Haven, CT: Yale University Press, 2008.

Thompson, C. "The Predictor." *The New York Times Magazine*, August 16, 2009, 20.

Thomson, J. J. "The Trolley Problem." In *Ethics: Problems and Principles*, edited by J. M. Fischer and M. Ravizza. Fort Worth, TX: Harcourt Brace Jovanovich, 1985: 6776.

Tienson, J. L. "About Competence." *Philosophical Papers* 19 (1990): 19–36.

Titmuss, R. M. *The Gift Relationship: From Human Blood to Social Policy*. New York: Pantheon Books, 1971.

Toch, H., and J. Klofas. "Alienation and Desire for Job Enrichment among Correction Officers." *Federal Probation* 46/1 (1982): 35–44.

Todorov, A., and A. N. Mandisodza. "Public Opinion on Foreign Policy: The Multilateral Public that Perceives Itself as Unilateral." *Public Opinion Quarterly* 68/3 (2004): 323–48.

Tomkins, S. S. *Affect, Imagery, and Consciousness: Vol. The Positive Affects*. New York: Springer, 1963.

Tomkins, S. S. *Affect, Imagery, and Consciousness: Vol. 2. The Negative Affects*. New York: Springer, 1963.

Tooby, J., and L. Cosmides. "The Psychological Foundations of Culture." In *The Adapted Mind: Evolutionary Psychology and the Generation of Culture*, edited by J. H. Barkow, L. Cosmides, and J. Tooby, 19–136. New York: Oxford University Press, 1992.

Torfason, M. T., and P. Ingram. "The Global Rise of Democracy: A Network Account." *American Sociological Review* 75/3 (2010): 355–77.

Totten, S,. ed. *Genocide in Darfur: Investigating the Atrocities in the Sudan.* New York: Routledge, 2006.

Trivers, R. L. "The Evolution of Reciprocal Altruism." *Quarterly Review of Biology* 46 (1971): 35–57.

Tuhus-Dubrow, R. "Sued by the Forest." *The Boston Globe,* July 19, 2009.

Turiel, E. *The Development of Social Knowledge: Morality and Convention.* Cambridge: Cambridge University Press, 1983.

Turner, J. C. *Social Influence.* Pacific Grove, CA: Brooks/Cole, 1991.

Turner, R. E., and C. Edgley. "Sociological Semanticide: On Reification, Tautology and the Destruction of Language." *The Sociological Quarterly* 21/4 (2005): 595–605.

Tyler, T. R., ed. *Legitimacy and Criminal Justice.* New York: Russell Sage Foundation, 2007.

Tyler, T. R. "Psychological Perspectives on Legitimacy and Legitimation." *Annual Review of Psychology* 57 (2006): 375–400.

Tyler, T. R. "Social Justice: Outcome and Procedure." *International Journal of Psychology,* 35 (2000): 117–25.

Tyler, T. R. *Why People Obey the Law.* Princeton, NJ: Princeton University Press, 1990.

Tyler, T. R., and J. Fagan. "Legitimacy and Cooperation: Why Do People Help the Police Fight Crime in their Communities?" *Columbia Public Law Research Paper* (2008)

Tyler, T. R., P. E. Callahan, and J. Frost. "Armed, and Dangerous (?). Motivating Rule Adherence Among Agents of Social Control." *Law and Society Review* 41 (2007): 457–92.

Tyler, T. R., L. W Sherman, H. Strang, G. C. Barnes, and D. J. Woods. "Reintegrative Shaming, Procedural Justice and Recidivism: The Engagement of Offenders." *Psychological Mechanisms in the Canberra RISE* (2007).

Ubel, P. A., J. Baron, and D. A. Asch. "Preference for Equity as a Framing Effect." *Medical Decision Making 21* (2001): 180–89.

Ulfstein, G., et al., eds. *Making Treaties Work: Human Rights, Environment and Arms Control.* Cambridge: Cambridge University Press, 2007.

Unger, P. *"Living High and Letting Die: Our Illusion of Innocence."* New York: Oxford University Press, 1996.

UN Committee on Economic, Social and Cultural Rights, General Comment 3.

United States Holocaust Memorial Museum, Mapping Initiatives: Crisis in Darfur (2008). Accessed August 19, 2008. http://www.ushmm.org/maps/projects/darfur/.

Universal Declaration of Human Rights, G.A. res. 217A (III), U.N. Doc A/810 (1948).

Uzzi, B. "The Sources and Consequences of Embeddedness for the Economic Performance of Organizations: The Network Effect." *American Sociological Review* 61/4 (1996): 674–98.

Van Berkum, J. J. A., B. Holleman, M. Nieuwland, M. Otten, and M. Jaap. "Right or Wrong? The Brain's Fast Response to Morally Objectionable Statements." *Psychological Science* 20 (2009): 1092–99.

Västfjäll, D., E. Peters, and P. Slovic. "Compassion Fatigue: Donations and Affect are Greatest for a Single Child in Need."*Personality and Social Psychology Compass* (in press).

Vedantam, S. *The Hidden Brain.* New York: Spiegel and Grau, 2010.

Viscusi, W. K. "Corporate Risk Analysis: A Reckless Act?" *Stanford Law Review* 52/3 (2000): 547–97.

Von Jhering, R. "Geist des romischen Rechts." Cited in Cohen, M. R. 1916: 1865–69.

Von Lang, J., ed. *Eichmann Interrogated: Transcripts from the Archives of the Israeli Police.* New York: Farrar, Straus and Giroux, 1983.

Von Savigny, F. C. *Of the Vocation of Our Age for Legislation and Jurisprudence,* translated by Abraham Hayward. London: Littleward and Co., 1881/1814.

Von Wright, G. H. *An Essay in Modal Logic.* Amsterdam: North-Holland, 1951.

Von Wright, G. H. *Norm and Action.* London: Routledge and Kegan Paul, 1963.

Waldmann, M. R., and J. Dieterich. "Throwing a Bomb on a Person versus Throwing a Person on a Bomb: Intervention Myopia in Moral Intuitions." *Psychological Science* 18/3 (2007): 247–53.

Wallack, L., L. Dorfman, D. Jernigan, and M. Themba. *Media Advocacy and Public Health: Power for Prevention*. Newbury Park, CA: Sage, 1993.

Walster, E., W. Walster, and E. Berscheid. *Equity: Theory and Research*. Needham Heights, MA: Allyn and Bacon, 1978.

Waltz, K. N. *Theory of International Politics*. New York: McGraw-Hill, 1979.

Warneken, F., and M. Tomasello. "Varieties of Altruism in Children and Chimpanzees." *Trends in Cognitive Sciences* 13/9 (2009): 397–482.

Warner, K. E. "Effects of the Antismoking Campaign: An Update." *American Journal of Public Health* 79/2 (1989) 144–51.

Warner, K. E. "Cigarette Smoking in the 1970's: The Impact of the Antismoking Campaign on Consumption." *Science* 211/4483 (1981): 729–31.

Watson, J. *Behaviorism*. New York: W. W. Norton, 1925.

Watts, D. J. *Six Degrees: The Science of a Connected Age*. New York: W. W. Norton & Company, 2004.

Watts, D. J. *Small Worlds: The Dynamics of Networks between Order and Randomness*. Princeton, NJ: Princeton University Press, 2003.

Watts, D. J., and S. H. Strogatz. "Collective Dynamics of 'Small-world' Networks." *Nature* 393/6684 (1998): 440–42.

Weaver, R. K., R. Y. Shapiro, and L. R. Jacobs. "Poll Trends: Welfare." *Public Opinion Quarterly* 39 (1995): 606–27.

Weber, E. H. *De pulsu, resorptione, auditu et tactu*. Leipzig, DE: Koehler, 1834.

Weber, R. J. "Approval Voting." *Journal of Economic Perspectives* 9 (1995): 39–49.

Weinrib, E. "The Case for a Duty to Rescue." *Yale Law Journal* 90 (1980): 247.

Wellings, K. "Evaluating AIDS Public Education in Europe: A Cross-national Comparison." In *Public Health Communication: Evidence for Behavior Change*, edited by R. Hornik, 131–46. Mahwah, NJ: Lawrence Erlbaum, 2002.

Wellman, B., and S. D. Berkowitz. *Social Structures: A Network Approach*. Cambridge: Cambridge University Press, 1988.

Wendt, A. "Anarchy is What States Make of It: The Social Construction of Power Politics." *International Organization* 46/02 (2009): 391–425.

Westermarck, E. *The Origin and Development of the Moral Ideas*, 2 vols. London: Macmillan, 1908.

Wheeler, N. J. "A Victory for Common Humanity? The Responsibility to Protect and the 2005 World Summit." *Journal of International Law and International Relations* 2 (2005): 95–105.

Wheeler, S. "Role Conflict in Correctional Communities." In *The Prison: Studies in Institutional Organization and Change*, edited by D. K. Cressey, 229–59. New York: Holt, Rinehart and Winston, 1961.

White, H. C., S. A. Boorman, and R. L. Breiger. "Social Structure from Multiple Networks. I. Blockmodels of Roles and Positions." *The American Journal of Sociology* 81/4 (1976): 730–80.

White, P. A. "Knowing More than We Can Tell: 'Introspective Access' and Causal Report Accuracy 10 Years Later." *British Journal of Psychology* 79/1 (1988): 13–46.

Wiebe, G. D. "Merchandising Commodities and Citizenship on Television." *Public Opinion Quarterly* 15/4 (1951) 670–91.

Wildschut, T., B. Pinter, J. L. Vevea, C. A. Insko, and J. Schopler. "Beyond the Group Mind: A Quantitative Review of the Interindividual-intergroup Discontinuity Effect." *Psychological Bulletin* 129 (2003): 698–722.

Wilkinson-Ryan, T., and J. Baron. "Moral Judgment and Moral Heuristics in Breach of Contract." *Journal of Empirical Legal Studies* 6/2 (2009): 405–23.

Williams, B. *Ethics and the Limits of Philosophy*. Cambridge: Cambridge University Press, 1985.

Williams, J., J. K. Wells, D. Reinfurt. "Increasing Seat Belt Use In North Carolina." *Journal of Safety Research* 27/1 (1996): 33–41.

Williamson, O. E. "Markets and Hierarchies: Some Elementary Considerations." *The American Economic Review* 63/2 (1973): 316–25.

Willinger, M., H.J. Hoffman, and R.B. Hartford. "Infant Sleep Position and Risk for Sudden Infant Death Syndrome." Report of meeting held January 13 and 14, 1994, National Institutes of Health, Bethesda, MD. *Pediatrics* 93 (1994): 814–19.

Wills, G. *Inventing America: Jefferson's Declaration of Independence.* New York: Doubleday, 1978.

Wills, G. "Lincoln's Black History." *The New York Review of Books,* June 11, 2009, 56.

Wilson, J. *The Works of James Wilson,* 2 vols. Edited by R. McCloskey. Cambridge, MA: Harvard University Press, 1967/1790–1791.

Wollstonecraft, M. *A Vindication of the Rights of Men, with A Vindication of the Rights of Woman, and Hints.* Edited by S. Tomaselli. Cambridge: Cambridge University Press, 1995/1790–1792.

Woods, A. K. "A Behavioral Approach to Human Rights." *Harvard International Law Journal* 51 (2010): 51–112.

Woods, A. K. "Moral Judgments and International Crimes: The Disutility of Desert." *Virginia Journal of International Law* 52 (2012): 633–81.

Young, L., F. A. Cushman, M. D. Hauser, R. Saxe. "Brain Regions for Belief Attribution Drive Moral Condemnation for Crimes of Attempt." *Proceedings of the National Academy of Science* 104/20 (2007): 8235–40.

Young, L., and R. Saxe. "The Neural Basis of Belief Encoding and Integration in Moral Judgment." *NeuroImage* 40 (2008): 1912–1920.

Young, R. M. *Mind, Brain, and Adaptation in the Nineteenth Century: Cerebral Localization and Its Biological Context from Gall to Ferrier.* Oxford: Clarendon Press, 1970.

Zajonc, R. B. "Feeling and Thinking: Preferences Need No Inferences." *American Psychologist,* 35/2 (1980): 151–75.

Zajonc, R. B. "On the Primacy of Affect." *American Psychologist* 39 (1984): 117–23.

Zelizer, B., *Remembering to Forget: Holocaust Memory through the Camera's Eye.* Chicago: University of Chicago Press, 1998.

Zimicki, S., R. C. Homik, C. C. Verzosa, J. R. Hernandez, E. De Guzman, M. Dayrit, A. Fausto, and M. B. Lee. "Improving Vaccination Coverage in Urban Areas through a Health Communication Campaign: The 1990 Philippines Experience." *Bulletin of the World Health Organization* 72/3 (1994): 409–22.

Zittrain, J. *The Future of the Internet —and How to Stop It.* New Haven, CT: Yale University Press, 2009.

Zuckerman, E. "Meet the Bridgebloggers." *Public Choice* 134 (2008): 47–65.

INDEX